Introduction to Criminal Justice

Thomas R. Phelps
Department of Criminal Justice
California State University, Sacramento

Charles R. Swanson, Jr.
Institute of Government
University of Georgia

Kenneth R. Evans
Director, State of West Virginia Law Library

Goodyear Publishing Company, Inc. • Santa Monica, California

MOTHER, TRACI, and KELLIE,
this book is for you with love

Library of Congress Cataloging in Publication Data

PHELPS, THOMAS R
    Introduction to criminal justice.

    Includes bibliographical references and index.
        1. Criminal justice, Administration of—United States.
2. Law enforcement—United States.   3. Criminal procedure—United States.   I. Swanson, Charles R., 1942–
joint author.   II. Evans, Kenneth R., 1938–   joint
author.   III. Title.
HV9471.P45   364'.973   78-31325
ISBN 0-87620-432-9

Copyright © 1979 by Goodyear Publishing Company, Inc., Santa
Monica, California

Current printing (last number):
10 9 8 7 6 5 4 3 2 1

ISBN: 0-87620-432-9
Y-4329-2

Printed in the United States of America

Contents

Preface   x

Chapter 1
Criminal Justice, Criminology, and Urban Violence   1

The Cost of Crime 1
The Amount of Crime 3
Criminal Justice and Criminology 10
Urban Violence 16
Terrorism 21
Study Questions 31
Notes 32

Chapter 2
Historical Perspectives on the Development of State and
Local Policing   33

Crucible: Our English Heritage 33
The Growth of Policing in America 40
London: The New Police 42
The New Police in America 46
The Frontier 49
The Emergence of State Police Organizations 53
Study Questions 55
Notes 56

Chapter 3
Federal Enforcement and Assistance   59

Federal Bureau of Investigation 61
Immigration and Naturalization Service 65
United States Marshals Service 67
Community Relations Service 67
Law Enforcement Assistance Administration 68
Drug Enforcement Administration 71
Department of the Treasury 74
Study Questions 82
Notes 88

Illustrative Careers in Federal Law Enforcement   **84**

Chapter 4
State, Local, and Private Policing   90

The State Role 90
Sheriff, Coroner, and Constable 97
Municipal Policing 105
Private Police 109
Study Questions 114
Notes 118

Illustrative Careers in State and Local Enforcement Agencies   **115**

Chapter 5
The Operating Milieu   120

The Societal Context 120
The Legal Context 122
The Organizational Context 131
Interface: The Police in the Criminal Justice System 140
Study Questions 145
Notes 145

Chapter 6
Innovation and Change in Policing   148

Women in Policing 148
Unions: The New Power Center 156
Crisis Intervention 165
Team Policing 171
Crime Prevention 175
Study Questions 180
Notes 181

Chapter 7
Criminal Behavior and Individual Rights   183

Motives in Criminal Behavior 183
Examples of Criminal Behavior 184
What Is a Crime? 185
Limiting the Power of the State 186
Jurisdictional Safeguards 186
Seasonal Safeguards: Time Limits 188
Interpretational Safeguards 189
Constitutional Safeguards 190
Study Questions 204
Notes 204

Chapter 8
Moving Through the Court System   206

The First Appearance: Preliminary Hearing 206
The Charging Process 210
Other Pretrial Proceedings 211
The Trial 213
Sentencing 221
Study Questions 223
Notes 224

Illustrative Careers in the Judicial Process   **225**

Chapter 9
The Court System: Its Dilemma Today   229

    Appellate Courts and the Role of Precedent 231
    Reform Proposals 232
    Inherent Power 233
    Federal Reform Proposals 245
    Epilogue 250
    Study Questions 250
    Notes 250

Chapter 10
Judicial Behavior   252

    The Function of the Trial Judge: General Principles 253
    Judicial Behavior: Pretrial Duties 255
    Judicial Behavior: Trial Duties 264
    Holding Judges Accountable 268
    Study Questions 268
    Notes 269

Chapter 11
Evidentiary Problems in Criminal Proceedings   271

    Eyewitness Identification Procedures 271
    Confessions: Miranda and the Out-of-Court Statement 278
    Confessions: The Non-Miranda Problems 288
    Confessions and Joint Trials: The Problem 290
    Character of the Accused 294
    Opinion Evidence 297
    Res Gestae and the Right of Confrontation 301
    Study Questions 302
    Notes 302

Chapter 12
Probation and Parole   305

    Probation 306
    Parole 310

Mandatory Release 325
Discharge from Prison 325
Pardons 326
Conclusion 328
Study Questions 328
Notes 328

An Illustrative Career in Probation and Parole   330

Chapter 13
Correctional Institutions   332

Jails—Justice or Injustice? 333
Prisons and Prisoners 339
Classification and Treatment 344
Study Questions 356
Notes 357

Illustrative Careers in Correctional Institutions   359

Chapter 14
Manpower Development and Corrections   362

Public Opinion 363
Careers in Corrections 364
Priorities for Corrections 372
Study Questions 377
Notes 378

Chapter 15
Delinquency and the Justice System   380

Criminal Behavior 380
Status Offenses 380
Age 382
Juvenile Court Process 383
Probation 392
Juvenile Institutions 394
Parole 398

Justice for Youth 399
Study Questions 402
Notes 403

Illustrative Careers in Youth Services   **404**

Glossary   **406**

Abstracts of Leading Cases   **421**

Fourth Amendment Cases   **421**

Application of the Fourth Amendment to the States 421
  Mapp v. Ohio (1961) 421
Probable Cause 422
  Aguilar v. Texas (1964) 422
Searches Without Warrants 423
  United States v. Robinson (1973) 423
  South Dakota v. Opperman (1976) 424
Challenging the Use of Seized Evidence 424
  United States v. Calandra (1974) 424
  Stone v. Powell (1976) 425

Fifth Amendment Cases   **426**

Self-Incrimination and the Right to Counsel 426
  Gideon v. Wainwright (1963) 426
  Escobedo v. Illinois (1964) 427
  Miranda v. Arizona (1966) 427
  United States v. Wade (1967) 428
  Gilbert v. California (1967) 429
  Stovall v. Denno (1967) 429
  Kirby v. Illinois (1972) 430
  Argersinger v. Hamlin (1972) 430
  Faretta v. California (1975) 430
  North v. Russell (1976) 431
  Brewer v. Williams (1977) 431
Double Jeopardy 432
  Bartkus v. Illinois (1959) 432
  Abbate v. United States (1959) 432
  Benton v. Maryland (1969) 433
  Ashe v. Swenson (1970) 434

Double Jeopardy and Imposition of Harsher Punishment 434
    North Carolina v. Pearce (1969) 434
Due Process 435
    Mempa v. Rhay (1967) 435
    Morrissey v. Brewer (1972) 435
    Gagnon v. Scarpelli (1973) 436
Forced Jurisdiction 436
    Ker v. Illinois (1886) 436
    Frisbie v. Collins (1952) 437
Discovery 437
    Williams v. Florida (1970) 437
    Wardius v. Oregon (1973) 438

Sixth Amendment Cases   **439**

Right to Confrontation 439
    Pointer v. Texas (1965) 439
    Bruton v. United States (1968) 439
Right to a Speedy Trial 439
    United States v. Marion (1972) 439
Jury Selection 440
    Swain v. Alabama (1965) 440
Unanimous Verdicts 440
    Apodaca v. Oregon (1972) 440
Guilty Pleas 441
    Boykin v. Alabama (1969) 441

Index   **442**

Preface

Today, criminal-justice programs in colleges and universities are enjoying a high growth period; law enforcement, courts, and corrections personnel are seeking new methods beyond proven procedures to control crime; and citizens are demanding greater accountability for services provided by local and state governments. Crime remains a serious community problem and criminal justice is viewed as a high priority item: California, for example, passed the first legislation for property tax reduction, but finds its citizens advising the legislature not to cut police and other related criminal-justice services.

This is an introductory textbook that offers a highly readable survey of the criminal-justice system. It is for the person interested in learning more about the people and agencies responsible for controlling crime. Chapter one introduces the reader to the problem of crime in this country, Chapters Two through Six investigate the role of police in the administration of justice, Chapters Seven through Eleven review the operations and activities of the courts, Chapters Twelve through Fourteen explore the field of corrections, and Chapter Fifteen focuses upon juvenile delinquency and the justice system. Helpful features in this book include a glossary of terms, abstracts of selected court cases, numerous examples of career opportunities, study questions, and suggestions for additional reading in areas of personal interest.

Because each of the authors was employed in some phase of the justice system before commencing an academic career, we are sensitive to the problems confronting the men and women responsible for criminal-justice agency operations. We believe the reader can find a high degree of satisfaction, as well as some frustration, in selecting criminal justice as a profession. This text suggests that adequate knowledge exists to minimize the crime problem, if only we will utilize it in our day-to-day decisionmaking. We trust that our book will motivate other people to upgrade this complex field that operates in crisis situations every day. We would like to thank several individuals for their invaluable assistance:

Susette Talarico, Department of Political Science, University of Georgia, used selected chapters in teaching an Introduction to Criminal Justice course and provided information on their reception by students. Len Wright, Criminal Justice Divison, Institute of Government, University of Georgia, reviewed portions of several chapters and gave incisive criticism that strengthened them, as did Neil Chamelin, Director, Florida Police Standards and Training Commission. William M. Sigmon, Institute of Government, University of Georgia, did yeoman's service in preparing the sections on careers in criminal justice, and R. Allen McCarteney, Crime Prevention International, Louisville, Kentucky, drafted the material on crime prevention in Chapter Six.

Photographs were graciously provided by Paula West in the Wyoming State Archives and Historical Department; Thomas C. Lyon of the Pennsylvania State Police; Clarence Kelly and Jay Cochran of the Federal Bureau of Investigation; E. Wilson Purdy of the Dade County, Florida, Department of Public Safety; R. F. Schillinger of the Berkeley, California, Police Department; John W. Warner of the United States Secret Service; Alfred J. Young of the New York City Police Department; Stephen Hatfield of the Los Angeles Police Department; John A. Craig from the Philadelphia Police Department; the United Nations Children's Fund; Lisa Cockran from the Library of Congress; Sue E. Clark, Superintendent, Purdy Treatment Center for Women, Gig Harbor, Washington; Duane Lowe, Sheriff, Sacramento County, California; and Associate Justice Wiley W. Manuel of the California Supreme Court.

One of the real pleasures in writing this book was the association with Hilda Spratlin, who served as typist and record keeper, always with great patience, a keen eye, and enthusiasm, and for whose many talents and contributions we are greatly appreciative.

Thomas R. Phelps
Charles R. Swanson, Jr.
Kenneth R. Evans

chapter one
Criminal Justice, Criminology, and Urban Violence

Crime is increasing and has become a threat to freedom of movement. Opinion polls reveal how deeply the public is concerned about the question. Crime is perceived as our fourth most serious problem after inflation, unemployment, and the energy crisis.[1] As crime increases, fear escalates. The National Crime Survey reports an estimated 40,483,000 victimizations of persons, households, and businesses for one year.[2] Individuals fear walking alone in their neighborhoods in the evening and many feel unsafe even at home. An effective criminal-justice system is required; without it, victims of crime will come to question the legitimacy and credibility of our crime-control efforts.

THE COST OF CRIME

The cost of crime, measured in losses to the economy, has been estimated to be $102.52 billion by the Joint Economic Committee of the United States Congress. This amount exceeds the annual appropriation for national defense. It requires an additional $22.7 billion in tax funds to operate the nation's criminal-justice system. The total costs of crime are $125.22 billion (see Figure 1-1). A seventy-nation survey conducted by Gallup International shows the United States to have the highest crime rate of all the major Western industrial nations.

The report of the Joint Economic Committee reveals the cost of certain crime categories to our society. White-collar crime costs us $44 billion each year as a result of bankruptcy, kickbacks, consumer fraud, computer-related crime, bribery, and embezzlement. Victimless crimes (narcotics, prostitution, and illegal gambling) divert $37.3 billion from the economy. Crimes against the person create financial hardship for survivors. An estimated $18 million of income is lost

1

Figure 1-1   The Costs of Crime

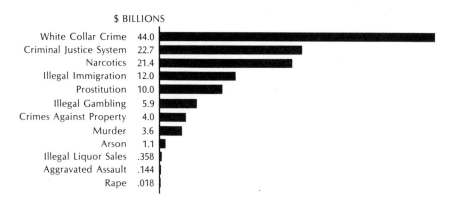

$ BILLIONS

White Collar Crime	44.0
Criminal Justice System	22.7
Narcotics	21.4
Illegal Immigration	12.0
Prostitution	10.0
Illegal Gambling	5.9
Crimes Against Property	4.0
Murder	3.6
Arson	1.1
Illegal Liquor Sales	.358
Aggravated Assault	.144
Rape	.018

Source: *The New York Times,* 2 January 1977, p. F–15.

each year because of forcible rape. Murder is responsible for a $3.6 billion loss to the economy and one-third of that amount represents income which would have been gainfully earned by the victims. The total social loss from crime cannot be calculated satisfactorily; however, these figures offer an unambiguous description of the estimated cost of crime to society as well as the cost of suppressing it.

Critics of the criminal-justice system like to emphasize the economic cost to the community of goods and services expended to control crime. They claim criminality diverts public funds to crime-control agencies, funds which might otherwise be available to satisfy more desirable needs. Presently, crime is uppermost in the public mind. This fact ought to lead to continued high-priority funding for criminal-justice agency operations.

The administration of criminal justice is carried out by many types of local, county, state, and national agencies. The system is composed of three subsystems operating independently and fulfilling different functions: law enforcement, the courts, and correctional agencies. The basic responsibility for crime control rests with the local level of government. It spends more for criminal-justice activities than the federal and state governments combined. The U.S. Department of Justice and the U.S. Bureau of the Census, using 1975 data, demonstrate the distribution of total direct expenditure for the criminal-justice system by activity and level of government. These data are shown in Table 1-1.

The criminal-justice system is composed of more than 57,000 agencies employing 1,128,569 persons.[3] The costs of operating law-enforcement agencies, courts, legal services and prosecutions, public

TABLE 1-1 Percent Distribution of Total Direct Expenditure for the Criminal-Justice System by Activity and Level of Government, Fiscal Year 1975

LEVEL OF GOVERNMENT	TOTAL	POLICE PROTEC- TION	JUDICIAL	LEGAL SERVICES	PUBLIC DEFENSE	CORREC- TIONS	OTHER CRIMINAL JUSTICE
Total	100.0	100.0	100.0	100.0	100.0	100.0	100.0
Federal	12.7	14.9	8.0	19.0·	31.0	5.6	23.9
State	26.7	15.5	24.1	23.1	23.4	57.1	37.9
Local	60.6	69.6	67.9	57.9	45.6	37.3	38.2

Source: U.S. Department of Justice, Law Enforcement Assistance Administration, and U.S. Bureau of the Census, *Expenditure and Employment Data for the Criminal Justice System: 1975* (Washington, D.C.: U.S. Government Printing Office, 1977), p. 3.

defense, police protection, jails and prisons, and other related activities has reached $71 for each man, woman, and child in the nation.[4] We have looked at the economic costs of crime and its control. Now let us consider the physical extent of crime as measured by arrest statistics provided by our law-enforcement agencies.

THE AMOUNT OF CRIME

The measurement of crime is essential to the study of criminology and to the administration of criminal justice. Law-enforcement statistics are the major source of information on the volume of reported crime. The Federal Bureau of Investigation serves as the national clearinghouse for such statistical information. This agency was assigned that role by Congress in 1930. Each state is responsible for the collection of data from its law-enforcement agencies which is then forwarded to the Federal Bureau of Investigation for inclusion in the Uniform Crime Reporting Program. The fundamental objective of this program is to produce a reliable set of statistics on a national basis for use in law-enforcement administration, operation, and management. All states use the crime classification procedures developed by the Committee on Uniform Crime Records of the International Association of Chiefs of Police. This association serves in an advisory capacity to the Bureau. Use of these procedures provides uniformity in reporting and allows the Bureau to coordinate and analyze statistics received from many jurisdictions. Two types of information are obtained: (1) the number of offenses reported to the police, and (2) the number of reported crimes cleared by arrest. This is published annually in *Uniform Crime Reports for the United States* or, as it is sometimes identified, *Crime in the United States*.

Crimes known to the police provide an accurate estimate of law violations. The Federal Bureau of Investigation has found that some

3

offenses are more likely to be reported than others. These serious and frequently occurring crimes have been identified as Crime Index, or Part I, offenses. This group includes four violent crimes and three property crimes. Violent crimes are: (1) criminal homicide (murder and nonnegligent manslaughter, or manslaughter by negligence; (2) forcible rape; (3) robbery; and (4) aggravated assault. Property crimes are: (1) burglary—breaking or entering; (2) larceny-theft; and (3) motor vehicle theft. The crime index, reported each year in the *Uniform Crime Reports,* is computed as the sum of police reports for the seven Part I offenses.

UNIFORM CRIME REPORTS SCORING SYSTEM

When a Part I offense comes to the attention of the police, it is counted in the class of "offenses reported or known to police," usually abbreviated "offenses reported." Those reported offenses which are determined to be false or baseless are counted as "unfounded complaints." The number of unfounded complaints is subtracted from the number of offenses reported, to yield the number of "actual offenses" or "actual offenses known" or "offenses known to police" or "offenses known." It is these "actual offenses known" which form the basis of the national reports issued annually by the FBI. If the police succeed in establishing the identity of the offender, charging him, and turning him over for prosecution, the offense is then said to be "cleared by arrest." If the police succeed in establishing the identity of the offender and his whereabouts, but arrest and prosecution are not possible because of some reason outside of police control, then the offense is said to be "cleared by exceptional means." Clearances by arrest and clearances by exceptional means are not separated in the reports. They are included in a single count: "offenses cleared by arrest or exceptional means." This category represents all clearances, whether the alleged offender is an adult or a juvenile. When the alleged offender is under eighteen years of age, a clearance is also counted separately in the category "clearances involving persons under eighteen years of age." In the FBI annual reports, *Crime in the United States,* the category "cleared by arrest or exceptional means" is often referred to simply as "cleared by arrest." Tabulations of clearances involving juveniles, defined in UCR as anyone under eighteen, are often entitled "cleared by arrest of juvenile." In addition to counts of offenses and clearances, the UCR also collects, for each Part I offense, data on individuals arrested and on those turned over for prosecution. For Part II offenses, data are not collected on offenses and clearances, but only on arrests and prosecutions; that is, Part II data are based on offenders rather than offenses.

Source: SEARCH Group, Inc., *Dictionary of Criminal Justice Data Terminology* (Washington, D.C.: U.S. Government Printing Office, 1976), p. 95.

Crimes known to the police, using Index offenses only, have risen in recent years. Since 1972, the volume of violent crime has increased 18 percent and property crime 39 percent. The change since 1967 is even more dramatic; violent crimes are up 97 percent and property offenses have increased 91 percent. The change in the incidence of specific offenses, since 1967, reveals the following rise: murder, 53.4 percent; forcible rape, 105.4 percent; robbery, 107.1 percent; aggravated assault, 90.9 percent; burglary, 89.3 percent; larceny-theft, 101.5 percent; and motor vehicle theft, 45.1 percent.[5]

The use of Crime Index offenses in estimating the extent of the crime problem has been criticized. The amount of unreported crime is estimated to be larger than that which is known to law-enforcement agencies. Studies of undetected crime and delinquency suggest that numerous adults and juveniles have committed offenses that are never reported. The Federal Bureau of Investigation is aware of this limitation and states: "The total number of criminal acts that occur is unknown, but those that are reported to law enforcement provide the first means of a count."[6] Hindelang has provided the following list of criticisms that have been made of the *Uniform Crime Reports* in the past:

1. Some offenses are never discovered.
2. Of those that are discovered, some are not reported to authorities.
3. Of those offenses reported to authorities, some are not transmitted to the Uniform Crime Reporting Program.
4. The offense categories used by the FBI are very broad and hence very dissimilar events can fall into the same category.
5. Because the definitions of offense categories vary so much from state to state—in spite of the FBI's efforts to stan-

dardize the categories by providing its own definitions— police agencies in different states will inevitably be using different referents when reporting on specific offense categories.

6. Methods of handling multiple offenses and multiple victims are too simplistic.

7. Population bases for computing rates—for example, using the number of females *and* males as the base for computing the rape rate—are sometimes inappropriate.

8. The use of crude rates rather than rates which are standardized along such dimensions as age, sex, and race may result in distorted areal and temporal comparisons.

9. Many important offenses—e.g., drug offenses—are not among those for which offenses known to the police are reported.

10. The overall measure of offenses known, the crime index, is a simple sum of the offenses known in several categories— irrespective of the various offense categories.

11. The summary nature in which the data are compiled unnecessarily wastes information about offenses.

12. Many of the procedures used by the U.C.R. in presenting results—the manner in which graphs are constructed, the use of time clocks, etc.—overemphasize the crime problem.

13. The manner in which the data are tabulated—for example, using different aggregates of geographic areas for different tables—often makes exact comparison of data from table-to-table and year-to-year impossible.

14. A good deal of important information about the nature of the offense—extent of injury and monetary loss, victim-offender relationship, etc.—is largely ignored by the UCR format.[7]

Determining the actual amount of crime in a community depends upon factors outside the control of a national agency whose task is gathering statistics. This assignment requires an intimate knowledge of the social planning and policy decision making of the local criminal-justice system, as well as knowledge of how state and federal guidelines on crime prevention and control can be implemented locally. In addition, there are numerous reasons why crimes are not reported to the police: the offender may be known to the victim but information is withheld because of friendship or fear of further harm; property losses may be considered minimal by the victim; or the person does not wish to become involved with the police because of apathy, inconvenience, fear, or loss of confidence in the criminal justice system. The reader who is dissatisfied with estimates of crime provided by the Crime Index will find a wealth of unanalyzed data available from the state-level criminal statistics agency, local law-enforcement agencies, criminal courts, probation and parole departments, and the state corrections agency. Many of the records are confidential but a majority of departments provide summary statistics which are helpful.

The second type of information found in the *Uniform Crime Reports* is the number of reported crimes cleared by arrest. A crime is cleared when an offender has been identified, charged with the offense, and taken into custody by a law-enforcement agency. Arrests are reported monthly to the Bureau for Part I offenses and for twenty-two additional offense categories which are known as Part II offenses. Crimes cleared by arrest are further analyzed by age, race, sex, and place of residence (i.e., city, suburb, and rural area).

Since 1969 the annual clearance rate for the Crime Index offenses has averaged 21 percent. In other words, only one-fifth of the serious crimes are cleared by arrest. Certain crimes have a higher clearance rate. In 1976, clearance rates by offense category revealed the following: murder, 79 percent; negligent manslaughter, 76 percent; aggravated assault, 63 percent; forcible rape, 52 percent; robbery, 27 percent; larceny-theft, 19 percent; burglary, 17 percent; and motor vehicle theft, 14 percent.[8]

A review of age, sex, and race profiles for the total number of persons arrested for all crimes in 1976 reveals this pattern:

1. Persons under eighteen years of age made up 25 percent of the total police arrests. This was a 6 percent decrease over the previous year.
2. Males accounted for 84 percent of the arrests. While crime remains predominantly a male activity there are new trends which suggest a changing pattern. The percentage change in arrests for males between 1975 and 1976 was a decrease of 6 percent, and for women a 7 percent decrease was recorded.
3. When race is considered, whites comprise 72 percent of all arrests.[9]

National arrest patterns may fail to reflect the situation in your own community. The decision to charge a person with an offense is governed by many variables that influence the policies of local criminal-justice agencies. And, as we mentioned earlier, only about one-fifth of crimes known to the police are cleared by arrest.

Arrest statistics mask the total number of persons taken into custody each year. For example, the same individual may be arrested for numerous crimes and be counted separately for each. It is important to trace individual offenders from the point of arrest through to the point of final disposition in criminal-justice proceedings. This is difficult because statistics collected by local, state, and federal agencies summarize information useful to only one agency—either the police, courts, or corrections. We require statistics that focus on four key items: offense, victim, defendant, and the court case. Figure 1-2 summarizes the information required for this approach.

A number of states have developed a computerized criminal-history system in order to learn more about the individual offender as he or she is tracked through the system. An example of such a system is the Offender-Based Transaction Statistics system (OBTS), which was first implemented in 1970. The criminal-history record describes each major contact that an individual has with the system by documenting such events as arrests, dispositions, sentences, and correctional commitments. This record is the informational thread that weaves together the functions performed by law enforcement, prosecutors, defense, courts, corrections, probation, and parole. What is significant about a criminal-history record is that data for each offender are recorded separately rather than in summary form. It shows what decisions are being made, where those decisions are made, and permits the consideration of determinations at one level in light of agreements made at other levels in the criminal-justice process. This approach highlights problem areas and identifies situations in which crime control effectiveness is limited. A sample OBTS file is shown in Figure 1-3.

Figure 1-2 Statistics Needed Regarding Four Key Units of Analysis

1. THE OFFENSE
- Follow from victimization through conviction.
- Analyze geographic patterns.
- Relate offenses to persons charged.

2. THE VICTIM
- Follow from victimization through conviction.
- Study reporting behavior.
- Survey victims to evaluate police or court treatment.
- Analyze impediments to witness cooperation.

3. THE DEFENDANT
- Follow from arrest through incarceration.
- Analyze recidivism — rearrest, reprosecution, reconviction.
- Identify most serious defendants.

4. THE COURT CASE
- Follow from arrest through disposition.
- Study the decision to file charges.
- Identify cases involving a serious offense or defendant.
- Study types of cases going to trial.
- Study reasons for dismissals.

Source: Institute for Law and Social Research, *Expanding the Perspective of Crime Data: Performance Implications for Policymakers* (Washington, D.C.: U.S. Government Printing Office, 1977), p. 18.

Critics of computerized criminal-history information systems point to the inaccuracies that can occur when records are maintained in crime data banks on a nationwide scale. Criminal-history information consists of notations of arrests, detentions, indictments, informations or other formal criminal charges, and any disposition stemming

Figure 1-3   Offender Based Transaction Statistics (OBTS)

IDENTIFICATION ELEMENTS

State Identification No.
FBI No.
State Record No.
Sex
Race
Date of Birth

POLICE/PROSECUTOR ELEMENTS

Arresting Agency No.
Sequence Letter
Date of Arrest
Charged Offense (Most Serious)
Police Disposition
Prosecutor Disposition
Police/Prosecutor Disposition Date

LOWER CRIMINAL COURT ELEMENTS

Court Identification No.
Initial Appearance Date
Disposition Date
Charged Offense (Most Serious)
Lower Court Disposition
Release Action
Release Action Date
Final Charge (Most Serious)
Type of Charge
Plea (at Trial)
Type of Trial
Date of Sentence
Type of Sentence
Confinement Term (Days)
Probation Term (Months)
Type of Counsel

COUNTY PROSECUTOR GRAND JURY ELEMENTS

Prosecutor Identification No.
Date of Filing
Type of Filing
Filing Procedure
Date of Arraignment
Charged Offense (Most Serious)
Initial Plea
Release Action
Release Action Date

FELONY TRIAL ELEMENTS

Court Identification No.
Trial Date
Trial Type
Final Plea
Trial Ending/Disposition Date
Final Charge (Most Serious)
Type of Charge
Court Disposition
Sentence Date
Sentence Type
Confinement — Prison (Years)
Confinement — Jail (Days)
Probation (Months)
Type of Counsel

CORRECTIONS ELEMENTS

Agency Identifier
Receiving Agency
Date Received
Status
Date of Exit
Exit

Source: Leonard Oberlander (ed.), *Quantitative Tools for Criminal Justice Planning* (Washington, D.C.: U.S. Government Printing Office, 1975), p. 84.

from such charges, including sentencing, correctional supervision, and release. The term also includes records of dismissals or decisions to drop charges. There have been a number of lawsuits resulting from the use of computerized information when individuals were unaware that a history was being kept. The ability of agencies to protect an individual's right to privacy will determine whether we succeed in identifying and tracing career criminals through the justice system. Computer security and accurate record keeping must stay abreast of technological advances to develop criminal-justice information systems. The Crime Control Act of 1973 mandates that states develop operational procedures to ensure privacy and security of criminal-history record information. Regulations implementing this requirement were issued in 1975. The U.S. Department of Justice and Law Enforcement Assistance Administration regulations refer to the following areas: (1) completeness and accuracy; (2) audit; (3) individual access and review; (4) limitations on dissemination; and (5) security.[10]

Measuring and recording the amount of crime occurring in this country is difficult. However, criminology and criminal justice are two areas of study which help us to better understand criminal behavior and the operations of rule-enforcing criminal-justice agencies.

CRIMINAL JUSTICE AND CRIMINOLOGY

During the past ten years the number of criminal-justice programs in academic institutions has expanded dramatically. There are numerous programs in two- and four-year colleges and universities. A number of departments began as police-science programs. The purpose of the new academic discipline of criminal justice is to prepare students to understand the operations and organization of the criminal-justice system with its many agencies—law enforcement, the courts, probation, correctional institutions, and parole. It concentrates on the criminal-justice process, which involves the apprehension of those accused of law violation, the determination of guilt or innocence, and, in the case of the guilty, the assignment of an appropriate sanction. The roles of the participants in this process are analyzed: defendant, arresting officer, prosecutor, defense counsel, judge, jail personnel, probation officer, institutional staff, parole board, and parole officer. The emphasis is upon crime control. The criminal-justice system is viewed in its entirety, not as isolated, discrete parts. We are concerned with the quality of justice provided by the system, the competency of the personnel employed within it, and the development and implementation of innovative ideas to correct inefficiency. James Q. Wilson challenges us when he asserts, "Above all, we can try to learn more about what works, and in the process abandon our ideological preconceptions about what *ought* to work."[11]

10

While criminal justice is concerned with decision making by control agencies, criminology as a field of study examines the underlying causes of criminal behavior and societal responses to crime and the offender. Fox tells us "there have been many approaches to the problem of crime from many different viewpoints with varying degrees of compatibility and agreement."[12]

Before 1700 there was great confusion in legal matters that was due primarily to vague definitions of what crime was and what proper punishment was. If questions did arise about the cause of crime they were likely to be answered by reference to such religious concepts as free will, sin, and natural law. There was intellectual sniping directed piecemeal against the criminal-justice system and existing laws. This culminated in a sweeping attack delivered by Cesare Beccaria. His essay *On Crimes and Punishments,* published in 1764, was the beginning of the end for the old system. This essay was widely distributed in Europe and helped create the mood for penal reform. The classical school emerged as a result of principles put forward by the young Italian lawyer Beccaria. A more calculated method of punishment was introduced. He conceived the idea of uniform punishment for crime and believed that pain and pleasure strongly determine the direction of human actions. The work of the sentencing judge was reduced to a legally calculated, administrative act. Punishments consisted of various penalties which were determined in advance by legislative mandate. There was no need for the sentencing judge to concern himself with the social background of the offender. But as time passed the application of systematic sentences brought additional injustice. It seemed fairer to apply differential sentences based upon an understanding of the individual and his crime. It was the beginning of individualized justice. This philosophy remained virtually unchanged until the nineteenth century and the advent of the positive school of criminology.

The founder of the positive school was an Italian physician named Cesare Lombroso. He claimed some individuals were born criminals. This theory was later refuted but it did lead to a new way of looking at crime: that is, the scientific study of the individual criminal. The emphasis shifted to the offender and away from the sentence. The impact of Lombroso on criminological thought can be seen in the popularity of his book *Criminal Man,* which was published in 1876 and revised or reprinted five times in the following twenty years.

The scientific study of criminals was the important goal of the positive school. Many years after this school of thought was established controversies raged among its adherents. However, it paved the way for many new explanations. Its followers stressed the role of biology, psychology, psychiatry, and sociology in understanding those who violate the established laws. If the criminal was influenced by

11

conditions within himself and his environment, then reformation was possible. Thus, the twentieth century became the age of criminal reform or "treatment to fit the offender." Later, the mood changed from treating the offender to adjusting the inequalities within American society.

A new school of criminology has developed within the past decade. It is identified as critical criminology, conflict criminology, or the "new criminology." Its followers claim that traditional criminology is conservative and supports the status quo by limiting study to conventional forms of crime. The critical criminologist is concerned with the oppressive use of power by the state in matters of law and criminal justice as well as the sociopolitical nature of crime. Tony Platt and Paul Takagi, two articulate spokesmen for this criminological viewpoint, state:

> The social sciences in North American universities have always *legitimated* the ruling ideology of monopoly capital and ruthlessly excluded or repressed any serious study of Marxism. Criminology, with its particularly close ties to the state apparatus, was originally developed as a science of repression; and the long-standing collaboration between criminology and the state have been even more strongly cemented in recent years with the help of massive investments and subsidies from the federal government and corporate think tanks.[13]

Conflict criminology declares that crime committed in the interest of the state is seldom to be found in official offense statistics. Lopez-Rey cautions us to keep in mind the realities of unconventional crime or governmental repression:

1. Out of 137 United Nations Member States barely 25 or 18 percent have democratic regimes if by this is understood the free exercise of the most fundamental human rights.
2. These undemocratic regimes usually have at their disposal large special police services and generally only a single political party is permitted.
3. Out of 85 developing countries in 65 or 77 percent, torture and the number of "persons missing" is on the increase.
4. The number of victims of terrorism and guerrilla warfare is steadily increasing.
5. Political, economic, and police corruption of a criminal character are not isolated phenomena but an expression of the decline of socioeconomic and political systems whatever the label attached to them.

12

6. In many countries, developed or developing, capitalist or socialist, the penal system, particularly the judiciary, is used for political or class purposes. By this is understood not only the justice "administered" to political dissidents or suspects but also that given in favor of privileged interests of many sorts.[14]

The sociological contribution to causation literature has received greater emphasis than other theoretical approaches. Courses such as social problems, criminology, delinquency, and corrections have been offered in sociology departments since the turn of the century. This instruction and the accompanying body of criminological writings are the result of steady interest by sociologists. They had traditionally evinced a sensitive concern for the individual tied to an environment of poverty. The cultural transmission of criminal and delinquent values between individuals and groups was viewed as a primary cause of deviant behavior.

A number of sociology departments pioneered in the development of criminology as an area of specialization. Among these were the University of Chicago, the University of Pennsylvania, and the University of Washington. The first sociology department in America was established in 1892 at the University of Chicago. The earliest sociological writings dealing with crime causation were the result of theses and dissertations written at Chicago. Thereafter, the study of crime and delinquency became a legitimate concern for sociologists. Faculty and student attention was directed toward the analysis of individual criminal careers as well as toward the environment in which they flourished. The first American textbook on criminology appeared in 1908. It was written by Maurice Parmelee and entitled *The Principles of Anthropology and Sociology in Their Relations to Criminal Procedure.* It offered further support to the premise that criminology was a specialization within the field of sociology.

The differential-association theory of the late Edwin Sutherland and the Richard Cloward and Lloyd Ohlin theory of delinquency and opportunity remain the most influential sociological contributions to criminology. Sutherland was a product of the "Chicago School" and was known for his studies of professional theft and white-collar crime. He authored a popular general text on criminology which is now in its tenth edition. He supported the premise that the acquisition of criminal behavior patterns is a social process. Sutherland introduced his theory of differential association in 1939. It has been refined by his former student, Donald Cressey, in recent years. The following is a recent elaboration of the theory:

1. *Criminal behavior is learned.* Negatively, this means that criminal behavior is not inherited, as such; also, the person

13

who is not already trained in crime does not invent criminal behavior, just as a person does not make mechanical inventions unless he has had training in mechanics.

2. *Criminal behavior is learned in interaction with other persons in a process of communication.* The communication is verbal in many respects but includes also "the communication of gestures."

3. *The principal part of the learning of criminal behavior occurs within intimate personal groups.* Negatively, this means that the impersonal agencies of communication, such as movies and newspapers, play a relatively unimportant part in the genesis of criminal behavior.

4. *When criminal behavior is learned, the learning* includes (a) techniques of committing the crime, which are sometimes very complicated, sometimes very simple; (b) the specific direction of motives, drives, rationalizations, and attitudes.

5. *The specific direction of motives and drives is learned from definitions of the legal codes as favorable or unfavorable.* In some societies an individual is surrounded by persons who invariably define the legal codes as rules to be observed, while in others he is surrounded by persons whose definitions are favorable to the violation of the legal codes. In our American society these definitions are almost always mixed, with the consequence that we have culture conflict in relation to the legal codes.

6. *A person becomes delinquent because of an excess of definitions favorable to violation of law over definitions unfavorable to violation of law.* This is the principle of differential association.[15]

Sutherland was concerned with the method by which criminal behavior is acquired by an individual. Criminal justice must evaluate current crime prevention and control policies in order to determine whether criminal careers can be terminated.

Poverty has continued to play a significant role in explanations for crime and delinquency just as it did in the earliest writings of the Chicago school. The Cloward and Ohlin theory of delinquency and opportunity is probably the most important contribution to the study of causation since Sutherland's differential association. Cloward and Ohlin, writing in 1960, stressed the uniformity of conventional success goals in our culture. They claim there is an emphasis upon financial success and the acquisition of material goods. Mass advertising campaigns reach everyone and most youngsters and young adults want the same things. However, there are artificial barriers against achievement and this is usually determined by social class position. Frustration occurs when personal goals cannot be achieved. When legitimate opportunities for goal acquisition are absent the person will seek alternatives. These may be criminal or delinquent solutions. This theory, articulated in *Delinquency and Opportunity,* was influential in the War on Poverty during the administrations of John F. Kennedy and Lyndon B. Johnson.[16] Wiley Manuel, California's first black Supreme Court justice, discussed the meaning of legitimate opportunity in a recent interview.

> Wiley Manuel is refreshingly unpretentious, a man seemingly unchanged by his success and a status.
> "I'm a guy who obviously came from relatively modest beginnings. I never developed any great political power. I started at the lowest rung and just about worked up to the highest—by being a craftsman."

Wiley W. Manuel, Associate Justice, Supreme Court of California.

Asked whether he felt a sense of special responsibility to blacks, as a role model, he replied:

"I hope I'm a model for all kinds of Americans—blacks, Chicanos, native Americans, Asian-Americans—who have to work their way up. A part of the problem for minorities is arriving at that point when they feel 'this is my society, too. I can do as good a job as anybody else.'"

"Kids today have to have images of people who soberly go about doing their work and move along. People in the ghetto are frustrated. They see the image of the superfly who earns quick money. It's important to stress that the legitimate norms and modes of getting things are available."

Asked whether he minds being referred to constantly as the first black on the California Supreme Court, Manuel smiled and thought for a moment.

"I think it's important to people out there to realize that there is a place to go. It may make a difference to a kid in Hunters Point or a kid in the Mission to know that I am black."

Source: *San Francisco Sunday Examiner & Chronicle,* 23 October 1977, p. A-4. Reprinted by permission.

Criminal justice can minimize the attractiveness of the illegitimate opportunity structure by reducing the benefits of crime. This can be accomplished by increasing the penalties for certain crimes, requiring mandatory incarceration for some offenders at the time of the first offense, reducing plea bargaining, and seeking speedy trials and immediate imposition of the sentence. These policies may make crime less attractive but no catalyst exists to expand legitimate opportunity as a crime-prevention measure. Communities mobilize resources more readily for control than they do for prevention programs. Both are needed. Familiarity with theoretical explanations for criminal behavior means that the worker in the field can identify and explore new leads which may have been overlooked in the processing of offenders in the criminal-justice system. Meanwhile, the problem of urban violence points to our failure in controlling crime.

URBAN VIOLENCE

Criminal-justice agencies and policymakers have to deal with the depth of public concern about the very real fear of street crime. People residing in urban areas know about the problem from incidents involving themselves or neighbors. Their fear is due to realistic external dangers. It results in a readjustment of life style or an altering of everyday behavior. This is done to reduce the likelihood of being victimized. An example of altered behavior is noted in a study of neighborhood fear in eight American cities where 45 percent of those questioned said they felt either "somewhat or very unsafe about being out alone in their neighborhoods at night."[17] Other forms of altered behavior include carrying weapons for self-protection, installing additional lighting and locking devices in residences, taking taxicabs instead of subways or city buses, and refusing to walk through neighborhoods alone.

Crimes known to the police provide a helpful estimate of the volume of crime; however, more information is needed if we are to calculate the amount of unreported crime and its social cost. A number of questions should be asked if a community is to possess adequate knowledge about the local crime problem and allocate police resources to respond to the seriousness of crime instead of merely to the number of reported offenses. These include the following:

1. How much street crime has there been in the past few months? Is it increasing or decreasing?

2. What portion of the street crime is committed for an apparent economic motive, such as holdups or purse-snatching?

3. Is economically motivated street theft changing at a faster or slower pace than street violence where economic gain is not involved, such as rape or assault?

4. How much street violence and theft is the result of a random encounter between strangers? Does street crime involve a significant number of victims and offenders who know each other in some social capacity?

5. When fewer people walk the streets due to real or imagined fear of crime, do street robberies rise because of the lessened mutual protection or deterrent effects that people provide from their sheer number and presence? Conversely, do street robberies decrease because fewer potential victims place themselves in the risk setting?

6. In what ways does fear modify behavior in regard to the use of mass transit, restaurants, downtown shopping, or other public services? How does this relate, if at all, to the actual occurrence of crime?

7. Where and when does street crime occur? Does it shift in time and space; if so, under what circumstances?

8. How much assaultive violence in the city streets is attributable to juvenile gangs? Is this phenomenon rising, cresting, or slackening?
9. Who are the victims of street attacks? Women? Men? The young? The old? Blacks? Whites?[18]

Since 1974 the U.S. Bureau of the Census has been involved in a statistical program known as the National Crime Panel for the Law Enforcement Assistance Administration. This victim survey is attempting to obtain meaningful data about crime in selected cities. A number of questions are asked including whether a person has been a victim of a crime, what the crime was, and whether it was reported to the police. The program has a general objective of developing insights into the impact of selected crimes upon victims. The findings of the National Crime Panel program are based on interviews with approximately 160,000 people living in 65,000 households and with 15,000 commercial businesses in the United States.

The advent of victimization surveys make possible for the first time the measurement of the volume of certain types of crimes that are not reported by victims to local law-enforcement agencies. The Panel, in studies of various cities, found the percentage of crimes reported to the police varied by offense. Crimes against the person are reported more frequently than property offenses by the victims. Recent National Crime Panel Survey Reports indicate these differences, which are shown in Table 1-2.

It is alarming to find that the most serious crimes committed against the individual are often unreported to the police. The reasons given by victims for withholding information include: the criminal event was not important enough to justify notification of law-enforcement authorities; nothing could be accomplished because of lack of proof; the physical harm was minimal; or the police would not want to be bothered or they would not do anything after receiving the report. These explanations suggest that the public has an inadequate knowledge of the operations of the criminal-justice system.

Victimization studies provide useful estimates of unreported crime. However, these surveys are relatively new in this field and they are expensive. Also, some methodological problems remain to be solved before unreported crime studies are used in formulating crime-prevention programs.

The victim has been described as the forgotten person in the criminal-justice system. Crime victims face a number of financial, legal, and emotional problems. Victim service centers are needed if we are to provide help to those requiring emergency medical and financial assistance. Most jurisdictions forbid police to transport victims to their homes even though apprehended criminals are taken

TABLE 1-2 Percent of Crimes Reported to Police by Victims

TYPE OF CRIME	PERCENT REPORTED TO THE POLICE		
	1974	1975	1976
Crimes of violence	47	47	49
Rape	52	56	53
Personal robbery	54	53	53
Robbery with injury	62	65	63
From serious assault	67	67	66
From minor assault	56	63	60
Robbery without injury	50	48	49
Assault	45	45	48
Aggravated assault	53	55	59
With injury	61	65	62
Attempted assault with weapon	50	50	57
Simple assault	39	39	41
With injury	46	48	46
Attempted assault without weapon	37	36	39
Crimes of theft	25	26	27
Purse snatching	46	49	52
Pocket picking	29	27	30

Source: *Criminal Victimization in the United States: A Comparison of 1974 and 1975 Findings,* U.S. Department of Justice, Law Enforcement Assistance Administration (Washington, D.C.: U.S. Government Printing Office, 1977), p. 32; and *Criminal Victimization in the United States: A Comparison of 1975 and 1976 Findings,* U.S. Department of Justice, Law Enforcement Assistance Administration (Washington, D.C.: U.S. Government Printing Office, 1978), p. 48.

away in a squad car. The victim, who may have been robbed of all cash and credit cards only moments before, must find his or her own way home. A well-known symphony conductor was the victim of a pickpocket while waiting to board his plane for New York City where he was to remain overnight before continuing on another flight for Germany. He discovered his loss while the plane was in flight to New York. No one would cash his personal check in New York City. He had to sleep in Central Park that evening and, fortunately, he was not robbed or assaulted in the park. We find most jurisdictions bill victims of violent crimes for ambulance services if they are injured. Many rape victims are turned away by hospitals and private physicians.

Victim-compensation laws have been passed in a number of states and these provide some financial help to victims. Unfortunately, such programs have serious limitations. Most victims are not aware of the law. It can take one or two years for the victim to receive compensation from the state. The victim must prove that he or she has suffered serious financial hardship as a result of the crime in some states. The majority of programs treat victims as welfare clients and require them to pass a means test as part of the eligibility requirements. In addition, compensation payments seldom cover all costs to the victim. The first state compensation program for victims of violent crime was established in California in 1965. Twenty states presently operate such programs and the number is increasing. Awards allowable under California law now total $23,500 per claim. There is a $10,000 maximum for medical or medically related expenses; $10,000 maximum for lost wages or support; $3,000 maximum for job retraining or similar employment-oriented rehabilitation services, and a maximum of $500 for attorney fees. No reimbursement is made for loss of personal property. To qualify, a claimant must be at least eighteen years of age and have been a resident of the state when the crime was committed. Application must be made within a year of the crime, unless an extension is granted by the State Board of Control which handles victim-compensation claims. If the victim was killed, anyone who assumes the burial or medical expenses may file. There are several tests which must be met before funds can be allowed. The person filing must have suffered an out-of-pocket loss as a direct result of the crime and show that as a result of physical injury he or she can no longer meet essential obligations or expenses either from income or assets available for such purpose. Victims of automobile accidents will not qualify unless the claimant was the victim of a hit-and-run driver or if the accident was caused by a person who was driving under the influence of drugs or alcohol. The claimant must have suffered a loss greater than $100 or equal to at least 20 percent of his or her net monthly income. After an application has been filed and research and investigation have been completed by the board staff and the staff of the office of the attorney general, a recommendation is made to the board allowing or denying the victim's claim. These procedures have taken as long as twenty-six months; the average time is thirteen months.

A number of organizations such as the National Organization of Victim Assistance are attempting to alert communities to the need for services to victims of violent crime. The U.S. House of Representatives approved the Victim of Crimes Act of 1977 on September 30 of that year. This represents the first federal crime-compensation law. Previously, the U.S. Senate had passed such bills five times, but each time the House of Representatives killed the legislation. The bill will reimburse the states having programs to compensate victims for 25 percent of the first $25,000 they pay each claimant.[19]

TERRORISM

Victims of violent crimes are no longer the forgotten people in the justice system. Federal and state legislation is correcting that problem. However, recent years have seen the growth of a new type of criminal. These are people who operate in large groups and use indiscriminate violence in order to achieve their goals. Many of them believe that society is the criminal, not they. The National Advisory Committee on Criminal Justice Standards and Goals, in its *Report of the Task Force on Disorders and Terrorism,* lists a number of leftwing and rightwing organizations whose members have been involved in one or more acts of terrorism or violence. The criminal acts of these individuals often injure or kill innocent victims. These organizations include:

Groups of Leftwing Political Orientation

1. Black Muslims—Primarily a religious and commercial organization, its believers differed from the orthodox Muslims in that only blacks were allowed to become members. Leader Elijah Muhammad's teachings, that all white men were devils and that blacks would rise up against them and establish a separate state, were carried to their extreme with the random killing of fourteen whites in San Francisco by the Muslim Zebra murderers. With the exception of the Zebra killings, the violence associated with the Black Muslims has involved shoot-outs with police and assassinations within the sect. With the death of Elijah Muhammad, more internal violence was feared, but Wallace D. Muhammad's succession as Supreme Minister was peaceful. Secular affairs (at least $46 million in assets) are run by a six-man committee, with Wallace's brother Hubert, and Muhammad Ali as members. In June of 1975, Wallace B. Muhammad announced that white people would be allowed to join the Black Muslims. *Muhammad Speaks,* the Black Muslim newspaper, has stopped demanding a separate black state. Thus the sect's potential for violence seems on the decline.

2. Student Nonviolent Coordinating Committee (SNCC)— Founded in the early 1960s, this small, multiracial group was primarily involved in voter registration in the South. In 1966, it was a staunch verbal advocate of black power—but by 1970 it had declined, with its leader H. Rap Brown still in prison, and its other major spokesman,

21

Stokely Carmichael, traveling around the world promoting Pan-Africanism.

3. Revolutionary Action Movement (RAM)—Organized in 1963, this group advocated militant self-defense for blacks. In June 1967, police in New York City and Philadelphia rounded up sixteen members and seized rifles, carbines, and shotguns. Two were charged with plotting to assassinate black moderates. Four more were later arrested in Philadelphia on charges of conspiring to foment a riot by poisoning the water supply. By 1968, the group had declined.

4. Republic of New Africa (RNA)—Founded in April 1968 with a few of its members formerly in RAM, this group had similar separatist goals. In August 1970, after a police raid on the residence of their leader, Imari, eleven members were charged with murder, assault, and waging war against the State of Mississippi.

5. Black Panther Party (BPP)—Founded in October 1966 by Huey Newton and Bobby Seale in Oakland, Calif., its membership swelled to several thousand with chapters in major U.S. cities. Their papers urged blacks to arm themselves for self-defense and liberation. On April 2, 1969, in a New York bomb plot case, twenty-one Black Panthers were indicted on charges of plotting to set off bombs in five midtown department stores. All were acquitted. On July 4, 1969, Stokely Carmichael, prime minister of the Black Panther Party, called a meeting to form a National Committee to Combat Fascism. The House Internal Security Committee stated on August 23, 1971, that the Black Panthers posed a danger to policemen but were "totally incapable of overthrowing the government." On January 30, 1972, Huey Newton said the party had abandoned the pick-up-the-gun approach. The violence associated with the Black Panthers has come out of confrontations with police, factional clashes within the party, and feuds with the rival black power group, the U.S. Cultural Organization (US). (The enmity between the BPP and US was allegedly encouraged by the FBI.) No longer instituting armed patrols in Oakland, the few hundred still active operate a shoe distribution program, an exterminating service, and health clinics.

6. U.S. Cultural Organization (US)—Based in Southern California, this black power group, led by Ron Karenga, competed with the Black Panthers to represent the radical

22

black community. Its members have been traced to at least two shoot-outs with the Black Panthers, in which three Panthers were killed.

7. Black Liberation Army (BLA)—Founded in 1971 as an offshoot of the Eldridge Cleaver faction of the Black Panthers, these more militant members have allegedly been responsible for several police killings in New York and San Francisco, and armed robberies to fund the organization. In New York numerous attempts have been made by BLA members to escape from prison. With the November 15, 1973, killing in New York City of Twymon Meyers, police believe that most BLA members have been either imprisoned or killed in shoot-outs with the police.

8. Fuerzas Armadas de Liberación Nacional Puertorriquena (FALN)—Although the main ideology of this group is the belief that Puerto Rico should be independent from the United States, many of its communiqués concern themselves with exploitation by bankers and stockbrokers (yanqui imperialists) of the working classes. The FALN introduced themselves on October 16, 1974, with the bombing of five banks in New York City. The bombings seem to occur in groups, with New York City as the central location. The FALN does not seem overly concerned with the preservation of life: they are responsible for booby-trapping an explosion for a police officer and the bombing of a crowded restaurant in New York City. The FALN is suspected of causing twenty-seven bombings in New Jersey, New York City, Chicago, Philadelphia, and Washington, D.C., resulting in four deaths and fifty-seven injuries.

9. Jewish Defense League (JDL)—Founded in 1968 to protest Soviet treatment of the Jews, its leaders were a lawyer named Bert Zweibon and an orthodox rabbi named Meir Kahane. Members were trained in karate and the use of weapons to defend themselves against anti-Semitism, their motto being "Never Again." During JDL's first three years they harassed Russians, Arabs, and Black Panthers with demonstrations and relatively harmless activities, such as letting loose mice and toads. Targets of their sabotage and bombings have been the offices of Soviet airlines (Aeroflot) and the trade agency (Amtorg). Their first reported bombing took place at Aeroflot and Intourist offices on November 25, 1970. One person died as a result of the bombing of agent Sol Hurok's office, an event that is widely attributed to JDL, though this was never proven. Early in 1976, a

group calling itself the Jewish Armed Resistance began claiming bombings in New York City directed at targets similar to those of the JDL. Though the JDL acts as a conduit for the Jewish Armed Resistance's communiqués, it disclaims any connection.

10. American Indian Movement (AIM)—This group of young, militant Indians has sought better treatment of American Indians through dramatic occupations. AIM first gained national prominence with its Trail of Broken Treaties to Washington, D.C., and the nonviolent occupation of the Bureau of Indian Affairs (BIA) building. AIM leaders Russell Means and Dennis Banks negotiated with a presidential commission set up in response to the occupation of Wounded Knee in 1973. The violence attributed to AIM is associated with shoot-outs with federal marshals or FBI agents or infighting with the more traditional tribal leaders at the Pine Ridge Reservation in South Dakota.

11. Students for a Democratic Society (SDS)—Founded in 1959, this loosely knit student organization did not emerge as a political force until Tom Hayden's and Al Haber's Port Huron Statement at the 1962 convention. The statement called for an alliance of blacks, students, peace groups, and liberal organizations to influence the Democratic Party. The first anti-Vietnam War march was organized by SDS in the spring of 1965, which resulted in a sudden growth of membership. In April and May 1968, black and white SDS members occupied Columbia University. At the 1969 SDS convention in Chicago, a serious dispute arose when the Maoist Progressive Party attacked the Black Panthers as being more nationalist than revolutionary. The factions that developed around this issue led to SDS's disintegration. One of the more militant factions was the Revolutionary Youth Movement I, most members of which became Weathermen. The "Weatherman Paper," sponsored by Bernadine Dohrn, Jeff Jones, Bill Ayers, Mark Rudd, et al., was delivered at this convention and called for guerrilla tactics to bring about the destruction of U.S. imperialism.

12. Weather Underground Organization (WU) (Changed from the original Weathermen because of its sexist connotations)—In 1969, the Weather Underground concentrated on recruiting high school students for their mass action in Chicago, by picketing high schools and rushing into classes screaming "jailbreak." Disappointed with the poor showing by radicals at their October 8–11, 1969, Chicago

24

Days of Rage, and angered by the killing of two Black
Panthers in a police raid, the decision was made to turn the
Weather Underground into an elite, paramilitary organization to carry out urban guerrilla warfare; thus it became
the grandperson of American revolutionary organizations.
On May 25, 1970, the *New York Times* received the first
communiqué from the Weather Underground, stating that
the group would go underground and that "within the next
fourteen days we will attack a symbol or institution of
American justice." With hardly a day to spare, the New
York police building was bombed on June 9.

    The only fatalities associated with the Weather Un-
derground (buildings are typically bombed late at night
and the bombing is preceded by a warning call) occurred on
March 6, 1970, when three Weatherpeople were killed in a
New York City townhouse after a series of explosions.
Police investigation revealed the townhouse was being
used as a bomb factory with the bombs manufactured being
of the kind used to kill or maim people rather than destroy
property. Some of the more spectacular incidents credited
to the group include the bombing of the Capitol on March
1, 1971, the bombing of the Pentagon on May 19, 1974, and
the freeing of Timothy Leary from a San Luis Obispo
prison on September 13, 1970. The Weather Underground's
bombing activities lessened considerably in 1972 (there
was only the Pentagon bombing) and 1973 (there were only
two bombings), but picked up again with four evenly
spaced bombings in 1974. In July 1974, copies of their
statement of revolutionary ideology and interpretation of
American history, "Prairie Fire," were distributed in the
San Francisco Bay Area and in Boston. The authors claim
credit for nineteen bombings in the United States since
1969. In terms of predicting future strategies of Weather
Underground activity, the document asserts that "legal and
clandestine struggle are both necessary; . . . peaceful
methods and violent methods . . ." will be used.

13. Sam Melville—Arrested in the act of bombing U.S. Army
trucks, he admitted to a number of 1969 bombings in the
New York City area; the United Fruit Co. pier, the Marine
Midland Bank, and the simultaneous bombings of the
General Motors building, the R.C.A. building, and a Chase
Manhattan Bank. A former plumbing hardware designer,
this thirty-three-year-old revolutionary typically positioned
his bombs so as to wreak the maximum amount of destruction. He was killed in the 1971 uprising at the Attica Correctional Facility.

14. Symbionese Liberation Army (SLA)—Formed out of associations between prison-reform-minded white radicals and members of a prison group called the Black Cultural Association at the California Medical Facility at Vacaville, the SLA emerged with the November 7, 1973, incomprehensible killing of Oakland school superintendent Marcus Foster. Their next act was to kidnap newspaper heiress Patricia Hearst on February 4, 1974. As the terms for her release, they demanded that $2 million in food be given to the poor of the Bay Area. When that food giveaway broke down into chaos, another distribution date was arranged; though it went much more smoothly, Patricia Hearst was not released. Through the taped communiqués sent to radio stations, Patricia Hearst appeared to be progressively more alienated from her parents until she eventually declared her new revolutionary identity as Tanya and took part in the April 15th robbery of the Hibernia Bank. On May 18, 1974, six SLA members died in a gun battle and ensuing fire in a suburb of Los Angeles, with Emily and Bill Harris and Patricia Hearst viewing the entire incident in a nearby motel. Aside from a suspected role in a Sacramento bank robbery, the SLA concentrated on anonymity until Patricia Hearst and the Harrises were recaptured in San Francisco on September 18, 1975.

    It is suspected that the remnants of the SLA have joined with the New World Liberation Front (NWLF). On February 12, 1976, San Simeon, the Hearst mansion, was bombed. The NWLF claimed credit for the bombing, and James Kilgore (former fellow house painter of Stephen Soliah, in whose apartment Patty Hearst was arrested, and also suspected in an SLA bank robbery in Sacramento) was identified as being on the tour that day at San Simeon.

15. New World Liberation Front (NWLF)—Based in the San Francisco Bay Area, this leftist group has adopted techniques similar to those of the Weather Underground—bombing accompanied by warnings and communiqués. The NWLF has developed the communiqué into an art form, to the point of having designated aboveground spokesmen. NWLF espouses a variety of leftist causes and directs its attacks primarily against major corporations or government buildings. In 1970, the NWLF published the late Brazilian revolutionary Carlos Marighella's *Minimanual of the Urban Guerrilla*. Their first recorded entry into violent action was the August 5,

26

1974, unsuccessful bombing of an insurance agency in Burlingame. In 1974, the NWLF claimed eight bombings; the majority of the targets were linked to International Telephone and Telegraph, which the NWLF claimed "drained the life of poor people" and "must . . . admit complicity in Chile's murderous coup." In 1975, twenty-two bombings were attributed to the group, many of them directed against utility towers belonging to Pacific Gas and Electric (PG&E). Their demands have ranged from better health care at the San Bruno jail to free utilities for retired people. The most active revolutionary group in the United States today, it is believed by some that the NWLF acts as an umbrella for other terrorist groups in California, such as the Chicano Liberation Front, the Red Guerrilla Family, and the remnants of the SLA.

16. Red Guerrilla Family (RGF)—This Bay-Area-based group emerged on March 27, 1975, with the bombing of the FBI office in Berkeley. Though less active than the NWLF, the bombings claimed by the Red Guerrilla Family have been more powerful. The similarities between the two groups (on two occasions they have bombed on the same day; their targets are similar) has led to speculation that either the Red Guerrilla Family is another name adopted by NWLF members to make revolutionary groups appear to be more numerous, or the two groups are working in cooperation with each other.

17. Chicano Liberation Front (CLF)—Another group with possible ties to the NWLF, this group was formed in the barrios section of Los Angeles in response to the deaths of Chicanos in an antiwar rally. Its targets have included banks, government offices, and supermarkets. Although it was very active in the early 1970s, the group declined after receiving a great deal of criticism for the killing of a Chicano employee in one of its bombings. It too is suspected of having joined with the NWLF.

18. Emiliano Zapata Unit (EZP)—Yet another San Francisco-based group, it appeared in October 14, 1975, with the unsuccessful bombing of a PG&E tower in Belmont, Calif. In October, a number of Safeway stores were bombed in the Bay Area. The Emiliano Zapata Unit claimed one of those bombings (in Oakland) on October 31. Three more bombings were claimed by the EZP until on February 17, 1976, while making an arrest for an attack on a home in Marin

27

County, the police traced the suspects to a group called the New Dawn Collective. The New Dawn Collective had described itself as an overground voice for revolutionary groups. From that arrest, agents and local police were able to raid a house in Richmond, Calif., on February 21, seizing 130 pounds of explosives and arresting six persons. Documents in the house linked the suspects with the Emiliano Zapata Unit.

Groups of Rightwing Orientation

1. Ku Klux Klan (KKK)—After a lull during World War II, the KKK returned to intimidating blacks, Jews, and Catholics through burning crosses, bombings, beatings, murders, and lynchings. The incidents occurred in waves, in 1945, 1948, and in 1950. the KKK responded to the civil rights movement with a new wave of such incidents in the early 1960s. FBI infiltration has undermined the secret organization, but it is still active in areas where racial integration is a major issue. A recent event for which KKK members were convicted was the bombing of school buses in Pontiac, Mich., on August 30, 1971.

2. Minutemen—A paramilitary, rightwing organization, their primary activity was harassing leftwing organizations, building up weapons arsenals, and threatening liberals with their insignia, the cross hairs of a rifle scope. Police arrested nineteen members as they reportedly prepared to sabotage three leftwing camps in New York State on October 30, 1966. On October 18, 1971, charges against the nineteen were dropped due to a court decision that held that the original search warrants were defective. Some members were alleged to have participated in at least one bank robbery to fund the organization. Strongest in the 1960s, the group declined by the end of the decade following the conviction of their leader, Robert DuPugh, for a federal firearms violation.

3. Legion of Justice—Between 1969 and 1971, this Chicago-based group reportedly beat and gassed anti-Vietnam War demonstrators and sabotaged theaters housing communist performers. Considerable controversy exists as to whether or not they were assisted in their efforts by law-enforcement authorities.

4. Breakthrough—Opposed to communism, socialism, and most leftwing causes, this Detroit-based group is repre-

28

sented by its ubiquitous chairman, Donald Fobsinger, who has been arrested on numerous occasions for disturbing the peace at leftwing rallies. A mayoral candidate, Mr. Fobsinger was convicted for assaulting a priest at an antiwar rally in 1973.

5. Secret Army Organization (SAO)—Based in San Diego and Arizona, this small group concerned itself primarily with harassing student radicals, to the point of shooting at them in one incident. One of its members, recruited by an FBI informer, was responsible for the bombing of an erotic theater. The SAO is noteworthy in that it represents the difficulties faced by the FBI in maintaining the credibility of its informers without allowing them to become agents provocateurs. Lawsuits have been brought against the FBI and governmental officials concerning the FBI's role in funding and directing the organization.

6. Cuban Action Commandos—This Los Angeles-based group is believed to have been responsible for numerous bombings of consulates of countries deemed friendly to Castro's Cuba. Active in the late 1960s, many of its members were imprisoned. Particularly active in 1975, this group also directs its attacks against leftwing bookstores.

7. Other Anti-Castro Groups—Most of these groups are social and fraternal organizations for Cuban exiles, who hope to return to a Cuba without Castro. Over 1,000 such groups have been formed in Miami alone, but approximately twenty are now still active. Few of the groups are actually violent, but their proliferation and ties with the Cuban community make those that are violent difficult to apprehend. Bombing targets are usually government agencies or firms doing business with Cuba. With hatred of Castro as the only unifying ideology, these groups are transient and have overlapping memberships. These groups often use fictitious names for the purpose of fund raising, and use another name for terrorist activities.

8. National Socialist Liberation Front (NSLF)—Led by the late Joseph Tommasi, this group broke off from the insufficiently violent fascist National Socialist White People's Party to pursue more violent tactics. Tommasi was shot and killed by a regular Nazi in the summer of 1975. The NSLF is suspected of having been responsible for four bombings against leftwing groups in the Los Angeles area

in 1975. With the death of Tommasi, its activities have declined.

9. Peace and Freedom Fighters—This Hungarian-exile group
   is based in Los Angeles. Police officials suspect the group
   has aligned itself with the Cuban Action Commandos and
   the National Socialist Liberation Front in actions against
   leftist organizations.

10. Posse Comitatus—Founded in Portland, Oreg., in 1968 in
    the home of Mike Beach, this vigilante group believes that
    the American Constitution has been subverted and that its
    members are justified in taking the law into their own
    hands. In their applications for charters, they state that
    they want "to aid the local sheriff in the exercise of his
    duties." Their literature asserts that federal income tax
    and all licenses (particularly those involving weapons) are
    unconstitutional, and that the county government is their
    highest authority. Though their potential for violence ap-
    pears to be considerable, only one incident of violence (the
    accidental discharging of a gun) has been attributed to the
    members of the organization. The Posse has been most ac-
    tive in the Northwest, in states like Montana, Idaho, and
    California.[20]

Terrorism is a form of violence which instills fear in others. This
is done by means of a threat of violence, individual acts of violence, or
a campaign of violence designed to terrorize a population. Terrorism
is violence for effect and it is aimed at the people watching a bombing, assassination, or airplane hijacking. The victim of terrorism is
usually unknown to those committing the act. The impersonal victim
may be a tourist, restaurant patron, security guard, airline passenger, or someone working late in an office building. It is important
that we learn to combat terrorism without destroying our civil liberties. This requires extensive and centralized intelligence gathering by
our law-enforcement agencies; specially trained police who can differentiate peaceful dissidents from people engaging in criminal acts
in order to facilitate social change; far-reaching security measures;
and a media campaign against terrorists and foreign governments
which offer asylum to terrorists.

Politicians exploit all aspects of the crime problem. Emotional
solutions are offered which do not take into account the role of
criminal-justice agencies in meeting the problem. The quality of
American life will be endangered if crime is not reduced. Deterrence
requires a greater effort by police, courts, and corrections. The appro-

priate utilization of manpower, adequate financial assistance, and proper evaluation of existing performance can make their work more effective.

STUDY QUESTIONS

1. Name the level of government on which rests the basic responsibility for crime control. Explain.
2. Has your community attempted to calculate the cost of crime? If so, how was this done?
3. What is the major source of information on the volume of crime?
4. Does your state operate a Uniform Crime Reporting Program? If not, who is responsible for compiling crime statistics?
5. Identify the agency which serves as a national clearinghouse for crime statistics. Name the annual publication which summarizes the information submitted to it.
6. Do crimes known to the police provide an accurate estimate of law violations? Explain.
7. Name the Part I offenses.
8. List reasons for the existence of unreported crime.
9. How many serious crimes do law-enforcement agencies clear by arrest? Is the clearance rate in your city higher than the national average? If so, why?
10. Differentiate the subject matter to be studied in a course entitled "Criminal Justice" from one identified as "Criminology."
11. Why should the criminal-justice system be viewed in its entirety and not as isolated, competing parts?
12. How is the field of criminology influenced by the *classical school* and the *positive school*?
13. How does traditional criminology differ from the "new criminology," which is sometimes called critical or conflict criminology?
14. Identify the two most important sociological theories of crime causation. Which theoretical formulation do you favor? Why?
15. What is meant by *altered behavior* as a response to urban violence? List three examples and discuss their effectiveness.
16. What kind of questions must you ask if you wish to possess adequate knowledge of the local crime problem? Have your local criminal-justice agencies answered your questions satisfactorily? If not, what are you proposing as a solution?

17. What is the major purpose of victim-compensation legislation?
18. Analyze recent activities of the leftwing and rightwing organizations listed in your chapter. Would you label their actions as terrorist acts? If so, why?

NOTES

1. *San Francisco Chronicle,* 16 April 1977, p. 6.
2. U.S. Department of Justice, Law Enforcement Assistance Administration, National Criminal Justice Information and Statistics Service, *Criminal Victimization in the United States: A Comparison of 1974 and 1975 Findings* (Washington, D.C.: U.S. Government Printing Office, 1977), p. 1.
3. U.S. Law Enforcement Assistance Administration and Bureau of the Census, *Trends in Expenditure and Employment Data for the Criminal Justice System: 1971–1975* (Washington, D.C.: U.S. Government Printing Office, 1977), p. 18.
4. Ibid., p. 10.
5. Federal Bureau of Investigation, U.S. Department of Justice, *Uniform Crime Reports for the United States, 1976* (Washington, D.C.: U.S. Government Printing Office, 1977), p. 35.
6. Ibid.
7. Michael J. Hindelang, "The Uniform Crime Reports Revisited," *Journal of Criminal Justice* 2 (Spring 1974): 2.
8. FBI, *Uniform Crime Reports, 1976,* p. 160.
9. Ibid., pp. 170, 172, 184, and 185.
10. U.S. Department of Justice, Law Enforcement Assistance Administration, *Privacy and Security of Criminal History Information: Summary of State Plans* (Washington, D.C.: U.S. Government Printing Office, 1977), p. 1.
11. James Q. Wilson, *Thinking About Crime* (New York: Basic Books, 1975), p. 208.
12. Vernon Fox, *Introduction to Criminology* (Englewood Cliffs, N.J.: Prentice-Hall, 1976). p. 28.
13. Tony Platt and Paul Takagi, "Intellectuals for Law and Order: A Critique of the New 'Realists,'" *Crime and Social Justice* 8 (Fall–Winter 1977): 10.
14. Manuel Lopez-Rey, "Criminological Manifesto," *Federal Probation* 39, no. 3 (September 1975): 18.
15. Edwin H. Sutherland and Donald R. Cressey, *Criminology,* 8th ed. (Philadelphia: Lippincott, 1970), p. 75.
16. Richard A. Cloward and Lloyd E. Ohlin, *Delinquency and Opportunity: A Theory of Delinquent Gangs* (New York: Free Press, 1960).
17. James Garofalo, *Public Opinion About Crime: The Attitudes of Victims and Nonvictims in Selected Cities,* U.S. Department of Justice, Law Enforcement Assistance Administration (Washington, D.C.: U.S. Government Printing Office, 1977), p. 19.
18. National Advisory Commission on Criminal Justice Standards and Goals, *Report on the Criminal Justice System* (Washington, D.C.: U.S. Government Printing Office, 1973), p. 200.
19. For more information on this topic, the reader should consult: Marvin Marcus, Robert J. Trudel, and Robert J. Wheaton, *Victim Compensation and Offender Restitution: A Selected Bibliography,* U.S. Department of Justice, Law Enforcement Assistance Administration (Washington, D.C.: U.S. Government Printing Office, 1975).
20. National Advisory Committee on Criminal Justice Standards and Goals, *Disorders and Terrorism* (Washington, D.C.: U.S. Government Printing Office, 1976), pp. 517–521.

chapter two
Historical Perspectives on the Development of State and Local Policing

CRUCIBLE: OUR ENGLISH HERITAGE

Along with their personal possessions the American colonists, who were predominantly English-speaking people, brought offices and patterns of policing long familiar to them; today these offices continue to exist in this country. Certain of the English precursors of these offices are at least ten centuries old; they are, then, not the product of a single mind, but rather the result of long years of experimentation, conflict, growth, and contraction. Our English heritage served quite literally as an institutional crucible. Over the next several decades there will be an acceleration of proposed and actual change to improve the delivery of police services with the attending consequence of eliminating or altering offices that have long been regarded as fundamental. To be able to make informed judgments—either as a practitioner in the criminal-justice system or as an active, interested citizen—requires that one understand the status quo as well as the nature of any changes proposed, and, additionally, possess a sound appreciation of the past.

Anglo-Saxon Contributions

To facilitate administration, to provide for the defense of the country, and to secure domestic order the Anglo-Saxon leader, Alfred the Great (871–900),[1] established a system which was local in nature and whose success depended upon the condition of mutual dependency.[2] In each shire (the rough equivalent of a county[3]) all free persons, except the exempt categories of women, clergy, and the disabled, between fifteen and sixty years of age were required to enroll in tithings, which were groupings of ten families. Each tithing elected one of

33

Alfred the Great, organizer of the frankpledge system, was born in 848 or 849. Upon the death of his father, Aethelwulf, shortly after Easter of 871, Alfred became king. He is also recognized in history as being a giver of laws and as having saved his people from the Danes. Courtesy of the Library of Congress.

its members "Headborough" to serve as their official spokesman.[4] Ten tithings formed a hundred and groupings of hundreds later constituted the basis for parishes. This system, termed "frankpledge," required that each man be responsible for, and to, his neighbors. When a crime was committed the hue and cry was raised—spreading from tithing to tithing, hundred to hundred, parish to parish, shire to shire—and each person enrolled in a tithing was required immediately to pursue the offender. This pursuit was to be maintained until the capture. Not to join the pursuit upon issuance of the hue and cry was regarded as a serious breach for which collective fines might be levied. In those cases where the hue and cry did not result in an apprehension, the remaining nine members of the violator's tithing were given a short period of time in which to produce him. The failure to do so could result in any of several courses of action. If the fugitive had a freehold (i.e., owned land) the fine might be assessed against it; if he was without a freehold his fellow freemen in the tithing might be assessed collectively.

The importance of the frankpledge system is unmistakable; that fact notwithstanding, however, the sheriff was the preeminent police figure in later day Anglo-Saxon England and for some time under the Normans. "The office of sheriff is one of the most familiar and most useful to be found in the history of English institutions. With the single exception of kingship, no secular dignity now known to English-speaking people is older."[5] Historical documents suggest that "the clearly recorded history of the sheriff begins . . . about the time of Edgar"[6] (959–975). The chief characteristic of Anglo-Saxon government was its local nature; this is not, however, to suggest that there were no attempts to exercise centralized control. Prior to the rise of the sheriff, groupings of shires were nominally headed by an alderman who identified more closely with local interests than with those of the crown.[7] In an attempt to change this situation, the king placed into each shire a king's "reeve," that is, a king's "keeper," whose administrative rank was inferior to that of the alderman.[8] Over a period of time the duties and responsibilities of the king's reeve grew steadily. By the time of Edward the Confessor (1042–1066) the king's reeve had emerged as the shire-reeve or sheriff, a figure of considerable power.

> He had become an important person. Already he may be seen going about his duties attended by an escort of horsemen. . . . It became his duty to proclaim the king's commandments and the enactments. . . . It was he that might be expected to execute a great part of such orders together with the decrees of the shire assembly. An occasional president of the hundred court, he exercised the customary criminal jurisdiction. He had authority to proclaim the

king's peace and to apprehend criminals. His was a responsibility for local defense and he led the forces of his shire
against Welsh attack or Norman invasion. . . . The collection of court fines increased his power. . . . When the king
made his visit to the shire the sheriff provided for his
safety, convenience, and various needs, like a household
official. . . . The sheriff of King Edward is shown due respect
when there rises the occasion to mention him. In a word,
the whole government of the shire was falling into his
hand.[9]

The sheriff of Edward's day had most government functions vested in
his office; he had judicial powers, enforced the criminal laws, collected
revenues, executed various types of legal papers, and was a key military figure. Moreover, through his power of *posse comitatus* he could
compel all free Englishmen between fifteen and sixty years of age
(save the exempt classes previously mentioned) to assist him in maintaining the peace. For about 125 years following the Battle of Hastings the sheriff enjoyed enormous power but, much like the relationship between the king's reeve and alderman, new figures appeared
that tended to steadily diminish the prerogatives of the office.

The Normans and After

The defeat of the Anglo-Saxon king Harold II by William, Duke
of Normandy, at the Battle of Hastings in 1066 brought with it the
winds of change. There was a strong similarity between the Anglo-
Saxon sheriff and the Norman office of vicecomes; the Norman con-
querors identified one with the other.[10] One of the most significant
Norman changes was to strengthen the role of national institutions,
making the crown a principle locus of power. By placing Normans
into the office of sheriff, the shift of power from local areas to the
crown was made both more swift and more certain. By 1071 Anglo-
Saxons in the office of sheriff were rare.[11]

The Normans retained the frankpledge system under the designation of "mutual security" and the headborough became known as
the *"praepositus."*[12] While old patterns of policing were retained, they
were administered harshly, especially by the vicecomes or sheriffs.

The visit of the Norman Sheriff generally resolved itself
into a demand for the payment of heavy fines, that might,
or might not, be legally due, and which too often were
heavier than the people could bear, for whereas the English
shilling had been worth about fivepence, the Norman shilling was equivalent to twelvepence, and amercements were
still calculated on the old scale without any allowance

36

being made for the change in the value of the coin. . . . The object of the vicecomes being to collect as many fines as possible, and to return to the king with some substantial evidence of his zeal.[13]

Moreover, other measures were applied heavily on the people of England. In the event that a Norman was found murdered, the local hundred was required to produce the perpetrator in five days or pay a fine, called murdum, of forty-six marks.[14] Any person found slain was presumed to be a Norman unless it could be satisfactorily demonstrated to be otherwise. Later the laws of Henry I (1100–1135) detailed the method by which such assumption of French national origin could be contravened. "If a hundred wishes to prove with respect to any slain person that he was not a Frenchman and it was consequently not murdum, the truth of this shall be established by the oaths of twelve substantial men of the hundred."[15] Ostensibly as a protection against fire, the practice of the curfew bell was instituted to prohibit the Saxons from moving about after dark to attend meetings at which the shortcomings of their oppressors might be discussed and ferment created.[16]

The sheriff's judicial powers were exercised in his Court of the Tourn, which was held in the various villages and towns as he moved about. Capriciously and severely administered, these courts were never accepted by the people. Over a period of time, lords having influence with the crown were able to establish locally controlled hundred courts. A writ from William II (1087–1100) illustrates the manner in which private jurisdiction was established to the exclusion of the sheriff with the revenue going to the franchise holder:

William, King of the English, to all the sheriffs and barons of Huntingdonshire, greeting. Known that I have granted the hundred of Normancross to the abbot and monks of Thorney to be held in fee-farm for an annual rent of 100 shillings . . . and order them to pay to my sheriff at Huntingdon. And I forbid any of my officers to do them injury or insult in respect of this.[17]

Thus, the Norman Sheriff, "famous for his extortion and oppression"[18] lost a degree of power as each private court franchise was awarded. By 1070 the acts of sheriffs reached such outrageous proportions that William I (1066–1087) established a commission to inquire into their conduct with respect to the theft of land belonging to the church. Urse of Abbetot, Sheriff of Worchester, was a particularly notorious despoiler.[19]

The Assize of Clarendon in 1166 is hailed as a landmark in the history of the jury as it supplies evidence of the jury's existence as a functioning unit in the administration of justice. The document, while reaffirming and extending the power of sheriffs, clearly reveals the beginning of a new relationship to the justices.

> And when a robber or murderer or thief or receiver of them has been arrested through the aforesaid oath, if the justices are not about to come speedily enough into the county where they have been taken, let the sheriffs send word to the nearest justice by some well-informed person that they have arrested such men, and the justices shall send back word to the sheriffs informing them where they desire the men to be brought before them; and let the sheriffs bring them before the justices. And together with them let the sheriffs bring from the hundred and the vill, where they have been arrested, two lawful men to bear the record of the county and of the hundred as to why they have been taken, and there before the justice let them stand trial.[20]

Upon his return from the Continent in 1170, Henry II (1154–1189) received so many complaints concerning the misconduct of sheriffs that it was necessary to have a group of barons conduct an inquiry. The charge to the commission contained thirteen articles, specifying both the matters to be investigated and the method by which information was to be obtained.[21] The result was the removal of all sheriffs from their office, although no further action was taken against them.[22] It is probable, however, that the findings of the barons contributed to the content of the Assize of Northampton in 1176 which substantially enlarged, at the sheriff's expense, the power of itinerant justices. The latter were formed into six groups that worked in newly delimited circuits.[23] An eyre of 1194 further restricted the sheriff's power by forbidding their acting as justices in their own shires;[24] this point was so critical that article twenty-three of the Magna Carta (1215) reiterated it. In 1194 and 1195 Richard I (1189–1199) dealt even further blows to the sheriff's power by creating the offices of coroner and peace knights; the latter were required to travel the country to assure that all males over the age of fifteen were sworn to the king. This meant that they were to take an oath to maintain the peace. The oath appears to have been based upon the laws of Canute and included a commitment to fulfill the ancient duty of responding to the hue and cry.[25] By 1253 the peace knights had been designated as peace wardens or conservators of the peace. In 1326 under Edward II (1307–1326) the office of justice of the peace emerged fully.[26] The early history of the office of coroner is somewhat obscure although it is known that three of these officers and one clerk[27] were assigned to keep "pleas of the crown," which were proceedings to determine which cases were to be tried by the king's officers rather than

38

by lesser courts. The duties of the coroner became clearer under Edward I (1272–1307).

> They were mainly concerned with felonies, especially involving homicide, and all with a view to the king's profit from the administration of law. They were required to hold inquests in cases of sudden death by accident, by violence, or in prison, viewing the body before it could be buried, and subsequently recording the value of property of any indicted persons, arresting these and taking their chattels into custody . . . reporting the names of jurors failing to attend the inquest . . . recording outlawries in the county court, from which chattels would be forfeited to the king. They also appraised wrecks . . . and treasure trove. From the government's point of view they formed a useful check on the activities of the sheriff. . . . If the sheriff were party to a suit or defaulted in his duty the coroners could execute royal writs in his stead. They could also assist or supersede the sheriff.[28]

In England the term "constable" has been applied to a variety of functionaries, both high and low, who had little in common beyond the fact that they all derived their authority from the Crown.[29] "It is likely that the offices of conservator of the peace and constable were often combined in the person of one man."[30] It was under Henry III (1216–1272), in the Assize of Arms in 1252, that some precision was used in defining the multiple uses of the title "constable."[31] This Assize established the watch and ward system in order to ensure the preservation of peace. Watches were to be kept

> in town and township by armed men, having power to arrest, and to pursue by hue and cry, strangers and suspects passing by night, for delivery to the sheriff. In each township a constable, and in each hundred a head constable was to be appointed, under whom all those sworn to arms were to be active in guarding the peace.[32]

In time we find the constable of the township developing into a parish or petty constable, a local peace officer, while the constable of the hundred or head constable was essentially a military figure. As the importance of the hundred as an administrative unit declined, the head constable's functions, which for a time included supervision of the petty constable, were gradually taken over by the justices of the peace.[33] The Statute of Winchester in 1285, under Edward I, further refined and gave vitality to the watch and ward; remarkably, it was not until 1793 that a committee of the House of Commons was to find that the Statute of Winchester no longer effectively served a nation which had moved increasingly from a rural, agrarian society to one characterized by urbanization and industrialization.

Thus, before the middle of the fourteenth century, the offices of sheriff, justice of the peace, coroner, and constable were all well known. By the time of the settlement of North America by English colonists in the early seventeenth century, the dynamics of power among these offices had been established. Further, the evils of centralizing too much power in an office not responsive to local control (as had been the case with the Norman sheriff) had reaffirmed the Anglo-Saxon tradition of peace maintenance as a function of local government.

THE GROWTH OF POLICING IN AMERICA

The Early Colonial Experience

The Massachusetts Bay Colony lost no time in installing the office of constable, which had by that time become the traditional local English peace officer. In the first year of the Colony one John Woodbury was chosen constable of Salem, "to contynue in that office for a yearee and after till newe be chosen."[34] As the population of the Colony slowly grew, each town was authorized to annually select from its "settled inhabitants and home-holders" a man suitable for the task. Other qualifications for the office were that he be at least twenty-four years of age, take a qualifying oath, be of "honest and good conversations," and have an estate valued at twenty or more pounds. The constable's broad powers and duties were set forth in great detail in a law of 1646 which subsequently was adopted by all the colonies.

> Every cunstable within our jurisdiction hath, by virtue of his office, full power to make, signe, and put forth pursuites, or hues and cries, after murtherers, manslayers, peace breakers, theeves, robers, burglarers, where no magistrate is at hand; also, to apprehend without warrant such as are overtaken with drinke, swearing, breaking the Saboth, lying, vagrant persons, night walkers, or any other that shall breake our laws, in any of these; provided, they be taken in the manner, either by the sight of the cunstables themselves, or by present information from others; as also to make search for all such persons, either on the Saboth dayes, or at any other time, when there shalbe occasion, in all houses licensed to sell beare or wine, or in any other suspected or disordered places, and those to apprehend, and keepe in safe custody, till oportunity serve to being them

40

before the next magistrate for further examination; provided, when any cunstable is implied [employed], by any of
the magistrates, for apprehending of any, he shall not do it
without warrant in writing.[35]

Over a period of time the constable's duties were steadily expanded; by 1658 they included informing the magistrates of "new-
comers," taking charge of the watch and ward, raising the hue and
cry, tallying votes for deputies to the general court, summoning jury-
men for duty, bringing before the court men and women not living
with their spouses, collecting taxes, and other sundry duties including the hanging of sheep-killing dogs where the owners refused to do
so themselves.

In 1643 the General Court created the four shires of Essex,
Middlesex, Suffolk, and Norfolk. Although the sheriff was an important English figure, he did not emerge in the Massachusetts Bay Colony until, or shortly after, 1691, when authorized by the Province
Charter.

Not later than 1650, the office of coroner was well established in
colonial Maryland. The coroner of each county was appointed by the
governor and the position was frequently held by prominent figures.
The coroner was responsible for conducting inquests into the deaths of
those who were murdered, drowned, or perished through some misad-
venture.[36] Justices of the peace were also well known during the same
time and, in support of their judicial functions, a central concern was
the desire to uphold the dignity of their office. When one Robert
Vaughan of Kent County insulted the justices of the peace by "oppro-
brious epithets" and other acts he was fined the extraordinary sum
of 1,000 pounds of tobacco. By a letter dated April 1, 1653, Vaughan
revealed himself to be properly chastened and contrite; the justices
remitted the fine.[37]

Prior to 1634 there was no mention of the office of sheriff in
Virginia; in that year, however, the Colony was divided by statute
into eight shires to be governed "like the English shires and to have
sheriffs with the same power as in England."[38] In rapid order the
records of that time show the establishment of the familiar offices of
justice of the peace, coroner, sheriff, and constable. The larger land-
owners monopolized these offices.

The American Need for a New Police

The development of municipal police forces, as exist presently in
this country, was a slow process. The first municipal peace-keeping
force appeared in Boston in 1631 when it was decreed that from sun-
set to sunrise a watch of four men would be kept every night.[39] In
New Amsterdam, later to become New York City, a citizen's night

41

watch existed as early as 1652. The first paid nocturnal police protection in New Amsterdam was provided in 1658 by a "Burgher Guard" created by Peter Stuyvesant. It consisted of a captain and eight men. But it was not until 1712 that paid watchmen emerged in Boston.[40] Between 1661 and 1784 New York City was alternately policed by paid watchmen, the military, and a citizen's watch; it was only with the appointment of James Duane as mayor by Governor George Clinton in February 1784 that full civil authority and normal judicial processes returned.[41] From the mid-1820s on, crime and disorders increased rapidly; the beginnings of industrialization, large-scale immigrations, slums, religious, racial, and ethnic rivalries, and the growth of machine politics all complicated New York City's problems.[42]

The situation in Boston (which in 1822 with a population of nearly 50,000 had been granted an act to incorporate by the General Court of Massachusetts) was somewhat different from that of New York City.[43] Although it was not convulsed with serious riots or victimized by a class of professional criminals, Boston's sense of propriety was assaulted by the fact that nearly two-thirds of its annual criminal convictions came in only four categories: common drunkenness, vagabondage, assault and battery, and lewd and lascivious conduct. What these four categories shared is high public visibility; their effect was to offend Bostonians' sensitivity about unruly conduct. The means of controlling crime still centered around the traditional figures of justice of the peace, sheriff, constable, and watchman. These authority figures had emerged when England was a thinly populated agrarian society and were ill-suited to policing a city with a burgeoning population. By the 1830s Boston, like other urban places of the time such as Philadelphia, Cincinnati, and Baltimore, was experiencing many of the negative conditions common to New York City from the mid-1820s. A new approach to policing America's cities was needed and England was to supply the concept.

LONDON: THE NEW POLICE

The history of policing in England—at least in London—from 1748 to 1829 is "the story of the way in which a medley of local parrish officers and watchmen came to be replaced by a single body of constables embodied into a police force, the governing principles of which were unity of control and professional excellence."[44] Improved agriculture methods, such as the dual introduction in 1730 of Charles Townshend's improved crop rotation system and Jethro Tull's four-coultered plow, made increased agricultural productivity possible. These and other agricultural advancements in turn made it possible for the farms to feed more people, freeing them to go to the cities as the Industrial Revolution began in the second half of the eighteenth century. As the population of England's cities grew, slums were created, crime increased, and disorders became frequent. Thus in no small measure the rise of England's professional policing was a by-product of the Agricultural and Industrial Revolutions.

The principal contributors to the creation, in London in 1829, of the first modern police force were Henry and John Fielding, William Pitt, Patrick Colquhoun, Jeremy Bentham, Edwin Chadwick, and Robert Peel.[45] Henry Fielding became chief magistrate of Bow Street in 1748 and set out with an abundance of energy, vision, and compassion to improve the administration of justice. His establishment in 1750 of a small group of nonuniformed houseowners to "take thieves" led to early inroads against crime. Within a few years this group of men evolved into the Bow Street Runners and are generally acknowledged to be the first detective force in the modern sense. Upon receipt of the report of a crime they would hasten to its location and begin an investigation. Beginning with "An Inquiry into the Causes of the Late Increase in Robbers" in 1751, he was to write a total of five pamphlets which establish him as a pioneer thinker on the control of crime. By 1752 he had begun to publish "The Covent Garden Journal" as a means of circulating the descriptions of wanted persons and educating the general public on penal issues. Upon his brother's death, John Fielding succeeded him as the chief magistrate of Bow Street and continued and expanded upon his brother's work, including more systematic dissemination of information about crime, the 1763 establishment of a night horse patrol of eight men to keep the roads leading into London clear of highwaymen, and the transition of the Bow Street Runners into a formal unit. In 1785 William Pitt caused a bill to be introduced into Parliament that incorporated much of the thinking of the Fielding brothers and foreshadowed Robert Peel's 1829 "Bill for Improving the Police in and Near the Metropolis." Pitt's bill provided for a single police structure that had nine divisions and was headed by three police commissioners; it was to service the entire London metropolitan area. Although Pitt's bill was withdrawn before a storm of adverse press, public opinion, and the displeasure of London's leaders, it remains a milestone of farsighted thinking. Patrick Colquhoun's *A Treatise on the Police of the Metropolis* addressed, often with detailed statistics, crime in London and touched on such subjects as burglars, highway robbers, cheats and swindlers, receivers of stolen goods, counterfeiters, and prostitutes. Moreover, Colquhoun did more than describe the malady; he advanced a compromise proposal which sought to bridge the span between the old parish system and that proposed in Pitt's ill-fated 1785 bill. Colquhoun envisioned a central administrative board of five commissioners who would employ a small cadre of professional police officers to be deployed to each parish to take charge of locally selected constables. The concept retained, even strengthened, the parish system while offering the advantages of some centralization. Colquhoun's treatise was generally well received and the chances of transferring its thoughts to reality seemed good, but inexplicably it was not to be. However, Colquhoun's observations did not go totally unnoticed. In his chapters 8 and 9, "On River Plunder" and "On Plunder in the Dockyards, etc." he had called attention to the enormous losses to criminal activity experienced by shipping firms and had suggested the need for preventive police. His point was not lost on the shipping industry; in 1798 a private marine police force was established with Colquhoun occupying a key post. By 1800 the success of the marine police was so evident that an act converted it into a public force, thereby creating London's first professional police force. Nevertheless, in 1816, 1818, and again in 1822, Parliament rejected the concept of a centralized professional police force for London. Strong philosophical forces were at odds; on the one hand were those who maintained that such a force was a direct threat to personal liberty, while the coalition around Bentham, Colquhoun, and Chadwick asserted that the greater risk to personal liberty was the absence rather than the presence of social control. Finally, on July 19, 1829, a Metropolitan Police Act was passed by the Parliament. However, it excluded one square mile in the heart of the City of London. Subsequently Peel selected Charles Rowan and Richard Mayne as commissioners and new principles were articulated.

1. The police must be stable, efficient, and organized along military lines.
2. The police must be under governmental control.
3. The absence of crime will best prove the efficiency of police.
4. The distribution of crime news is essential.
5. The development of police strength both by time and area is essential.
6. No quality is more indispensable to a policeman than a perfect command of temper; a quiet determined manner has more effect than violent action.
7. Good appearance commands respect.
8. The securing and training of proper persons is at the root of efficiency.
9. Public security demands that every police officer be given a number.
10. Police headquarters should be centrally located and easily accessible to the people.

Sir Robert Peel (1788–1850), the distinguished British statesman who was twice home secretary and prime minister. His seven-year effort to create a competent police force in London resulted in Parliament's 1829 approval of The Metropolitan Police Act. Courtesy of the Library of Congress.

11. Policemen should be hired on a probationary basis.
12. Police records are necessary to the correct distribution of police strength.[46]

Recruiting manpower for the force was difficult due to the high standards set; during the first three years of operations there were 5,000 dismissals and more than 6,000 resignations, most of which were forced,[47] an indication of the strong effort made to develop a professional force that would enjoy the public's confidence and support. However, when the force began operation on September 29, 1829, it was not under the best of circumstances. The public was suspicious, even hostile, because of the oppression experienced in France under centralized police. The English people taunted the new officers as "Bobbys," initially a derisive play on Peel's first name, Robert; it became a term of respect and affection in later years. The *London Times* viewed the organization as potentially a high patronage machine and Peel was maligned from some quarters as a potential dictator. Within a few short years, however, the unarmed force won a reputation for composure, fair play, and courage which turned the tide of public opinion in its favor.

THE NEW POLICE IN AMERICA

The success of Peel's reform in England did not go unnoticed in this country. In Philadelphia, Stephen Girard had left that city the sum of $33,190 to assist in developing a "competent police." That bequest resulted in an 1833 ordinance creating America's first paid daylight police service.[48] Although the ordinance was repealed only three years later, the innovation would appear again as riotous conditions and appalling incidences of crime swept the cities. In 1836 Mayor Lawrence forwarded a proposal to New York's Common Council advocating the reorganization of that city's police department along the lines suggested by Peel. A committee of the council rejected the proposal:

> Though it may be necessary, at some future period, to adopt a system of police similar to that of London ... the nature of our institution is such that more reliance may be placed upon the people for aid, in case of any emergency, than in despotic governments.[49]

Between 1841–1844 several plans were submitted for the organization of a London style police in New York City, but none commanded sufficient support for adoption. Finally in 1844 the New York State Legislature passed a law creating this country's first unified day and night police force, although the measure was not implemented until a year later. Until this time, in the areas where day police forces had existed, they were treated as entirely separate organizational entities from their night counterparts. Other cities following New York City's lead included Chicago in 1851, New Orleans and Cincinnati in 1852, Baltimore and Newark in 1857, and Providence in 1864.[50] By 1880 virtually all of the major cities had police departments of the type pioneered by New York City.

Many of the difficulties faced during the period 1830–1880 by the emerging municipal police departments were caused by gross political interference. Selection standards were often nonexistent, patronage frequently dominated appointments and promotions, and occasionally attempts were made to use the police to curtail the activities of the opposing political party. In an attempt to alleviate these and other problems various cities experimented with several approaches.

This photograph of a group of early Philadelphia police officers was taken sometime between 1896 and 1898. Courtesy Philadelphia Police Department.

New York City police officers, circa 1865, of the 32nd precinct, which was then located at West 135th Street on 10th Avenue. Note that ranking officers wear double-breasted coats while the patrolmen wear single-breasted. Courtesy Alfred J. Young Collection.

Personnel of the Berkeley Police Department circa 1914. The person seated third from the left is August Vollmer, the innovative police administrator. Courtesy Berkeley Police Department.

Responsible leaders created police administrative boards to replace the control exercised over police affairs by mayors or city councils. These boards were given the responsibility of appointing police administrators and managing police affairs. Unfortunately, this attempt to cure political meddling was unsuccessful, perhaps because the judges, lawyers, and local businessmen who comprised the administrative boards were inexpert in dealing with the broad problems of the police. . . . Another attempt was made at police reform during the close of the nineteenth century. Noting that poor policing tended to occur mainly in urban areas, the state legislatures required that police administrators be appointed by authority of the state. Thus state control became an alternative to local control of law enforcement. This move brought little success, for many problems had not been anticipated. . . . For one thing, the theory of state control . . . was not uniformly applied. It was primarily directed at the larger cities, by legislatures seeking to perpetuate rural domination in public affairs.[51]

Shortly after the turn of the century American municipal policing started to overcome the legacy of gross political interference and began its long journey toward professionalization; many of the early contributions came from the Berkeley Police Department. August Vollmer, an imaginative person totally dedicated to improving policing, was appointed chief of police of that organization in 1909 and it was he who conceived such innovations as the world's first motorized police force, the idea of distributing patrolmen in proportion to the variance of crime, the recruiting of college-educated people, and the systematic study of the police organization to improve performance.

THE FRONTIER

Manifest destiny, the lure of rich lands, economic incentives, increasing congestion in the east, and the natural restlessness of a young nation all contributed to the westward movement. James Marshall's discovery of gold in California in 1848, the Washoe Valley, Nevada, silver strike of 1859, the gold finds of 1860 at Orofino Creek, Idaho, and of 1863 at Alder Gulch, Montana, all tapped man's age-old fantasy of getting rich quickly. Since not all chose honest means the need for police protection moved west along with the settlers and miners.

The westward movement of the frontier did not alter the customary roles of coroner and justice of the peace. However, the sheriff now tended to concentrate his efforts upon the rural areas, although he remained the primary law-enforcement officer of the country despite the fact that police officers had emerged in the larger cities and

49

city marshals in the towns. But the frontier was a vast area to cover and it was virtually impossible to achieve anything approaching equitable justice. "In the diggings racially prejudiced 'miners' courts' dispensed a cruel brand of alleged justice, wasting no time in stringing up a suspected offender if he chanced to be a Mexican."[52] Vigilante groups were also active, such as the one which hung Henry Plummer, the outlaw sheriff of Virginia City, Montana, in 1864. In addition to state organizations, the quilt of frontier policing was further developed by the excellent work of the Pinkertons, Wells Fargo detectives, and Union Pacific operatives.

No _P.N.D.a. - 15~97._

Name _Geo Cassidy alias Butch Cassidy alias_

Alias _Ingerfield. right name Robt. Parker._

Age _32_ Height _5 ft 9"_ Weight _165_

Complexion _Light._ Hair _Flaxen_

Eyes _Blue._ Beard _____ Teeth _____

Nationality _American_

Marks and Scars _2 cut scars back head_
Small red scar under left eye.
Eyes deep set. Small brown
mole calf of leg.

Arrested _for Grd. Lar. Fremont Co. Wyo._

Remarks _July-15-94. Pardoned Jan 19-9_
by Gov. Richards
Home is in Circle Valley. Utah
Sandy beard & Mustache if any.

Robert Leroy Parker, alias Butch Cassidy, as he appeared at the time of an arrest in 1894, along with his Pinkerton's record. He was the acknowledged leader of the Wild Bunch which operated largely in Wyoming, Utah, and Colorado. Although there are conflicting accounts it is generally believed he, along with Harry Longabaugh, the Sundance Kid, were killed in a gun battle with Bolivian soldiers at San Vincente in 1909. Courtesy of Wyoming State Archives and Historical Department.

51

FRONTIER JUSTICE 1835 STYLE

This man was a resident of Hinds County . . . his character previous to this had been reputed good . . . from the multiplicity of evidence introduced to establish his good character and the circumstances not being sufficiently strong . . . could not punish him, but [rather] determined on requesting him to leave the state in a short a time as was convenient; which request he has complied with . . . [for] after his discharge he was taken by some citizens and lynched.

> *from H. R. Howard,*
> The History of Virgil A. Stewart
> (New York: Harper & Brothers, 1838),
> pp. 255–256.

While stagecoach robberies were frequent in England, they appear to have been less common in the eastern United States. For example, in 1684 the *London Gazette* reported weekly holdups of the Bristol to London stage during one month, while a single such incident in 1818 near Baltimore was sensational news.[53] In the west, however, a different picture prevailed. One of the most prolific stage robbers was Charles E. Boles, alias "Black Bart" who struck twenty-eight Wells Fargo stages between 1875 and 1883, along with some number of stages from less well-known lines. Impish, Boles was given to leaving notes at the scene of his robberies.

> I've labored long and hard for bread,
>   for honor and for riches,
> But on my corns too long you've tread
>   You fine haired sons of bitches.
>
> *Black Bart, the PO8*[54]

Finally apprehended by Wells Fargo detective Harry Morse, Boles served a term of years and disappeared from the public eye around 1888.

While those who attacked stagecoaches were referred to as "road agents," the term "car robbers" was used to designate those who victimized trains. While the James-Younger gang is popularly believed to have been the first to rob a train—at Adair, Iowa, on July 21,

1873—that dubious distinction belongs to another group.[55] John Reno's gang committed the first train robbery in this country near Seymour, Indiana, on October 6, 1866.[56] Despite the sensational character of the acts of outlaws—reported in newspapers and romanticized in popular publications such as Richard F. Fox's pink-sheeted *Police Gazette*—the heyday of the frontier bandit was a short period historically and even shorter for its practitioners, many of whom died violent deaths.

THE EMERGENCE OF STATE POLICE ORGANIZATIONS

Various writings claim that Massachusetts, Texas, or Pennsylvania had the first state police force. How is it that the examination of historical evidence could lead to such disparate conclusions? The answer to that question is not that historical facts differ, but rather that the definition of "state police force" varies.

The precursor of state police forces was formed in 1835 when the General Council of the Provisional Government of Texas authorized the raising of three ranger companies "who shall be subject to the orders and directions of the commander-in-chief of the regular army"[57] of Texas. With the entrance of Texas into the Union in 1845, the rangers became the first state police force.

"In the midst of the gold rush, California briefly experimented with its own rangers. Terror attributed to Joaquin Murieta led to legislative approval in 1853 of a small company of twenty men under Harry Love. In less than three months the California rangers destroyed Murieta's gang and were themselves disbanded."[58] While the Arizona rangers were established in 1901 and the New Mexico mounted police in 1905, state police forces were by no means a phenomenon peculiar to this country's west.

> Between Reconstruction and World War I several American jurisdictions experimented with various forms of state police. Massachusetts recognized "Constitutes of Commonwealth" in 1865 to demand observance of vice laws; the force eventually became a small detective force under central control. Connecticut formed a similar unit in 1903.[59]

In 1905 Governor Samuel Pennypacker signed legislation creating the "Department of State Police of the State of Pennsylvania." The pressure to create such a force is traceable to the Anthracite Strike of May 12–October 23, 1902. This strike destroyed the peace of seven Pennsylvania counties, cost miners $25,000,000 in lost wages,

A Pennsylvania State Police officer in 1906 dress uniform; note the "Rough Rider" style hat. President Teddy Roosevelt was so impressed with the Pennsylvania State Police that he observed "I feel so strongly about them that the mere fact that a man is honorably discharged from this force would make me at once, and without hesitation, employ him for any purpose needing courage, prowess, good judgment, loyalty, and entire trustworthiness." Courtesy Pennsylvania State Police.

and deprived the coal companies and coal-transporting companies of about $74,100,000 in lost earnings. Although the national guard had been mobilized to maintain order during the strike, the state had also used the coal and iron police toward the same end. The coal and iron police were unpopular with strikers because the state sold commissions for one dollar apiece, thereby conferring police powers upon individuals selected and employed by the corporations. The net result was that, instead of being neutral, the power of the state was utilized in a highly partisan manner by employers. Ultimately, the federal government entered the issue, establishing the "Anthracite Coal Strike Commission" as an arbitration board to resolve the conflict between the United Mine Workers and the corporations. Recognizing the ills associated with selling police commissions to private industry, the first of the general recommendations offered by the Strike Commission was the creation of a state police force.[60] The unit which arose subsequently became a prototype for modern state police organizations, emulated in 1917 by New York and Michigan, and in 1919 by Delaware.

During the early years of the state police they tended to be regarded with a jaundiced view by labor interests, due to the widely held belief that they were "strike busters on management's side." In 1921 Governor Edwards of New Jersey vetoed a bill which would have created the New Jersey State Police on the grounds that "various labor organizations had opposed the measure as a vehicle for oppressing labor and he was inclined to accept that view."[61] Although the veto was rapidly overridden, the image of the state police as an antilabor entity remained.

Although "the American Civil Liberties Union was later to initiate court suits to test the legality and constitutionality of many forces ... state forces survived this early controversy and, in time, [became] a necessary and desirable institution."[62] Today every state, with the exception of Hawaii, has some form of state police.

STUDY QUESTIONS

1. Summarize the operation of the frankpledge system.
2. Trace the history of the development of the offices of sheriff, justice of the peace, coroner, and constable in England.
3. What is the importance of the Assize of Clarendon?
4. What impact did the Normans have upon the administration of justice in England?
5. What conditions in this country led to the recognition that the traditional and long-familiar English offices which had been

adopted to administer justice needed to be supplemented by a "new police"?

6. Identify and discuss the contributions of the Fieldings, Pitt, Colquhoun, and Peel.

7. How was the concept of London's "new police" applied in this country?

8. Who was Vollmer and what were his important innovations?

9. Pennsylvania's State Police became a prototype for modern state police organizations; what brought about their creation?

10. Why did state police forces, during the early years of their formation, have an anti-labor reputation?

NOTES

1. The date of Alfred's death is cited as 900 or 901 in most contemporary works; C. W. Previte-Orton identifies the event as occurring October 26, 899; see *The Shorter Cambridge Medieval History,* vol. 1 (Cambridge: University Press, 1952), p. 385. In the *Anglo-Saxon Chronicle* 900 is given; see David C. Douglas, ed., *English Historical Documents,* vol. I (New York: Oxford University Press, 1952), p. 189.

2. In Melville Lee's *A History of Police in England* (Montclair, N.J.: Patterson Smith reprint, 1971) and other authoritative works, credit is invariably given to Alfred for creating the frankpledge system. However, elements of the system existed for several centuries prior to Alfred; William Stubbs suggests that rather than regarding him as innovator it would be more proper to think of Alfred as organizer. See William Stubbs, *The Constitutional History of England,* vol. 1 (New York: Barnes & Noble, 1967), p. 108. Moreover, the Hundred Ordinance (939–961) is generally attributed to Edgar (959–975). For detailed insight into the operation of the Hundred after 1066 see Helen M. Cam, *The Hundred and Hundred Rolls* (New York: Burt Franklin, 1930), p. 296.

3. Stubbs notes that a shire *system* (emphasis mine) had been established in Wessex as early as the reign of Ine (688–694), but that the arrangement of the whole kingdom into shires could not have been completed until Edgar's time; see Stubbs, *Constitutional History,* vol. 1, pp. 123–124. In the laws of Athelstan (924–939) the term "shire" is specifically used; see Douglas, *English Historical Documents,* vol. I, pp. 383 and 389. It has been suggested that the shires generally tended to take the geographical dimensions of the old petty kingdoms. However, W. A. Morris discounts—except in a very few cases—the notion that shires are earlier kingdoms mediatized, holding instead that shires tended to be territorial divisions on one or more ancient kingdoms. See W. A. Morris, *The Medieval English Sheriff to 1300* (Manchester: Manchester University Press, 1927), p. 292.

4. In various periods the office of headborough is also identified as chief frankpledge, tithingman, and borsholder; all refer to the same position.

5. Morris, *Medieval Sheriff,* p. 1.

6. Ibid., p. 21. Stubbs notes that the Laws of Ine (688–694) contain mention of an official, the scir-man, who might be a very early sheriff; see Stubbs, *Constitutional History,* vol. 1, p. 126. In Douglas, *English Historical Documents,* vol. 1, p. 66, support for Morris' position is found: "The title is used in Canute's reign (1017–1035) and a shire-man, which represents the same official, occurs in a document between 964–988."

7. Bede (672–735), author of the multivolume *Historia Ecclesiastica Gentis Anglorum,* vol. 10, p. 624, observed that "these same old Saxons . . . have not a king but a great number of satraps set over their nation, who in any case of

56

imminent war cast lots equally; and on whomsoever the lot falls, him they all follow as leader during the war; him they obey for the time; but, when the war is over, all the satraps again resume their equal power." The condition noted by Bede continued for some time; thus one should not gain the impression that at this time there was one national Anglo-Saxon king. This figure emerged only with Edward the Confessor (1042–1066), a distinction promptly lost by his successor Harold II (1066) to William, Duke of Normandy.

8. Morris, *Medieval Sheriff*, p. 3. Other writers have maintained that when the king's reeve first appeared he was placed alongside, rather than subordinate to, the alderman; the weight of evidence supports Morris' position. By Ethelred's reign (866–871) the alderman had become the ealdorman and Canute (1017–1035) substituted the title "earl," his geographic area being termed an "earldom." Normally an earldom consisted of a number of shires although for a time after the Conquest William's few earls were of single counties. See Previte-Orton, *Shorter Cambridge Medieval History*, p. 589.

9. Ibid., p. 34.

10. Ibid., p. 41.

11. Ibid., p. 44.

12. Lee, *History of Police in England*, p. 14.

13. Ibid., p. 15.

14. Ibid., p. 16. However, in L. J. Downer, trans., *Leges Henrici Primi* (Oxford: Clarendon Press, 1972), p. 285, 91-1, Henry I (1100–1135) provided for a period of seven days in which the murderer was to be brought forward. This section also provided that of the forty-six marks to be paid "forty marks shall belong to the king and six to the relatives of the slain man."

15. *Leges Henrici Primi*, 92-11, p. 291.

16. Lee, *History of Police in England*, p. 16.

17. Douglas, *English Historical Documents*, vol. 1, p. 433.

18. Morris, *Medieval Sheriff*, p. 68.

19. Douglas, *English Historical Documents*, vol. 1, pp. 431–433.

20. Ibid., p. 408. In Article 5 the king claims sole rights to the profits arising out of jurisdiction. In 1066 there were 600 private hundreds operated as fee-farms in Wiltshire, by 1275 the number had dwindled to 27; see A. Harding, *The Law Courts of Medieval England* (London: Allen & Unwin, 1973), p. 35.

21. Stubbs, *Constitutional History of England*, vol. 1, p. 510. On October 11, 1274, the behavior of sheriffs again is central in a fifty-one-article inquiry.

22. Ibid., p. 511. A few members of the Curia Regis, such as Ranulf Glanvill and William Basset, who were removed as sheriffs were later reinstated to that office.

23. Douglas, *English Historical Documents*, vol. 1, p. 411.

24. Stubbs, *Constitutional History of England*, vol. 1, p. 544.

25. Lee, *History of Police in England*, p. 44 and Stubbs, *Constitutional History of England*, vol. 1, p. 546.

26. Stubbs takes the position that the *existing* (emphasis mine) functions of the office of justice of the peace date from the time of Edward III (1327–1377); see Stubbs, *Constitutional History of England*, vol. 1, p. 546. He is correct in that Edward III extended their power considerably. However, the creation of the office is properly attributable to Edward II.

27. Helen M. Jewell, *English Local Administration in the Middle Ages* (New York: Barnes & Noble, 1972), p. 153.

28. Ibid., p. 155.

29. Lee, *History of Police in England*, p. 55. Little is known of the early functions of the office of constable; the name was derived from the Comes Stabuli of the Byzantine Court and appeared in the west as early as the days of Gregory of Tours; see Stubbs, *Constitutional History of England*, vol. 1, p. 383.

30. John Coatman, *Police* (London: Oxford University Press, 1959), p. 20.

31. Sidney and Beatrice Webb, *English Local Government*, vol. 1 (Hamden, Conn.: Shoe String Press, 1963 reprint), p. 26.

32. R. Stewart-Brown, *The Sergeants of the Peace* (Manchester: Manchester University Press, 1936), pp. 71–72.

33. Jim Hart, *The British Police* (London: Allen & Unwin, 1951), p. 23.

34. For an excellent overview of the administration of justice in colonial Massachusetts during the period 1620–1692 see Edwin Powers, *Crime and Punishment in Early Massachusetts* (Boston: Beacon Press, 1966), especially chapter 13, "Criminal Justice in Operation," pp. 424–454. The Massachusetts Bay Colony should not be confused with the Plymouth Colony, which preceded it somewhat; the administration of justice in the two colonies is not differentiated.

35. Ibid., p. 425.

36. Raphael Semmes, *Crime and Punishment in Early Maryland* (Baltimore: Johns Hopkins Press, 1938), p. 311. For viewing the body of a deceased person coroners could place a claim against the estate for 250 pounds of tobacco, tobacco being a key to the economics of the colony.

37. Ibid., p. 35.

38. Cyrus Karraker, *The Seventeenth-Century Sheriff* (Chapel Hill: University of North Carolina Press, 1930), pp. 64–68.

39. Nathaniel B. Shurtleff, ed., *Records of Massachusetts, 1628–1641*, vol. 1 (New York: Ams Press, 1853), p. 85.

40. James F. Richardson, *The New York Police* (New York: Oxford University Press, 1970), p. 8. However, in 1801 Boston became the first American city to require a permanent night watch.

41. Ibid., pp. 8–13.

42. Ibid., p. 15.

43. Roger Lane, *Policing the City: Boston 1822–1885* (Cambridge, Mass.: Harvard University Press, 1967), pp. 3–7.

44. T. A. Critchley, *A History of Police in England and Wales* (Montclair, N.J.: Patterson Smith, 1972), p. 29.

45. Ibid., pp. 29–55. Also see Leon Radzinowicz, *A History of English Criminal Law*, vols. 1–3 (New York: Macmillan, 1948–1957).

46. A. C. Germann, Frank D. Day, and Robert R. J. Gallati, *Introduction to Law Enforcement and Criminal Justice* (Springfield, Ill.: Charles C. Thomas, 1970), pp. 54–55.

47. Lee, *History of Police in England*, p. 240.

48. Raymond Fosdick, *American Police Systems* (Montclair, N.J.: Patterson Smith reprint, 1969), pp. 63–64.

49. Richardson, *New York Police*, p. 37.

50. Fosdick, *American Police Systems*, pp. 66–67.

51. President's Commission on Law Enforcement and Administration of Justice, *Task Force Report: The Police* (Washington, D.C.: Government Printing Office, 1967), p. 6.

52. Harry Sinclair Drago, *Road Agents and Train Robbers* (New York: Dodd, Mead, 1973), p. 7.

53. Eugene B. Block, *Great Stagecoach Robbers of the West* (Garden City, N.Y.: Doubleday, 1962), pp. 16–17.

54. Drago, *Road Agents*, pp. 48, 56, and 256–257.

55. James D. Horan, *Desperate Men* (New York: Bonanza Books, 1949), pp. 66–67.

56. Ibid., p. 66 and Carl W. Breihan, *Badmen of the Frontier Days* (New York: Robert M. McBride Company, 1957), p. 75.

57. Bruce Smith, *The State Police* (Montclair, N.J.: Patterson Smith reprint, 1969), p. 37.

58. Frank Richard Prassel, *The Western Peace Officer* (Norman: University of Oklahoma Press, 1972), p. 160.

59. Ibid.

60. Katherine Mayo, *Justice to All* (New York: Putnam, 1917), pp. 1–5.

61. Leo J. Coakley, *Jersey Troopers* (New Brunswick, N.J.: Rutgers University Press, 1971), p. 26.

62. William J. Bopp and Donald O. Schultz, *Principles of American Law Enforcement and Criminal Justice* (Springfield, Ill.: Charles C. Thomas, 1972), p. 80.

chapter three
Federal Enforcement and Assistance

At the time our nation was founded the federal government maintained jurisdiction over only a handful of crimes, such as piracy, treason, postal crimes, and revenue and customs offenses, while the subunits of the states exercised the major responsibility for the control of crime. This pattern continues today and, as has been seen, the growth of law enforcement at the state level during the first quarter of this century served to further emphasize the relatively limited jurisdiction of the federal agencies. Thus, contrary to popular belief, the powers of law-enforcement agencies of our national government are finite rather than infinite, being limited to jurisdiction over only some 900 provisions of the federal criminal code.

Despite the fact that federal agencies are responsible for a relatively circumscribed number of statutes, the efforts to enforce those statutes are distributed widely over many units of our national government, including often-overlooked activities in the departments of agriculture, interior, labor, defense, transportation, and health, education and welfare. There are also enforcement personnel in such independent agencies as the Nuclear Regulatory Commission, the Federal Deposit Insurance Corporation, and the Securities and Exchange Commission.[1] Altogether there are about fifty law-enforcement agencies in the federal government. Despite the fact that there are so many law-enforcement agencies scattered through various units of national government, it is fair to say that the locus of the federal enforcement activity is in the Departments of Justice and Treasury; it is to these that the balance of this chapter is devoted. It should also be noted that, in addition to its enforcement role, the federal government provides a significant amount of financial, training, and technical assistance to state and local units of government.

Figure 3-1 Organization of the United States Department of Justice.

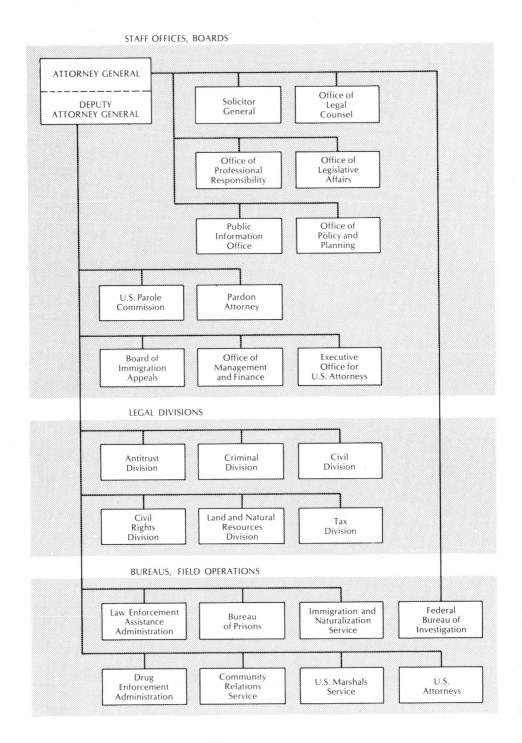

60

FEDERAL BUREAU OF INVESTIGATION

In 1908 the embryo of what was to become the FBI was formed when Attorney General Charles Bonaparte ordered that investigations by the Department of Justice be handled by a special group. In 1924 J. Edgar Hoover assumed leadership of the trouble-ridden Bureau of Investigation and eleven years later the Congress passed a measure redesignating it as the Federal Bureau of Investigation.

J. Edgar Hoover (1895–1972) entered the Department of Justice in 1917; two years later he was appointed special assistant to the attorney general and from 1921 to 1924 he served as assistant director of the Bureau of Investigation. During his tenure as director, 1924–1972, he served under eight presidents and seventeen attorneys general. Courtesy of the Federal Bureau of Investigation.

61

Although under increasing criticism during the last years of his stewardship of the FBI, it was under Director Hoover that the agency achieved a widespread reputation for professionalism. His continual stance to limit the role of the FBI is to the benefit of all citizens; even his critics concede that the Watergate scandal would have been brought under public scrutiny far more rapidly had he still been director. At least some of the criticism seems warranted; Hoover's over-concentration upon the Communist party, his tardy recognition of the existence and impact of organized crime, and his personal attention to minor administrative details are matters of record. In sum total, however, the man was a tireless public servant who caused a peerless investigative agency to rise, like a phoenix, from its scandal-ridden predecessor, the Bureau of Investigation.

With an annual operating budget of $513,377,000 and 19,665 total employees (about half of whom are special agents), the FBI serves as the chief investigative arm of the Department of Justice.[2] It performs its responsibilities through 59 major field offices and nearly 500 smaller resident agencies distributed throughout the United States. Its legal jurisdiction is strictly limited to the enforcement of some 185 violations of the Federal Criminal Code such as kidnapping, crimes on government and Indian reservations, interstate transportation of stolen goods or vehicles, fraud against the government, thefts from interstate shipments, bank robbery, crimes on the high seas, and interstate gambling offenses. While the protection of the president is a responsibility of the Department of the Treasury's Secret Service, it is the FBI's responsibility to investigate violence against a federal officer (including the president), be it assault, kidnapping, murder, or conspiracy to commit any of these acts.[3] Additionally, the Bureau investigates complaints alleging deprivation of rights that are secured by federal civil-rights statutes and locates individuals who flee from one state to another to escape prosecution or confinement or to avoid giving testimony where a state felony is involved. The fulfilling of the FBI's statutory responsibilities generates a considerable workload. In one recent year it entailed $528,723,113 in fines, savings, and property recoveries, 17,544 convictions, and the apprehension of 32,206 fugitives.[4]

In order to augment the law-enforcement effort at the subnational level, the FBI provides state and local police agencies with a variety of services on a fee-free basis. Upon request the FBI will provide assistance in the investigation of a criminal homicide of a non-federal police officer. The Bureau provides instruction in some 10,000 law-enforcement schools attended by more than 300,000 officers from throughout the nation.[5] Moreover, at its modern eleven-building National Academy complex in Quantico, Virginia, the FBI annually trains more than 8,000 police officers from across the country; some of

A Federal Bureau of Investigation laboratory technician conducting a chemical extraction. Courtesy of the Federal Bureau of Investigation.

these are given its prestigious National Academy course. The FBI's crime laboratory is one of the finest in the world; it provides services ranging from analysis of hairs and fibers to decrypting gambling codes. In 1976 the FBI examined more than 470,000 specimens of evidence; about 33 percent of that number were studied cost-free for other federal, state, and local agencies.[6] The laboratory also maintains the National Fraudulent Check File. It assists in the identification of professional check passers through its computerized PROCHECK program, which in one annual period assessed 56,286 items resulting in 24,891 identifications.[7] The Identification Division gathers and maintains identification data such as fingerprint records —which currently number 165,727,564—from other agencies of criminal justice; the access to this information is strictly limited to official uses by appropriate government bodies.[8] A subunit of the Identification Division, the Disaster Squad, is available upon request to assist in determining the identity of those losing their lives in major tragedies such as airline accidents. Some of the most frequently used services are those provided by the National Crime Information Center. The NCIC is a computerized information system linking law-enforcement agencies throughout the nation; the system stores data on stolen property and persons wanted for serious crimes. This system enables police personnel in the field to determine within seconds whether a particular article has been stolen or if a person is wanted, thereby eliminating a suspect's traditional advantage of being able to markedly lessen the likelihood of apprehension by fleeing from one jurisdiction to another. Inquiries to NCIC now exceed 234,303 daily. Of these, some 900 daily are "hits" or positive responses to inquiries.[9] NCIC capabilities are complemented by state and local systems; these systems generally maintain, in addition to the significant local information entered in NCIC, data not enterable in the national system such as warrants for arrest on traffic charges. A final major service provided by the FBI is the publication of crime statistics. Each year the FBI releases data voluntarily submitted by individual police departments and states; this information is summarized in the publication titled *Crime in the United States* and covers the preceding calendar year. Often referred to as the *Uniform Crime Reports,* it organizes the data on the basis of UCR Part I and UCR Part II offenses. UCR Part I offenses are used in computing the index of crime for this country because they are serious crimes common to all jurisdictions and because they are considered to be those most likely to be reported to the police. UCR Part I offenses include: (1) murder and nonnegligent manslaughter, (2) forcible rape, (3) robbery, (4) aggravated assault, (5) burglary, (6) larceny of cash or property valued at $50 or more, and (7) auto theft. The UCR Part II offenses are: (8) other assaults, (9) arson, (10) forgery and counterfeiting, (11) fraud, (12) embezzlement,

(13) stolen property, (14) vandalism, (15) weapons violations, (16) prostitution, (17) sex offenses, (18) narcotic drug law violations, (19) gambling, (20) offenses against the family and children, (21) driving under the influence of alcohol or drugs, (22) liquor-law violations, (23) drunkenness, (24) disorderly conduct, (25) vagrancy, (26) all other violations, except traffic, (27) suspicion, (28) violating a curfew and loitering, and (29) being a runaway juvenile. The *Uniform Crime Reports* are important to practitioners, students, the public, and researchers because historically they have been the only centralized source for national crime data.

IMMIGRATION AND NATURALIZATION SERVICE

Created in 1891 and transferred to the Department of Justice in 1940, the Immigration and Naturalization Service is the federal government agency responsible for the administration and enforcement of laws pertaining to the admission, exclusion, deportation, and naturalization of aliens. To carry out these duties the INS, with 10,071 employees, conducts five main programs that consume about 80 percent of its annual budget of 266.4 million dollars.[10] These programs involve: denying entry to thirty-one categories of people deemed inadmissible under the Immigration and Nationality Act, including those convicted of crimes of moral turpitude; detaining and deporting people who enter the United States illegally; investigating the status of aliens to identify those engaged in criminal behavior; maintaining records on all persons granted or denied admission; and operating the uniformed Border Patrol to prevent penetration of this country by groups such as smugglers and illegal entrants.

The Border Patrol operates regularly between various ports of entry; due to the high activity level their largest concentrations of manpower—81 percent—are in the Southwest, primarily around Chula Vista, California, and El Paso, Texas. Border Patrol personnel often work alone under harsh conditions in remote areas of the country. Access to these areas is often available only by foot, horse, four-wheel-drive vehicle, or airplane. These conditions are described in the following case histories.

> Border Patrol agents received information from an airfield that a small plane heavily loaded—and with a characteristic odor of Mexican refined gasoline—had just refueled and was about to depart a local airport. One of the sector pilots, airborne some thirty miles north, was contacted. With the assistance of radar approach control personnel at Davis-Monthan Air Force Base, he intercepted the suspect plane

west of Tucson and maintained visual contact until re-
lieved by a Bureau of Customs plane [which] followed the
suspect to a landing at Palm Springs, California, where the
Bureau of Customs pilot, with the assistance of the local
Sheriff's Office, apprehended the pilot and seized 797
pounds of marijuana.

During a snowstorm, a Canadian smuggler tried to guide
an illegal entry party of three Chinese crewmen through a
wild, wooded area near Mooers, New York. The party became lost and spent two nights exposed to bitter cold. Two
of the Chinese were found wandering around lost in the
border area by Border Patrol officers. The third Chinese
and the smuggler died of exposure and their bodies were
not found until the spring thaw. The smuggler's clothing
still contained some of the $700 paid to him, although he
had burned part of the money trying to start a fire.[11]

Despite the staggering task of conducting more than 237 million in-
spections annually at 400 ports of entry and patrolling nearly 6,000
miles of territory along our Canadian and Mexican borders the INS
enjoys considerable success. In one recent year it located 875,915
deportable aliens, including 773,460 persons who had entered this
country illegally at points other than official ports of entry; the vast
majority of these surreptitious entries were made across the Mexican border.[12]

San Ysidro, California: The truck in the background was used in an attempt to
smuggle forty-one aliens into this country. Courtesy of the Immigration and
Naturalization Service.

UNITED STATES MARSHALS SERVICE

United States marshals are appointed by the president, subject to the advice and consent of the Senate, for terms of four years. This office was created by the Judiciary Act of 1789.[13] One marshal serves in each of the ninety-four geographic areas constituting the federal judicial districts which cover the fifty states, Guam, the District of Columbia, Puerto Rico, the Virgin Islands, and the Canal Zone. Administrative direction is provided by the Executive Office for United States Marshals headed by the service's chief marshal. Marshals serve as agents of the executive branch of government and as executive officers of their court. More specifically their duties include, with respect to the federal courts: responsibility for the custody of 147,000 arrested persons annually until their release or delivery to a correctional institution; providing for the security of the court's physical plant; extending protection to jurists, principal witnesses and their family members in the event of attempts to intimidate; the execution of warrants on persons to be extradited, arrested for alleged criminal activities or parole violations; and providing for the personal safety of judges. While marshals are responsible for extending protection to federal judges, should one actually be assaulted or killed, the ensuing investigation would be conducted by the Federal Bureau of Investigation. Additional responsibilities of marshals include serving of summonses issued by congressional committees, government agencies, and the courts and, pursuant to court orders, seizing, guarding, and disposing of personal or real property. In fulfilling these responsibilities a United States marshal is assisted by a staff of deputy marshals who are career employees; at the present the total personnel complement of the United States Marshals Service is 2,187; its annual budget is $39,471,000.[14]

COMMUNITY RELATIONS SERVICE

The Community Relations Service, with only 104 employees, including 70 professional staff members, and an annual budget of $5,059,000, is the smallest of the federal agencies to be treated in this chapter.[15] However, its diminutive size and lack of direct law-enforcement responsibilities and authority belay the significant contributions made by the CRS. Created by the Civil Rights Act of 1964, and transferred from the Department of Commerce to the Department of Justice in early 1966, the CRS assists communities in resolving dispute or open-conflict situations which arise out of alleged or real social or ethnic discriminations. To do this the CRS uses an interdisciplinary staff with training in such diverse fields as education, economics, law, and housing. An excellent example of their crisis-conciliation assistance occurred in a large midwestern city.

Chicanos staged two large-scale demonstrations in protest against alleged police harassment and mistreatment. The first march was a "dry run" for the larger march set for twenty-two days later. As it turned out, 1,500—instead of 100—marchers were involved in the first march which resulted in several altercations between marchers and police along the march route. Some thirty Chicanos were arrested following a melee of rock-throwing and window-smashing. There were no deaths. By the time the second march was set to get underway, tension reached a peak. CRS conciliation teams accompanied each march segment, opening communication channels between marchers and officials of communities along the march route, and resolving sporadic disputes between marchers and community residents.[16]

In defusing potentially explosive situations the CRS attempts to provide a forum in which conflicting parties may air their complaints, concerns, and viewpoints in an orderly, constructive fashion as a prelude to the development of a responsive solution acceptable to all.

The CRS does not, however, merely react to difficult situations which have already surfaced; it also pursues a proactive strategy of technical assistance which is designed to prevent or ameliorate such situations before they become solidified. Past efforts of this type include helping citizens of New York City establish a Puerto Rican Legal Defense Fund and working with the Oakland Police Department in the coordination of police/community-relations programs and the recruiting of minority police.

LAW ENFORCEMENT ASSISTANCE ADMINISTRATION

In 1968, Congress passed the Omnibus Crime Control and Safe Streets Act creating the Law Enforcement Assistance Administration.[17] LEAA serves as the primary vehicle for delivering massive amounts of federal assistance to state and local governments in their efforts to stabilize and reduce the growth of crime. During the first four years of its existence LEAA was appropriated some $1.5 billion by the Congress, the bulk of which, excluding the administrative needs of LEAA, went to the states. Its designation as the Law Enforcement Assistance Administration is a misnomer because "law enforcement" in conjunction with the administration of LEAA programs is defined by the Act as meaning all activities "pertaining to the crime prevention or reduction and enforcement of the criminal law." Thus, this legislation is actually concerned with improving the entire fledgling system of criminal justice. As in the case of the CRS, LEAA has no direct law-enforcement responsibilities or authority.

The basic philosophy behind the Safe Streets Act is that while crime is a problem of national dimensions, it is most effectively and appropriately addressed at the state and local levels with the financial support of the more abundant resources of the federal government; a variety of techniques are employed to implement this philosophy. Large block grants of monies are provided—largely on the basis of their populations—to the fifty states, Guam, Puerto Rico, the District of Columbia, American Samoa, and the Virgin Islands to carry out various programs to prevent and combat crime. Examples of law-enforcement projects funded in past years are grants to improve the capabilities of the Honolulu Police Department's crime laboratory; support of an interagency metropolitan organized-crime investigation unit in Detroit; the development of a research and planning capability for the Massachusetts State Police; a helicopter project in Dallas; assistance in consolidating the files of two large agencies in Los Angeles County; underwriting police training in Puerto Rico; and a police/community-relations effort in Sante Fe.

To be eligible for funding, programs formulated must be documented in a comprehensive plan and submitted to LEAA before implementation to ensure conformance with various legal and procedural requirements. Since the control of crime must proceed on a broad front to be successful, the LEAA review, which entails the effort of many of its 732 employees, also assists the local jurisdictions in identifying and correcting any omissions or disproportionate allocations in their applications. The fifty-five participating jurisdictions also receive some funding to retain a professional staff to help administer the Safe Streets Act.

The Law Enforcement Education Program encourages both the continued professional growth of those currently employed in criminal-justice agencies and the preservice development for such careers by making educational grants and loans available to interested parties. In the Pilot Cities Program in San Jose, Des Moines, Omaha, Albuquerque, Rochester, Charlotte, Dayton, and Norfolk, LEAA utilized the expertise of university-based interdisciplinary teams to improve the planning capability, and the actual functioning, of criminal-justice agencies. There was special emphasis on the change process. These eight cities were selected because they met the criteria of being medium-sized jurisdictions with representative crime patterns; having an existing minimum-planning capability; and having an articulated commitment to systematically improve the delivery of services.

The National Institute of Law Enforcement and Criminal Justice is LEAA's research arm. It contracts with individuals, universities, and special-capability private firms to develop new concepts and approaches, to conduct pilot projects, and to independently evaluate projects conducted by recipients of grant awards. The National Criminal Justice Reference Service provides a means of compiling and disseminating information about current research and publications. Persons engaged in criminal-justice activities can complete a "Registration for Services" form that indicates their area of interest; periodically, the NCJRS forwards to each registrant annotated bibliographies of recent publications, many of which are available free from the NCJRS upon request.

The National Criminal Justice Information and Statistics Service is responsible for the gathering of data designed to facilitate greater understanding of the criminal-justice system and to provide

THE POLITICS OF CRIMINAL JUSTICE

Mayor Rizzo had been making overtures to the president . . . about his interest in supporting Mr. Nixon for reelection in 1972. The president was smitten with the idea of Rizzo supporting him and carrying the state of Pennsylvania. Mr. Ehrlichman instructed me in 1972 to do all that was necessary to get Rizzo's programs on narcotics and law enforcement on the line as soon as possible. I was told to make sure that checks for federal funds (from the Law Enforcement Assistance Administration) were transmitted to his office as fast as possible.

Donfeld (a staff assistant to Krogh) was given a seventy-two-hour deadline to prepare the application grant, have it sent to Washington, signed, and transmitted back to Philadelphia. I received a call from Mr. Ehrlichman at Camp David, who asked me, prior to the deadline, whether the check . . . as I recall for one million dollars . . . had gone yet. . . . Mr. Ehrlichman said it was the president's decision that the check was to go out by the deadline and that there would be no excuses. Accordingly, the check was transmitted to Rizzo, and he was able to announce very shortly thereafter a greatly expanded mechanism in Philadelphia.

Egil Krogh, Jr., former Deputy Counsel
to the President as quoted by Edward
Jay Epstein,
"The Krogh File —
The Politics of Law and Order,"
The Public Interest, Spring 1975

technical assistance to states desiring to develop parallel or comple-
mentary statistics centers. Significant publications of this unit include the *Directory of Criminal Justice Agencies, National Prisoner
Statistics, Annual Expenditure and Employment Data for the Criminal Justice System,* and the *National Jail Census.* The Systems Development Division has a strong interest in discovering applications
of systems analysis which might be useful in improving the administration of criminal justice. This division provides further service
through maintenance of various national-level information systems
supporting the administration of LEAA programs and by extending
technical assistance to state and local governments seeking to apply
computer technology. A vital part of the latter involves helping to
establish privacy and confidentiality criteria to be applied to auto-
mated records systems. Through its unsolicited proposal program
LEAA makes awards to conduct research for which other funding
mechanisms do not provide and which are of significant importance.

LEAA was subject to criticism from a number of quarters during
its first few years; critics voiced comments such as: monies were being
spent disproportionately on a "shopping list" basis for "hardware"
items, primarily cars and related equipment; the problems of the
large cities were not being adequately addressed; little actual long-
range planning was being done; the overuse of studies and consultant
firms led to an inability to translate plans into action rapidly; there
was a failure to maintain adequate records; grants were made on the
basis most beneficial to political encumbents; and the agency failed to
evaluate the benefits derived from its expenditures. In the early years
one or more of these deficiencies was to be found in some degree in
each of the fifty-five participating jurisdictions. As time has gone on,
however, the program has matured in terms of its direction and focus
to such a degree as to overcome many of these problems.

DRUG ENFORCEMENT ADMINISTRATION

Until the creation of the Drug Enforcement Administration on July 1,
1973, the effort to enforce federal laws pertaining to narcotics and
dangerous drugs was fragmented between several agencies. This condition was noted in 1949 by the Hoover Commission which, along
with subsequent bodies, recommended that—to eliminate duplication,
working at cross-purposes, and other ills—the federal narcotics enforcement effort be unified under a single command structure in the
Department of Justice. In 1968, this was partially accomplished by
the creation of the Bureau of Narcotics and Dangerous Drugs (BNDD)
and finally was more fully realized with the inception of the DEA.

The basic responsibility of the DEA is the control of the abuse of
narcotics and dangerous drugs; toward this end it operates a network

of 2,200 special agents[18] throughout the United States and in more than sixty-five foreign cities in over forty countries.[19] The DEA has identified some ten major international drug trafficking systems affecting this country and regards the penetration and disruption of them as the priority activity. While interdiction of narcotics and dangerous drugs at our borders is primarily a DEA function, the disruption of intercity distribution systems is a cooperative effort with state and local officials. At the present the DEA is engaged in cooperative task force efforts with state and local police officers in at least thirty-three major cities.[20]

TWO VIEWS OF DEA UNDERCOVER WORK
The Heroin Deal

One evening, in a fashionable restaurant in a major East Coast city, two men—Antonio and George—nursed Scotch whiskeys and talked about a heroin deal.

The conversation was amiable, the kind one would expect between two men who were "friends" as well as business acquaintances. George had bought heroin from Antonio several times during the past year.

After about thirty minutes of conversation, George said: "Antonio, I want you to be cool and don't get excited. I'm going to lay something heavy on you."

George slowly pulled a leather case from his rear pocket. He opened it for Antonio to look at. Inside was the blue-and-gold badge of a federal narcotics agent.

"Jeez, Georgie, where'd you get that? Those things are worth a lot of money on the streets!" Antonio exclaimed.

"It's mine," said George. "Uncle Sam gave it to me. I'm a federal agent, and you're under arrest."

A Ripoff

The greatest threat to the undercover agent is the criminal who intends to conduct a "ripoff." He may or may not be a real drug trafficker. But in the "ripoff" his intention is not to sell drugs but solely to rob an agent of "buy" money. Agents take careful precautions . . . to guard against such a robbery. Sometimes, however, precautions are of little use. The rip artist simply pulls a gun and kills the agents.

Once, two agents held an undercover meeting with two traffickers beneath a bridge in a large city. One agent, George, carried $13,500 as buy money for a cocaine transaction.

As the traffickers were arriving in their car, the agents later learned, they passed a uniformed policeman . . . nearby in his patrol car. The suspects had planned to kill the agents with a rifle and take the money. When they saw the patrol car, they told the agents, "Follow our car, and we'll take you to the main man." After driving up and down many city blocks, the suspects motioned for the agents to park.

"He's in an apartment just around the corner. Come with us," said one suspect.

As they rounded the corner, one suspect dropped back a pace, pulled a pistol, and announced "O.K., this is it, FBI!"

The suspect reached into George's belt and grabbed the agent's pistol. His partner disarmed the other agent, Tommy.

"You're no FBI agents," Tommy snarled.

"Shut up, Tommy, let them have the money," said George.

Suddenly Tommy leaped for the suspect's gun. Shots narrowly missed him and George. The second suspect, armed with the agents' guns, backed up with both weapons blazing.

George whipped a concealed pistol from the small of his back and shot the second suspect in the torso. The man went down behind the car. . . . In a moment, the suspect popped up again and this time George shot him through the head, fatally wounding him. George wheeled to aid Tommy, who was still struggling to disarm the first suspect. George pulled the trigger on his fifth and last round, killing the man instantly.

from Crime Control Digest, *vol. 11,*
No. 44, November 7, 1977, pp. 8–10.

A significant DEA responsibility is preventing the diversion of drugs from legitimate sources. "In the United States today there are approximately 400,000 doctors, veterinarians, pharmacists, and other professionals registered to handle controlled narcotics and drugs";[21] additionally, there are some 5,000 drug-producing and distributing firms. Preventing illicit diversions from such sources is the principal responsibility of compliance investigators.

The ability of units of state and local government to combat illicit drug trafficking and use is enhanced by the DEA's extensive training programs for both investigators and forensic chemists; the DEA conducts schools of this type at such diverse points as Mexico, Australia, Peru, and the Philippines to improve indigenous police capabilities in those countries. As a further means of advising foreign governments on ways to improve their enforcement capabilities, thereby reducing the flow of narcotics to this country, over 150 special agents are assigned abroad.[22] The benefits to be derived from multinational cooperation are well illustrated by an actual case.

> It was determined that French traffickers were driving automobiles to Spain, then shipping them to Mexico where they were driven into this country. As a result of cooperation between agents of the Spanish and United States governments a shipment of 248 pounds of heroin—destined for New York City—was seized in an automobile in Valencia, Spain, and two major system subjects were arrested.[23]

The DEA operates regional laboratories—in New York, Miami, San Francisco, Dallas, Chicago, San Diego, and the District of Columbia—to analyze and evaluate substances seized as possible narcotics evidence. The services of these laboratories—which are staffed by 120 chemists who analyze 45,000 separate evidence submissions annually—and expert testimony on conclusions reached about suspected drug substances are provided to nonfederal enforcement agencies without cost.[24]

DEPARTMENT OF THE TREASURY

Secret Service

It has been estimated that during the early portion of the American Civil War as much as one-third of the paper money in circulation was counterfeit.[25] This happened because each of the 1,600 state banks designed and printed their own currency, producing 7,000 varieties of genuine notes which were often difficult to distinguish from the 4,000 species of counterfeits. In 1863 the federal government, desirous of bringing the problem under control, adopted a national currency which became popularly known as "greenbacks." This, too, became subject to widespread counterfeiting and in 1865 the United States Secret Service was established, under its first director, William Wood, to combat the menace. Within its first year of existence the Secret Service arrested some 200 counterfeiters. In 1867 it made one of its most important early apprehensions with the arrest of Lewis Roberts, who may have passed as much as $3 million in bogus money during a five-year period. Today counterfeiting remains a serious problem; in one recent year counterfeiters produced $26.8 billion in bogus currency, 87.1 percent of which was seized before it could be passed to the public. In that same year the Secret Service made 1,766 arrests for counterfeiting.[26] A case history illustrates the magnitude

A comparison of counterfeit and genuine paper currency. Note how much finer are the details of the specimen on the right, printed by the government. Courtesy of the Secret Service.

of potential loss which could be experienced by the public in the absence of effective Secret Service investigations.

> During February 1971, an undercover Secret Service agent was introduced to a suspect in Los Angeles, California, who was offering counterfeit notes for sale. The agent made a small purchase of these notes and arranged for a larger purchase. Three days later, the suspect was arrested while making a $600,000 delivery to the agent. A second suspect at the site of the latter delivery was also arrested and later identified as the printer of the notes. The total seizure amounted to $1.6 million with only $320 being passed on the public.
>
> While awaiting trial, the printer produced a new counterfeit and delivered $100,000 to a second undercover agent. Consequently, three months after his arrest for the first offense, the printer was again arrested. The seizure in the second case totaled $660,000 with only $940 passed on the public.[27]

In addition to enforcing laws pertaining to the counterfeiting of currency, the Service's responsibilities today—with some 3,600 employees, of which approximately 2,700 are enforcement positions, and an annual budget of $123 million—include the enforcement of laws pertaining to the forging of bonds and government checks.[28]

After President William McKinley was assassinated in 1901 by Leon Czolgosz, a disappointed office seeker, the Secret Service was assigned its presidential protection function. Five years later the Congress provided formal legislation authorizing the practice, subject to annual approval; following the ill-fated attempt to assassinate President Harry S. Truman, the protective responsibility was permanently mandated to the Service by the Congress. Over a period of time marked by the separate assassinations of President John F. Kennedy and Senator Robert F. Kennedy, the protective jurisdiction grew to include presidents and their families, vice-presidents, presidents- and vice-presidents-elect, former presidents and their wives, major candidates for the presidency and vice-presidency, the widows of presidents until their death or remarriage, and the children of former presidents until they reach sixteen years of age. The difficulty of providing protective service when, for example, the president travels, is a task of considerable magnitude requiring close coordination with local law-enforcement agencies. Advance teams must visit and survey the area to identify manpower and equipment needs; designate emergency sites such as hospitals, evacuation routes, and regrouping points; and provide for patrol and control of special vantage points. Additionally, various types of tactical and strategic intelligence must be collected and evaluated with respect to individuals or groups representing actual or potential threats to the subject's safety.

There are two uniformed divisions within the Secret Service: the Executive Protective Service and the Treasury Security Force. The former succeeded the White House police and is responsible for the security of the White House, those buildings in which presidential offices are maintained, and the diplomatic missions of foreign governments located in the Washington, D. C. metropolitan area. The latter force provides the same services for the main Treasury Building and the Treasury Annex.

Annually the Secret Service offers in excess of 6,000 man hours of training to personnel from other law-enforcement agencies, typically in techniques of protective services and the examination of questioned documents.[29]

Interpol

As travel beyond national borders was made increasingly swift it also became more frequent by all types of individuals, including criminals. Thus in 1923, an Austrian, Dr. Johann Schober, revived the idea of an international police organization, the concept having first received serious attention at the First International Criminal Police Congress of 1914 in Monaco.[30] With the newly formed League of Nations providing a cooperative atmosphere, Dr. Schober's invitations brought together 130 delegates from 20 countries. The objective of the new organization, the International Criminal Police Commission, was to provide systematic mutual assistance. The ICPC was not to be a functioning police unit with international arrest powers but rather would be a focus for the dissemination of information and rendering of assistance to member countries in apprehending suspects of common crimes. These functions were not to be applied to individuals involved in political, racial, or religious controversies. ICPC membership was on a national basis with each member nation paying support for the organization on the basis of one Swiss franc for each 10,000 units of population. From the outbreak of World War II until 1946 the ICPC was inactive; when it was revitalized it retained its designation as the International Criminal Police Commission until 1956, when Dr. Giuseppe Dosi, an Italian delegate, proposed the current title International Criminal Police Organization. That title was approved by ICPC's General Assembly.

Today Interpol is headquartered in Saint Cloud, France. Its operating costs are borne by member nations, who contribute on the basis of assessments voted upon by Interpol's general assembly.

Dr. Johann Schober (1874–1932), whose distinguished public career also included service as the police commissioner of Vienna and twice being the Austrian chancellor. Courtesy of the International Criminal Police Organization.

Interpol establishes and maintains identification files on known international criminals and conducts and prepares various types of studies, reports, and intelligence evaluations with regard to their activities. The rapid transmission of requests for, and receipt of, this type of information is facilitated by sophisticated communications systems.

In this country—which has been a member nation of Interpol since 1938—requests for assistance from any of the 111 member nations of Interpol are coordinated through the National Central Bureau in Washington, D.C., which is staffed by personnel from the United States Secret Service and Bureau of Customs. The National Central Bureau is a subunit of the Department of the Treasury which has, since 1958, been designated as our representative to Interpol. Requests for service may range from checks on possible criminal records, to the conducting of actual investigations, to evidence seizure, to the apprehension of fugitives. In recent years the use of Interpol's services, especially by local units of government, has increased steadily by significant margins.

Internal Revenue Service

Since it was established in 1862, the Internal Revenue Service has grown until today it has an annual budget of $1,862,240,000; 2,809 special agents; and 772 internal security inspectors. All of this money and personnel are used by the Internal Revenue Service to administer federal tax provisions.[31] The major source of revenue for the operation of the federal government and its programs is derived from income taxes, both individual and corporate. Other major revenue sources include excise, estate, gift, and employment taxes. Overall, the gross revenue receipts collected by the IRS exceed $300 billion per year, most of it raised by the honest self-reporting and voluntary compliance of those taxed.

Annually, however, a small percentage of the more than 125 million persons filing tax returns attempt various forms of willful noncompliance with the tax laws, such as endeavoring to produce unreported income gained through involvement in illicit activities or trying to improperly influence any of the 75,252 IRS employees. Where any of these conditions appear to exist they become the subject of an investigation. The IRS executes its law-enforcement responsibilities through its intelligence, audit, and internal security divisions.

The intelligence division is responsible for the investigation of possible criminal violations of most tax laws—including those pertaining to excise, estate, gift, and income—and the associated stat-

79

utes pertaining to interference, aiding and abetting, and conspiracy to violate the tax laws. The offenses with which this division must deal most frequently are willful nonfiling of returns and attempts to evade full payment of taxes. The history of the division is traceable to 1919, when then-Commissioner Daniel Roper established an effort to root out bribe-acceptance and extortion by service employees. Subsequently, in 1952, this function was given to what was to become the internal security division, charged with the responsibility to investigate efforts to compromise or corrupt the service. Today the intelligence division conducts two major enforcement operations: the general enforcement and the special enforcement programs. The former is directed at cases involving legitimate persons and businesses, while the latter focuses upon those who obtain unreported income from illegal activities including narcotics trafficking, bribery, and extortion. In 1971 the IRS initiated one of its most effective special enforcement programs, the Narcotics Traffickers Project, whose fundamental objective was to ensure that tax provisions were being applied to major narcotics traffickers and financiers.[32] Individuals selected for tax examination or investigation generally occupy such significant operational or financial positions in the narcotics-distribution system that they are ordinarily well protected from having substantive narcotics charges brought against them. However, many such suspects are living well beyond their reported income, thus indicating a violation of internal revenue laws. Individuals become subject to tax investigations on the basis of intelligence reviewed by a target selection committee, which is composed of representatives from the DEA, Department of the Treasury, and the intelligence and audit divisions of the IRS. During the first three years of operation NTP produced recommendations for 425 prosecutions and assessments of $210,650,000 in additional taxes and penalties.

The audit division seeks to promote the highest possible level of voluntary compliance with tax laws. To do so it conducts an extensive program of intensively scrutinizing tax returns, at the rate of 1,625,445 per year. A total of more than 80 million are reviewed annually. Such reviews may reveal issues that are civil only, but where a deliberate intent to defraud the government is indicated, the case will be referred to the intelligence division for investigation.

Bureau of Customs

Although the collection of customs revenue was authorized in 1789, it was not until 1927 that the Bureau of Customs was created. The broad responsibilities of the Bureau, with 14,029 employees,[33] include the expected customs revenue collection; the control of car-

MARK TWAIN AND THE IRS

When the Internal Revenue presented Mark Twain with an 1864 tax bill for $36.82, plus a $3.12 delinquency penalty, he wrote his editor, "I am taxed on my income. This is perfectly gorgeous. I never felt so important in my life."

Albert B. Paine, ed.,
Mark Twain's Letters
(New York: Harper & Row, 1917).

riers and merchandise imported into, or exported from, this country; the suppression of smuggling; the prevention of pilferage from imported cargoes while at ports of entry; the enforcement of laws prohibiting the shipment of animals under inhuman conditions; the prevention of infiltration of import-export firms by criminal elements; and the examination of incoming foreign mail for contraband and dutiable merchandise. During one fiscal year the Bureau's personnel screened more than 80,000 vehicles, 11,570,000 mail packages, and 6,260,000 units of cargo.[34] From this staggering workload 58,615 pounds of marijuana, 3,027 pounds of hashish, 18 pounds of cocaine, 29 pounds of heroin, 5 pounds of opium, and 4,300,000 dosage units of other dangerous drugs were detected, thereby removing some $192.5 million in "street prices" of narcotics from circulation. While the investigative role of customs has been modified with the advent of the DEA, statutory responsibilities to control smuggling, including narcotics, remain unchanged. In other types of narcotics cases the Bureau of Customs will contact the DEA to either handle the investigation itself or to ask a local enforcement agency to handle the case, depending on its nature and magnitude.

The prevention of importation frauds and subsequent revenue losses is another Bureau responsibility. In one recent year some 1,900 fraud cases came under the Bureau's investigation, including the illegal entry of a Raphael portrait valued in excess of $600,000. The Bureau of Customs also provides training and assorted types of technical assistance to units of government throughout this country and in other nations.

81

Bureau of Alcohol, Tobacco, and Firearms

The relationship between the distilling of spirits and taxation is nearly as old as this country. Boston's first saloon opened in 1625 and by 1633 the Massachusetts Bay Colony began to regulate the sale of liquor by licensing. Monies raised from our first internal revenue law, passed in 1791, paid for one-third of the Revolutionary War debt and produced the celebrated Whiskey Rebellion. From 1803 onward, measures affecting the tax status of liquor were instated and repealed by the Congress several times, but were finally given permanence to meet the unprecedented revenue needs created by the Civil War.[35] Thus the history of the Bureau of Alcohol, Tobacco, and Firearms may be said to date from 1862, when the first Commissioner of Internal Revenue was appointed and three detectives were employed to suppress the illegal manufacturing of distilled spirits with its attendant loss of income for the federal government.

In 1952 the enforcement of the tobacco tax was transferred to the agency known as the Alcohol Tax Unit; it was then redesignated the Alcohol and Tobacco Tax Division. The passage of the Gun Control Act of 1968 created an increased emphasis on firearms control and brought about another title change, this time to the Alcohol, Tobacco, and Firearms Division. Subsequently, on July 1, 1972, the unit was transferred out of the IRS and given its present bureau status within the Department of the Treasury. With an annual operating budget of more than $92 million, the responsibilities of this bureau center upon suppressing traffic in spirits on which the appropriate taxes have not been paid and preventing or reducing the illegal possession of firearms, explosives, and other destructive devices. In one recent annual period these activities resulted in the seizure of 2,272 illicit distilleries and the arrest of 3,195 persons along with the confiscation of 7,995 illegal firearms and the apprehension of 2,223 firearms-law violators.[36]

The Bureau assists state and local police agencies through an extensive training program and by making the services of its forensic laboratory available on a fee-free basis. Additionally, it provides expert testimony regarding evidence examined by the laboratory whenever such testimony is required.

STUDY QUESTIONS

1. Attack or defend the proposition that federal law-enforcement agencies have virtually unlimited power.
2. Which departments represent the locus of federal law-enforcement activity?

3. What is the legal jurisdiction of the FBI?

4. What is NCIC and how does it operate?

5. What are the main criticisms of UCR statistics?

6. What are the responsibilities of the Immigration and Naturalization Service?

7. How are United States marshals selected and what are their duties?

8. What is the CRS?

9. Discuss the operation of the LEAA.

10. Why was the DEA created and what are its functions?

11. What are the protective responsibilities of the Secret Service and to whom do they extend?

12. Trace the development of Interpol. What are its present contributions?

13. What are the roles of the IRS's audit and intelligence divisions?

14. What is the relationship between the Bureau of Customs and the DEA?

15. What federal agency did the Gun Control Act affect most?

ILLUSTRATIVE CAREERS IN FEDERAL LAW ENFORCEMENT

THE FEDERAL BUREAU OF INVESTIGATION

Personnel

Of the approximately 20,000 people working with the FBI, about half are criminal investigators, referred to as Special Agents. While some special agents are assigned to the headquarters office in Washington, D.C., most of them work in the field offices and resident agencies located throughout the nation. The balance of FBI employees are the clerks and technicians who work to support the field operations of the Bureau. The majority of technical and clerical personnel are located in Washington, D.C., and hold such positions as computer programmer, translator, and laboratory technician.

Entry Requirements

All personnel seeking a position with the Federal Bureau of Investigation must meet the following general employment qualifications:

1. have United States citizenship
2. be a high school graduate or its equivalent
3. be at least sixteen years of age
4. be able to meet the physical requirements for the position
5. be able to pass a thorough background investigation

In addition to these general employment qualifications, applicants for the position of special agent must meet additional qualifications: they must be between the ages of twenty-three and thirty-five; they must be able to pass strenuous physical examinations; and they must have excellent vision, hearing, and health. Educational requirements are higher for special agent positions than for other positions. A college education has long been established as a requirement for special agents as has been a degree in law or the attainment of recognition as a certified public accountant. Over the years, this has been occasionally liberalized to admit persons with a baccalaureate degree and three or more years of professional or specialized investigative experience. Special agents must also pass the very rigorous background investigation.

84

Assignments

Special agents are given extensive training at the FBI Academy in Quantico, Virginia, for fifteen weeks. Following the completion of training, agents are assigned to one of the field offices or resident agencies and are occasionally rotated from one office to another.

Career Development

Each of the major position classes within the FBI has an established career ladder which provides increasing responsibility for demonstrated ability. Special agents begin at a GS-10 rating, which under the October 1977 pay schedule means a starting salary of $16,618. Pay raises within the grade or rating level may be as much as $507 annually. In addition, special agents are expected to work overtime, for which they are paid at a rate amounting to 20 percent of the base salary. For other positions there is also career progression. Fingerprint examiners begin at a starting salary of $7,930 annually. After six months of acceptable performance, the Fingerprint examiner is raised to grade GS-4 at $8,902 and thereafter to a GS-7 level at $12,336. The first promotions come at yearly intervals and are followed by promotion at more extended intervals. For positions as laboratory specialists and computer programmers the entry salary is based on education, training, and experience. For most advanced positions in these jobs, the rating is GS-11, with an annual base salary of $18,258.

BUREAU OF ALCOHOL, TOBACCO, AND FIREARMS

Personnel

ATF Special Agents are assigned to over 200 field offices throughout the United States. Investigators are called upon to perform a variety of investigations and enforcement duties ranging from raiding a distillery to preparing material for court proceedings.

Entry Requirements

General requirements for employment in the ATF are similar to those of other federal enforcement agencies. The requirements for employment include American citizenship, age between twenty-one and thirty-five, and the ability to pass a rigorous background investigation of personal history, character, and associates. For the position of ATF Special Agent, there are additional qualifications which must be met, including a bachelor's degree from a college or university and a qualifying score on the Treasury Enforcement Examination. Because of the nature of the work, special agents are required to be in excellent physical health. They must pass a comprehensive medical examination by a licensed physician prior to appointment to the service.

Assignments

Special agents for ATF begin their assignment with eight weeks intensive training at the Federal Law Enforcement Training Center at Glynco, Georgia. This training covers basic law-enforcement skills and is supplemented by the ATF Special Agents Basic School, which provides specialized training in ATF operations. Operations by ATF agents involve surveillance, participation in raids, interviewing suspects and witnesses, making arrests, obtaining search warrants, and searching for physical evidence. Agents must maintain close working relationships with other national, state, and local law-enforcement agencies. The activities of ATF agents frequently require regular unscheduled hours and involve personal risks. Exposure to all kinds of weather, arduous physical exertion under rigorous and unusual environmental conditions, as well as overnight travel are all part of the job for the ATF agent.

Career Development

Special agents in ATF normally enter at GS-5 or GS-7, depending on their education and experience. Under the 1977 revision of the General Schedule, personnel at GS-5 begin at a salary of approximately $9,959, those at the GS-7 level at $12,336. Like FBI agents, ATF investigators earn 20 percent of their base pay for overtime work. Promotions to higher rank are dependent upon satisfactory performance as determined by supervisory recommendations. Promotions require at least one year in each grade before advancement to the next higher grade. The journeyman level for special agents in ATF is a GS-11 with a base salary of $18,258 annually. Supervisory positions are available as vacancies occur for agents at the journeyman level and opportunities for promotion are numerous.

UNITED STATES BORDER PATROL

Personnel

The border patrol is a highly trained, uniformed patrol corps of approximately 2,000 officers. It actively seeks applicants who speak and understand the Spanish language. Entry requirements for positions with the U.S. Border Patrol reflect the nature of the work that is required.

Entry Requirements

Work in the border patrol frequently involves strenuous patrol activity in remote places. Physical requirements include generally excellent health as certified by a qualified physician, and uncorrected binocular vision of 20/50 with no single vision of less than 20/70. In addition to the physical requirements, applicants must be able to pass a rigorous background investigation. All applicants must be under the age of thirty-five and possess a valid driver's license. After all the preliminary conditions for employment have been met, the applicant must establish an eligible rating on a written examination. Examination for border patrol officer positions are administered by the U.S. Civil Service Commission. After qualifying on the written examination, the applicant must then appear before an examining board for an oral interview.

Assignments

Border patrol officers begin their assignments as trainees. They are initially appointed to a duty station along the Mexican border. Shortly after the initial assignment, they report for sixteen weeks of training at the Federal Law Enforcement Training Center at Glynco, Georgia. In addition to the basic training for all federal law-enforcement investigators, border patrol officers receive specialized instruction in Spanish, operation and procedures of the Border Patrol and Immigration Service, immigration and nationality law, and other related subjects. Following training, the border patrol officer is returned to his initial duty station on the Mexican border.

Career Development

Border patrol officers enter the service at GS-5, a salary of $9,959 at the levels of the October 1977 adjustments and earn 25 percent of their base salary for overtime work. They are subsequently promoted to the GS-7 and GS-9 levels. At least one year must elapse before promotion to the next higher grade. At present, GS-9 (with a $15,090 base) is the journeyman grade for border patrol officers. After reaching the journeyman grade, supervisory and other positions in the U.S. Border Patrol and Immigration and Naturalization Service are available on a competitive basis to those who qualify.

NOTES

1. *The Attorney General's First Annual Report, Federal Law Enforcement and Criminal Justice Assistance Activities* (Washington, D.C.: Government Printing Office, 1972). This and subsequent attorney general's annual reports have been freely consulted in the preparation of this chapter.
2. Testimony of Director Clarence M. Kelley before the House Subcommittee on Appropriations, March 18, 1978, p. 2.
3. There are several exceptions to this; for example the Department of the Treasury handles such investigations affecting its employees and by agreement with the Postal Service that agency conducts such investigations if the incident occurs upon postal property.
4. Federal Bureau of Investigation, *1976 Annual Report*, p. 10.
5. Testimony of Director Kelley on March 18, 1978, p. 40.
6. *Attorney General's Annual Report, 1976*, pp. 157–158.
7. *Attorney General's Annual Report, 1972*, p. 201.
8. Testimony of Director Kelley on March 18, 1978, p. 43.
9. Ibid., pp. 46–47.
10. Information supplied by the Immigration and Naturalization Service's Public Information Officer in response to a letter dated November 23, 1977; the figures pertain to FY'78.
11. *Attorney General's Annual Report, 1972*, pp. 241–242.
12. *Attorney General's Annual Report, 1976*, p. 207.
13. There are two exceptions to this statement. In the Virgin Islands the United States marshal is appointed by the attorney general and in the Canal Zone the term of office is eight years.
14. The workload data were taken from the *Attorney General's Annual Report, 1976*, pp. 231–237.
15. These data are taken from the Community Relations Service's *Annual Report 1976*, p. 59. The budget figure is accurate, but because the CRS reported its staffing for both professional and clerical by monthly fluctuations, the figure of 104 represents a typical total personnel complement.
16. *Attorney General's Annual Report, 1972*, p. 258.
17. Ibid., pp. 214–231 and *Attorney General's Annual Report, 1976*, pp. 167–195.
18. "Interview with the Administrator," *Drug Enforcement* (Summer 1974): 2.
19. "The Mission before Us," *Drug Enforcement* (February/March 1974): 1.
20. "Interview with the Administrator," p. 2.
21. "Diversion Investigative Units," *Drug Enforcement* (February/March 1974): 15.
22. Ibid., p. 2.
23. *Attorney General's Annual Report, 1972*, p. 205.
24. John W. Gunn, Jr., "Role of the DEA Laboratories," *Drug Enforcement* (February/March 1975): 5.
25. For an excellent history of the Secret Service see Walter S. Bowen and Harry Edward Neal, *The United States Secret Service* (Philadelphia: Chilton, 1960), p. 205.
26. *Attorney General's Annual Report, 1972*, pp. 297–298.
27. Ibid.
28. John W. Warner, Jr., Assistant to the Director, United States Secret Service to Charles R. Swanson, 13 December 1977, private collection.
29. *Attorney General's Annual Report, 1972*, p. 30.
30. Michael Fooner, *Interpol* (Chicago: Henry Regnery Co., 1973), pp. 13–27.
31. These data were provided by the IRS Public Information Officer in response to an inquiry dated November 23, 1977, and pertain to FY'78. Much of the workload data in this section are taken from the Commissioner of Internal Revenue's *Annual Report: 1976*.
32. John J. Olszewski, "IRS: Taxing the Trafficker," *Drug Enforcement* (Summer 1974): 13–14.
33. *Sourcebook of Criminal Justice Statistics* (1976), Table 1.15, p. 84.

34. Vernon D. Acree, "This Is Customs," *Drug Enforcement* (Spring 1974): 10–11.
35. Miriam Ottenberg, *The Federal Investigators* (Englewood Cliffs, N.J.: Prentice-Hall, 1962), p. 192.
36. *Attorney General's Annual Report, 1972,* p. 294.

89

chapter four
State, Local, and Private Policing

THE STATE ROLE

The state's most visible law-enforcement role is that of providing and supporting direct police services. Such services are often treated under the designation of "state police" which, as popularly used, is an imprecise term covering many very different agencies.[1]

Technically, the term "state police" refers to a body which has general police powers and distributes its efforts between the investigation of criminal matters and traffic safety and enforcement programs. This is true of the state police of Alaska, Delaware, Pennsylvania, Vermont, Kentucky, Michigan, and New Jersey. In other areas the state police focus upon traffic safety and enforcement almost to the exclusion of criminal matters and are most often referred to as "state highway patrol" or "state patrol." In Alabama, California, North Carolina, Oklahoma, and South Carolina such units typically spend 88 percent of their time on matters relating to traffic. California is unusual in that it has both state police and highway patrol units.

In jurisdictions with traffic-oriented patrols, there is a need to provide for the delivery of criminal investigation services; this is accomplished through separate organizations. For example, both Florida and North Carolina have uniformed state patrols that focus on traffic matters, while criminal investigations are handled by their plainclothes Department of Criminal Law Enforcement and the State Bureau of Investigation, respectively.

The patterns of authority exercised by state investigative units are also diffuse, but generally three are recognizable: they may have the authority to originate an investigation of any actual or potential criminal matter; their function may be limited to providing assistance only upon request by key local government officials or at the direction of the governor; or such agencies may have jurisdiction over a very limited number of offenses, such as arson and corruption of public officials, and may act in other matters only upon the issuance of a request for such services or on the direction of the governor. State patrol and criminal investigation units may be located in the same organizational structure, such as the Department of Public Safety in Idaho, Utah, and Illinois, or be placed in different divisions, as is the case in Colorado, South Dakota, and Wyoming.

In addition to providing direct enforcement services, states also offer a number of support services: maintenance of files; collection and dissemination of intelligence; operation of high-speed information and communications systems; collection, tabulation, and publication of crime statistics; and operation of forensic laboratories.

Other types of "state police" include personnel assigned the investigative function in alcoholic beverage commissions, departments of agriculture, and racetrack boards. While such individuals may possess general police powers, they tend to focus on only a few selected matters such as cattle rustling, license investigations, or tax frauds.

While the provision of direct and supportive services is an important and highly visible role, states, through their inherent legal powers, also have considerable impact upon the police function. Through minimum-standards legislation, pioneered by California some twenty-five years ago, the state defines the criteria required by those to be employed as police officers. The requirements prescribed by statute in North Carolina are fairly representative. This statute requires that a police officer must:

1. Be a citizen of the United States.
2. Be at least twenty years of age.
3. Be of good moral character as determined by a thorough background investigation as prescribed.
4. Be fingerprinted and a search made of local, state, and national files to disclose any criminal record.
5. Not have been convicted by any military, local, state, or federal court of any offense involving moral turpitude.
6. Be a high-school graduate or have passed the General Educational Development Test indicating high-school equivalency.
7. Be examined by a licensed physician and meet the physical requirements necessary to properly fulfill the responsibilities of a law-enforcement officer.[2]

Minimum-standards requirements are administered through an organization frequently designated as the Police Officer Standards and Training Commission (POST). In addition to the seven general

Figure 4-1 The organization of the Pennsylvania State Police. Note that a great deal of information is provided about structural relationships, but that the chart only implicitly addresses the activities that these units actually perform.

PENNSYLVANIA

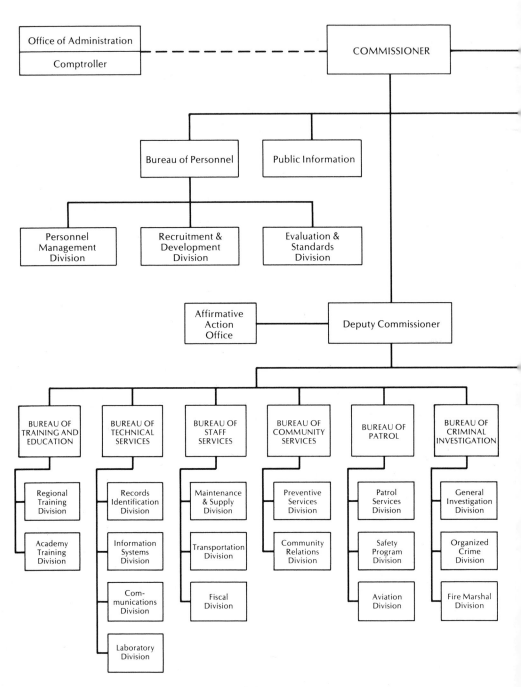

STATE POLICE

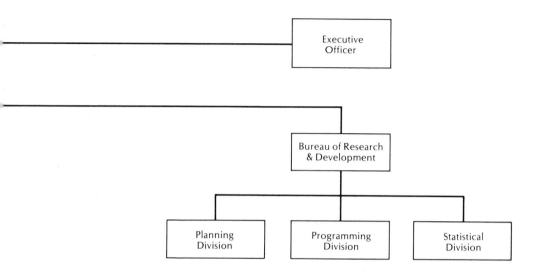

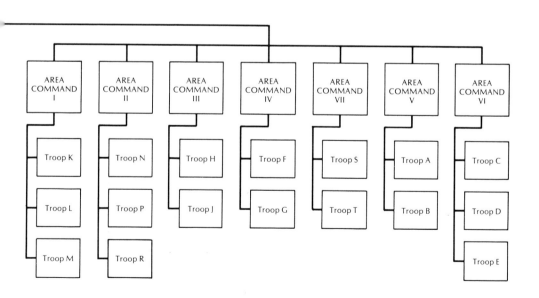

December 21, 1976

93

Figure 4-2 A functional organizational chart depicting the California Highway Patrol. Unlike a simple organizational chart, this type of representation provides a clear notion of the functions performed, but with some loss of detail about structural relationships. Ordinarily large agencies have both organizational charts and functional organizational charts.

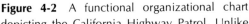

```
COMMISSIONER
DEPUTY COMMISSIONER

ASSISTANT COMMISSIONER
CHIEF OF STAFF
```

PLANNING AND ANALYSIS DIVISION

- Operational plans for the use of uniformed personnel, equipment, and facilities.
- Coordinate with the Attorney General on matters relating to Departmental policies.
- Data and information through the application of applied research techniques.
- Design and administer statistical services.
- Provide statistical reports.
- Provide electronic data processing services.
- Manage and coordinate the State-wide Integrated Traffic Records System.
- Review and provide input to Federal agencies on proposed traffic safety standards.
- Project management for nonoperational projects.
- Special funding project coordination.
- Assistance to transportation planning agencies.

ADMINISTRATIVE SERVICES DIVISION

- General administrative consultation to executive management.
- Budget preparation and fiscal management.
- Special legal, contractual, and management studies.
- Coordinate with the Attorney General on civil litigations.
- Personnel Management.
- Personnel and manpower planning.
- Liaison with the State Personnel Board.
- Employee development.
- Career opportunity development.
- Injury and disability claims.
- Liaison with S.C.I.F., W.A.C.B., and P.E.R.S.
- Class and pay studies.
- Employee recruitment.
- Logistical support, planning, management, and services to field operations in the areas of facilities, vehicle transportation, communications, supply distribution, etc.
- Accept and coordinate service of claims, complaints, subpoenas, summonses, and writs.
- Records management and publication control.

ENFORCEMENT SERVICES DIVISION

- Inspection of passenger, commercial and farm labor vehicles, school buses, and carrier terminals.
- Safe loading and transportation of regulated materials including hazardous commodities.
- Engineering service, and standards for automotive equipment.
- Operation of Departmental aircraft.
- Reduction of motor vehicle noise emissions.
- Prevention and control of vehicle theft.
- Issuance of permits and licenses. required for operation of specialized or emergency vehicles.
- Development and adoption of technical administrative regulations.
- Planning, organizing, coordinating, and evaluating the Statewide Vehicle Abatement Program.
- Direct dispersal of funds to cities and counties conducting local vehicle abatement programs under contract with the Department.

TRAINING DIVISION

- Training services for the Department, State, and allied agencies.
- Academy operations.
- Book and Film library services.
- Film and graphic art services.

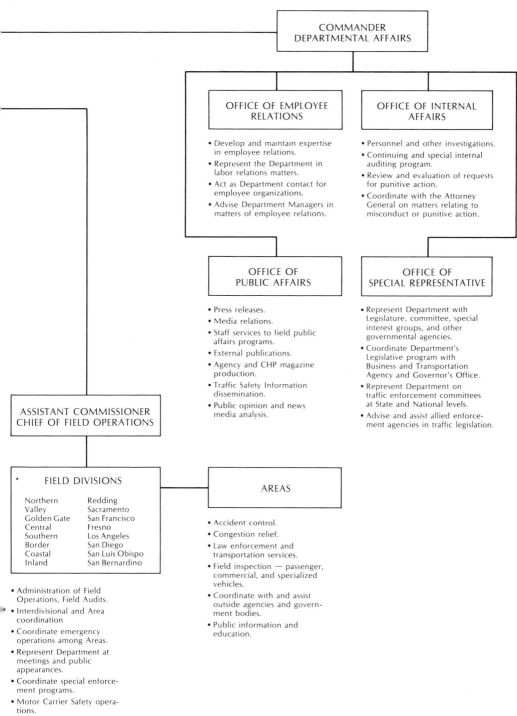

COMMANDER
DEPARTMENTAL AFFAIRS

OFFICE OF EMPLOYEE
RELATIONS

• Develop and maintain expertise in employee relations.
• Represent the Department in labor relations matters.
• Act as Department contact for employee organizations.
• Advise Department Managers in matters of employee relations.

OFFICE OF INTERNAL
AFFAIRS

• Personnel and other investigations.
• Continuing and special internal auditing program.
• Review and evaluation of requests for punitive action.
• Coordinate with the Attorney General on matters relating to misconduct or punitive action.

OFFICE OF
PUBLIC AFFAIRS

• Press releases.
• Media relations.
• Staff services to field public affairs programs.
• External publications.
• Agency and CHP magazine production.
• Traffic Safety Information dissemination.
• Public opinion and news media analysis.

OFFICE OF
SPECIAL REPRESENTATIVE

• Represent Department with Legislature, committee, special interest groups, and other governmental agencies.
• Coordinate Department's Legislative program with Business and Transportation Agency and Governor's Office.
• Represent Department on traffic enforcement committees at State and National levels.
• Advise and assist allied enforcement agencies in traffic legislation.

ASSISTANT COMMISSIONER
CHIEF OF FIELD OPERATIONS

* FIELD DIVISIONS

Northern	Redding
Valley	Sacramento
Golden Gate	San Francisco
Central	Fresno
Southern	Los Angeles
Border	San Diego
Coastal	San Luis Obispo
Inland	San Bernardino

• Administration of Field Operations, Field Audits.
• Interdivisional and Area coordination
• Coordinate emergency operations among Areas.
• Represent Department at meetings and public appearances.
• Coordinate special enforcement programs.
• Motor Carrier Safety operations.
• Vehicle theft investigations.

AREAS

• Accident control.
• Congestion relief.
• Law enforcement and transportation services.
• Field inspection — passenger, commercial, and specialized vehicles.
• Coordinate with and assist outside agencies and government bodies.
• Public information and education.

*effective January 1, 1977

requirements, police applicants must also complete a course of such content and length as POST may require. While the lengths of such basic or entry-level training varies, it is not unusual to find courses exceeding 400 hours and, as is indicated by Table 4-1, much longer courses are not uncommon. Additionally, under the aegis of the minimum-standards legislation, states with increasing frequency are requiring preservice psychological screening and refresher training programs at various intervals following completion of the recruit course, coupled with required programs of study for supervisors, middle managers, and executive-level personnel. There is variance among the states with POST programs—presently forty-five—as to compliance with requirements; in some it is voluntary and in others mandatory, the latter being the most frequent. One of the contributing factors central to this variance was the resistance in some states, especially by those in predominantly rural areas, to mandatory requirements. It was perceived as a hardship upon smaller organizations to have to release an officer from normal duties for four or more weeks of "nonproductive" classroom work. With the advent of the Law Enforcement Assistance Administration's grant program, some states with voluntary POST requirements saw an administrative means to encourage compliance by refusing to make grants to police departments which did not adhere to the voluntary requirements. As a future trend we may anticipate the gradual widening of Police Officer Standards and Training organizations to Criminal Justice Standards

TABLE 4-1 A Sample of Longer-than-Average Police-Recruit Training Programs

AGENCY	DURATION
Dayton, Ohio	960 hours
Seattle, Washington	880 hours
Jacksonville, Florida	448 hours
Richmond, Virginia	16-weeks live-in
Michigan State Police	16-weeks live-in
Dade County, Florida	949 hours
Baltimore, Maryland	640 hours
Royal Canadian Mounted Police	910 hours
Chicago, Illinois	1,040 hours
Kansas City, Missouri	640 hours
Madison, Wisconsin	420 hours
Los Angeles Sheriff's Office	1,040 hours

Source: National Advisory Commission on Criminal Justice Standards and Goals, *Police* (Washington, D.C.: Government Printing Office, 1973), p. 393.

and Training Commissions with responsibility for requirements affecting all personnel employed in the administration of justice.

After police personnel have been properly trained, their effectiveness can be increased by various interstate agreements, such as the Arkansas-Mississippi and Arkansas-Tennessee boundary compacts covering criminal jurisdiction on the Mississippi River and the New England State Police Compact which provides for mutual assistance in emergencies and for centralized criminal records. States also provide various types of technical assistance to local units of government ranging from guidance in establishing records systems to complete management audits. The nature of the long-familiar offices of constable, coroner, and sheriff are shaped by the states, which determine whether they are to be constitutional or statutory, elective or appointive, and establishes limits to succession and the length of terms of office. The states further enhance the local police function by the establishment of uniform minimum-pension systems and by financially underwriting minimum-standards training programs. Moreover since 1968, under the Omnibus Crime Control and Safe Streets Act establishing the Law Enforcement Assistance Administration, the states have played a key role in criminal-justice planning. Finally, states define what constitutes a crime and how crime must be investigated to ensure for lawful searches, seizures, or interrogations.

SHERIFF, CORONER, AND CONSTABLE

Sheriff

With the exceptions of Hawaii and Alaska, the office of sheriff has been established, either by state constitution or statutory law, in every state of this country.[3] In forty-six states the prevailing practice is to elect sheriffs as county officers; in Connecticut sheriffs are selected by the county electorate, but as state officers. In Rhode Island, sheriffs are appointed by the governor.

Delaware, Indiana, Kentucky, West Virginia, Illinois, Tennessee, and New Mexico impose limits to succession by sheriffs. "Sheriffs serve two-year terms in eleven states, three-year terms in New York and New Jersey, a six-year term in Massachusetts, and four-year terms in thirty-three states."[4] In Rhode Island, sheriffs serve at the pleasure of the governor.

Even in states where the prevalent practice is election, a limited number of counties, such as Dade County, Florida; Nassau County, New York; and Multnomah County, Oregon, have sheriffs who are appointed by the chief executive of the county, subject to the approval of the commissioners, or by the commissioners themselves. The principal advantage of an appointed sheriff is that—given the existence of

Figure 4-3 The Organizational chart of the well-organized Dade County Department of Public Safety.

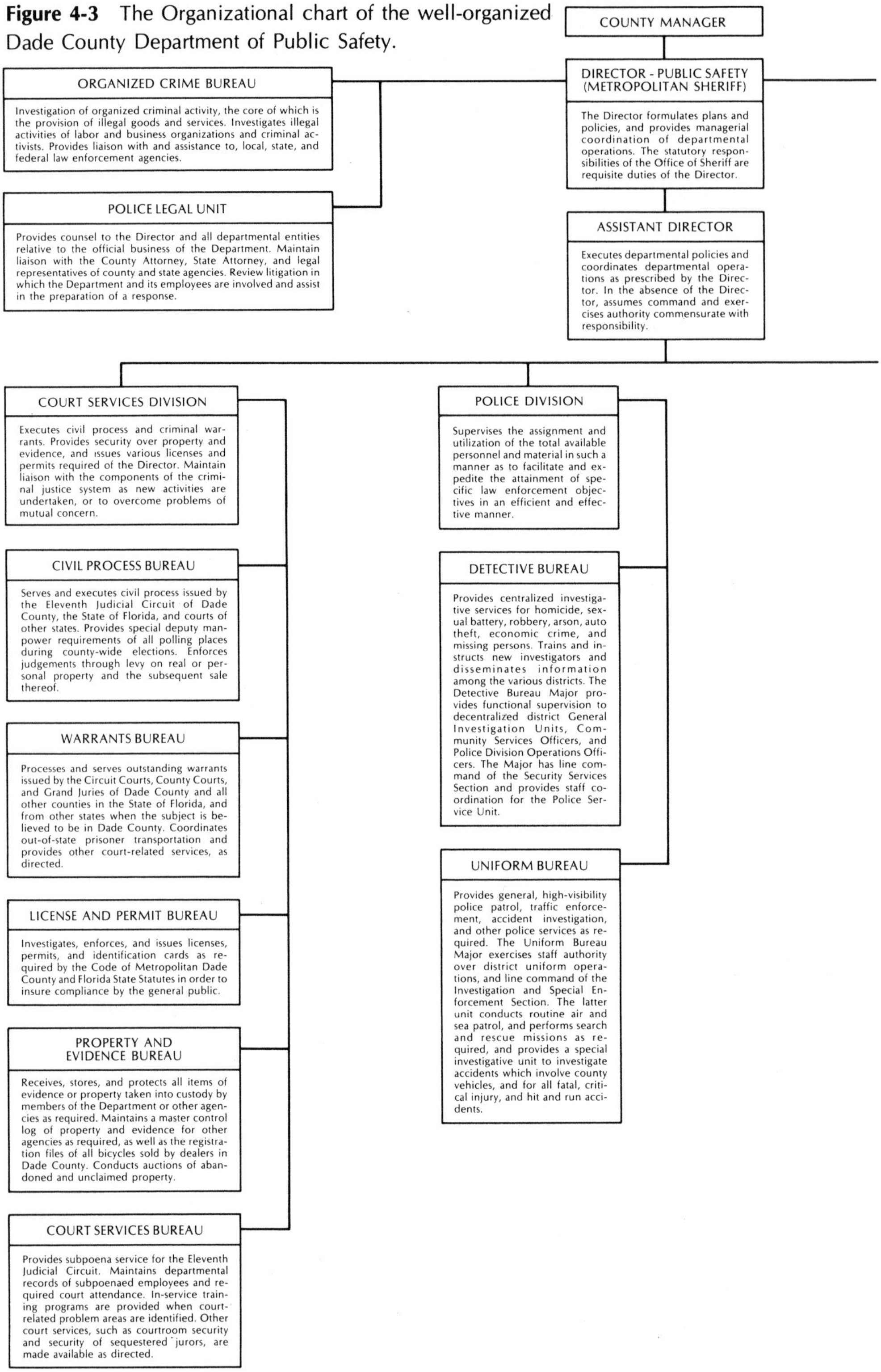

COUNTY MANAGER

DIRECTOR - PUBLIC SAFETY (METROPOLITAN SHERIFF)

The Director formulates plans and policies, and provides managerial coordination of departmental operations. The statutory responsibilities of the Office of Sheriff are requisite duties of the Director.

ORGANIZED CRIME BUREAU

Investigation of organized criminal activity, the core of which is the provision of illegal goods and services. Investigates illegal activities of labor and business organizations and criminal activists. Provides liaison with and assistance to, local, state, and federal law enforcement agencies.

POLICE LEGAL UNIT

Provides counsel to the Director and all departmental entities relative to the official business of the Department. Maintain liaison with the County Attorney, State Attorney, and legal representatives of county and state agencies. Review litigation in which the Department and its employees are involved and assist in the preparation of a response.

ASSISTANT DIRECTOR

Executes departmental policies and coordinates departmental operations as prescribed by the Director. In the absence of the Director, assumes command and exercises authority commensurate with responsibility.

COURT SERVICES DIVISION

Executes civil process and criminal warrants. Provides security over property and evidence, and issues various licenses and permits required of the Director. Maintain liaison with the components of the criminal justice system as new activities are undertaken, or to overcome problems of mutual concern.

POLICE DIVISION

Supervises the assignment and utilization of the total available personnel and material in such a manner as to facilitate and expedite the attainment of specific law enforcement objectives in an efficient and effective manner.

CIVIL PROCESS BUREAU

Serves and executes civil process issued by the Eleventh Judicial Circuit of Dade County, the State of Florida, and courts of other states. Provides special deputy manpower requirements of all polling places during county-wide elections. Enforces judgements through levy on real or personal property and the subsequent sale thereof.

DETECTIVE BUREAU

Provides centralized investigative services for homicide, sexual battery, robbery, arson, auto theft, economic crime, and missing persons. Trains and instructs new investigators and disseminates information among the various districts. The Detective Bureau Major provides functional supervision to decentralized district General Investigation Units, Community Services Officers, and Police Division Operations Officers. The Major has line command of the Security Services Section and provides staff coordination for the Police Service Unit.

WARRANTS BUREAU

Processes and serves outstanding warrants issued by the Circuit Courts, County Courts, and Grand Juries of Dade County and all other counties in the State of Florida, and from other states when the subject is believed to be in Dade County. Coordinates out-of-state prisoner transportation and provides other court-related services, as directed.

LICENSE AND PERMIT BUREAU

Investigates, enforces, and issues licenses, permits, and identification cards as required by the Code of Metropolitan Dade County and Florida State Statutes in order to insure compliance by the general public.

UNIFORM BUREAU

Provides general, high-visibility police patrol, traffic enforcement, accident investigation, and other police services as required. The Uniform Bureau Major exercises staff authority over district uniform operations, and line command of the Investigation and Special Enforcement Section. The latter unit conducts routine air and sea patrol, and performs search and rescue missions as required, and provides a special investigative unit to investigate accidents which involve county vehicles, and for all fatal, critical injury, and hit and run accidents.

PROPERTY AND EVIDENCE BUREAU

Receives, stores, and protects all items of evidence or property taken into custody by members of the Department or other agencies as required. Maintains a master control log of property and evidence for other agencies as required, as well as the registration files of all bicycles sold by dealers in Dade County. Conducts auctions of abandoned and unclaimed property.

COURT SERVICES BUREAU

Provides subpoena service for the Eleventh Judicial Circuit. Maintains departmental records of subpoenaed employees and required court attendance. In-service training programs are provided when court-related problem areas are identified. Other court services, such as courtroom security and security of sequestered jurors, are made available as directed.

INTERNAL REVIEW SECTION

Investigates complaints and allegations of improper activities which involve employees of the Department. Conducts background investigations of applicants for special-deputy commissions. Investigation of lawsuits directed against the Department and other investigations as requested by the Director.

COMMUNITY SERVICES SECTION

Identifies and evaluates the needs of the community and the Department in order to establish and maintain meaningful communications and a responsive working relationship.

CENTRAL SERVICES DIVISION

Provides crime laboratory and related services as well as central records and identification service for the Department and other governmental jurisdictions. Provides central communications services for the Department, other county departments, and municipal subscribers.

CRIME LABORATORY BUREAU

Provides crime laboratory services including firearms identification; comparative micrography; bomb disposal; crime scene processing; analysis by chemical, biological, and instrumental methods; photography; questioned document examination; and chemical tests for intoxication.

RECORDS AND IDENTIFICATION BUREAU

Provides records and identification services for the Department and other law enforcement agencies, and support-terminal control for National Crime Information Center and local Criminal Justice Information System. Maintains latent fingerprint and voiceprint analysis as well as certain photographs.

COMMUNICATIONS BUREAU

Provides dispatching and complaint services via radio and telephone. The Center receives and transmits information for the Department and municipal subscribers via computer terminals through the local, state, and national systems. Provides emergency maintenance and operation of communications repair facilities for all county departments and municipal subscribers.

ADMINISTRATIVE DIVISION

Performs departmental supply, fiscal, budget, and personnel functions; coordinates transportation requirements; conducts studies for organizational improvement; and develops managerial, operational, and procedural plans for the Department and various divisions. Administers, directs, and conducts training for departmental and municipal personnel.

MANAGEMENT ANALYSIS BUREAU

Long-range planning to develop comprehensive programs which are responsive to the departmental mission and based on internal and external resources. Analyzes, develops, and evaluates administrative procedures, operational methods, and management systems to promote efficiency and effectiveness.

TRAINING BUREAU

Administers, directs, and supervises training for the Department. Budgets, controls, and coordinates all educational travel requests. The departmental library is maintained within the Bureau as well as the Department's closed circuit television studio and equipment. Administers the Department's police reserve training and student internship programs.

DATA SYSTEMS BUREAU

Provides the informational needs of the Department. Utilizes data processing for informational and research purposes and issues reports for use by all divisions to more effectively distribute manpower and equipment. Statistical compilations of data derived from crime reports, traffic accidents, and calls for police service.

PERSONNEL BUREAU

Recruitment and screening of employees for the Department's respective functions consistent with equal employment opportunity and affirmative action guidelines. Personnel records management, compilation and maintenance of attendance data, and payroll preparation are performed. Assists employees with department-related personnel matters.

99

any reasonable competency of county leadership—a professionally educated and experienced administrator may be retained, whereas an elected sheriff may have to be less of a professional and more of a politician. The sheriffs have not been insensitive, nor unresponsive, to such criticisms and have instituted a number of training programs, such as the one at the University of Southern California, through the National Sheriffs' Association. Moreover, acting individually, many sheriffs have taken the initiative by attending workshops and seminars designed to impart greater professional competency.

Most states provide that the sheriff is the chief law-enforcement officer in his county, with countywide jurisdiction. As a practical matter, with the rise of municipal police forces, the sheriff generally restricts the scope of his activities to the unincorporated areas of the county.

The major functions usually undertaken by a typical sheriff's office include operation of the jail, patrol services, and criminal investigation. "In addition, the sheriff is assigned a multitude of civil duties as a ministerial officer of the court"; although the duties go on at some length, a few of the more common are:

1. Certifying lists of juror's names for jury duty.
2. Conducting executive sales of confiscated and unclaimed property.
3. Arresting and detaining civil prisoners.
4. Serving civil writings and legal processes.
5. Executing court orders such as attachments, seizures, and sequestering property.
6. Endorsing processes and various kinds of legal notices.[5]

As presently constituted in many jurisdictions the office of sheriff is an anachronism, overburdened by very different and difficult major functions. Moreover, because of the paucity of requirements to be eligible for the office, it is occasionally found that the politically astute, but not necessarily professionally prepared, are elected. This often leads to a questionable quality of administration. This is not to accuse such administrations of corrupt practices, but rather to note that the level of performance may well be below that consistent with the public welfare.

If necessary, the removal of a sheriff from office is ordinarily regulated by the state constitution or statutory law. One pattern provides for suspension from office by the governor, subject to an impeachment hearing by the legislature. Among the more frequent grounds for removal are:

1. Corruption in office.
2. Conviction of a felony or crime involving moral turpitude.
3. Misfeasance, nonfeasance, or malfeasance in office.
4. Intemperance in the use of drugs or alcohol.
5. Failure to perform statutory duties adequately and correctly.[6]

Alternate means of delivering local police services need to be explored. They may be defined briefly as reorganization of police service-delivery patterns through combining the resources of more than one unit of government, a pattern we can expect to see with increasing frequency in the coming years. Whenever some type of consolidation is considered, a key and politically sensitive issue becomes, "What shall be done with the office of sheriff?" There are basically five options which might be followed. One option is to make the sheriff exclusively an officer of the court with responsibility for detention facilities, as in Fulton County, Georgia. A second possibility is to divest the office of all nonpolice functions, which was the course followed in Multnomah County, Oregon. A third option would be to eliminate the office, as in St. Louis County, Missouri, accompanied by assigning the duties elsewhere in county government.[7] A fourth alternative, currently under strong consideration in a growing number of counties, is to reduce the functions of the office of sheriff to one, serving civil processes, and to create a county law-enforcement agency to handle police matters, with the administration of detention facilities under a separate county department. In Dade County, Florida, a fifth option is seen; the sheriff's office is responsible for police matters and for serving civil processes, with a separate Department of Corrections running the detention facilities.

As the public seeks to find relief from existing and ever-increasing high tax levels, a collateral effect will be an increased emphasis upon achieving efficiency in government. The future of the office of sheriff in large measure lies with the ability of individual sheriffs—with the assistance of the National Sheriff's Association and other resources—to continue to professionalize and to adapt the office to a largely urban society.

Coroner

Historically the office of coroner is bound up, in various ways, with other offices of criminal justice. Today the office of coroner retains its ancient responsibility for conducting hearings, termed "coroner's inquests," on deaths resulting from violent acts or occurring under suspicious circumstances. "The mere fact that a body lies

101

dead does not give the coroner jurisdiction, even though death was sudden. . . . Moreover a coroner's inquest is required to be held only when the circumstances of death are suspicious in nature and only where the cause of death is problematical or in doubt; if it is clear and manifest that the death was felonious an inquest is unnecessary."[8] The courts have differed in their opinions of whether coroners function in a judicial capacity; they have alternately described the role as "judicial," "partly judicial," "quasijudicial," and "ministerial."[9] Unless conferred by statute, a person suspected of having committed an act resulting in a felonious death does not have the right to be represented by counsel or to cross-examine witnesses at a coroner's inquest. Statutory provisions require a coroner to summon a jury whose duty it is to diligently inquire how the deceased came to die, to investigate all material circumstances connected with the death, and to deliver a verdict to the coroner.[10] The finding of the jury is merely advisory, creating no duties on the part of the public officials charged with the administration of the criminal law. Neither does it create any rights or liabilities, either criminal or civil.[11]

In a number of states, when the office of sheriff becomes vacant through death, resignation, or the prescribed removal process the coroner of the county is authorized to perform all the duties of the office of sheriff until such time as another person is appointed. Since coroners are county officers, they are subject to removal in the same manner as sheriffs. However, most serve out their full terms, usually two or four years.

In twenty-five states the coroner is elected on a county basis; in Connecticut, Tennessee, and West Virginia he or she is appointed by county officials; in sixteen states the office has been abolished in favor of a medical-examiner system, and in the remaining states it continues to exist supplemented by a medical examiner-system.[12] One of the chief criticisms of the coroner system is that it fails to ensure that competent medical authority is consistently brought to bear upon analysis of, and judgments pertaining to, deaths occurring under unusual circumstances; this criticism is supported by the fact that only two states require coroners to possess medical degrees. Statewide medical-examiner systems, staffed by appointed medical authorities, respond to this deficiency and also provide the virtue of eliminating a costly and time-consuming process, the coroner's inquest. It is likely that by the end of the century the office of coroner will cease to exist or will be regarded as an oddity. The coroner's successor will be the medical examiner.

An incident in the bizarre Patricia Hearst case underscores the benefits to be derived from the application of forensic medicine. On February 4, 1974, Patricia Hearst was kidnapped by members of the Symbionese Liberation Army (SLA). Some eight days later her father, Randolph Hearst, owner of the *San Francisco Examiner,* received a demand to provide $70 worth of food to every needy person in California—at a projected total cost of $400 million—in exchange for the release of his daughter. While Randolph Hearst apparently made a good-faith attempt to meet the demand, the SLA did not release his daughter. The events which followed suggest that, for whatever reasons, she had committed herself to the SLA. On May 17, 1974, in Los Angeles a gun battle broke out between heavily armed members of the SLA and the police; this battle resulted in the suicide or death of six members of the SLA. The stucco house in which they had barricaded themselves suffered heavy fire damage during the course of the conflict. The fire evidently resulted from an explosion of fumes from gasoline the fugitives were using to make Molotov cocktails. All six bodies were severely burned. For each of the families involved there was the agony of not knowing whether their daughters and sons were dead or alive. On the part of the police there was a need to know who had perished so that further investigation could be properly directed at the still-living members. Fortunately, resources existed that could provide immediate assistance. The Chief Medical Examiner of Los Angeles County was Dr. Thomas Noguchi, one of the world's leading forensic pathologists. He was able to establish not only the identities of the deceased, based upon dental records, but also the sequence and means in which they had died. Of all the words spoken and written about the Hearst case up to that point, none were awaited more anxiously than Dr. Noguchi's expert conclusions. Although most medical examiners will never have the opportunity to handle a case of this dimension, their daily work makes a contribution that is no less important.

Constable

In most states the constable is an elected county officer; in Maryland and South Carolina county officials appoint the constable. In all states that have constables their primary function is to execute the law-enforcement duties of the local justice of the peace. The office is provided for, either by statute or by the state constitution, in forty states; it does not exist in Virginia, Alaska, New Mexico, Colorado, New Jersey, Ohio, Maine, Illinois, Delaware, and Hawaii.[13] The term of office ranges from one year in Vermont to a maximum of six years in California; most frequently, as is the case in sixteen states, the term of office is two years. In a few states, such as Florida, Washington, and Louisiana, individual counties may abolish the office of constable.[14] From the vantage of the present, it seems the future of the office of constable is inexorably bound up with that of justice of the peace and sheriff. As unified court systems develop at the state level the office of justice of the peace may virtually disappear, thereby raising the question of whether the office of constable should be continued

Dr. Thomas T. Noguchi (b. 1927), Chief Medical Examiner of Los Angeles County, a leading forensic pathologist and a key figure in the aftermath of the 1974 SLA barricade situation.

to serve some segment of the judiciary or whether it might be more sound to abolish the office and transfer the function to the sheriff.

MUNICIPAL POLICING

The Magnitude of Municipal Policing

In sheer numbers of personnel employed, dollars expended, and the number of agencies in operation, the policing function in America is overwhelmingly municipal; as used here "municipal" includes villages, towns, and true municipalities. During one recent year, of the 670,724 persons employed in policing by all levels, 500,536 (74.6 percent) worked for local government, primarily municipalities. In financial terms, 81 percent of the $7.7 billion expended annually for local police services comes from municipalities, which outspent counties by about a four to one margin.[15] Further, while there are only some 50 federal law-enforcement agencies, 200 state agencies, and 3,050 county forces, police agencies in municipalities number approximately 37,000.[16] What do these data mean? Examined in the aggregate they suggest that municipal law enforcement is a large and well-financed social institution; implicit in that judgment is the assumption that these agencies are functionally sound. However, the sheer statistical frequency of agencies produces a gross fragmentation of resources and duplication of effort. While fewer than 150 large cities employ roughly one-half of all police personnel, the balance are spread over the remaining 36,850 village, town, and municipal forces. The net effect is that while the largest number of police officers work for large city departments, the most statistically frequent situation is the small town department consisting of fewer than twenty officers. This condition applies to at least two-thirds of all "municipal" forces. As a function of their limited size many of these small departments cannot provide twenty-four-hour patrol and radio-dispatch services, let alone sophisticated investigative services. Such departments also represent a burden on their large, well-endowed neighbors by initiating frequent requests for various types of assistance. Recognizing this, one prestigious government commission recommended that "police agencies that employ fewer than ten sworn employees should consolidate for improved efficiency and effectiveness."[17]

Delivering Police Services

Policing is a function of the executive branch of government. Generally in municipal government the chief of police, who is appointed, reports directly to the mayor or city manager and is at least equal to other department heads in terms of prestige and influence. A variation of this is seen where departments of public safety exist, headed by an appointed director who is responsible to the mayor or city manager. In this system the fire chief and chief of police are subordinate to the director of public safety.

There are three broad divisions of police services: line, auxiliary, and staff. Line units are those which seek to achieve directly the broad goal prescribed for the police: the protection of life and property, the prevention of acts of criminality, and, where failing this, the rapid detection of the offense, followed by identification and apprehension of the violator. The primary line unit is the uniformed patrol division where all the manpower is assigned in departments of up to ten officers and where about 45 percent of a large city force will be assigned. Other line units include the traffic and investigation divisions. There are auxiliary elements which are immediately supportive of the line units; these are responsible for the operation of the detention facility, communications, the crime laboratory, records and criminal-identification files, and evidence storage. Staff services also support the line function, but in a less direct fashion than do auxiliary services. Staff services include training, fiscal management, recruitment and selection, planning and research, and public-information efforts. Only police departments in the largest cities have the full range of line, auxiliary, and staff elements; even medium-sized municipalities with a quarter to a half a million residents may lack one or more elements such as a crime laboratory, while the smallest police departments will have only the patrol element.

The American Bar Association has identified certain major current responsibilities of local police departments.

1. To identify criminal offenders and criminal activity and, where appropriate, to apprehend offenders [to] participate in subsequent court proceedings.
2. To reduce the opportunities for the commission of some crimes through preventive patrol and other measures.
3. To aid individuals who are in danger of physical harm.
4. To protect constitutional guarantees.
5. To facilitate the movement of people and vehicles.
6. To assist those who cannot care for themselves.
7. To resolve conflict.
8. To identify problems that are potentially serious law-enforcement or governmental problems.
9. To create and maintain a feeling of security in the community.
10. To promote and preserve civil order.
11. To provide other services on an emergency basis.[18]

A careful reading of this list leads one to question how much of the police officer's function actually involves enforcing the law. A study of radio dispatches made by the Syracuse Police Department revealed that only 10.3 percent of the time was a law-enforcement activity involved; in the remaining cases the focus of activity was gathering information, providing services such as vehicle escort, finding lost persons, and maintaining order, including the difficult task of settling domestic quarrels.[19] Traditionally, recruit training has given disproportionate emphasis to the enforcement function. More than 80 percent of recruit curriculum has been devoted to preparing the individual for what is admittedly an important, but limited, part of his total range of responsibilities. To solve the problems caused by this gap between training and responsibilities, the options would be to divest the patrolman of at least certain of his functions or to make significant curriculum alterations. During the past few years there has been a steady increase in the amount of social-science content in recruiting training programs, but clearly more is needed.

Alternative Methods of Delivering Local Police Services

As has been noted, the delivery of police services in this country is overwhelmingly a function of local units of government; it is accurate to depict service delivery at this level as characterized by gross fragmentation and duplication of effort. "Although law-enforcement officials speak of close cooperation among agencies, the reference often simply means a lack of conflict."[20] The absence of close and continuous cooperation has some high costs, for it contributes to inefficiency by creating a parochial attitude which focuses almost exclusively upon police problems within a narrowly defined geographic setting. This is a condition that is consistently taken advantage of by our highly mobile criminal population.

If significant improvements are to be made in the quality and quantity of police services it will be necessary to reorganize service delivery based upon combinations or recombinations of resources from more than one unit of government. This may be accomplished by regionalizing certain types of services or through consolidation of police agencies or whole governmental units. There are five widely recognized types of resource manipulation. (1) Intergovernmental contracts, in which one unit of government agrees to provide certain stipulated levels of service, such as two one-man cars, twenty-four hours per day, for a fixed fee. These contracts can be developed in several different ways. The Connecticut resident-trooper plan is a state-to-municipal arrangement. In Georgia, a city-to-county service arrangement existed between the city of Atlanta and the unincorporated portions of Fulton County until 1975 when a separate Fulton

107

County Police Department was created. In Los Angeles a county-to-city pattern prevails, with the sheriff's office providing total police services to twenty-nine of seventy-seven incorporated municipalities. (2) Comprehensive governmental reorganizations, producing a structure termed "metropolitan," have largely been limited to a handful of jurisdictions such as Jacksonville, Florida, Nashville-Davidson County, Tennessee, and Dade County, Florida. In this latter case, the county provides all governmental services in unincorporated areas and selected services on a countywide basis. Administrative responsibility for the police function is vested in an appointed director of public safety, whose office may generally be equated to that of sheriff. Municipalities in Dade County remain as separate units of government; virtually all of them provide a minimum of basic police services and a few units provide, in addition to line services, auxiliary and staff functions. In contrast, in Nashville-Davidson County since 1962, police services have been provided throughout the county by the metropolitan police department in both urban and general-service districts with urban residents, due to the service level, paying operating costs at a higher rate than their rural counterparts in the general-service districts. (3) Special police districts, which are rare in this country, represent the creation of a new, single-purpose unit to provide service districts. This is not a reorganization of existing government but rather the creation of a new unit based upon geographic boundaries which emphasize the single service to be delivered without respect to existing political boundaries. Such districts may be financed by revenues raised through user or property assessments. (4) Suffolk and Nassau counties, New York, represent county subordinate-service district patterns, although the details of the respective operations emphasize different considerations. The county subordinate-service district system provides for policing of both incorporated and unincorporated areas of a county. Ordinarily the entire county receives the same level of service, financed from general tax revenues, except that particular geographic areas, termed "subordinate districts," may receive higher levels of service financed by *ad valorem* property taxes. The amount of these taxes is determined by the level of higher police services received. County subordinate-service districts are distinguished from special police districts in that the former are units of an existing multipurpose governmental structure, the county, whereas the latter must be created as new single-purpose governmental units. (5) Regionalization patterns which essentially are cooperative efforts among two or more units of government to improve the quality of police services. Such efforts generally focus upon combining elements of line, auxiliary, or staff functions. The Kansas City area metro unit is an excellent example of regionalized investigative services for line functions. The unit consists of 291 officers drawn from 41 separate departments located in two states. In the Phoenix and Tucson metropolitan areas cooperative arrangements exist to make available a particular auxiliary function, crime-laboratory services. Chicago and Philadelphia both provide training assistance, a staff function, on a cooperative basis to smaller agencies in their respective areas.

Regardless of the form taken, both consolidation and regionalization or cooperative efforts tend to be issues which arouse the emotions of those who may be affected. Although initially they appear to have little impact on how police services are currently delivered, efforts to combine resources will meet progressively more resistance as they develop in staff, auxiliary, and line functions. Such resistance invariably centers around two factors: pride and control. A recent study sought to determine how police services in a county of 80,000 inhabitants might be improved. In all seven of the incorporated areas within the county being studied government leaders voiced some opposition to regionalization of line services or consolidation. The reason for the opposition is clear.

> We don't want just any policeman coming into Black Elm and starting to give tickets for just any little old thing. The boys we got know everybody. . . . Usually if something is wrong stopping them and talking is about all that's needed.

> We're small, but I'll tell you one thing . . . Cooper City is proud as hell and we'll take care of our own . . . and [we] got the money to do it.

In attempting to sell these concepts, advocates of consolidation and cooperation emphasize the savings by virtue of the fact that duplicate efforts need no longer be maintained. As a rule of thumb the savings actually experienced tend to be minimal since more funds are spent on increasing the quality and quantity of other types of services. Over the next two decades we can anticipate a steady increase in the incidence of resource manipulation among various levels of government.

PRIVATE POLICE

Nature and Extent

"Private police" is a general term which includes a variety of nonpublic organizations or individuals such as those providing guard, patrol, lie detection, armored-car transportation, or alarm services. When one begins to analyze private policing two facts become apparent rapidly: (1) despite intermittent treatment in the news media and the attention of a task force on private security operating under the

National Advisory Committee on Criminal Justice Standards and Goals private police have, with the exception of an excellent five-volume study by the Rand Corporation, largely escaped systematic, empirical study and (2) it is an industry of considerable dimensions.[21] There are two general types of private police: contract forces, which provide services for a fee and proprietary or in-house forces, which provide services exclusively to one employer.[22] Unless commissioned, private security personnel generally do not possess powers any greater than those of other citizens, but by virtue of their positions such personnel are more knowledgeable about and more likely to take fuller advantage of their powers as citizen.[23]

Presently more money is expended annually on private police than on public police. Figure 4-4 indicates the types of expenditures made for security by categories. There are over 4,000 private establishments providing contract guard and investigative services. In one recent year the ratio of total private-sector, crime-related security personnel to total public-sector, law-enforcement and guard personnel was about four to seven. However, if one includes government guards, who do not have general peace-officer powers, with private security forces, the ratio of security personnel to those with peace-officer powers becomes about one to one. Despite the large number of private establishments only four firms—Pinkerton's, Burns, Wackenhut, and Globe—account for 50 percent of the industry's earnings.[24]

Figure 4-4 Expenditures for Private Security Services and Products

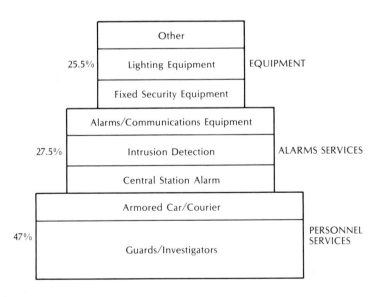

Source: A.D. Little, Inc., "Estimates of Sales to End User—1975," *Outlook for the U.S. Safety, Fire Protection and Security Business* (January 1973).

"During the nineteenth century and until . . . the FBI came into existence, public police were local in nature, and law enforcement beyond local boundaries was provided mainly by private detective agencies."[25] With the rise of the FBI, technological advancements permitting high-speed communication, and increased interlocal cooperativeness, private police began to shift their focus from quasipublic investigative functions to guard services. In terms of sheer numbers of personnel the primary employment function in the private security industry today is providing guard services. The following factors are generally regarded as being the primary forces in spurring the strong and continual growth of private security.

1. The general level of all types of reported crime throughout the country.

2. Increasing public awareness and fear of crime.

3. The federal government's need for security in its space and defense activities during the past decade and, more recently, for protection against violent demonstrations, bombings, and aircraft hijackings.

4. The continuing trend toward specialization of all or many types of services.

5. A general lack of confidence in the ability of overburdened public-sector police to cope with crime.

6. Rising fire and casualty loss claims to insurance companies coupled with the withdrawal of some insurers from the market and the rising insurance rates, often extended only with the proviso of requiring the use of certain types of private security systems or allowing premium discounts where used.

7. Increased technological sophistication resulting in the development of new security devices and markets.

8. Marked overall increases in the growth of corporate and individual incomes resulting in new acquisitions with the collateral ability to pay for their protection.[26]

Role Perspectives

Private security services may be classified on the basis of their service objective or function: (1) information-gathering activities such as preemployment background checks, insurance-claim investigations, antipilferage undercover work in retail and industrial establishments, credit-application checks, and marital investigations; (2) maintaining order on, and controlling access to, private property on which sporting events or other recreational activities are conducted; and (3) protection of persons and property including guarding and patrolling apartment complexes, model communities, and industrial centers, armored car transportation of valuables, antishoplifting surveillance in retail stores, and alarm-system monitoring and response.[27] In meeting these service objectives private police create certain role obligations for themselves which are usually distinctive from, but occasionally overlap with, the public police function.

1. Public police have the primary responsibility for maintaining order, enforcing the laws, preventing and investigating crimes, and apprehending violators.
2. Public property is policed primarily, although not exclusively, by public police.
3. Policing private property is the primary responsibility of the owner, management, or the householder, all of whom have the option to provide or purchase private security services and equipment.
4. Private police are primarily concerned with crime prevention and detection rather than criminal investigation and apprehension.
5. Both private and public police act in the role of consultants in advising persons how to prevent or reduce the likelihood of becoming a crime victim.[28]

Personnel and Training

The manpower of private security firms may be divided into two broad groups. The first consists of investigators and executives who frequently have degrees in criminal justice or an allied field, are professionally experienced, receive sound compensation along with a full range of fringe benefits, and tend to be younger than their counterparts in the second group, the guards, who are far more numerous.

The typical private guard is an older white male with less than a high-school education and with low earnings.[29] Depending upon his employer and the region of the country in which he is employed, he has the following characteristics. He is about forty-seven years of age with a few years of experience in private security. He tends to be overwhelmingly Caucasian, not because of employer prejudice but because more nonwhites are subject to arrest or conviction and are therefore discouraged from applying to private police agencies or are rejected because of their records. The average guard has a tenth- or eleventh-grade education; in some of the larger companies, such as Wackenhut, a high-school degree or its equivalent is currently required. Some of the better small and midsized firms have the same requirement. Typically guards must labor forty hours per week and ordinarily earn only the minimum hourly wage. Fringe benefits, such as life insurance and retirement plans, are generally much smaller for private police than for their public counterparts. At the better medium and large firms the fringe-benefit package seldom exceeds 10 percent of wages paid by employers and contract security employees often have no benefits. Since annual turnover rates range from 10 percent in some in-house forces to over 200 percent in some contract firms, even where fringe benefits are provided many employees never receive them because they do not work the six months or one year required for eligibility. Guards have diverse backgrounds; many are retired lower-level civil-service or military personnel. Part-time guards are frequently students, teachers, and enlisted men on active duty; they generally work for the minimum hourly wage for sixteen to twenty-four hours per week, often without any fringe benefits.

While larger guard forces generally have structured programs it is a harsh reality that the majority of such operations in this country do not have any formal programs. Typically private police receive no more than eight to twelve hours of training and even armed guards may be placed on duty without any more instruction than can be accomplished in two hours.[30] The lack of training is not without some very serious implications. The Rand Corporation conducted a survey in which 275 private security guards completed a questionnaire which sought to elicit their reactions to hypothetical situations. The questionnaire contained a total of forty-four situations in which errors might be made; twenty of these potential mistakes were so major that they could have possibly produced civil or criminal liabilities. The results produced by the hypothetical situations were staggering: an excess of 99 percent of the security workers made at least one mistake and the average was ten errors. More importantly, over 97 percent made at least one major mistake, with the average being three and a half major mistakes. The conclusions of the Rand study are even more disturbing when one notes that the sample was biased in favor of higher paid and better educated security personnel.

Executives of contract security forces recognize both the need and importance of training their personnel properly, but they are inhibited in the pursuance of that goal by such constraints as high turnover rates and strong price competition.

The Future of Private Policing

There are two diametrically opposed views on private police. One holds that they provide valuable services which public law-enforcement agencies and their personnel are not able to provide by virtue of legal, procedural, or resource restrictions. The second view is that private police are poorly selected, non- or ill-trained, inadequately supervised, nourished by the public's fear of crime, and an unnecessary public hazard and nuisance. Each of these views is, for

113

the present, correct, depending on what particular company's services are under discussion. Increasingly, we can anticipate that Police Officer Standards and Training Commissions will require completion of approved training before a person is certified to be employable as a guard or investigator in the private security industry. There are, however, two criteria which the public police officer must meet which his private counterpart may not have to: maximum employable age and the passing of an extensive physical examination. These are required in the public service as indications of sufficient health and potential years of service to sustain a career, which is not ordinarily a concern in the private sector.

STUDY QUESTIONS

1. How are the terms "state police" and "state patrol" properly distinguished?
2. Which state pioneered police minimum-standards legislation?
3. What is the difference between voluntary and mandatory POST programs?
4. In which states does the office of sheriff not exist?
5. What is the singular advantage of using the appointive method for selecting sheriffs?
6. If consolidation of police services takes place, what are the five options regarding the office of sheriff?
7. Discuss the relationship between the coroner and medical-examiner systems.
8. What is the statistical profile of municipal policing?
9. What are the three elements of police services?
10. What are the major responsibilities of local policing?
11. How do consolidation and regionalization differ from each other?
12. What is the magnitude of private policing in this county?
13. What are "contract" and "in-house" forces?
14. What social conditions produced private policing?

ILLUSTRATIVE CAREERS IN STATE AND LOCAL ENFORCEMENT AGENCIES

FLORIDA HIGHWAY PATROL

A career as a Florida State Trooper provides a rich opportunity for public service. The enormous number of vehicles on our nation's roads produces a clear need for traffic control. The State Trooper helps to assure the safety of motorists on public roads throughout the state. A principal duty is to patrol the state's highways in such a way as to regulate, control, and direct the movement of traffic on these highways. State Troopers have primary enforcement responsibility for motor vehicle traffic laws throughout the state and are responsible for accident investigation. Often the trooper is the first person to arrive at the scene of an accident and occasionally must render life-saving first aid to victims. They are also responsible for complex investigative work in the area of vehicle theft. State Troopers also provide valuable assistance to county and municipal police agencies in various matters, including such varied activities as traffic task force operations and civil disorder control.

Entry Requirements

The standards of the Florida Highway Patrol illustrate the requirements imposed by state highway patrol agencies throughout the United States. Entry standards are an attempt to measure the potential fitness of an applicant for the kinds of major activities involved in enforcement work. The following summarize the key minimum entry level requirements for the Florida Highway Patrol: applicants must be between the ages of eighteen and thirty-five, but cannot have reached their thirty-fifth birthday at the time the application is initiated; they must be able to pass the Patrol physical examination and a physical performance test; they must be high-school graduates or its equivalent and have completed sixty semester college hours or have three years of responsible employment experience.

Career Development

The new recruit begins his career with a thirteen-week instructional program at the Florida Highway Patrol Academy in Tallahassee. Instruction in the academy covers such topics as traffic law enforcement, accident investigation, search and seizure law, narcotics law, and related subjects.

115

Training in the academy develops the skills necessary for effective performance once assigned to field duties. Graduation from the academy results in designation as a Trooper I, with an annual salary of $10,670. The Florida Highway Patrol has a well-developed rank structure which is the basis of their career ladder. Promotion in grade is largely dependent on supervisory ratings. The rank structure extends from Trooper to Colonel and promotion in rank is dependent upon one's performance on competitive examinations.

NEW JERSEY STATE POLICE

Entry Requirements

The selection standards of the New Jersey State Police are rigorous. In a recent year there were approximately 10,000 applicants for appointment and from that number, 60 recruits were ultimately graduated from the State Police Academy. Applicants must be between eighteen and thirty-five years of age, possess a high-school diploma or its equivalency, and undergo an intensive background check that is designed to ensure a candidate's fitness for law-enforcement work. A competitive examination is administered to all applicants. This examination is a general aptitude test of verbal and numerical abilities. The test is a good indication of an individual's ability to perform the work of the police academy. Following this initial aptitude test there is a test designed to measure an individual's psychological fitness to perform the tasks of a police officer. For the applicant who successfully completes these tests and procedures, there is an oral interview board which must approve potential recruits before they are sent to the academy.

Career Development

The New Jersey State Police Academy is the beginning of a career with the State Police. The academy sessions are four months in length. The role of the academy is to provide basic knowledge, skills, and abilities vital to police officers today. The first field assignment of a New Jersey State policeman comes when he and a veteran officer are paired for one month's intensive supervision. Following this "trooper-coach" period the new trooper is given his first solo assignment. For the next two years his performance is rigorously evaluated with reports being filed every six months. Five years from initial entry the trooper attains tenure and is given full status as a trooper. After seven years service as a trooper, an individual becomes eligible to take the Sergeant's Examination. Promotion through the ranks is attained by supervisory ratings and performance on competitive examinations. Salaries in the New Jersey State Police begin at $14,000 for the entering trooper. There is a pattern of merit promotion in New Jersey State Police. This allows for increasing responsibility to be given as merit is demonstrated. In a comprehensive enforcement unit such as the New Jersey State Police there is a great variety of assignments. After the individual has served his initial five years of duty there are opportunities for assignment to specialized investigative units.

GEORGIA GAME AND FISH DIVISION

Throughout the United States there are uniformed, sworn peace officers who have protective and enforcement responsibilities for state owned lands and waterways. These peace officers are often referred to as rangers. Rangers have primary responsibility for the conservation of natural resources in state owned lands. While conservation is a primary task for these rangers, they have definite responsibility for the enforcement of game and fish regulations, boating laws and regulations, and litter laws. Patrol of an assigned area, usually in a state park or forest is the principal mission of these rangers. In addition to patrol and enforcement responsibilities, rangers serve to provide public information as well as educational programs about outdoor safety, safe boating, and conservation in general.

Entry Standards

The outdoors nature of the work is such that physical requirements are rigorous. In addition to the medical examination, applicants are required to pass a physical endurance and agility examination. Individuals must be at least twenty-one years of age to apply. The educational requirements are similar to those for other state law-enforcement employees. Applicants must possess a high-school diploma or equivalency certificate. In addition to this general education requirement, applicants are required to pass a specially designed examination which tests both general aptitude and specific knowledge of Georgia Fish and Game Law, boating law, and other conservation subjects.

Career Development

The Game and Fish Ranger begins his career with a mandatory training program for all the state peace officers. He then undergoes specialized training that is provided by the Department of Natural Resources. This training is designed to provide basic familiarity with the operations and policies of the Game and Fish Division. Salary for a Cadet Ranger is $7,782 annually while for a full ranger, it is $9,102. The salary grades increase with promotions. A Major in the Game and Fish Division earns $15,342. Promotion after initial appointment requires a year of experience within each succeeding rank. As with other law-enforcement agencies, the rank structure provides a career ladder of positions and responsibilities.

117

NEW YORK CITY POLICE

The New York City Police Department is the nation's largest with more than 30,000 sworn officers who provide services to the city's inhabitants. While the New York City Police Department has a greater number of administrative and specialized personnel than smaller departments, the basic entry level position is that of patrol officer.

Entry Requirements

All applicants must be between twenty-one and twenty-nine years of age, possess a high-school diploma or its equivalent, agree to reside within the city or in a surrounding county, pass a competitive written examination, and meet the medical and physical standards.

Career Development

Police recruits begin their career with training at the Police Academy, which gives them the skills and understanding they need. Following graduation from the Academy, "rookies" are assigned to the uniformed patrol force. Starting salary for New York City police officers is $17,450. The basic civil service ranks of Police Officer, Sergeant, Lieutenant, and Captain are achieved through competitive Civil Service examination. Other designations, such as Detective, are made by the Police Commissioner.

Retirement benefits may begin after twenty years of service at a pension of 50 percent of the employee's annual salary. While an officer is employed, he receives unlimited sick leave with pay and twenty-seven working days vacation annually after three years of service. Additionally, there is a city-supported welfare fund, a medical and hospitalization plan, a blood credit program, and longevity pay after each five years of service through twenty years.

NOTES

1. Advisory Commission on Intergovernmental Relations, *State-Local Relations in the Criminal Justice System* (Washington, D.C.: Government Printing Office, 1971), pp. 82–87.
2. For a detailed analysis of this and related topics see Leonard Territo, C. R. Swanson, and Neil C. Chamelin, *The Police Personnel Selection Process* (Indianapolis: Bobbs-Merrill, 1977).
3. Advisory Commission, *State-Local Relations in Criminal Justice*, pp. 82–83.
4. Ibid., p. 82.
5. George T. Felkenes, *The Criminal Justice System: Its Functions and Personnel* (Englewood Cliffs, N. J.: Prentice-Hall, 1973), p. 56. For a different view of the functions of the office of sheriff see Roger Handberg, Jr., and Charles M. Unkovic, "Southern County Sheriffs: Multifaceted Law Enforcement Agencies"

(Paper delivered at the annual meeting of the Academy of Criminal Justice Sciences, New Orleans, Louisiana, March 8–10, 1978).

6. Felkenes, *Criminal Justice System*, p. 60.
7. David L. Norrgard, *Regional Law Enforcement* (Chicago: Public Administration Service, 1969), p. 56.
8. George S. Gulick and Robert T. Kimbrough, eds., *American Jurisprudence,* vol. 18 (San Francisco: Bancroft Whitney, 1965), p. 521.
9. Ibid., p. 522. Also see C. Granger, "Crime Inquiries and Coroners Inquests: Individual Protection in Inquisitorial Proceedings," *Ottawa Law Review* 9 (1977): 411–473.
10. Gulick and Kimbrough, *American Jurisprudence,* p. 525.
11. Ibid., pp. 523 and 529.
12. Advisory Commission, *State-Local Relations in Criminal Justice,* p. 276. For an evaluation of the medical examiner's and coroner's function and problems see Kenneth Fields et al., *Assessment of the Personnel of the Forensic Sciences Profession* (Washington, D.C.: Law Enforcement Assistance Administration, 1977).
13. Advisory Commission, *State-Local Relations in Criminal Justice,* p. 275.
14. Ibid., p. 276.
15. Law Enforcement Assistance Administration, *Expenditure and Employment Data for the Criminal Justice System 1976* (Washington, D.C.: Government Printing Office, 1978), extracted or computed from data in Table 3, p. 23 and Table 6, p. 30.
16. President's Commission on Law Enforcement and Administration of Justice, *Task Force Report: The Police* (Washington, D.C.: Government Printing Office, 1967), p. 7.
17. National Advisory Commission on Criminal Justice Standards and Goals, *Police* (Washington, D.C.: Government Printing Office, 1973), p. 108.
18. American Bar Association, *The Urban Police Function* (New York: American Bar Association, 1972), p. 8.
19. James Q. Wilson, *Varieties of Police Behavior* (Cambridge, Mass.: Harvard University Press, 1968), pp. 18–19.
20. Norrgard, *Regional Law Enforcement.* On cooperation and conflict between police agencies see Knowlton W. Johnson, "Police Interagency Relations: Some Research Findings" (1977), Sage Professional Papers in Administration and Policy Studies, and James C. McDavid, "The Effects of Interjurisdictional Cooperation on Police Performance in the St. Louis Metropolitan Area," *Publius* 7, no. 2 (Spring 1977): 3–30.
21. Law Enforcement Assistance Administration, *Private Police in the United States,* vols. 1–5 (Washington, D.C.: Government Printing Office, 1971). This excellent work was later updated by James S. Kakalik and Sorrel Wildhorn and published as *The Private Police: Security and Danger* (New York: Crane, Russak, 1977). See also Law Enforcement Assistance Administration, *Report of the Task Force on Private Security* (Washington, D.C.: Government Printing Office, 1976).
22. Law Enforcement Assistance Administration, *The Law and Private Police* (Washington, D.C.: Government Printing Office, 1971), p. 7.
23. Law Enforcement Assistance Administration, *Private Police in the United States,* (Washington, D.C.: Government Printing Office, 1971), p. 3. See also Stanley R. Steinberg, "Private Police Practices and Problems," *The Law and Social Order* (1972): 585–604 and Stephen Spitzer and Andrew T. Scull, "Privatization and Capitalist Development: The Case of the Private Police," *Social Problems* 25 (October 1977): 18–29.
24. Ibid., pp. 10–12.
25. Ibid., p. 17.
26. Ibid., p. 15.
27. Ibid., p. 24.
28. Ibid., p. 18.
29. Law Enforcement Assistance Administration, *The Private Police Industry* (Washington, D.C.: Government Printing Office, 1971), pp. 67–93.
30. Law Enforcement Assistance Administration, *Private Police,* pp. 34–37.

chapter five
The Operating Milieu

The fact that the responsibility for policing is divided between the three levels of government, the burgeoning private sector, and the variety of government offices has produced a system of enforcement with unique characteristics. This system functions in a daily operating milieu which can be studied by viewing it as occurring within three specific contexts: the societal, where the chief value served by policing is to be found and its relationship to our form of government established; the legal, which shapes the authority exercised by the police; and the organizational, with its key variables being the individual, service-delivery styles, and interface with other institutions involved in the administration of justice.

THE SOCIETAL CONTEXT

The institutions of society may be viewed fundamentally as building blocks; they are the things of which societies, however simple or complex, are made. At least four major clusters of social institutions are generally recognized: political, concerning the exercise of power; economic, involving the production and distribution of goods and services; expressive-integrative, including the arts and drama; and kinship, focusing mainly on regulating sex and family functions.[1]

Given that institutions within these clusters are the building blocks of society, the cement which binds them together is the social order. The regular fulfillment of the role obligations of the various members of society is the sine qua non of the social order. Acts or omissions which violate society's expectations of an individual's behavior may be viewed as constituting deviance. One has only to stand on any street corner to witness an incredible range of overt deviance: people jaywalking, profanity spicing the conversations of passersby, cars being parked illegally, drivers making improper turns and other vehicular violations, individuals littering the streets, vendors selling fruit, pencils, and flowers without display of the required licenses, groups assembling unlawfully, and an occasional drunk or beggar. Additionally, there are numerous incidents of covert deviance which elude most observers. Examples of these are: carrying a concealed weapon, driving without an operator's license, shoplifting, possessing narcotics, writing worthless checks, consuming alcoholic beverages while underage, and price fixing. Whether the deviance is overt or covert, it is one of two major types: statistical deviance, in which the departure from normative standards is relatively minor, or social deviance, in which the act is of such magnitude that the larger society seeks to prevent, control, and eliminate it.[2] In the case of statistical deviance, if any sanctions are invoked they would be informal and of a minor nature such as withholding approval. The same, however, cannot be said of social deviance where violations are met with the invocation of formal sanctions, the severity of which reflects the intensity of desire to ensure against transgressions. Figure 5-1 depicts the relationship between overt, covert, statistical, and social deviance.

The police, courts, and corrections are the political institutions charged with controlling social deviance as defined by the legislative branch of government. The primary benefit gained by the existence of the police is preserving the social order. The police function as initiators of the process of justice; they are also the most visible evidence of government. Yet, paradoxically, "the police more than any other institution exhibit an antagonism, both in concept and practice, to some of the basic precepts of a democratic society."[3] First, democracy is predicated upon consensus, but the police officer's role begins where consensus has not been achieved; the less consensus the more abundant and difficult the task of the police. Secondly, the principle of equality is at odds with the virtual monopoly on the legitimate use of

Figure 5-1 A Typology of Deviance

	STATISTICAL	SOCIAL
OVERT	Ignoring a greeting, refusing to shake hands, or faulty table manners.	Robbery, unlawful assembly, or assault and battery
COVERT	Daydreaming while supposedly listening to someone, not wearing underwear, or drinking immoderately in private	Carrying a concealed weapon, possessing narcotics, or price fixing

121

force which has been given to the police. Thirdly, the element of freedom is constrained by police authority; in relations between equals, either one has the right to cancel the relationship. This contract aspect is unidirectional in policing; the officer may withdraw but frequently the citizen may not because he or she is the object of unwanted police services, i.e., subject to arrest for a violation of the criminal law.

THE LEGAL CONTEXT

The Pivotal Dichotomy: Felony Versus Misdemeanor Offenses

A crime may be defined as the commission or omission of any behavior prohibited or required by the organized political state in its penal code and for the breach of which penalties may be imposed. Many of the statutory provisions of the criminal codes of the respective states reflect with great faithfulness our English heritage. However, to be utterly sure of what constitutes a specific crime one is frequently compelled to examine the statutes and attending decisions of the courts of a particular state. Criminal statutes must clearly define in advance what forms of behavior are punishable.

The single most important distinction between types of crimes is whether they are felonies or misdemeanors; this distinction is pivotal to the entire process of administering justice. A felony is an act punishable, upon conviction, by imprisonment in the state penitentiary for a term of one or more years. The test to determine if a person has been convicted of a felony is not whether he or she was actually imprisoned for such a period of time following conviction, but if the sentence could have been envoked. All criminal acts not deemed to be felonies are misdemeanors, which are lesser offenses. In a broad sense the distinction between misdemeanors and felonies is important on the following grounds.

1. More severe sanctions are associated with felonies.
2. The social stigma attached to a felony conviction is greater than that associated with a misdemeanor.[4]
3. Historically, fewer procedural rights have been associated with misdemeanors.

State codes deal primarily with felonies but also, to a lesser extent, with misdemeanors. Upon conviction of a state misdemeanor the sanctions which may be applied are ordinarily of the same weight as those attached to violations of local ordinances. The punishment frequently is six months incarceration and/or a fine not to exceed $500.

Police Arrest Authority

For the police the distinction between misdemeanors and felonies is critical because it defines the circumstances under which they may effect an arrest and delineates the amount of force which may, if required, be employed. A police officer is empowered to use deadly force as a last resort in making a felony arrest; this is not true for a misdemeanor arrest. Generally, a police officer acting without a warrant may initiate an arrest under the following conditions.

1. When the person to be arrested has committed a felony or misdemeanor in his presence.
2. When a felony has in fact been committed, and he has reasonable grounds to believe that the person to be arrested has committed it.
3. When he has reasonable grounds to believe that a felony has been, or is, being committed and reasonable grounds to believe that the person to be arrested has committed or is committing it.[5]

Reading these conditions is a good bit less difficult than applying them. For example, what does "reasonable grounds" mean? A generally accepted definition is what a prudent person would believe under the same or similar set of conditions. However, the police officer is not afforded the leisurely opportunity to render his judgment of whether reasonable grounds exist; the cognitions of a few seconds represent the paucity of data upon which the officer must act, at least occasionally. His action may subsequently be subject to months-long scrutiny by the U.S. Supreme Court and even then only be sustained or invalidated by a margin of five to four.

Arrest Authority and Client Reactions

Contrary to frequently held public opinion, the arrest authority of the police is relatively circumscribed. Formal variables which limit it include statutes and ordinances, court rulings, and departmental policy. In some instances the limitations are not understood by victims of crime, many of whom interpret a lack of police action as disinterest.

For purposes of illustration, let us assume that two uniformed officers are dispatched to a residence to handle a domestic quarrel, the event having come to the attention of the police by a neighbor's anonymous telephone call.[6] The wife of the household alleges that the husband physically mistreated her and she does, in fact, have a bruised face. Further, the husband readily admits the actions alleged. Under these circumstances the police could not make an immediate arrest in a number of states. What has occurred is an assault and battery, which is a misdemeanor. Since the officers did not witness it, they cannot initiate an arrest. If, however, the wife signs a complaint and secures a warrant, the officers could then take the husband into custody. Having explained to the wife the course of action available to her, the officers would attempt to prevent further incidents by giving the couple advice. This might be by suggesting that further difficulties would be likely to have an adverse effect upon the couple's children emotionally or by appealing to the couple's pride by saying that further violence would cause them embarrassment in the neighborhood. However, to the woman assaulted, who has heard her husband acknowledge his actions to the officers, all of this may make little sense; in fact, the counseling may be greeted on her part with derisive comments about the willingness of the police to render a service. Not infrequently, despite patient reexplanations of the limitations on police arrest authority, the woman will be left with very negative feelings about the police. However, if the police were to arrest the husband under the circumstances described above, both they and the unit of government they represent could incur legal liabilities.

The opposite of the preceding case is when the police arrest an individual who rejects their claim of lawful authority over him. Angered by their claim the client may attempt to flee, resist physically, or may call upon those standing nearby to free him from the police. When people deny the lawful arrest authority of the police, there is the potential for an ugly incident which tends to reinforce negative stereotypes of both the police and of segments of the public.

Statements defining police arrest authority are straightforward, perhaps disarmingly so when we attempt to determine if "reasonable grounds" exist. However, arrest authority is not only fraught with legal difficulties but also offers the potential for the police—while acting entirely properly—to be seen as "wrong" by the public.

The Need to Acknowledge Police Discretionary Power

What is, and will be, legislated into a criminal code is influenced by a series of factors such as changing social conditions, emerging interests, desire to protect the status quo, and changing perceptions of what is in the "public interest."[7] Due to the distance between those formulating the criminal law and those empowered to enforce it, variations develop because the criminal law does not detail the manner in which it is to be implemented. Furthermore, it is impossible to

124

LOOKING AT POLICEMEN

The only way to police a ghetto is to be oppressive. None of Commissioner Kennedy's policemen, even with the best will in the world, have any way of understanding the lives led by the people. They swagger about in two's and three's controlling. Their very presence is an insult, and it would be, even if they spent their entire day feeding gumdrops to children.

> James Baldwin, "Fifth Avenue,
> Uptown," Man Alone, Eric and Mary
> Josephson, editors (New York: Dell
> Publishing Co., Inc., 1962), p. 352.

The policeman is a "Rorschach" in uniform as he patrols his beat. His occupational accouterments—shield, nightstick, gun, and summons book—clothe him in a mantle of symbolism that stimulates fantasy and projection.

> Arthur Niederhoffer, Behind the Shield
> (Garden City, New York: Anchor Books,
> 1967), p. 1.

enforce the criminal code fully. Local conditions such as community expectations, the ideology of the police, and actor-victim-situation variables all dilute the possibility of a policy of full enforcement.[8] In the final analysis whether or not a criminal arrest will be made frequently rests upon the discretionary judgment of a single officer working alone in the field.

The fact that individual officers must use discretionary judgment in situations which could produce an arrest places considerable responsibility on police officers. This fact notwithstanding, police officials have traditionally been reluctant to deal with the issue in explicit policy terms for at least four reasons.

1. Lawmaking bodies may construe such action as a fundamental perversion of legislative intent.
2. Special interest groups may litigate over the limits prescribed by policy.

3. Widespread knowledge of tolerance limits could lead to confrontations between officers and offenders seeking to escape arrest by claiming exemption under the tolerance provisions of the applicable policy.
4. Public knowledge of tolerance limits may lead to individuals adjusting their behavior to the tolerance limits rather than to the actual laws.[9]

Figure 5-2 represents the four types of discretionary situations experienced by the police; each case offers a different degree of discretion for the patrol officer, the department, or both.[10] The patrol officer has great discretion in cases I and IV; the difference between them is that in the former instance it can be brought under departmental control and in the latter it cannot. The patrol officer has the least discretion in case II, except where juveniles are involved as suspects; in that case the degree of discretion is substantial unless it is subject to strong administrative policies and organizational control. The remaining case, III, is intermediate in both the degree of discretion and the possibility for departmental control.

The most numerous detailed studies on the use of police discretionary power in situations where an arrest may or may not result deal with encounters between the police and juveniles.[11] If the offense is sufficiently serious—which is true in roughly 10 percent of the cases—an arrest will be made and referred to the juvenile or family court. However, for lesser offenses a number of variables may be considered before making the decision of whether or not to arrest.

1. What type of offense is involved and what was the youth's role?
2. What prior record does the juvenile have?
3. What preference does the victim have?
4. What is the home life situation of the violator?
5. What community resources exist?

Figure 5-2 Wilson's Four Kinds of Discretionary Situations

NATURE OF SITUATION	BASIS OF POLICE RESPONSE	
	Police Invoked Action	Citizen-Invoked Action
Law Enforcement	I	II
Order Maintenance	III	IV

6. What action does the officer anticipate by the juvenile or family court if the youth is arrested?

7. What characterological assessment does the officer make of the juvenile; that is to say, is he seen as a "good boy" or a "bad guy." The research suggests that this assessment, except when a serious offense is involved, may be a critical variable and would include such components as: does the youth show respectful deference to the officer? What is the youth's physical appearance, i.e., does he have long hair, dirty levis, and a "gang-type" jacket?

That the police will and must exercise discretionary authority in arrest situations is inescapable. To narrowly and vigorously enforce the criminal law would be to steadily erode the very foundation upon which police in free societies rest—the voluntary compliance with the laws by the majority of the people most of the time. Thus the question becomes what choices—and attendant outcomes—exist concerning the use of discretionary authority? There are two fundamental alternatives. First, we may let "sleeping dogs lie" and do nothing, thereby giving tacit approval to such behavior as arrest dispositions being made about juveniles on the basis of characterological assessments. The second alternative is to recognize not only the existence of but also the need for and legitimacy of discretionary authority that is exercised as provided for by written policy. Better managed police departments see the second alternative as not only desirable but also essential. Such departments are investing considerable organizational effort in policy formulation. In the more professionally operated police departments officers have less discretionary power than they may believe they do; it is certainly nothing approaching the power wielded by their counterparts in less rigorously managed departments.

Further impetus was given to efforts to control discretionary powers by a national commission which stated:

Every police chief executive should establish policy that guides the exercise of discretion by police personnel in using arrest alternatives. This policy:

a. Should establish the limits of discretion by specifically identifying, insofar as possible, situations calling for the use of alternatives to continued physical custody;

b. Should establish criteria for the selection of appropriate enforcement alternatives;

c. Should require enforcement action to be taken in all situations where all elements of a crime are present and all policy criteria are satisfied;

127

    d. Should be jurisdictionwide in both scope and application; and

    e. Specifically should exclude offender lack of cooperation, or disrespect toward police personnel, as a factor in arrest determination unless such conduct constitutes a separate crime.[12]

The formal recognition of police discretionary powers in arrest situations has and undoubtedly will continue to cause difficulties for the police on occasion. This problem may have a positive side-effect by reducing the existence of invisible justice through enhancement of the public's understanding of the police role. The public's increased knowledge may help establish appropriate limitations on discretionary power.

The Police and the Supreme Court: The Due-Process Revolution

During the period 1961–1969—a period frequently referred to as the "due-process revolution"—the United States Supreme Court took an activist role, becoming quite literally givers of the law rather than interpreters of it. The Warren Court's activist role in the piecemeal extension of the provisions of the Bill of Rights, via the due-process clause of the Fourteenth Amendment, to criminal proceedings in the respective states may have been a policy decision.[13] Normally the Supreme Court will write opinions in about 115 cases during any particular term. During the 1938–1939 term only five cases appear under the heading of criminal law; a scant three decades later, during the height of the due-process revolution, about one-quarter of each term's decisions related to criminal law.[14] The Supreme Court could scarcely have picked a worse period in which to undertake the unpopular role of policing the police; a burgeoning crime rate far outstripped population increases and many politicians were campaigning on "law and order" platforms which all too often dissolved into rhetoric upon their election. The problem of crime increasingly came to the public's eye through the media. In sum total, the high court acted to extend procedural safeguards to defendants in criminal cases precisely at a point in time when the public's fear of crime was high and there was great social pressure to do something about crime.

On at least three earlier occasions the Supreme Court had incurred the general wrath of the country.[15] In the Dred Scott decision of 1857 it had refused to free a Negro slave who crossed over from slave to free territory. In the celebrated legal tender case of 1870, Congress gave President Ulysses Grant the power to print additional paper money to pay Civil War debts. The Court ruled four to three against the constitutionality of the act, whereupon Grant, the same day, appointed two new judges to the bench and shortly thereafter received a favorable five to four verdict. In 1895 the Court displayed a rapid .turnabout from sparing the new income-tax law to declaring it unconstitutional; that maneuver resulted in a later era's needing a constitutional amendment to implement the income tax. As learned men, the Supreme Court justices in the 1960s had to be sensitive to these historical perspectives, but their collective judgment led them to undertake a program of sweeping impact upon the administration of criminal justice. The reaction of the country was swift; "Impeach Warren" billboards dotted the landscape and by 1968 a Gallup poll revealed that 63 percent of the people felt the courts were too lenient.[16] Why did the Supreme Court undertake its activist role? What decisions were key in arousing the country's ire? In what manner did the decisions affect police work? How did the police react?

Fundamentally the Supreme Court's role in the due-process revolution was a response to a vacuum in which the police themselves had failed to provide the necessary leadership. The era of strong social activism by various special-interest groups was not yet at hand and neither the state courts nor the legislatures had displayed any broad interest in reforming the criminal law. What institution was better positioned to undertake this responsibility? The Court may even have felt obligated by the inaction of others to do so. Therefore it became the Warren Court's lot to provide the reforms so genuinely needed but so unpopularly received. The high court did not move into this arena until after it had issued warnings which, to responsive and responsible leaders, would have been a mandate for reform.

Among the key decisions in the due-process revolution were Mapp v. Ohio, Gideon v. Wainwright, Escobedo v. Illinois, and Miranda v. Arizona. For present purposes the facts of these and related cases are less important than their focus and effect. Their focus was upon the two vital areas of search and seizure and the right to counsel; the effect was to markedly extend the rights of defendants. The impact upon police work was staggering; the use of questionable and improper tactics was eliminated, thereby creating the need for new procedures in such areas as interrogations, line-ups, and seizure of physical evidence. In general the reaction of the police to this whirlwind of due-process decisions was one of wariness tinged with occasional outcries that they were being "handcuffed" and could not adequately perform their job. Many people felt that the decisions went beyond seeking a fair trial in quest of a perfect one. As indicated in Table 5-1, the *Uniform Crime Reports* reveal that during the period of the due-process revolution police effectiveness dropped while reported crime increased. In part this may be due to a decreasing public tolerance of crime which resulted in more offenses being reported, including more crimes which the police were less likely to solve. While we cannot assert that the Court's decisions caused the shifts noted in Table 5-1, the two factors are closely correlated and in the minds of

Earl Warren (1891–1974), the liberal fourteenth Chief Justice of the United States Supreme Court, whose span of service on the bench (1953–1969) included the years of the due-process revolution. A former California governor, attorney general, and local office holder, Earl Warren was also an unsuccessful candidate for vice-president on Thomas Dewey's 1948 Republican ticket. Courtesy of the Library of Congress.

TABLE 5-1   Police Effectiveness at the Onset and Conclusion of the Due-Process Revolution

FACTOR	UNIFORM CRIME REPORTS PART I OFFENSES PER 100,000 UNITS OF POPULATION	PERCENT UNIFORM CRIME REPORTS PART I OFFENSES CLEARED BY ARREST	PERCENT UNIFORM CRIME REPORTS PART I OFFENSES IN WHICH DEFENDANT CHARGED WAS ACQUITTED OR HAD CHARGES DISMISSED
1961	1,053	26.7	12.2
1969	2,471	20.1	15.9

Source: Federal Bureau of Investigation, *Uniform Crime Reports—1961* (Washington, D.C.: Government Printing Office, 1962), pp. 3, 85, and 86, and Federal Bureau of Investigation, *Uniform Crime Reports—1969* (Washington, D.C.: Government Printing Office, 1970), pp. 5, 28, and 102.

many people they are inexorably bound together. By the early 1970s many police executives had come to recognize that, while the Supreme Court's decisions in the previous decade could be correlated with some indicators of reduced police efficiency, these decisions also had the subtle effect of hastening the development of professional policing. This happened because the decisions forced the police to abandon the use of both improper tactics and at least some traditional approaches while virtually mandating continuous sophisticated training in order to implement innovative techniques and programs.

THE ORGANIZATIONAL CONTEXT

The Individual in the Organization

In administrative terms, becoming a police officer entails meeting the requirements prescribed by the applicable Police Minimum Standards legislation and the specific additional requirements of the particular state or local government; satisfactorily completing a basic training course; and rendering an acceptable performance during the probationary period, which is frequently twelve months. However, becoming a police officer also involves being socialized into a virtual subculture.

Metamorphosis: Socialization into the Police Subculture

Despite the growing number of women in policing, the recruit officer typically is a white male, twenty-four years of age, married, a military veteran, has been interested in the field as a career for less

131

than two years, and is heavily influenced in his decision by acquaintances or friends who themselves have police backgrounds. Further, the rookie is at least a high-school graduate—with some college credits in 33 percent of the cases—who has previously done shift work and possesses long-standing ties to the community in which he is to be employed. Often the recruit comes from a job which requires clerical or craftsman skills, the kind of position—unlike policing—which did not fundamentally entail working directly with people. The product of a lower-middle or upper-working-class family, the new officer stands to increase his annual salary by joining the force.[17] Upon completion of the basic recruit-training course—which may be as short as two weeks or as long as nine months, depending upon the jurisdiction involved—the probationary officer is usually assigned to the uniformed patrol division.

> The recruit reports with some anxiety, but in general
> ready to practice what has been preached to him at the
> academy. According to the general code of deportment
> which covers the behavior of the newcomer, he is expected
> to be a good listener, quiet, unassuming, and deferential
> without being obsequious toward his superior officers. . . .
> For a month or so, he receives lenience . . . for routine mis-
> takes. After that he is on trial and carefully watched to see
> how he measures up to the challenge of police patrol. His
> reputation is made in the next weeks. . . . On these cases
> the new patrolman must resolve the dilemma of choosing
> between the professional ideal of police work he has
> learned in the academy and pragmatic approach. It is no
> great feat for a policeman working in an upper-class
> neighborhood to protect the rights of his white clientele. It
> is much more difficult in a lower-class community. In a
> slum area the professional ethic loses most of the time: the
> civil rights of lower-class individuals do not count as much
> as the necessity to accomplish a staggering amount of
> police work as expeditiously as possible.[18]

Essentially the new recruit is confronted with the tension between normative values and empirical realities. Many of the lessons learned in the academy take on dimensions that seem unreal. The admonition "never to lose your temper" is difficult to grip firmly if the rookie is spat upon and then reviled by an intricate series of epithets which simultaneously question his lineage and manhood. The rule "to only use such force as is necessary to effect an arrest" is immediately confronted by the informal working norm "that if your partner gets hurt then the person that did it better get some lumps." The desire to be a fair person becomes prey to the necessity of avoiding being seen as soft. The need to operate scrupulously under rule of law is consistently at war with the need to maintain order, frequently under the most difficult of situations. Hourly, the new officer is rapidly exposed to people who are not at their best or who have suffered the worst; abused and neglected children, tavern brawlers, obnoxious drunks, sick or beaten people, and those who are bent on suicide are all familiar figures in scenes that are part of the rookie's daily working life. The public is not anxious to be a part of the officer's dirty and at least occasionally dangerous job and the rookie rapidly learns this reality. If these circumstances were not enough to create a gap between the police and the public, the authority wielded by police officers further reinforces the distance between him and others; gradually the new officer undergoes a transition.

> As the rookie experiences contacts with the public, he becomes emotionally involved with policing's informal rules of behavior. For the protection of his self-esteem he begins to believe "you gotta make them respect you." He generally formulates this rule as a duty to make the public respect the law. He begins to recognize ... that his interests lie with his fellow officers and begins to differentiate himself from non-policemen. Thus, the stories and instruction he received from older partners ... become empowered with the emotional force of experience. The rookie has become a cop and the group has gained a new member.[19]

Set apart from the conventional world by the elements of danger and authority, the police officer becomes a member of the police group or subculture in more than just a loose sense.[20] To an unusual extent police officers tend to live in the same neighborhoods, to participate with other officers and their families in recreational activities, and to find their closest friends within the circle drawn by their occupation. Thus, the metamorphosis from being a police officer only in administrative terms to being one in all areas of one's life is completed.

Other Determinants of Police Behavior

A job-analysis study in the Chicago Police Department sought to identify the elements and functions common to the police role and the associated attributes required to competently execute those functions. That study found that a good police officer must:

1. Endure long periods of monotony and yet react quickly and effectively to problem situations.
2. Gain knowledge of the physical characteristics, events, and behavior patterns of people in a patrol area.

133

3. Exhibit initiative, problem-solving capacity, effective judgment, and imagination in coping with complex situations.

4. Make prompt and effective decisions.

5. Demonstrate mature judgment in deciding to make an arrest, give a warning, or use force.

6. Demonstrate critical awareness in discerning signs of unusual conditions or circumstances.

7. Exhibit a number of complex psychomotor skills.

8. Adequately perform communication and record-keeping functions.

9. Have the facility to act effectively in extremely divergent interpersonal situations.

10. Endure verbal and physical abuse from citizens and offenders.

11. Exhibit a professional, self-assured presence and a self-confident manner.

12. Be capable of restoring equilibrium to social groups.

13. Be skillful in questioning suspected offenders, victims, and witnesses.

14. Take charge of situations yet not unduly alienate participants or bystanders.

15. Be flexible enough to work under loose supervision in some situations and under direct supervision in other situations.

16. Tolerate stress in a multitude of forms.

17. Exhibit personal courage in the face of dangerous situations.

18. Maintain objectivity while dealing with a wide variety of people and groups.

19. Maintain a balanced perspective in the face of constant exposure to the worst side of human nature.

20. Exhibit a high level of personal integrity and ethical conduct.[21]

If these are the types of behavior and attributes to be sought in prospective police officers, one must ask what effect such factors as fatigue, stress, type of call, and citizen behavior have upon the performance of the police. A six-month study in Miami, Florida, observed and analyzed over 1,000 police-citizen interactions involving over 1,400 citizens. Although there is a need for replication studies, the results of the Miami study are instructive.

134

On the average 4.45 police-citizen interactions occur per shift, representing 41 percent of the policeman's working time; in 62 percent of the cases the contacts were initiated as the result of being dispatched by a radio call. The patrolmen studied spend by far the majority of their time in general-service and peace-keeping operations, with very little time devoted to actual crime-fighting activities. Precall stress, as evidenced by such factors as changes in rate of speech and muscle tension, occurs in up to 20 percent of the cases. However, in terms of performance at the scene of a request for police service in which precall stress was observed, the stressfulness of the situation produced minimal effect on the policeman's behavior in 1.5 percent of the cases and in less than 1 percent of such contacts did it lead to a measurable performance deterioration. The most striking finding in the analysis of data with regard to stress is that it is simply the number of citizens, rather than any particular attribute of the citizen, which causes stress for the policeman. Encountering two citizens is significantly more stressful than encountering one, and encountering three is significantly more stressful than encountering two. Stress induced by citizen contact with policemen is largely a function of sheer numbers.

Police-citizen interactions involve very little violence. Almost all of the physically aggressive behavior on the part of the policeman toward the citizen occurs either in making an arrest or in handling a drunk. The police use weapons in only 3 percent of contacts and 66 percent of such use involves handcuffs. Conversely, citizens are physically assaultive on the police in less than .5 percent of contacts. These data, taken with other data from the study, show that negative, racial, and other stereotypes of the citizens about the police and the police about citizens derive from a relatively infrequent number of bad episodes rather than from the absolute frequency with which injury or potential injury results in a police-citizen interaction.

Boredom and inactivity are major determinants of police behavior. Officers are less controlling and "cooler" in handling citizens when they are kept busy, e.g., on Saturday night. That is, an officer will exhibit more controlling behavior toward any single citizen when he has had few citizen contacts and spends most of his time simply riding around in a patrol car. Inactivity also produced fatigue; the greatest and most consistent increments in fatigue at the end of a shift clearly occurred when the policeman had the least number of citizen contacts.

Analyses of police and citizen behavior in three ethnically "pure" areas—black, Caucasian, and Cuban—found no large differences. There is, therefore, a wide disparity between what policemen and citizens may say about each other versus actual behaviors. Policemen may voice, for example, fairly severe anti-black sentiment, but when they actually get into a ghetto they behave in a way consistent with their behavior in a white neighborhood. The same statement would hold true for black citizens and their attitudes and behaviors toward policemen.

An analysis of single-citizen episodes revealed the following: poorly dressed citizens are uncooperative, medium-dressed citizens are more cooperative, well-dressed black citizens are quite cooperative, but well-dressed white citizens are less cooperative. Police perceive the most stressful citizens to be large-sized teenagers, and the least stressful to be small-sized teenagers. The least cooperative citizen group of all are large-sized teenagers, regardless of race. In comparing older black, older white, and younger white officers, there were no younger black officers in the observed sample, it was found that older, more experienced officers of either race tend to be more sympathetic, but also more controlling, toward members of their own race. All citizens tended to be more cooperative with the older black officers. Younger white officers tended to find encounters with single black citizens more stressful than older officers of either race.[22]

Departmental Styles of Policing

James Q. Wilson has identified three fundamental organizational orientations for delivering police services: the legalistic, the service, and the watchman.[23] In the legalistic style the police executive uses such control as he has over patrol officers' behavior to induce them to handle less serious matters as if they were matters of law enforcement. The police responsibility simply becomes comparing a particular behavior with a clear legal standard and effecting an arrest where that standard has been violated. A department with a legalistic orientation will divert fewer juveniles from formal processing, issue more traffic citations, make more arrests for misdemeanors, encourage the arrest and prosecution of shoplifters, vigorously enforce the vice laws, and in general produce more arrests. Since certain groups within our society are arrested at disproportionately high rates (for example, in one recent year blacks constituted 12 percent of our nation's population and 27 percent of all arrests), the legalistic police department is likely to develop a racial or harassment reputation with certain segments of the community.[24] The legalistic department is not one dominated by zealots; its personnel do not regard all laws as equally important nor do they love the law for its own sake. The legalistic style is produced by strenuous administrative efforts to get officers to do what they otherwise might not; almost invariably a legalistic department was once corrupt or at least magnanimous in granting favors. A legalistic approach reduces both the suspicion of, and prospects for, corruption.

In communities with police departments reflecting a service orientation requests for service are approached seriously but—especially in the case of relatively minor offenses—are less likely to produce the envocation of formal sanctions. Juveniles are referred to the family court less frequently, verbal warnings will often be issued in lieu of traffic citations, and the police will often arbitrate public or quasipublic disputes. Service-style departments consciously employ those who will be least likely to produce citizen complaints; the community expects its officers to be courteous and neat in appearance and to display a generally deferential manner. The service style is—unlike the legalistic—most often found in homogeneous middle- and upper-class communities where there is wide consensus about what constitutes proper public order. With the exception of the few serious crimes, the chief focus of activity for such departments is protecting residents from the minor and occasional threats created by unruly youths and outsiders. The ultimate rationale for a service-style department is political, not in the partisan sense, but rather in terms of being in contact with, and having high regard for, community feelings. Because of this factor extensive special-purpose units are often found in these departments as they attempt to display and maintain a high level of responsiveness.

The predominate emphasis of the watchman style is maintaining order. The patrol officer is allowed and often encouraged to follow the path of least resistance in the course of his daily business. Watchman-style departments ignore many minor violations—especially those involving youths and traffic offenses—and uses the law, in contrast to the legalistic approach, as a means of regulating conduct informally. The character of the individual or the group has a significant bearing on how a particular matter is handled; community notables are often routinely excused in minor matters because of their influence. Minority groups are often seen by the police as wanting and hence deserving less law enforcement because they appear to have a low level of morality and to be hostile and uncooperative. Private disputes among minority groups and friends are treated informally or ignored unless police authority is flouted. Thus the watchman style, beyond simply ignoring many minor violations, applies the law unevenly based in part upon the socioeconomic composition of its clientele.

In summary, the legalistic department seeks to uniformly apply the criminal law to lessen the likelihood or suspicion of corruption at the occasional cost of being accused of pursuing racist policies due to the fact that certain segments of our population represent high risks for arrest. The service style applies the law uniformly subject to variations produced by common definitions and perceptions produced by the homogeneous middle- or upper-class communities they serve. In contrast, the watchman style simply ignores many minor violations, using the law to maintain order on the basis of differing standards of public order and morality which often are affected by the community's socioeconomic composition.

Individual Styles of Policing

Muir, drawing upon Weber's notion of the professional politician, has identified four individual styles of policing.[25] According to Weber, the politician's susceptibility to corruption—in the sense of banality, cowardice, or wickedness—is limited by a combination of two personality characteristics: passion, defined as the capacity to integrate coercion into morals and perspective, meaning intellectual objectivity. Figure 5-3 depicts the Weber-Muir attitudinal model.

The tragic perspective incorporates three themes: that all humankind is of one substance, that establishing causality is very complex, and that human interdependence is precarious but necessary. In contrast, the cynical perspective reflects a simple conception of causality, an indifference, and a view of humankind as two warring camps. In Figure 5-3, "morality of coercion" is either integrated or conflicted. In the first case, the person has resolved the contradiction of achieving just ends through the use of coercive power; in the second, this is unresolved.

Figure 5-3 Muir's Individual Styles of Policing

	MORALITY OF COERCION	
PERSPECTIVE	Integrated	Conflicted
TRAGIC	Professional	Reciprocator
CYNICAL	Enforcer	Avoider

Within this framework, a police officer must have two virtues to be considered a "good," that is a professional, officer. He or she must intellectually grasp the nature of human suffering, and he or she must have morally resolved the contradiction of achieving just ends with coercive power. Developing a tragic sense and moral equanimity leads to growth on the job and produces more confidence, skill, sensitivity, and awareness. In contrast, the avoider has an ethical "disinclination to hurt," moral conflict in the exercise of power, and low self-defense skills resulting in low self-confidence. The reciprocator has sufficient interpersonal skills to exchange official leniency to obtain something of value in return from a party with whom there is some familiarity and a kind of agreed-upon balance of power. The enforcer, operating with increasingly meager and biased information, loses contact with the complex realities around him and comes to hold an enhanced belief in the efficacy of coercion.

Muir defines coercion as a means of controlling the conduct of others through threats to do harm. This abstract model of the coercive relationship is called the extortionate transaction and it reveals certain paradoxes of coercive power: dispossession (the less one has, the less one has to lose), detachment (the less the victim cares about preserving something, the less the victimizer cares about taking it), face (the nastier one's reputation, the less nasty one has to be), and irrationality (the more delirious the threatener, the more serious the threat; the more delirious the victim, the less serious the threat). Muir relates these paradoxes to the police.

> The policeman's authority consists of a legal license to coerce others to refrain from using illegitimate coercion. . . . But the reality, and the subtle irony, of being a policeman is that, while he may appear to be the supreme practitioner of coercion, in fact he is first and foremost its most frequent victim. The policeman is society's "fall guy," the object of coercion more frequently than its practitioner. Recurrently he is involved in extortionate behavior as victim, and only rarely does he initiate coercive actions as victimizer. If he is vicious, his viciousness is the upswing of the vicious cycle inherent in an extortionate relationship.
>
> Contrary to the more unflattering stereotypes of the policeman, it is the citizen who virtually always initiates the coercive encounter. What is more, the citizen tends to enjoy certain inordinate advantages over the policeman in these transactions. The advantages derive from the four paradoxes of coercion. The citizen is, relative to the policeman, the more dispossessed, the more detached, the nastier, and the crazier. Add to these natural advantages the fact that most police-citizen encounters are begun under

139

circumstances which the citizen has determined, and the reader may begin to feel some of the significant limits placed on the policeman's freedom to respond in these encounters.[26]

The paradigms for departmental and individual styles of policing are more than just useful conceptual devices for summarizing complex realities. For example, Ferdinand used the Wilsonian model to study the Rockford, Illinois, Police Department records covering a period of ninety years and found fluctuations in the amount of reported crime as that agency moved from a service to a legalistic style.[27] Significantly, as the Rockford Police Department developed the legalistic style, the clearance rate for serious crimes declined, perhaps due to the loss of the close ties to the community which had existed while the service style was utilized. Presently researchers[28] using the interactive model portrayed in Figure 5-4, are analyzing the data generated by a sample of patrol officers drawn from 18 different-sized police departments in 15 states to answer such questions as: Does the enforcer have higher job satisfaction when working in a legalistic, as opposed to the watchman, style department? Does the avoider in a legalistic department experience any sense of a lack of social integration? How do those who identify themselves as avoiders, reciprocators, enforcers, and professionals differ with respect to age, educational achievement, years of service, and other such variables? How can administrators ensure that their philosophy of policing is actually being executed by working police officers? Where the stream of thinking and research on individual and departmental styles of policing leads is perhaps less important than an underlying point—that the social sciences must play a key role if our understanding of crime and criminal justice is to be steadily enlarged.

INTERFACE: THE POLICE
IN THE CRIMINAL-JUSTICE SYSTEM

Implicit in this section's subheading is the judgment that there is in fact a criminal-justice system. However, there is not unanimity of opinion with respect to that position. One writer observes:

> The system, however, is a myth. A system implies some unity of purpose and organized interrelationship among component parts. In the typical American city and state, and under federal jurisdiction as well, no such relationship exists. There is, instead, a reasonably well-defined criminal process. . . . The inefficiency, fallout, and failure of purpose during this process is notorious.[29]

Figure 5-4 Model of Interactive Styles of Policing

	INDIVIDUAL STYLES OF POLICING				
	AVOIDER	RECIPROCATOR	ENFORCER	PROFESSIONAL	Totals:
WATCHMAN	19	22	11	101	153
LEGALISTIC	24	32	23	130	209
SERVICE	48	43	23	163	277
Totals:	91	97	57	394	

Therefore before one explores the position of the police in the criminal-justice system one must address the issue of whether or not such a system actually exists. Those who support the "nonsystem" view note that organizations are created to facilitate human purpose and should, therefore, be both effective and efficient; these critics argue that since agencies involved in the administration of the criminal law do not regularly achieve their respective goals, they lack effectiveness. In those cases where the goals are realized, the amount of resources required to produce that state is such that efficiency can scarcely be claimed. The aforegoing are serious issues which cannot —and should not—be cast aside easily. There are, however, other perspectives to consider.

What Is a System?

"Systems are man-created inventions for serving specific human objectives; they are purposeful, deliberate, and rational, and they are also subject to modification so that their value may be increased."[30] A system may be defined as a collection of entities which receives certain inputs and is constrained to act concertedly upon them to produce certain outputs with the objective of maximizing some function of inputs and outputs.[31] Schematically a system might be represented as depicted in Figure 5-5. Inputs may be classified in several ways: the "raw material" upon which the process or operation is to be performed, which constitutes the "load" of the system; the environment, which affects the manner in which the processing is conducted; and the component placement or replacement, such as material, energy, or information.[32] Process represents channels through which inputs must pass; accordingly the process must be so arranged that the inputs are acted upon in the proper and timely sequences. Output represents the system's record of accomplishment and must possess two features: (1) reliability, meaning that it is operationally consistent and minimizes error and (2) stability, meaning that a low-error unit

141

Figure 5-5 A Simple System

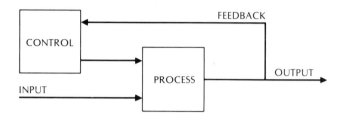

of output is provided continually. The final element, control, is the mechanism which ensures that the output will be maintained at certain desired and prespecified levels. It serves to regulate resources in order to produce reliability and stability and is dependent upon data flowing to it from the feedback loop.

Criminal Justice as System

If criminal justice is a system then it consists of three substantive subsystems: (1) the police, responsible for the functions of prevention, detection, investigation, apprehension, protection of the suspect's rights, property recovery, and diversion; (2) the courts, responsible for prosecution, defense, protection of the accused's rights, determination, sentencing, and prevention; and (3) corrections, responsible for protection of the offender's rights, probation, institution-based corrections, community-based programs, parole and other post-release services, and prevention. It should be noted that certain states may assign the responsibility for executing the probation or parole function to the courts rather than to corrections.

The fact that there is not a single, unified department for the administration of justice does not invalidate the concept of criminal justice as a system. Those who argue that to qualify as a system a monolithic structure is required fail to recognize that their proposal is "antithetical to democratic precepts and to the constitutional doctrine of separation of legislative, executive, and judicial powers."[33]

Using the schematic of a system given previously, the criminal-justice system could be grossly represented as indicated in Figure 5-6. If, as was suggested by Winston Churchill, one of the most unfailing tests of the civilization of any country is its treatment of criminals, then surely the focus of any such analysis must be upon the controls which are placed on agencies involved in the administration of justice. Figure 5-6 suggests that there is a sufficient degree of control on America's justice system to ensure that methods unacceptable in a

Figure 5-6 Criminal Justice as a System

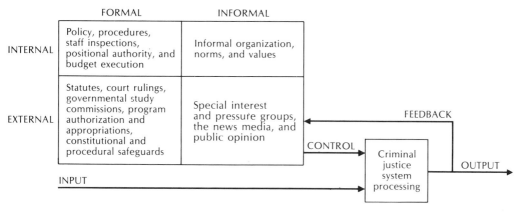

free and democratic society are used infrequently and that, upon detection, they will be subject to redress.

Figure 5-7 demonstrates the relationship of the three subsystems. Previously four elements of a system were identified: input, process, output, and control. To treat in a meaningful way the question of whether or not criminal justice is a system requires that current functioning be examined against the fabric of these four elements. Three broad classes of systems are generally recognized: machine to machine, human to machine, and human to human. The administration of justice is a human-to-human system and the basic raw material constituting the inputs are human beings. The second element, process, requires that the inputs are acted upon in proper and timely sequences. The police can only process those they apprehend; the courts receive their material to be processed from the police; and corrections agencies are only able to act upon those individuals who are remanded to their custody following adjudication.

Output has been defined as the system's record of accomplishment; it is here that the argument for definition of criminal justice as a "nonsystem" has its greatest merit. Overall the police are only able to apprehend a small percentage of all violators, the courts stand accused of failing to dispense justice equitably, and the inability of corrections to habilitate or rehabilitate is an often-heard charge. Thus, the system fails to provide a high degree of reliability and stability; that is to say that it does not approach being error free and cannot, therefore, produce overall anything even approximating a regular error-free-minimizing level. The final component, control, seeks to ensure that the desired outcomes are produced regularly. Feedback in

143

Figure 5-7 The Police and Other Substantive Units of the Criminal Justice System.

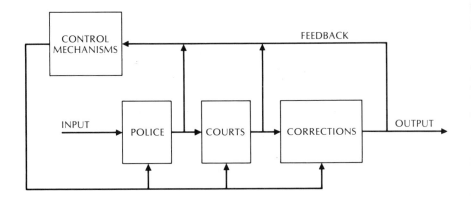

the criminal-justice system consists of informational flows to the appropriate governmental bodies and constituencies. These bodies, in turn, exercise prerogatives in efforts to maximize performance by the various substantive units.

Thus the most damaging evidence against criminal justice as a system lies in its inability to perform with some degree of consistency on a regular basis. This evidence fails, however, to consider several important facts: (1) criminal justice is a human-to-human system which, given our present state of technology, must be expected to be less reliable and stable than the two other classes of systems; (2) our society places a high value on the protection of the individual's rights and this contributes in no small measure to lower performance levels, but it is a trade-off that our society willingly accepts; and (3) the concept of criminal justice as a system is less than fifty years old and it is only since the early 1960s that the term has enjoyed any currency.[34] Established systems are those in which conditions can be specified and predicted with sufficient data to generally control outcomes.[35] In contrast, emergent systems lack one or more of the conditions of established systems. Criminal justice must be regarded as an emerging system. Therefore, the proposition that criminal justice is a "non-system" may be technically correct but it is situated on a very narrow perceptual base. The chief barriers to criminal justice becoming a classical system lie in the present lack of stability and reliability. This condition is in part due to the fact that our present state and federal criminal-justice systems grew, not out of conscious design, but through a process of accidental historical developments.

STUDY QUESTIONS

1. Identify and discuss the three contexts in which policing occurs.
2. What factors impinge upon the policy of full police enforcement of all criminal laws?
3. What was Wilson's contribution to understanding police discretionary power situations?
4. What was the due-process revolution and what effect has it had upon law enforcement?
5. Examine the conflict between normative values and empirical realities which confronts the police recruit.
6. What elements tend to separate the police from the conventional world?
7. Identify and discuss the legalistic, service, and watchman styles of police service.
8. Outline and briefly discuss Muir's notion of individual styles of policing.
9. What are the essential components of arguments for and against regarding the administration of criminal justice as a system?

NOTES

1. Alex Inkeles, *What Is Sociology?* (Englewood Cliffs, N.J.: Prentice-Hall, 1964), p. 67.
2. Ibid., p. 80.
3. George E. Berkley, *The Democratic Policeman* (Boston: Beacon Press, 1969), pp. 1–4.
4. In groups, however, where criminality tends to be normative, convictions may actually be an asset. See Erving Goffman, *Stigma: Notes on the Management of Spoiled Identity* (Englewood Cliffs, N.J.: Prentice-Hall, 1963).
5. *Florida Statutes,* Sec. 901.15; the Florida statute essentially parallels provisions in other states. For further insights into this subject see Wayne R. LaFave, *Arrest: The Decision to Take a Suspect into Custody* (Boston: Little, Brown, 1965).
6. On patterns in family disturbances, see G. Marie Wilt et al., *Domestic Violence and the Police: Studies in Detroit and Kansas City* (Washington, D.C.: Police Foundation, 1977).
7. Richard Quinney, *The Social Reality of Crime* (Boston: Little, Brown, 1970), p. 18. See also Erik Beckman, "Criminal Justice and Politics in America: From the Sedition Act to Watergate and Beyond," *Journal of Police Science and Administration* 5, no. 3 (1977): 285–289.
8. Quinney, *Social Reality,* p. 19.
9. These factors are fundamentally those in the President's Commission of Law Enforcement and Administration of Justice, *Task Force Report: The Police* (Washington, D.C.: Government Printing Office, 1967), p. 17. See also Theodore K. Moran, "Judicial-Administrative Control of Police Discretion," *Journal of Police Science and Administration* 4, no. 4 (1976): 412–418 and C. W. Thomas and W. A. Fitch, "Exercise of Discretionary Decision-making by the Police: An

Inquiry into Its Correlates, Consequences, and Control," *North Dakota Law Review* 54 (1977): 61–95.

10. See James Q. Wilson, *Varieties of Police Behavior* (Cambridge, Mass.: Harvard University Press, 1968), pp. 85 and 89.

11. A number of studies have been drawn upon in preparing this section. See William F. Hohenstein, "Factors Influencing the Police Disposition of Juvenile Offenders," in Thorsten Sellin and Marvin E. Wolfgang, editors, *Delinquency: Selected Studies,* Nathan Goldman, *The Differential Selection of Juvenile Offenders for Court Appearance* (New York: National Council on Crime and Delinquency, 1963); Irving Piliavin and Scott Briar, "Police Encounters with Juveniles," *American Journal of Sociology* 70 (September 1964): 206–214; Carl Werthman and Irving Piliavin, "Gang Members and the Police," in David J. Bordua, ed., *The Police: Six Sociological Essays* (New York: Wiley, 1967), pp. 56–98; Joseph A. Paquin, "Characteristics of Youngsters Referred to Family Court Intake and Factors Related to Their Processing" (Ph.D. diss., State University of New York at Albany, 1977); and John R. Hepburn, "The Impact of Police Intervention upon Juvenile Delinquents," *Criminology* 15, no. 2 (1977): 235–262.

12. National Advisory Commission on Criminal Justice Standards and Goals, *Police* (Washington, D.C.: Government Printing Office, 1973), p. 21.

13. In a legal sense the Supreme Court opted for a piecemeal application when they rejected the "shorthand doctrine," i.e., making a blanket application of the federal bill of rights provisions binding on the states, when they considered *Hurtado v. California* 110 U.S. 516 (1884); therefore, the author's statement should be read in the context that the activist role was a policy decision.

14. Fred P. Graham, *The Self-Inflicted Wound* (New York: Macmillan, 1970), p. 37. For a recent look at the police and due process see A. T. Quick, "Attitudinal Aspects of Police Compliance with Procedural Due Process," *American Journal of Criminal Law* 6 (1978): 25–56.

15. Graham, *Self-Inflicted Wound,* p. 3.

16. Ibid., p. 8

17. James W. Sterling, *Changes in Role Concepts of Police Officers* (Gaithersburg, Md.: International Association of Chiefs of Police, 1972), pp. 30–49.

18. Arthur Niederhoffer, *Behind the Shield* (Garden City, N.Y.: Anchor Books, 1969), pp. 55–58.

19. William A. Westley, *Violence and the Police* (Cambridge, Mass.: MIT Press, 1970), p. 160.

20. For a further discussion of these elements see Jerome H. Skolnick, *Justice Without Trial* (New York: Wiley, 1966).

21. Melany E. Baehr et al., *Psychological Assessment of Patrolman Gratification in Relation to Field Performance* (Chicago: Industrial Relations Center, University of Chicago, 1968), pp. II–3–5.

22. Daniel Cruse and Jesse Rubin, *Determinants of Police Behavior: A Summary* (Washington, D.C.: Government Printing Office, 1973), pp. 1–9.

23. See Wilson, *Varieties of Police Behavior* for in-depth treatment.

24. See Walter C. Reckless, *The Crime Problem* (New York: Appleton-Century-Crofts, 1973), p. 83 and Steven Spitzer, "Conflict and Consensus in the Law Enforcement Process: Urban Minorities and the Police," *Criminology* 14, no. 2 (1976): 189–212.

25. William Ker Muir, *Police: Streetcorner Politicians* (Chicago: University of Chicago Press, 1977). In preparing this section material has also been drawn from C. R. Swanson, "Review of *Police: Streetcorner Politicians,*" *Crime and Delinquency* 24 (April 1978): 238–239.

26. Muir, *Police,* pp. 44–45.

27. Theodore N. Ferdinand, "From a Service to a Legalistic Style Department: A Case Study," *Journal of Police Science and Administration* 4, no. 3 (1976): 302–319.

28. C. R. Swanson, Institute of Government, and Susette Talarico, Department of Political Science, University of Georgia. The results of this research will be reported at a series of professional meetings and in various journals beginning in 1979.

29. *Law and Order Reconsidered,* a staff report to the National Commission on the Causes and Prevention of Violence, Milton S. Eisenhower, chairman (Washington, D.C.: Government Printing Office, 1969), p. 266; the full argument is to be found in pp. 265–284.
30. Stanley Young and Charles E. Summer, Jr., *Management: A Systems Approach* (Glenview, Ill.: Scott, Foresman, 1966), p. 16.
31. Ibid., pp. 15–16.
32. Ibid., pp. 16–18.
33. Advisory Commission on Intergovernmental Relations, *State-Local Relations in the Criminal Justice System* (Washington, D.C.: Government Printing Office, 1971), p. 13.
34. In fact the systems concept only began to gain real momentum and visibility during the early 1950s; it was only after the turn of the century that the term "criminal justice" enjoyed even a modicum of use. Among the early works are: James P. Kirby, *Criminal Justice* (New York: Wilson, 1926); Howard Pendleton, *Criminal Justice in England* (New York: Macmillan, 1931); Roscoe Pound, *Criminal Justice in America* (Cambridge, Mass.: Harvard University Press, 1945); and Hermann Mannheim, *Criminal Justice and Social Reconstruction* (London: Routledge and Paul, 1949).
35. Robert Goguslaw, *The New Utopians: A Study of System Design and Social Change* (Englewood Cliffs, N.J.: Prentice-Hall, 1965), pp. 7–9.

chapter six
Innovation and Change in Policing

The future of policing will, like the larger society it serves, be marked with rapid and continuous change. The nature of many of these changes is for the present obscured by time, even to the farsighted. However, there are recently developed concepts and practices which are of considerable prominence in the field and will be so for some time. Among these are the role of women in policing, the union movement, crisis intervention, team policing, and crime prevention.

WOMEN IN POLICING

The movement for women police in this country began during the mid-nineteenth century under the sponsorship of a variety of organizations including the National League of Women Voters, the Chicago Juvenile Protective Association, the American Social Hygiene Association, and the National Women's Christian Temperance Union; several men's groups were also active in this cause, most notably the men's city clubs of Chicago and Philadelphia.[1]

The first recorded use of women in police work in this country was in 1845, when the American Female Reform Society secured the appointment of six women as matrons in New York City.[2] Women were used as matrons only sparingly until nearly four decades later, when genuine progress was made, largely due to efforts by the Women's Christian Temperance Union. Finally, between 1880 and 1886, the larger cities, including Chicago, Boston, Philadelphia, Baltimore, St. Louis, Denver, Milwaukee, Cleveland, San Francisco, and Detroit, employed numerous women as matrons, marking the first widespread official recognition that females in police custody should be cared for by women.[3]

The earliest appointment of a woman with full police powers— as opposed to a matron with custodial duties—was in Chicago in

1893; Marie Owen, a patrolman's widow, was assigned to the detective bureau, with responsibility for assisting in cases involving women and children.[4] In 1905 in Portland, Oregon, Lois Baldwin was given police power to deal effectively with social conditions threatening the moral safety of young girls and women. Although preceded by Marie Owens and Lois Baldwin, Alice Wells, employed by the Los Angeles Police Department in September 1910, became known as the first policewoman in this country because her position was classified under civil service the year following her appointment.[5] By 1917 the movement had spread to thirty cities; following World War I the figure grew to 220 local units of government. Among the factors contributing to this rapid expansion were the manpower drain caused by the "war to end all wars," the new political status of women, growing activism by women in all phases of public affairs, and their growing social and economic freedom.[6]

Alice Wells, graduate theology student and social worker who became known as the first woman police officer in the United States.

THE STATUS OF WOMEN: PEONAGE AND PROGRESS
A School Teacher's 1928 Contract

I promise to take a vital interest in all phases of Sunday-school work, donating of my time, service, and money without stint for the benefit and uplift of the community.

I promise to abstain from all dancing, immodest dressing, and any other conduct unbecoming a teacher and a lady.

I promise not to go out with any young men except insofar as it may be necessary to stimulate Sunday-school work.

I promise not to fall in love, to become engaged or secretly married.

I promise to remain in the dormitory or on the school ground when not actively engaged in school or church work elsewhere.

I promise not to encourage or tolerate the least familiarity on the part of any of my boy pupils.

I promise to sleep at least eight hours each night, to eat carefully, to take every precaution to keep in the best of health and spirits in order that I may be better able to render efficient service to my pupils.

I promise to remember that I owe a duty to the townspeople who are paying me my wages, that I owe respect to the schoolboard and to the superintendent who hired me, and that I shall consider myself at all times the willing servant of the schoolboard, and the townspeople, and that I shall cooperate with them to the limit of my ability in any movement aimed at the betterment of the town, the pupils, or the school.

Stanley Ewing,
"Blue Laws for School Teachers,"
Harpers Magazine *(1928). pp. 329–338.*

Sail'er Inn V. *Kirby* (1971): The Pedestal as Cage

Sex, like race and lineage, is an immutable trait, a status into which the class members are locked by the accident of birth. What differentiates sex from nonsuspect statuses such as intelligence or physical disability and aligns it with the recognized suspect classification is that the characteristic frequently bears no relation to ability to perform or contribute to society. The result is that the whole class is relegated to an inferior legal status without regard to the capabilities or characteristics of its individual members. Where the relation between characteristics and evil to be prevented is so tenuous, courts must look closely at classifications based on that characteristic lest outdated social stereotypes result in invidious laws or practices.

Laws which disable women from full participation in the political, business, and economic arenas are often characterized as "protective" and beneficial. Those same laws applied to racial or ethnic minorities would readily be recognized as invidious and impermissible. The pedestal upon which women have been placed has all too often, upon closer inspection, been revealed as a cage. We conclude that the sexual classifications are properly treated as suspect, particularly when those classifications are made with respect to a fundamental interest such as employment.

The California State Supreme Court

Former Patterns in Assignments

Although a 1969 study of 1,330 law-enforcement agencies revealed that only 34 percent had any fulltime sworn women officers,[7] there was a growth between World War I and 1972 in the employment of women as police officers. Unfortunately, the prevailing pattern was to assign female officers to specialized units, such as youth or vice, or to use them in jobs traditionally held by women such as clerk, secretary, or switchboard operator. At one time in the recent past well over half of the seventy-four policewomen employed in Indianapolis, including most of the five sergeants, were used as secretaries, even though they had received the same training as male officers. The policewomen enjoyed more status than did civilian clerical help, but there was no attempt to disguise the reality that their work was secretarial.[8] For example, the department directory listed policewomen as secretaries to each division chief. Until very recently women were underrepresented on police forces and were not utilized for general assignments such as uniformed patrol work.

The limited role for women in policing developed out of past practices.[9] Recruiting by most departments was exclusively male-oriented, thereby creating a de facto quota system even though it would have been discriminatory to have a de jure quota system. A 1969 survey revealed that women constituted only 2 percent of the police labor force. Differential entrance requirements were applied in the past; since only a few women were to be hired, agencies wanted the best and required a college degree for female applicants when the parallel requirement for males was a high-school degree. The specialization syndrome effectively exiled women to positions or functions they were thought to handle better than men, such as being

151

secretaries and handling juveniles. They were consistently denied the opportunity to demonstrate their capacity to perform as well as men in other roles, including patrolling. The lack of both promotion opportunities and equal pay for equal work tended not only to discourage female applicants but also to displace to other occupations a number of those women who had at one time gained employment as police officers.

Present Assignment Practices

While police agencies initially resisted the employment of women, except in limited capacities, that position was not viable for several reasons.[10] Women wanted employment with diverse assignments and increasingly had the backing of groups such as the National Organization for Women. Further, many police departments were unable to fill vacancies and the employment of women represented one means to do so. Additionally, it was inevitable that society in general and women in particular would not accept a status quo which was legally untenable. In 1972, Title VII of the Civil Rights Act of 1964 was amended so that its administering agency, the Equal Employment Opportunity Commission, could take action against any state or local government which discriminated against women. It is now illegal to deny a woman the opportunity to compete with a man for any police position in local or state government solely on the basis of sex. Such discrimination could have two costly results for a police department: liability under Title VII and loss of valuable grants awarded by the Law Enforcement Assistance Administration. Finally, the unwillingness to assign women in the same fashion as men resulted in the lack of the empirical data necessary to answer important questions about the performance of women in general assignments.

The Policewomen-on-Patrol Experiment

In 1972 the national barrier to allowing females access to "policemen's work" was broken in Washington, D.C., when Chief Jerry V. Wilson hired a substantial number of women for patrol duty. Working with the Police Foundation a policewoman-on-patrol experiment was designed to compare the performances of eighty-six new officers of each sex who were closely matched; Table 6-1 compares the two groups on the basis of several characteristics. Based upon one year's experience the following conclusions were reached.

Performance

1. Comparison men handled somewhat more patrol incidents per tour, primarily because they initiated more traffic incidents (usually, issuance of written citations).

TABLE 6-1 Descriptive Data on Eighty-six New Policewomen and a Like Number of Comparison Males in the Washington, D.C., Policewomen-on-Patrol Experiment

	YEARS EDUCATIONAL ACHIEVEMENT	CIVIL SERVICE TEST SCORES	NUMBER OF PREVIOUS JOBS	PERCENT BLACK	AVERAGE HEIGHT	AVERAGE WEIGHT
WOMEN	12.8	82	3.5	68	5'7.8"	138
MEN	12.9	82	3.5	42	5'10.3"	170

Source: Peter B. Block et al., *Policewomen on Patrol: Final Report* (Washington, D.C.: Police Foundation, 1974), p. 1.

2. New women patrolling alone tended to handle more service calls assigned by police dispatchers than did men patrolling alone.

3. New women and comparison men responded to similar types of calls while on patrol and saw similar proportions of citizens who were dangerous, angry, upset, drunk, or violent.

4. New women obtained results similar to those of comparison men in handling angry or violent citizens.

5. Comparison men made more felony arrests and misdemeanor arrests than did new women.

6. Arrests made by new women and comparison men were equally likely to result in convictions.

7. New women and comparison men worked well with their partners in two-officer units. The two partners shared the driving about equally, took charge with about the same frequency, and were about equal in giving instructions to the other.

8. New women and comparison men received the same amount of "back-up," or assistance, from other police units.

9. New women and comparison men showed similar levels of respect and general attitude toward citizens.

10. New women and comparison men received similar performance ratings from the police department in its standard review of police officers after the first year of performance.

11. New women and comparison men were given similar performance ratings in several patrol skills on a special rating form. However, men received higher ratings on their ability to handle various violent situations and on general competence to perform street patrol.

12. Police officials in an anonymous special survey gave new women lower ratings than comparison men on ability to handle domes-

153

tic fights and street violence, and on general competence. Women were rated equal to men in handling upset or injured persons.

13. There was no difference between new women and comparison men in the number of sick days used.

14. There was no difference between new women and comparison men in the number of injuries sustained or the number of days absent from work due to injuries.

15. New women were more likely than comparison men to be placed on light duty due to an injury.

16. There was no difference between new women and comparison men in the number of driving accidents in which they had been involved since joining the police force.

17. New women, on the average, needed two weeks longer than comparison men to pass the police driving test.

18. Comparison men were more likely than new women to have been charged with serious unbecoming conduct.

19. Similar numbers of new women (twelve) and comparison men (eleven) resigned from the police department.

20. Citizens showed similar levels of respect and similar general attitudes toward new women and comparison men.

21. Citizens interviewed about police response to their calls for assistance expressed a high degree of satisfaction with both male and female officers.

22. Citizens who had observed policewomen in action said they had become somewhat more favorably inclined toward policewomen.

Attitudes

Citizen Attitudes

1. Citizens of the District of Columbia, regardless of their race or sex, were more likely to support the concept of policewomen on patrol than to oppose it.

2. Citizens believed that men and women were equally capable of handling most patrol situations, but they were moderately skeptical about the ability of women to handle violent situations.

3. The police department was highly rated by citizens in 1972, and this rating has not been affected by the introduction of women into the patrol force.

Police Attitudes

The following attitudes of police officials, patrolmen, and patrolwomen about the "satisfactoriness" of specific patrol skills possessed by the two groups involved in the patrol experiment were found to exist.

1. Patrolmen doubted that patrolwomen were the equal of men in most patrol skills.

2. Patrolwomen felt that their patrol skills were as good as patrolmen's in most cases.

3. Police officials were more likely than patrolmen to say that men and women were equally able to handle important patrol situations, but officials were not as positive about patrolwomen's skills as the women themselves.

4. Patrolmen, patrolwomen, and police officials agreed that men were better at handling disorderly males, that women were better at questioning a rape victim, and that there was no difference between men and women in skill at arresting prostitutes.

5. Police officials agreed with patrolmen that patrolwomen were not as likely to be as satisfactory as men in several types of violent situations.

6. Patrolmen had a definite preference for patrolling with a male partner and patrolwomen had a slight preference for patrolling with a male partner.

7. Patrolwomen felt they received a greater degree of cooperation from the public than patrolmen did.

8. Patrolwomen felt that police supervisors were more critical of patrolwomen than of men. Patrolmen felt there was no difference.

9. Black police officials and black policemen were somewhat less unfavorable toward policewomen than white male officials and policemen.

10. Patrolmen assigned to the same two districts as the new women were slightly more negative toward them than patrolmen assigned to the two comparison districts, which had no new women.

11. Male patrol officers who said that women "should not be a regular part of the patrol force" had less formal education and were more likely to believe in arrests as a performance measurement than other patrolmen.

12. Police officials were somewhat more positive toward policewomen in 1973 than they had been during the initial months of the experiment in 1972.

13. There was little change in the attitudes of patrolmen toward policewomen between the start and the conclusion of the experiment.[11]

In 1978 the Law Enforcement Assistance Administration released a follow-up study to the Washington, D.C., policewomen-on-patrol experiment.[12] The patrol performance of forty-one female police officers was compared to that of forty-one male police officers in New York City. These males and females were matched by length of time on the force, patrol experience, and type of precinct. Direct observation by police and civilian personnel was the principal research method. The findings add to the growing literature justifying assignment of women to patrol.[13] In general, male and female officers performed similarly: They used the same techniques to gain and keep control and were equally unlikely to use force or to display a weapon. However, small differences in performance were observed. Female officers were judged by civilians to be more competent, pleasant, and respectful than their male counterparts, but they were observed to be slightly less likely to engage in control-seeking behavior or to assert themselves in patrol decision making. Compared to male officers, females were less often named as arresting officers, less likely to participate in strenuous physical activity, and more likely to take sick time. Some of the performance disparities appeared to be rooted in morale- and deployment problems resulting from departmental layoffs, social conventions, and role expectations. Situationally and socially engendered differences between the performance of male and female officers might be remedied by different deployment and training policies.

Sufficient interest exists among women to ensure that their influx into policing will continue. Present barriers will continue to be overcome through positive leadership and occasional litigation. The research on the performance of women is still limited but impressive, suggesting that men and women perform patrol work in a generally similar manner. Within the next decade women will occupy significant leadership positions from which they will make notable contributions to both police philosophy and actual programs.

UNIONS: THE NEW POWER CENTER

Although in this country the earliest record of a labor dispute dates from 1636, when a group of fishermen mutinied over withheld wages, and the first union was established in 1792 by a society of Philadelphia shoemakers,[14] police unionism is a relatively recent phenomenon.

Unions and collective bargaining were widely believed to be incompatible with the duties of the police and, therefore, were resisted both in the community and in city hall. Despite this condition police officers were organized in thirty-seven cities by the early 1900s.[15] However, the Boston police strike of September 1919—which was marked by rioting, looting, violence, and the dismissal of some 1,500 striking officers—ended the burgeoning union movement. Congress banned unions in the protective services (police and fire) in the District of Columbia, and many state and municipal governments followed suit.[16] For nearly twenty years following the Boston strike— which historically is often treated as a revolt against public authority rather than as a labor dispute—the police labor movement lay dormant; it was revived when the American Federation of State, County, and Municipal Employees (AFSCME) charted its first police local in Portsmouth, Virginia, in 1937.[17] While experiencing slow growth over the next several decades the AFSCME made progress and by December of 1970 claimed:

> to represent approximately 11,000 policemen and sheriff's department employees. Ten thousand of these were in some 90 local police unions in 20 states. The remaining 1,000 policemen held membership in 36 locals in 15 states; each local represents police along with other public employees ... with Membership centers in Colorado, Connecticut, Illinois, Maryland, Massachusetts, Michigan, Minnesota, Nebraska, New York, Oregon, Tennessee, and Wisconsin.[18]

Police Collective Bargaining: Different Times and Views
1944

Let us examine closely the application of the union principle to police forces. Union benefits to private employees are usually termed collective bargaining in matters pertaining to wage and working conditions, the closed shop, the check-off system, and the strike to enforce these benefits.

1. *Collective Bargaining.* This benefit is denied to police employees, since courts of the nation have declared that a municipality, county, or state is without power to enter into collective bargaining agreements with its employees. Appropriations for police salaries are fixed by statute or through certain statutory provisions. The legislative body of the state, county, or municipality cannot bargain away or delegate its statutory powers and responsibilities.

157

2. *The Closed Shop.* The closed shop benefit is denied to police employees. Statutes, charters, civil service rules and regulations stemming from statutory provisions, departmental rules, or other instruments define the procedure under which police employees are selected and appointed. In public employment there can be no discrimination of citizen against citizen, or union member against nonunion member, where other eligibility requirements are met. This has been declared by courts of the nation.

3. *The Check-off System.* The check-off system provides that the employer shall deduct at stated intervals the union membership fees of a union member. This cannot apply to police union members, since state or local governments cannot be used as an agency for the collection of private debts.

4. *The Strike.* Police union members cannot hope to exercise the right of strike to enforce demands. In almost every instance where there has been agitation for a labor union, or where such union has been organized, the constitution contains a no-strike clause. The American Federation of Labor in March 1943, at [a] meeting of the General Executive Board of the American Federation of State, County, and Municipal Employees, directed that a no-strike provision be included in all charters issued to affiliated local unions which comprise police officers. Public opinion is so overwhelmingly against strikes by police officers that to exercise this weapon of private employees would bring immediate disaster to the group. It was demonstrated in Jackson, Mississippi, when thirty-six officers were dismissed for failing to withdraw from a police union. It was demonstrated in Boston in 1919.

Therefore, if the original tenets and expressed objectives of a recognized trade or labor union are to be adhered to, there is very little advantage, if any, offered to police officers by union membership. Police employees, along with other public employees, are now contributing generously to charitable and welfare causes in addition to deductions for retirement benefits, and perhaps the only privilege afforded them by union membership would be that of adding union dues to their already sizeable contribution list.

> *International Association of Chiefs of Police,* Police Unions and Other Police Organizations *(Washington, D.C.: September 1944) pp. 29–30.*

1975

In earlier times, collective bargaining for policemen was deemed inappropriate, even though employees in both the private and public sectors were permitted—even encouraged—to employ the practice. Prohibitions against law-enforcement officers utilizing the same devices that other working groups employed to upgrade pay and to improve working conditions were based upon the parochial management view that policemen were outside the normal framework of occupations because of their "special" role in society. Now, however, collective bargaining is becoming institutionalized in law enforcement. Officers no longer accept traditional administrative dogma about the "pedestal" position of policemen, especially when there has not been an improvement in the economic or social status of officers that would sufficiently reinforce this position. Policemen are now engaging in collective bargaining nationwide, although there are still some areas of the country where the concept has not made serious inroads.

> *Charles W. Maddox,*
> Collective Bargaining in Law
> Enforcement *(Springfield, Illinois:*
> *Charles C. Thomas, 1975) p. 3.*

In general, organizations which seek to organize police officers may be divided into three broad categories: subdivisions of industrial unions, independent government-employee associations, and independent police-only associations.[19]

Industrial Unions as the Parent Organization

AFSCME is the largest all-public-employee organization with an industrial union as parent. While police officers are bargained for separately, they belong to locals comprised of a variety of public employees. AFSCME's police strength lies primarily in Michigan, Connecticut, and Maryland. AFSCME is an American Federation of Labor-Congress of Industrial Organizations (AFL-CIO) affiliate.

Among federal workers the American Federation of Government Employees (AFGE) is AFSCME's counterpart and is also an AFL-CIO affiliate. AFGE was founded in 1932, four years before AFSCME got its AFL-CIO charter. It presently represents personnel from a number of agencies including the DEA, the Border Patrol, protective officers with the General Services Administration, and deputy federal marshals. Like AFSCME, AFGE is an all-public-employee union.

The Service Employees International Union (SEIU) has been involved in organizing police officers two ways. The first was through a subordinate organization, the National Union of Police Officers (NUPO), while the second has been to directly charter autonomous police locals. SEIU, unlike AFSCME and AFGE, is a mixed union

159

admitting both private- and public-sector employees. NUPO was formerly designated the International Brotherhood of Police Officers but was forced to change its name because an organization by that name already existed. Knowledgeable observers characterize NUPO as nearly defunct, with less than one-third the members it had in 1969. SEIU has about thirty police locals, primarily in Michigan, Louisiana, Missouri, South Carolina, and the Virgin Islands.

The International Brotherhood of Teamsters, Chauffeurs, Warehousemen, and Helpers of America (IBT or Teamsters) has had some interest in organizing the police for about two decades. The IBT either places police officers in mixed locals or in all-public-employee locals, such as Local 310 of the state of Minnesota, which includes state, county, and municipal employees. The Teamster's greatest success in organizing police officers has been in rural, suburban, and western areas of the country.

Independent Government-Employee Associations

The National Association of Government Employees (NAGE) was founded in 1961 and organizes police officers through its subordinate arm, the International Brotherhood of Police Officers (IBPO). IBPO was founded in 1964 in Rhode Island and affiliated with NAGE in 1970. While IBPO's main strength is in New England, it also has locals in Texas, Utah, and California.

It is difficult to assess the extent of police membership in the Assembly of Government Employees (AGE). Founded in 1952, AGE organizes on a governmentwide basis with most of its affiliates being at the state level, such as the 12,000-member Colorado State Employees Association. However, it is clear that some number of police officers do belong, although they are believed to be only a very small percentage of the total 700,000 members claimed by AGE.

Independent Police Associations

Independent police associations limit their membership to police personnel and may be national, statewide, or local in nature.

For the twenty years following its founding in 1953 the International Conference of Police Associations (ICPA) was an association of associations with the purpose of exchanging information about police-employee organizations. In 1973, however, ICPA decided to become a police union and to charter locals. Presently it represents about 182,000 officers in some 400 locals with heavy membership in New York, Illinois, New Jersey, and California. The Fraternal Order of Police (FOP) has historically resisted labeling as a union. As a practical matter, however, where it represents police officers as a bargaining agent it is a de facto union. Founded in 1915, the FOP is not militant, largely because the lodge leadership positions tend to be dominated by low-ranking officers with long years of service. At least occasionally this creates some dissatisfaction with younger, more militant officers who sometimes form rival organizations. In general, FOP membership is concentrated in the northeast and southern states.

Some state police associations are independent, such as the Massachusetts Police Association, while others, such as the Police Conference of New York, are affiliates of ICPA. Typically, state associations are not directly involved in negotiations. Instead they provide services to their substate affiliates such as legal counseling, disseminating information, lobbying, and conducting wage and benefit surveys.

Due to the activeness of ICPA, IBT, and SEIU, the success of these groups in displacing independent police locals, and the advantages of affiliation of some type, we may expect the future to bring some erosion of the number of independent police locals. There are and probably will continue to be locals such as the Buffalo Silver Shield Club and Local 1, Omaha Police Union. But affiliation will probably become increasingly prevalent. We should expect that affiliations of independent police associations will be with umbrella-type organizations, such as statewide police associations, which permit a great deal of local autonomy, as opposed to the more centralized character of IBT or AFL-CIO affiliates.

Factors Producing Police Unionism

Collective bargaining in this country emerged in the private sector during the middle of the nineteenth century; by 1900 it was increasingly pervasive throughout industry. Management and labor, the former accustomed to having its way and the latter with an appetite for self-betterment, were often in sharp conflict. This conflict resulted in at least the occasional use of the ultimate job action, the strike. The police role in these confrontations earned them two things: a reputation as strike-breakers and the long-lasting hostility of unions. However, "it did not go unnoticed among policemen that the country's labor force was making substantial headway in its self-help campaign, especially since police officers were generally of the same ethnic and class background as workers."[20] After 1910 police officers increasingly sought unionization to acquire the benefits held by industrial workers. However, their reputation with labor was a serious impediment and by that time most unions forbade police membership. Labor's position was altered, reluctantly, in 1919, by Samuel Gompers of the American Federation of Labor. However, the ill-fated Boston strike rapidly laid the police labor movement to rest until 1937; it was not until the tumultuous 1960s that it really regained its vitality.

As if in conspiracy with history three unique factors converged in the mid-1960s to create an atmosphere in which police unions could experience rapid growth: (1) social conditions such as a steadily escalating crime rate, apparent public hostility or indifference to police programs, the success of activism by minority groups, and the rising level of police-directed violence; (2) institutional alienation by the police, chiefly due to the strictures of the due-process revolution and a sense of profound isolation in carrying the war against crime forward; and (3) organizational estrangement produced by a leadership unprepared for a decade of change of unprecedented swiftness, including the influx of bright young officers unencumbered by the anchor of tradition.

The reaction of the police was human and, from the safe vantage secured by hindsight, fairly predictable. If they were not to be freely given working conditions, pay, and fringe benefits—which they considered fairly theirs—they would aggressively seek their demands. Unions and collective bargaining came to be the vehicles to that end.

Overview of the Collective-Bargaining Process

"Police collective bargaining is grounded on the assumption that police officers laboring at even the lowest operational levels have an inherent right to exert an influence on certain departmental affairs that control their personal and professional destinies."[21] The process by which this influence is exercised is collective bargaining, which entails negotiations between representatives of a political entity and a recognized police-employee organization. The purpose of these negotiations is to produce a bilateral agreement which regulates selected aspects of the working relationship.[22]

The collective-bargaining process, due to the many different actions, agencies, practices, and statutes involved, does not lend itself readily to description. Despite this fact collective bargaining may be characterized broadly in terms of four major elements.[23] First, a group to represent the employees in bargaining must be established. It does not follow that because the majority of police officers in a particular department belong to the same association that it is empowered to represent them in collective bargaining. The right to representation must be conclusively established on the basis of the association's membership vote or by their written consent; in either case a simple majority is ordinarily sufficient. Once this legitimacy is established the association must inform management of its intent to be the bargaining agent for the department or a specific segment thereof and to demonstrate the basis upon which their legitimacy was established. The final step is electing the negotiating team from among the association's membership. Frequently key officers in the association will automatically become part of the negotiating team. The second point is to determine the focus of negotiations. While seemingly simple, this task can often be extraordinarily complex. Labor's right to negotiate with respect to conditions of employment and management's tenacious maintenance of its prerogatives, may come into conflict due to differing philosophies and definitions. Third, the actual negotiations must be conducted. These may be characterized as informal, with rigidity decreasing and realism increasing as negotiations progress. If both parties have bargained in a spirit of good faith, mutually making concessions, then an agreement can be reached. When negotiations break down and deadlocks develop it may be necessary to ask the help of a neutral third party to get the negotiations moving again and reach a successful conclusion. The fourth and final element is composed of ratification of the contract by the employees represented, acceptance of its terms by government officials, and the actual administration of the contract during its life.

While the elements of legitimacy, focus, negotiations, and ratification-acceptance are fairly clear, the reader is reminded that the collective-bargaining process in actual operation is less clear, since it is fraught with opportunities to create division and conflict. Union members may find difficulty in reaching consensus about what issues should be negotiated and what the priority items are. Conversely, management may lack agreement on what constitutes its prerogatives and what power is bargainable, that is, to be shared. Moreover, the mayor, city manager, or legislative unit may pressure management to take certain positions, positions which may be untenable in the face of union demands. Finally, while government will ordinarily accept an equitable contract, labor may feel the negotiating team has not attained any measure of success and may, therefore, fail to ratify it.

The Impact of Unions

Already unions have had considerable impact upon policing, most notably in the areas of professionalization, executive prerogative, policy, and intradepartmental race relations.

To the extent unionization continues to drive a wedge between low-ranking officers and ranking personnel, such as lieutenants and captains, forcing a continual rethinking of different responsibilities, it will foster a high degree of professionalization in the management of police departments.[24] Unions are threatening to many police executives because their effect has been to narrow managerial prerogatives that have too often been exercised injudiciously; unions have contributed to the elimination of such practices by hastening the development of improved personnel practices. The impact of unions upon policy must be judged in terms of both direct and indirect influences.[25] Direct impact has been seen in alienating or thwarting the implementation of civilian review boards, successful legislative lobbying, the sponsorship and election of law-and-order candidates, the

163

influencing of weapons-use policy, and hampering efforts to lower entrance standards as a means of increasing minority representation among police officers.[26] The indirect impact is more difficult to assess but may, over the years, be more important than the direct. One example of this would be those situations in which executives have failed to act or have been moved from their preferred course of action because of anticipation of a strong union reaction.[27] Also, unions may, perhaps only marginally, have contributed to some degree to racial polarization in various communities by the unions' opposition to review boards, coroners' inquests for shootings by the police, and restrictive guidelines on the use of force. Such opposition may be perceived as hostile and racist acts by minority communities. Some incidents suggest that the advent of unions may also have occasionally worsened intradepartmental race relations.

> Incidents that have served to widen the gulf between black and white policemen have occurred in cities throughout the country. The issues involved have varied: endorsement of George Wallace for United States president by the national president of the Fraternal Order of Police; support by police associations of white mayoralty candidates in contests with blacks; charges of police brutality, use of dogs, and excessive firepower against blacks; Mayor Daley's shoot-to-kill order to Chicago policemen in dealing with looters; use of epithets by white policemen in referring to black members of the force; alleged discriminations against blacks in upgrading and promotions; and a brawl between white and black policemen at an annual FOP picnic. . . . These and similar incidents have helped to convince black policemen that they need their own organizations to represent them. . . . Black policemen more than any other public employee occupational group have tended to form their own organization.[28]

The Future

Unions have steadily become an established part of the police organization. Their presence was in part secured by the findings of major reports. In 1972 the American Bar Association made the following statement

> policemen have a proper collective interest in many aspects of their job such as wages, length of workweek, pension, and other fringe benefits. To implement this interest, the right of collective bargaining should be recognized. However, due to the critical nature of the police function within government there should be no right to strike.[29]

A 1973 government study made a similar recommendation.

> Every police agency and all police employees should be al-
> lowed, by 1975, to engage in collective negotiations in ar-
> riving at terms and conditions of employment that will
> maintain police service effectiveness and ensure equitable
> representation for both parties.... Legislation enacted
> by states to provide for collective bargaining ... should
> include provisions to prohibit police employees from par-
> ticipating in any concerted work stoppage or job action.[30]

Another major factor favorable to unions was various court decisions. In 1969 in *Atkins* v. *City of Charlotte,* a federal district court
ruled that a North Carolina statute prohibiting membership in a
labor organization was an abridgement of the freedom of association
guaranteed by the first and fourteenth amendments to the United
States Constitution. The court, however, also ruled that while
employees may organize, the state of North Carolina could, as a matter of public policy, prohibit collective bargaining. In 1971 a federal
district court ruled as unconstitutional, in *Melton* v. *City of Atlanta,* a
Georgia statute making it a misdemeanor for a police officer to join or
belong to a labor union.[31] Two years later a Colorado court required
the reinstatement of a deputy sheriff who had been suspended because of a refusal to indicate whether he would disaffiliate with the
union.[32] Other indications for the continued growth of unionism include the example of their successes to date, their generally sound
quality of leadership, the strong support of their membership, and the
frequent legitimacy of their demands.

CRISIS INTERVENTION

Among the more frequent types of calls for police service are general
disturbances and domestic disturbances. Tragically, such calls often
end in an assault upon, or the death of, the officer assigned. In one
recent year, 18 percent of the police officers killed in the line of duty
and 31 percent of all assaults on police officers were associated with
such complaints.[33] Five major factors produce these statistics: (1) the
term "disturbance" is a convenient label to be applied to an incoming
call for service but it fails to provide the officer responding to it with
adequate information about the behaviors and mental sets of the
people involved; (2) the judgment of one or more of those people is
distorted by strong emotions, often complicated by the use of alcohol;
(3) although frequently it is a wife who initiates the call, she will
often attack the police officer if he or she attempts to arrest the husband, resulting in a two-party assault upon the officer; (4) usually

the male involved does not welcome third-party intervention; (5) the police traditionally have been ill equipped to effectively handle tense emotional confrontations because they have not been taught how to defuse a charged atmosphere. Moreover, the officer who has not been adequately prepared for this function may actually behave in ways that increase the likelihood of a tragic ending.

As hazardous as these situations are for the police, they are even more so for the people involved. Of all reported murders in any given year nearly one-quarter will involve family members and about half are lovers' quarrels, romantic triangles, or other personal arguments. Aggravated assaults—defined as an unlawful attack on the person of another for the purpose of inflicting grave physical harm—have a profile similar to murders with respect to circumstance, perpetrator, and victim. Beyond their statistical frequency, the fear created, and the grief caused, murder and aggravated assault are important social problems in economic terms. Recently these two crimes resulted in annual losses of approximately $3 billion, including medical bills and loss of earnings.[34]

The New York City Crisis-Intervention Project

Recognizing the facts in the preceding paragraphs, the New York City Police Department embarked upon a unique program to train police in family crisis intervention.[35] Fundamental to the program was the belief that a family in a crisis grave enough to require police assistance might present a state of openness which would permit a dramatic response to skilled intervention and that, if properly trained, the police could play a key role in crime prevention and community mental health.

During the preparatory phase of the project eighteen police volunteers were selected; all of them had at least three years of service and evidenced the motivation and aptitude for family crisis intervention. The personnel selected formed the Family Crisis Intervention Unit (FCIU) and received 160 hours of specialized training including lectures, field trips, and role playing. New York's 30th precinct was designated as experimental, that is, the one in which the FCIU would first operate. The control precinct, in which domestic disturbances would be handled as before by officers who had not received specialized training, was the 24th. The experimental and the control precincts were somewhat similar with respect to population composition.

During the two-year operational phase the eighteen officers in the FCIU were able to provide virtually continuous coverage to the 30th precinct. They were dispatched on all complaints that could be

166

Morton Bard, professor of psychology and director of the Center for Social Research at the City University of New York, who conducted the pioneering research on family crisis intervention. (Photograph by Ralph Tornberg).

predetermined to involve a family disturbance. The project's final phase, evaluation, produced the following conclusions.

1. Sensitive and skillful police intervention in family disturbances may serve to reduce the occurrence of family assaults and homicides.
2. The presence of police specialists trained in family crisis intervention may have a positive effect upon police community relations.
3. The use of sophisticated psychological techniques can greatly increase the personal safety of police officers when dealing with highly charged human conflict situations.
4. The professional identity of police officers can remain intact despite their acquisition of skills and techniques usually associated with the helping professions.
5. Policemen occupy an unusual position for the early identification of pathological human behavior and, if trained, can play a critical role in crime prevention and mental health.

6. Officers can operate as patrol generalists, yet simultaneously they may require behavioral knowledge and function in highly specialized capacities.

7. Members of the academic and policing communities can successfully collaborate to improve the quality of service citizens receive.

The success experienced in the family-crisis-intervention project suggests that police departments—which typically expend about 90 percent of their time in providing various types of social services—can profitably expand the concept from a narrow focus on the family to include assisting crime victims in adjusting to stress reactions (while simultaneously eliciting information useful to the investigative process) and handling victims of the temporary stress disorders which normally accompany large-scale disasters such as tornadoes, earthquakes, and floods. Additionally, the police must often provide notification of death or serious injury to a family; under these circumstances they can be both the precipitators of crisis and agents of resolution.

A domestic-crisis-intervention chart is depicted in Figure 6-1; note that at the decision point the police have five options from which they can select a course of action. Referral represents the most promising option for long-term amelioration, with the possible exception of immediate successful mediation by the officer. However, referral is one of the most difficult options to put into operation. A police department cannot mandate that a person seek professional assistance from mental-health agencies; the police can merely suggest it and forward a written report to the agency to which referral has been made, hoping that if the people involved do seek assistance they will be given priority. Table 6-2 illustrates this problem; the chief cause of the large number of "unknowns" was that mental-health agencies failed to respond or made incomplete responses to police inquiries. In such situations the police themselves were properly reluctant to initiate a follow-up contact out of respect for their client's civil rights.

Models of Implementation

The legitimacy of allocating police organizational resources to crisis intervention has steadily grown. Presently departments are implementing such programs under three different models: generalist-specialist, generalist, and specialist. The latter is the least desirable, for reasons discussed below.[36] The model employed in New York City's FCIU was the generalist-specialist, in which a selected group of specially trained officers handled all family disturbance calls within a specific geographical area. These officers operated in uniform, on all tours of duty, and maintained regular patrol responsibilities when not

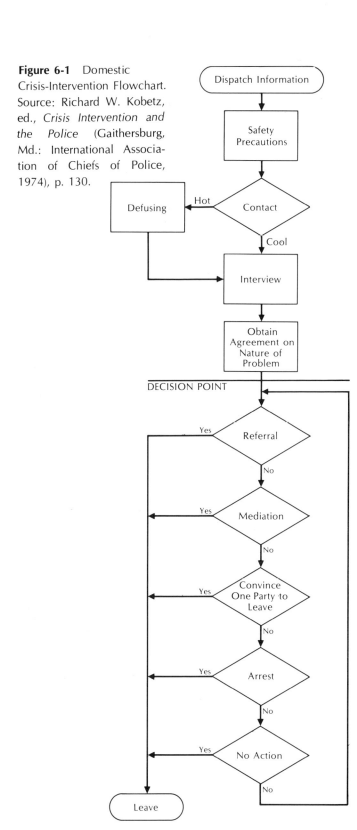

Figure 6-1 Domestic Crisis-Intervention Flowchart. Source: Richard W. Kobetz, ed., *Crisis Intervention and the Police* (Gaithersburg, Md.: International Association of Chiefs of Police, 1974), p. 130.

TABLE 6-2   Action Taken with Respect to Referral by Families Visited by the 30th
Precinct FCIU

	NUMBER OF FAMILIES REFERRED	APPLIED	*FAMILY ACTION* DID NOT APPLY	UNKNOWN
TOTAL	719	69	277	373
PERCENT OF TOTAL	100	9.6	38.5	51.9

Source: Morton Bard, *Training Police as Specialists in Family Crisis Intervention* (Washington, D.C.: Government Printing Office, 1970), p. 32, Table 7.

engaged in crisis work. The generalist-specialist model ensures that in both the eyes of the public and of his or her colleagues an officer's professional identity as a "real cop" remains intact. Some other advantages of this first model are that delivery of service is improved without draining manpower from general patrol coverage and that the patrol officer does not have to be all things to all people, since specialists are available. The success of this program implies that such an approach could be used in other areas, such as the handling of youths, with officers given the specific functional expertise necessary. This model also enhances the morale of patrol officers by acknowledging their area of expertise and giving them appreciation for it by fellow officers and the public. The generalist model requires that all patrol personnel be trained in techniques of crisis intervention; this second model is well suited to small departments that have too few officers to allow for generalist-specialists on each shift. The generalist model avoids a pitfall of the generalist-specialist orientation by emphasizing crisis intervention as an ongoing patrol responsibility. At least occasionally the generalist-specialist model generates feelings that particular complaints are the responsibility of a select group of officers. A disadvantage, however, is that the quality of service in the generalist model shows greater variance than in the generalist-specialist, because the former trains all patrol personnel, regardless of aptitude, while the latter trains a selected group. The specialist model is encumbered by three significant disadvantages. First, it is through this model that organizational ambivalence is most likely to be expressed. The delivery of the service becomes the exclusive responsibility of the specialist and satisfies only the policy decision to implement the program with no reference to the broader operating responsibilities of the organization. Second, it tends to create two classes of officers within the organization; those who do "real" police work and those who do social work. This encourages the public to think of the police as being either "bad guys" or "good guys," that is, those who are "enforcers" and those who are more "humane." Lastly, it is ultimately destructive to morale and hence destructive to the function of the specialist. The specialist feels alienated from his colleagues and may become confused in his identity as a police officer if his functions are restricted to a single service. A case in point is the derisive designation in many departments of juvenile specialists as "kiddie cops."

TEAM POLICING

The 1960s were a time of considerable strain on our police forces; it was a period marked by urban upheavals, a burgeoning crime problem, and the due-process revolution. As the public's anxiety grew, so did their demands for more effective police services. The police response was to attempt to provide additional increments of traditional services; this approach was perceived as unsatisfactory and unresponsive by many communities. By the late 1960s the gulf between the police and their respective communities was considerable. That situation was antithetical to the proposition that maximum citizen cooperation is fundamental to crime control in a free society. Recognizing this fact, police departments began team policing efforts to "reduce isolation and induce community support in the war on crime."[37]

The Organization of Team Policing

Presently at least sixty different-sized cities are using some form of team policing. Total team policing consists of five elements: combining all line functions of patrol, traffic, and investigation into a single unit under common supervision; blending generalists, such as patrolmen, and specialists, such as homicide investigators, to form teams; establishing geographical stability by the continuous assignment of particular teams to particular areas; making the teams responsible for the delivery of all police services in their area; and maximizing communication between team members and neighborhood residents.[38] The differences between this approach and traditional policing are significant and may be contrasted as to size, supervision, time responsibility, assignments, coordination, community interface, planning, and service orientation, as follows.[39]

Size   The grouping of patrol officers in the traditional organization is on the basis of precincts or large divisions; either of these will often contain 100–250 persons. Teams typically consist of 20–40 officers.

171

Supervision   Team policing relies upon professional supervision which is characterized by the delegation of considerable decision-making authority to the patrol officers, using mistakes as a learning rather than a fault-finding exercise; an openness to suggestions and criticisms from subordinates; and interpersonal communications occurring in an atmosphere of trust and confidence. Traditional supervision tends toward centralization of decision-making power; its stated preference for close supervision in the field subtly incorporates a depreciated view of the capabilities of subordinates, thereby neglecting a rich source of innovative contributions.

Time Responsibility   Traditional patrol service is delivered on eight-hour tours of duty with twenty-four-hour responsibility vested only in the precinct or division commander; this more than occasionally produces unevenness in styles, levels, or types of services. In contrast each individual team commander is responsible for all police services on an around-the-clock basis.

Assignments   The prevailing method of assigning patrol officers incorporates rotation to new geographical areas, precincts, or assignments. Team policing, because of its dependency upon detailed knowledge of the area and maximum interaction with citizens, utilizes fairly stable assignments.

Coordination   Total team policing blends specialists and generalists together under the unified leadership of the team commander. The traditional method of patrol services leaves the patrol officer—a generalist—in need of support services from specialists in other divisions, often resulting in bureaucratic fencing over prerogatives and credit and in fragmentation of organizational effort.

The Community Interface   Police community-relations programs were an effort to lessen the racial tensions of 1960–1968; while some departments conducted meaningful programs, others often used them as window dressing and instead conducted public-relations campaigns. The existence of such programs often created the mental set among patrol officers that community relations was solely or primarily the responsibility of a particular unit, rather than a departmentwide responsibility. Team policing views community relations as an essential ongoing effort of all officers, stressing the need for friendly contacts and attendance at meetings of neighborhood groups.

Planning   The traditional method of policing relies upon planning that is heavily centralized; innovation—such as may occur—flows from the top of the organization. Team policing emphasizes decentralization of planning with key contributions coming from team commanders and their subordinates, subject to review and approval by senior officials.

Service Orientation   Team policing is proactive; maximum positive interaction with the community produces the knowledge and support necessary to conduct anticipatory programs to prevent crime. Traditional policing is heavily, but not exclusively, reactive, responding to calls after the fact. It makes use of programs which are often abrasive to the neighborhood, such as aggressively conducted field interrogations or stop-and-frisk encounters.

The Response to Team Policing

The first well-known team policing project was started in 1968 in Syracuse; other jurisdictions which have since implemented it include: St. Petersburg, New York City, Dayton, Los Angeles, Detroit, Albany, Cincinnati, Culver City, and Tucson.[40] Detroit subsequently discontinued the program. In Detroit, the team commander, team detectives, and most team members supported the program; it was eliminated because a new police commissioner disliked the concept.[41] While Detroit abandoned their team policing program, the overall reaction in other cities has been favorable with the departments and with the residents; it is fair to say that there have been no fiascoes. Efforts to implement team policing are occasionally met with resistance within departments. Team policing represents change, which is often threatening to senior officials. Patrol officers who see themselves as enforcers view certain elements of team policing as an attempt to make social workers out of them—a serious attack upon their role concept. Others resist it out of a concern that maximum informal contact with the community offers too much potential for corruption. Finally, the implementation of this method may significantly alter the organizational structure and, thus, the existing career paths; those with a strong military orientation or heavy career investment may subvert team policing on the basis of their predisposition or because it threatens their vested interest.

The Kansas City Study and Its Implications

A year-long study in Kansas City possesses implications for team policing. The police department there sought to determine the effectiveness of the traditional strategy of routine preventive patrol by conspicuously marked vehicles. "Police patrol strategies have always been based on two unproven but widely accepted hypotheses: first, that visible police presence prevents crime by deterring potential offenders; second, that the public's fear of crime is diminished by such police presence."[42]

From October 1, 1972, to September 30, 1973, the Kansas City Police Department, with the support of the Police Foundation, sought to test whether routine patrol had any measurable impact upon crime or upon the public's sense of security. Beats are limited areas of geographical responsibility which are ordinarily patrolled by marked vehicles operated by one or two uniformed officers. As depicted in Figure 6-2 a total of fifteen beats, representing a thirty-two-square-mile area with a 1970 resident population of 148,395, were involved. Beats were designated as being reactive, proactive, or control. Reactive beats did not receive preventive patrol; officers entered the area only upon citizens' requests for service. When not responding to calls reactive units patrolled the boundaries of their beats or adjacent proactive beats. In proactive beats the amount of routine preventive patrol was intensified some two to three times its usual level. The normal amount of patrolling was conducted in control beats. The evaluation of the experiment was as follows:

1. The amount of reported crime between reactive, control, and proactive beats showed only one statistical significant variation "other sex crimes," which excludes rape while including such offenses as exhibitionism and molestation, was higher in reactive than control areas. However, the judgment of the project evaluators was that the statistical significance was probably a random occurrence.

2. As crime is considerably underreported a victimization study was conducted to determine if fluctuations could be detected in levels of crime which were not officially reported to the police; no

Figure 6-2 Schematic Representation of the Fifteen-Beat Experimental Area

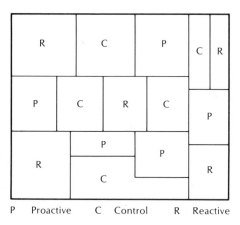

P   Proactive   C   Control   R   Reactive

Source: George L. Kelling et al., *The Kansas City Patrol Experiment* (Washington, D.C.: Police Foundation, 1974), p. 9.

174

statistically significant differences were found between the three types of areas.

3. Crimes citizens and businessmen said they reported to the police showed statistically significant differences between reactive, control, and proactive beats in only five of forty-eight comparisons, and these differences showed no consistent pattern. In two instances the change was greater in control beats, twice it was greater in the proactive beats, and only once was it greater in reactive beats.

4. There were no statistically significant differences in arrests between the three types of beats.

5. Citizen fear of crime was not significantly altered by changes in the level of routine preventive patrol.

6. Variations in the level of patrolling did not significantly alter the security measures taken by citizens or businesses.

7. Little correlation was found to exist between level of patrol and citizen and business persons' attitudes toward the policing.

8. The amount of time taken by police in answering calls was not significantly altered by variations in the level of routine preventive patrol.

9. There was no significant effect upon the incidence of traffic accidents due to differing levels of service.

The interpretations and findings of the Kansas City study are highly controversial and there is not agreement on them.[43]

Upon learning the results of the study, some local government leaders felt that further increases in police manpower were not warranted and that decreases might be justified. Such persons failed to consider that just because the prevailing method of preventing crime—routine preventive patrol—was not effective, it did not follow that no strategy of prevention would work. The bridge between the Kansas City Study and team policing is tenuous. However, the findings suggest that administrators may move into team policing, diverting significant manhours from routine patrol to the community interface function, without producing an intolerable crime rate and with the genuine possibility of lowering it.

CRIME PREVENTION

Its Roots

The prevention of crime is a prominent theme throughout history. Both Aeschylus (525–450 B.C.) and Sophocles (495–400 B.C.)

175

associated the prevention of future crime with punishment directed at the perpetrator.[44] Aristotle (384–322 B.C.) presented a similar notion, emphasizing that crime would only be prevented if the offender received pain and loss.[45] In a similar vein, Plato (428–348 B.C.) stated that the sole purpose of punishment is to prevent crime in the future.[46] Thucydides (460–400 B.C.), in his work on the Peloponnesian War, noted that the psychological properties of a person must be changed if the future is to be different from the past.[47] Such action usually took the form of making the transgressor an example of what would happen to others if they chose similar behavior. Herodotus (484–425 B.C.) records an extreme case of example making in the events surrounding the appointment of a judge. A newly appointed judge was reminded of the punishment applied to his father, who had preceded him in that post. The father had been found guilty of accepting a bribe for the imposition of a lenient sentence. Darious had the father killed and his skin cut into strips. These strips were stretched across the chair in which the son was to sit while hearing cases and passing judgment—the same chair the father had once occupied. Having done this, Darious reminded the newly appointed judge of the manner in which his chair was cushioned.[48] St. Thomas Aquinas (1225–1274) also made reference to the relationship between crime prevention and punishment: "Punishment is meant as much for others as for the punished."[49] Tacitus (55–117) observed that "laws indeed punish crimes committed; but how much more merciful would it be to the individual, how much better to our allies, to provide against their commission."[50] His observation underscores the very heart of the presently prevailing definition of crime prevention, which appears later in this section.

The development of the modern concept of crime prevention is in large measure attributable to the work of the Fielding brothers, Colquhoun, and William Pitt, and to the good wrought by the Peelian reform of 1829. Indeed, the first order of the Metropolitan Police Act discussed the importance of crime prevention.

> It should be understood, at the outset, that the principal
> object to be attained is the prevention of crime. To this
> great end, every effort of the police is to be directed. The
> security of person and property, the preservation of the
> public tranquility, and all the other objects of a police establishment, will thus be better effected, than by the detection and punishment of the offender, after he has succeeded
> in committing the crime. This should constantly be kept in
> mind by every member of the police force, as the guide for
> his own conduct. Officers and police constables should endeavor to distinguish themselves by such vigilance and activity as may render it extremely difficult for anyone to

commit a crime within that portion of the town under their charge.[51]

The American Experience

Douthit offers one of the most concise accounts of the development of crime prevention in this country from 1900 to 1940.[52] Although he was some fifty years premature, the Chief of Police in Rochester, New York, told fellow officers in 1913 that "the time is at hand when the efficiency of the police will be judged—not by the number of criminals apprehended but by the amount of crime in the community, and the popular police will no longer be the catcher of criminals, but the one who foresees crime and prevents it." Oakland, California, in 1915 declared that police departments could no longer afford to be concerned with the arrest and conviction of criminals alone, but must become a constructive power for the prevention of crime in a larger and broader sense. In 1919, August Vollmer, at an International Association of Chiefs of Police Conference, presented a paper entitled "The Policeman as a Social Worker." This paper urged that the police make more efficient use of local social-service agencies in an effort to prevent crime and delinquency. About 1920 Arthur Woods initiated a youth-oriented crime-prevention program in the New York City Police Department.

In the 1920s and 1930s August Vollmer continued to try to interest the police and the public in the social dimensions of police work. In 1925 the Berkeley Crime Prevention Division was established because of interest generated in that community. The newly formed division concentrated on personal counseling, investigation, and referral work. As early as 1936 Vollmer argued that "police organizations constitute . . . the logical agencies for the coordination of the resources of the community in a concentrated effort toward crime prevention."

By the 1930s, some thirteen cities reported having crime-prevention divisions within their organizations. But confusion existed then, as it does now, concerning the functions of a crime-prevention division and the application of its resources in an entire community. For example, O. W. Wilson observed in 1939 that crime prevention in general was associated with physical recreation and character-building programs for the youth of the community more so than any other program.

Despite the efforts being made, crime prevention, both in this country and in England, began stagnating due to a lack of focus.

The Revival in England

Attention to the concept of crime prevention revived in England about 1948. Localized crime-prevention exhibitions took place in the smaller towns of England. Such programs usually consisted of posters, limericks, films, and other aspects of the mass media designed to educate the public about the various methods of protecting their property. W. J. Hutchinson, Chief Constable of Brighton, was one of the key proponents of crime prevention during this period. England's first national crime-prevention campaign was in 1950. This effort was inspired by a report that Swedish insurance companies and the police had joined together and created a Crime Prevention Advisory Bureau.

Following the Swedish lead, insurance companies in England worked with the Home Office and agreed to donate 2,400 pounds to the cost of creating a crime-prevention exhibition. A crime-prevention program was developed by the Central Office for Information. Several noted products emerged, including a short film entitled *Help Yourself,* a touring exhibit termed "The Burglar and You," and a collection of posters highlighting burglary techniques and short captions indicating how to prevent such acts. About 2,000 such poster sets were produced and distributed. This first national crime-prevention program was officially opened on May 1, 1950, and ran until the fall of 1951. This program had an estimated cost of 25,000 pounds, with a 25 percent allocation for film production.

Prior to 1961 the use of uniform widespread publicity in England was practiced. This publicity centered around two-minute filler films for television and theater, a continuation of the poster-printing program, and the manufacture of window displays for demonstration purposes. Subsequently, varied programs were developed to have impact upon the specific crime problems of particular locations.

Also, under the direction of the Home Office, crime-prevention training was given to local police officers. Training began at Stafford during 1963. From its inception to 1971, 1,045 police officers were trained at Stafford's four-week training program. After completion of the program, the officer returned to his or her own jurisdiction and began or supported an existing prevention effort. Three-day discussion seminars were created on the direction of the Home Office at the Stafford facility in 1969. Twenty-one Chief Constables attended the first crime-prevention discussion seminar. The program was expanded to include line officers in 1970. Advanced techniques were taught to officers in jurisdictions already having crime-prevention programs.

The British Insurance Association and the Home Office agreed in 1966 to provide a crime-prevention course for the insurance industry. A tightening of regulations resulted when the insurance surveyors and the police exchanged ideas and problems.

A standing committee for crime prevention was established in the Home Office in 1967. The purpose of this committee was to provide a forum for those who had an interest and desire in participating collectively in the advancement of crime-prevention knowledge. Several national campaigns were also undertaken from 1965 to 1968.

A crime-prevention newsletter was published beginning in March of 1969; it is still a viable communication vehicle in the United Kingdom and the United States. This newsletter provides local crime-prevention officers with information concerning programs and projects that have proven successful in other jurisdictions. Even more importantly, the officer is informed of the programs and projects which did not produce the intended results, so that he is better able to choose programs best suited to his particular needs and budget. One of the most important contributions of the Training Institute at Stafford, England, is the currently accepted definition of crime prevention. It is important because it provided a long-needed focus. Chief Superintendent Fred Hudson of the British Home Office Crime Prevention Training Unit at Stafford stated that "crime prevention is the anticipation, the recognition, and appraisal of a crime risk and the initiation of some action to remove or reduce it."[53]

Progress in America

Several institutes specializing in crime-prevention training have been developed in the United States; the first—and still most notable—is the National Crime Prevention Institute in Louisville, Kentucky. Since its inception in 1971 NCPI has trained an estimated 2,300 police officers from almost every state and from several foreign nations. Both basic and advanced crime prevention are offered in programs ranging from one to four weeks in length. Many other states have excellent programs, including Texas, North Carolina, and California. Kentucky provides one week in-service crime-prevention training to all police officers.

The National Advisory Commission on Criminal Justice Standards and Goals investigated many means by which the community and police could join in an effort to halt crime before it occurred. This commission concluded that all Americans must make a personal contribution to the reduction of crime by increased citizen participation, expanded employment, support for juvenile programs, provisions for the treatment of drug offenders, establishment of statewide anticorruption programs, and development of career programs for students.

Crime-prevention training for police has led to the development of several successful crime-prevention programs throughout the country. Operation ID, also known as "Brand It," "Mark It," and "Tatoo," encouraged home owners and businesses to inscribe a particular, unique reference number on easily fenceable property, such as radios, tape recorders, and calculators. Numbers used in the past include social security, driver's license, numbers randomly assigned by the police department, and an alphanumerical combination developed by a New York-based corporation. Approximately 33 percent of the police departments that have crime-prevention divisions and that responded to the National Crime Prevention Institute's survey of 1976 indicated that they use this program.[54] Many departments include, as a public service, on-site security surveys. The survey is designed to inform the occupant of structural and procedural deficiencies which an offender could take advantage of during an attack. Of particular importance in residential surveys are doors, locks, lighting, visibility from the street, and alarms. Commercial surveys are concerned with such variables as cash on hand, employee pilferage, lighting, visibility, hold-up alarms, doors, locks, and key control. Neighborhood Watch is a program intended to develop a community relationship. The people form an unofficial pact to observe and report to the police suspicious activity in or about their neighbors' homes. Community talks by crime prevention personnel have greatly enhanced the police community-relations effort by reducing the "nameless police" to a person they know. The usual audience for such community programs includes senior-citizens' groups, merchant associations, service clubs, and ladies auxiliaries. Many police departments have developed unusual programs to cope with special problems. One department registers snow skis due to the high incidence of theft; another implants colored confetti into feed and grain to identify it if stolen; and other agencies initiated programs against burglary, robbery, bicycle theft, bombs, rape, and assaults on the elderly.

As to the future of crime prevention, all indications are that insurance companies, private security organizations, social and service groups, and business will become increasingly active in selective programs appropriate to their particular needs.

STUDY QUESTIONS

1. Discuss the history and role of women in policing from 1845 until the Policewomen-on-Patrol experiment.
2. What liabilities may befall a police department which denies a woman—solely on the basis of sex—the opportunity to compete with males for any position?
3. What effect did the Boston Police Strike have upon unions in public-sector protective services?
4. What factors produced the rapid growth of police unionism in the 1960s?
5. What have been the direct and indirect impacts of unions upon local policing?
6. Historically, why have domestic-disturbance calls been so difficult and dangerous for the police?
7. Discuss the consequences of both the generalist and specialist models for implementing crisis intervention.

8. How is team policing differentiated from the traditional method of delivering police services?

9. If you were a chief of police confronted with a mayor or city manager who threatened to cut your budget on the basis of the Kansas City patrol study, what would your reply be?

10. Trace the development of crime prevention.

NOTES

1. Chloe Owings, *Women Police* (Montclair, N. J.: Patterson Smith, 1969), p. 97.
2. Ibid., p. 98.
3. Ibid., pp. 98–99.
4. Ibid., p. 99.
5. Ibid., pp. 99–100.
6. Gary Perlstein, *An Exploratory Analysis of Certain Characteristics of Policewomen* (Ph.D. diss., Florida State University, 1971), p. 57.
7. Catherine Milton, *Women in Policing* (Washington, D.C.: Police Foundation, 1972), p. 16.
8. Ibid., p. 63.
9. These factors are essentially those identified in Milton, *Women in Policing,* pp. 16–26.
10. Ibid., pp. 34 and 43–46.
11. Peter B. Block et al., *Policewomen on Patrol: Final Report* (Washington, D.C.: Police Foundation, (1974), pp. 5–7.
12. Joyce L. Sichel et al., *Women on Patrol: A Pilot Study of Police Performance in New York City* (Washington, D.C.: Government Printing Office, 1978)
13. For example, see Kenneth W. Kerber, Steven M. Andes, and Michele B. Mittler, "Citizen Attitudes Regarding the Competence of Female Police Officers," *Journal of Police Science and Administration* 5, no. 3 (1977): 337–347 and JoAnn McGeorge and Jerome Wolfe, "A Comparison of Attitudes Between Men and Women Police Officers: A Preliminary Analysis," *Criminal Justice Review* 1, no. 2 (1976): 21–33.
14. Allen Z. Gammage and Stanley L. Sachs, *Police Unions* (Springfield, Ill.: Charles C. Thomas, 1972), pp. 8 and 9.
15. Ibid., p. 30 and William J. Bopp, *Police Personnel Administration* (Boston: Holbrook Press, 1974), p. 342.
16. Jack Stieber, *Public Employee Unionism* (Washington, D.C.: The Brookings Institution, 1973), p. 56.
17. Gammage and Sachs, *Police Unions,* p. 44. For an analysis of contemporary police strikes see Richard M. Ayres, "Case Studies of Police Strikes in Two Cities—Albuquerque and Oklahoma City," *Journal of Police Science and Administration* 5, no. 1 (1977): 19–31.
18. Ibid., p. 49.
19. This material is drawn from Charles R. Swanson, Jr., "A Typology of Police Collective Bargaining Employee Organizations," *Journal of Collective Negotiations in the Public Sector* 6, no. 4 (1977): 341–346.
20. Bopp, *Police Personnel Administration,* p. 322.
21. Ibid., p. 343.
22. Ibid.
23. Ibid., pp. 344–354.
24. Hervey A. Juris and Peter Feuille, *The Impact of Unions* (Washington, D.C.: Government Printing Office, 1973), p. 8.
25. Ibid., p. 10. See also J. P. Morgan and Richard J. Korstad, *The Impact of Collective Bargaining on Law Enforcement and Corrections* (St. Petersburg, Fla.: Public Safety Research Institute, 1976).
26. Juris and Feuille, *Impact of Unions,* pp. 11–12.
27. Ibid., p. 12.

28. Stieber, *Public Employee Unionism,* pp. 60 and 62.
29. American Bar Association, *The Urban Police Function* (New York: American Bar Association, 1972), pp. 170–171.
30. National Advisory Commission on Criminal Justice Standards and Goals, *Police* (Washington, D.C.: Government Printing Office, 1973), p. 457.
31. 324 F. Supp. 315 (N.D. Ga. 1971).
32. *Lontine* v. *Vancleave,* 80 LRRM 3240, D. Colo 1972, Aff'd. 483 F. 2d 966 (10th cir. 1973).
33. Federal Bureau of Investigation, *Uniform Crime Reports—1976* (Washington, D.C.: Government Printing Office, 1977), pp. 283 and 288.
34. *U. S. News and World Report* (December 16, 1974): 32.
35. Morton Bard, *Training Police as Specialists in Family Crisis Intervention* (Washington, D.C.: Government Printing Office, 1970) from which this description of the project is drawn. For a more generalized view see Morton Bard and Joseph Zacher, *The Police and Interpersonal Conflict: Third-Party Intervention Approaches* (Washington, D.C.: Police Foundation, 1976).
36. Morton Bard, *Family Crisis Intervention: From Concept to Implementation* (Washington, D.C.: Government Printing Office, 1973), pp. 9–10.
37. National Advisory Commission, *Police,* p. 154.
38. Ibid., Lawrence W. Sherman et al., *Team Policing* (Washington, D. C.: Police Foundation, 1973), pp. 4–6.
39. Adapted from Peter B. Block and David Specht, *Neighborhood Team Policing* (Washington, D.C.: Government Printing Office, 1973) p. 2.
40. Ibid., p. 1.
41. Ibid. For detailed information on the Detroit experience and six other communities see Sherman et al., *Team Policing.*
42. George L. Kelling et al., *The Kansas City Preventive Patrol Experiment* (Washington, D.C.: Police Foundation, 1974), p. v; the summary of the research is taken from this document.
43. For example, see Richard C. Larson, "What Happened to Patrol Operations in Kansas City?" and Tony Pate, George L. Kelling, and Charles Brown, "A Response to What Happened to Patrol Operations in Kansas City," *Journal of Criminal Justice* 3, no. 4 (1975): 267–297 and 299–320 and John F. Schnelle et al., "Patrol Evaluation Research: A Multiple-Baseline Analysis of Saturation Police Patrolling During Day and Night Hours," *Journal of Applied Behavior Analysis* 10, no. 1 (1977).
44. Aeschylus *The Persians* Lines 736 to 812. Sophocles *Oedipus the King* Lines 828 to 949. The section was contributed by R. Allen McCartney, Crime Prevention International, Louisville, Kentucky.
45. Aristotle *Rhetoric* 1. 12.
46. Plato *Protagoras* 323–325.
47. Thucydides *The Peloponnesian War* 9. 46–49.
48. Herodotus *The History* 23–29.
49. Thomas Aquinas *Summa Theologica* 1.
50. P. Cornelius Tacitus *The Annals* 3.
51. Charles Reith, *A New Study of Police History* (London: Oliver and Boyd, 1956), pp. 135–136.
52. Nathan Douthit, "Enforcement and Non-Enforcement Roles of Police," *Journal of Criminology and Criminal Law* 3, (1975): 343–344.
53. This widely accepted definition of crime prevention can be found in a number of locations, e.g., "The History of Crime Prevention," mimeographed (Washington, D.C.: National Crime Prevention Institute, n.d.), p. 4.
54. These statistics were developed by R. Allen McCartney, Director of Research, Crime Prevention International, Louisville, Kentucky.

chapter seven
Criminal Behavior and Individual Rights

MOTIVES IN CRIMINAL BEHAVIOR

Law leaves the "why" of criminal behavior to the behavioral sciences. For this reason, the rule has long been that motive is not an essential part of the proof of a crime. This is not to be taken as an absolute prohibition against the use of motivating evidence. It simply means that if the state proves its case beyond a reasonable doubt the defendant is guilty regardless of motive. There are times when motive is used as one circumstance, along with other reasonable inferences, to prove the "who" of a crime. Standing alone, however, it is not enough.

Before criminal law was adopted, the entire redress for personal grievances was based on a motive system. At one time, personal vendettas were quite acceptable. Vengeful individual behavior brought such havoc that an alternative system was created—criminal law.

America's experience with both vigilantes and, more recently, the militants of the 1960s has demonstrated once again how unwise it is to allow motive to determine and possibly to excuse the resolution of grievances. Exercising the option for order, as opposed to chaos, seems sound. Dissent must be channeled into orderly means of objecting to oppressive behavior.

The fact that motive is not the key to determining which behavior is or is not acceptable does not mean that motive goes unnoticed. Motive can legitimately be taken into account after a person has been found guilty. Sentencing standards give judges discretionary power based on various factors, including motive.

EXAMPLES OF CRIMINAL BEHAVIOR

Criminal law is that device through which we seek to protect ourselves from antisocial behavior. Society sets norms which are the parameters of acceptable behavior. Going outside these norms brings to bear on the individual the full force of society. Although there is some hope that the sanctions of criminal law will prevent undesirable behavior, that is not the prime purpose for the criminal law.

The purpose of criminal law is not to "cure" antisocial individuals of the conditions that cause or contribute to their criminal behavior, but to prevent individuals from offending, by either severely affecting their pocketbooks (fines) or restricting their mobility (imprisonment).

Considered in this light, very few excuses for antisocial behavior are tolerated. Despite the efforts of psychiatrists, psychologists, and others to encourage society to excuse and cure, most subdivisions of American government recognize only one test for totally avoiding criminal penalties. This test, M'Naghten rule, says that to be excused for his conduct, a defendant must not have known the difference between right and wrong at the time of the act. Accepting lesser mental impairments as reason for not receiving further penalties would allow freedom to individuals who are dangerous.

Perhaps the most antisocial act is that of criminal homicide. Severe penalties exist for this conduct; however, there is one type of murder for which society extends limited sympathy for the offender. This is called "manslaughter." The law recognizes that sometimes people are brought to a point of justifiable rage. When murder is committed under this circumstance, it cannot be excused, but the penalty for it can be reduced. For example, when a spouse finds another person having sexual intercourse with the spouse's mate and kills one or both of them, the charge is usually manslaughter.

The charge of manslaughter rather than of murder is not arrived at out of sympathy or as a general or arbitrary decision. There are strict definitional parameters on manslaughter. The "hot blood," the lack of a "cooling" period, the spontaneity, and the relationships of those involved are all taken into account, as are the defendant's alternatives to manslaughter. The father who finds his child being molested and reacts by grabbing the offender and choking him to death had no time to "cool off." Yet if that same father waits several hours, plans, purchases a gun, and then shoots the offender, the charge will be murder, although the motive was the same. The father might have brought acceptable, or legal, alternatives to bear against the child-molester.

The law is not callous toward people with mental deficiencies. If because of mental illness a defendant does not understand the nature of the charges against him, he will not be tried until he can understand. If a defendant becomes mentally ill after trial but before sentencing, he will not be sentenced until he can understand the sentencing process.

Consent to searches and incriminating statements taken from those unable to understand what they have done cannot be used against them. Of course, ignorance or a mere lack of formal education is not sufficient. A mental deficiency at the time of the consent or statement must be proved. Courts have held that persons giving statements during drug withdrawal or while suffering delirium tremens cannot have those statements used against them at trial.

WHAT IS A CRIME?

A crime is composed of two elements, the act (called the *actus rea*) and the intent. Unless the act and the intent come together at the same time, the conduct is usually not considered "criminal." Suppose a person's worst enemy darts in front of that person's car and is killed. This conduct, an accident, cannot be defined as murder. This is true even if a day before the driver would have been glad to run down this enemy or was happy about the death once it occurred.

Those crimes which require an intent and an act are usually referred to as *mala in se* (bad in themselves). Government also seeks to protect its citizens from lesser types of behavior. It enacts certain laws and provides sanctions if those laws are broken no matter what the mental attitude of the violator was. These lesser offenses are called *mala prohibita* (bad because they are prohibited). Traffic violations are the most common example of *mala prohibita*. Because some of the penalties for *mala prohibita* offenses are stiff and because custodial arrests can be made, these offenses are treated as crimes. The right to counsel has been extended for the most serious of these offenses. Recent decisions allowing a full search of the individual in connection with a traffic offense[1] and the upholding of an inventory conducted of an auto towed for illegal parking[2] point out the wisdom of no longer making the pure crime distinction.

Prior to these decisions, conduct labeled as criminal by legislatures was given varying treatment by courts in relation to the officer's search powers. These artificial distinctions were created more as public relations efforts. The Supreme Court, by saying a crime is a crime, brought common sense to the area. If a person is arrested for a crime (whether murder, driving while intoxicated, or running a stop light) that person is subject to a full field search. Some states, faced with this logic, decriminalized certain traffic offenses. Other states, through their courts, returned to the old distinctions by interpreting their own constitutions as requiring a different and more liberal standard.

185

LIMITING THE POWER OF THE STATE

It would be easy for society to get carried away with its self-protective mechanism. Built-in safeguards restrict runaway activity by the state. There are jurisdictional, seasonal, interpretational, and constitutional safeguards.

JURISDICTIONAL SAFEGUARDS

Before a conviction can be upheld, it must be proved that a court has the power to enforce the pertinent laws. This power is called "jurisdiction." Jurisdiction is concerned with three elements: the subject matter, the individual, and the territory. These are considered separately.

Subject Matter   As to the subject matter, it must be shown that the purported conduct actually offended the laws. If the conduct is not specifically prohibited, the state is without power to act. This is no major problem for states that have rejected the common law. They say that unless the prohibited behavior is actually spelled out by statute, there is no violation. If it cannot be found in black and white it is not a crime.

However, some states still have a common-law base. In these states there may be two levels of prohibited conduct. There are statutes as in the other states. Yet these states still recognize the unwritten offenses which were decreed by common-law courts to exist, despite the absence of a statute. Although this may seem unfair, it is not, as long as the organic source of rights (the Constitution) permits it. In that case each individual is on notice of the existence of such crimes, despite the absence of specific statutes prohibiting them.

Wisconsin was one of the first states to do away with the hidden, unwritten, or common-law crimes. Following their lead, the Model Penal Code of the American Law Institute was proposed and has been adopted by a number of states.

Either the statute or common law must have been in effect at the time of the purported crime. It is unconstitutional to pass a law to prosecute a person for past conduct. There can be no ex post facto laws.

For an act to be defined as a crime, not only must the state law be offended in the broad sense, but the court before which the defendant is taken must have subject-matter jurisdiction. This is illustrated by the fact that the federal district courts have no power to grant divorces. Even if a husband and wife were to consent to a federal judge granting a divorce, it would not be valid.

Some courts are given jurisdiction only over misdemeanors. These are referred to as courts of limited jurisdiction. Other courts are given power over all offenses. These are courts of general jurisdiction. Any judgment rendered by a court on a matter not a part of its subject-matter jurisdiction is null.

Jurisdiction of the Individual   The second area the courts control is that of the individual, called personal jurisdiction. Jurisdiction is obtained when the charging process (indictment, information, or affidavit of complaint) has been properly issued and served. The defendant does not have to be present, however. There are innumerable instances when the state can try the defendant *in absentia*. If the defendant absents himself by escape from the territory this does not mean the state has lost a trial right. Although defendants have a right to be tried in person, this right, like others, may be waived.

This may seem a bit rough, but any injustice can be corrected later. The general rule is that the court, for jurisdictional purposes, does not care how that jurisdiction was established. If it was illegally obtained, then either the evidence procured can be declared inadmissible or those who arrested the defendant can be charged with criminal or civil misconduct or both. Nonetheless, personal jurisdiction has been established.[3]

Territorial Jurisdiction   The third aspect of jurisdiction involves the place where the crime occurred. At one time the whole offense had to take place within the court's territorial limit. Given free mobility from one state to another, a crime often begins in one state and is consummated in another. This fact has caused legislative reaction.

The general rule is that if any element of a crime is committed within the boundaries of a state, that state has jurisdiction to try the offender. The other state or states involved also have that right if they have a similar law.

"Venue" is a confusing term because it is both jurisdictional and procedural in nature. The state has to prove the venue to show they are in the right court in the state. If they fail to prove this, they have no jurisdiction. Venue is procedural in that the defendant is given the right to be tried at the place where the crime occurred. This keeps the state from holding the trial at strange places and at inconveniently long distances. Defendants can ask for a change of venue if they feel they cannot get a fair trial where the crime was committed. If the change is granted, the venue procedural right is waived, preventing the defendant from a further change of mind. The new venue is selected by the court.

187

SEASONAL SAFEGUARDS: TIME LIMITS

There are certain seasonal requirements that have to be met before a conviction can be upheld. These requirements include satisfying the statute of limitations and the right to a speedy trial.

The statute of limitations is the legislatively prescribed time limit within which the state must begin its prosecution. If it fails to do so within the prescribed time, the trial is void. Ascertaining the prescribed time is not a simple matter. Two questions are inherent: When does the statute begin to run? What conduct extends the time limit of the statute?

The statute of limitations begins to run from the date of the crime. Unless the prosecution is begun within the statutorily specified time limit following that date, the prosecution is void. There are two exceptions. If the crime was begun beyond the time for prosecution but continues over a period of time, the prosecution would be valid. Crimes such as child desertion, neglect, conspiracy, unlawful possession of firearms, selling alcoholic beverages without a license, concealment of assets, fraudulent schemes, and various other crimes have been found to be continuing offenses throughout the United States. The crux of continuing offenses is the interrelationship between each offense which can be said to make one series of events one crime. For example, the crime of concealing stolen goods continues as long as the goods are knowingly in the defendant's possession. Therefore the last date on which they were held can be used as well as the date they were first concealed.

The second exception involves attempts by the defendant to "toll the statute" by becoming a fugitive until the statute of limitations has been reached. To be a fugitive the defendant must intend to avoid prosecution by his absence. When a defendant hides from the police he or she is a fugitive, whether or not the defendant leaves the boundaries of his or her home state.

Akin to this exception is the rule followed in most states that the statute is tolled while the defendant is absent from the state. One federal court found that sporadic and intermittent trips outside the state were not enough and that those days spent outside the jurisdiction could not be added to the toll calculation.[4] Practicality is the byword. In a Pennsylvania case, a student worked in another state each summer but at all other times lived in Pennsylvania. The court said the summer absences could not be assumed as intention to conceal his whereabouts or to avoid arrest.[5] Both state and federal courts have held that time spent in a penitentiary of another jurisdiction will toll the running of the statute.[6]

There is one final complication to consider. Suppose an indictment is made on a felony charge within the correct time limit, but the defendant is found guilty on a lesser included offense for which the statute of limitations has run out. Can that verdict of guilty stand or should the defendant be discharged? The general rule is that one cannot be convicted of a lesser offense upon prosecution for a greater crime commenced after the statute has run out on the lesser offense.[7]

In addition to the timeliness of the prosecution, the defendant is entitled to a speedy trial. Justice delayed is justice denied. To meet the problem of delay, several states as well as the federal courts have responded with speedy-trial provisions and rules implementing these. The major policy statement concerning speedy trial was published by the American Bar Association (ABA) in its project for minimum standards for criminal justice.[8]

These standards require that priority be given in the scheduling of criminal cases. Prosecutors have to make regular reports. Continuances are to be granted with the public interest in mind. There are a host of other rules. All speedy-trial rules begin "clocking" after the defendant has been formally charged.

There is another speedy-trial problem. Suppose the prosecutor has all the information he needs to charge the defendant within one week of the crime's completion. However, he waits until the last week of the statute of limitations to bring the formal charge (indictment or information). Can the defendant successfully charge denial of speedy trial? This was the question in *U.S.* v. *Marion.* Justice White, speaking for the Court, said:

> There is thus no need to press the Sixth Amendment into service to guard against the mere possibility that pre-accusation delays will prejudice the defense in a criminal case since statutes of limitation already perform that function.[9]

However, the Court left the door open when it spoke of the possibility of the case where actual delay caused real prejudice. Thus if it were proven that the prosecutor acted in bad faith (for example, in the hope that a defense witness would die), then the Court might view the charging delay as a denial of a speedy trial. Proof of such conduct would be almost impossible, however.

INTERPRETATIONAL SAFEGUARDS

Though space does not permit a full exploration of all rules of statutory construction and presumption, the guiding principle of such rules is of utmost importance. The general rule is that all statutes dealing with criminal law must be strictly construed against the state and liberally in favor of the defendant.

189

This is the court's way of balancing the power. The strict-construction rule applies to procedural rules as well. If the state is trying to introduce evidence based upon a search warrant and the warrant and affidavit have inconsistent dates (as where the warrant predates the affidavit), the court will strictly construe the date requirement against the state and find it to be a blank date, thus voiding the warrant. The evidence gathered, unless admissible on another basis, would be suppressed.

If a statute is vague and ambiguous as to what conduct is prohibited, the statute would be declared unconstitutional because of the "void-for-vagueness" doctrine. This was the fate of many vagrancy laws.

One of the more perplexing problems is that of constitutional interpretation. The United State Supreme Court is the final arbiter of the meaning of the U.S. Constitution. When the Supreme Court sets parameters for a constitutional limitation the state courts cannot interpret the Constitution more liberally in favor of the defendant or more restrictively against the state. However, the state can interpret its own constitution more liberally in favor of the defendant.

The states cannot interpret their own constitutions more severely against the defendant. The U.S. Constitution thus becomes the limiting device setting the boundaries of state conduct.

One of the great interpretational tools is the presumption of innocence. Unlike many civil-law nations, the U.S. system presumes every person innocent until proved guilty. This presumption is a result of interpreting the Fifth Amendment's proscription against self-incrimination.

CONSTITUTIONAL SAFEGUARDS

The heart of individual rights comes from the Fourth, Fifth, Sixth, and Eighth Amendments to the United States Constitution as applied to the states through the due-process clause of the Fourteenth Amendment. The remainder of this chapter will be devoted to these rights.

Fourth Amendment

Through the Fourth Amendment, the individual has the right not to have illegally seized evidence used against him. If a warrant was issued, it must not be like the hated general warrant in use in colonial days. The general warrant was based on suspicion and usually failed to describe the place to be searched or the things to be seized. It was quite official looking and resistance to it meant jail or worse.

190

An unreasonable search and seizure, whether with or without a warrant, is one based on suspicion and not on probable cause. Whether probable cause existed at the time of the search is the question. How the search turned out is not relevant.

What is probable cause? There is a standard definition; probable cause exists where the facts and circumstances within the officer's knowledge and of which he has reasonably trustworthy information are sufficient in themselves to warrant a belief by a person of reasonable caution that a crime is being committed or has been committed. This is a practical, nontechnical definition affording the best compromise that has been found between rash police action and individual rights.

The amount of evidence needed for probable cause could be characterized numerically as something more than 50 percent in favor of believing criminal conduct occurred or is occurring. It is less evidence than is required for conviction. Conviction requires proof "beyond and to the exclusion of every reasonable doubt." Therefore it is possible for probable cause to exist where there is not enough evidence to convict.

Fifth Amendment

The Fifth Amendment has four divisions dealing specifically with criminal procedure. The first division concerns the requirement that no one should be tried for a capital offense or other infamous crime without the action of a grand jury.

Grand Jury   At the time this amendment was proposed, a criminal action could be started by the single affidavit of an individual citizen, no matter how serious the charge. The intent of the Fifth Amendment was to require the information used to commence a criminal proceeding to be tested by a group of citizens intelligently weighing the probabilities. It was felt that capricious action could be avoided in this way.

There appears to be no satisfactory definition of the phrase "other infamous crime." In some states all charges except misdemeanors must be brought by the grand jury. The majority of the states require only capital cases to follow the grand-jury process, allowing other felonies to be begun by information (a charging process issued by the chief prosecutor of the jurisdiction).

Double Jeopardy   The second division of the Fifth Amendment is concerned with the problem of double jeopardy. A person cannot be tried by the same sovereign twice for the same offense.[10] There are a multitude of exceptions to this rule, however. If a defendant appeals his case to a higher court and wins, the jeopardy of the first trial is erased and he can be tried again.[11]

191

However, if two sovereign laws have been offended by the same act, each can try the offender. In actual practice, this is not often done if the state first trying the offender successfully convicts him or her. When a federally insured bank is robbed, both state and federal laws have been broken. It has been the practice for the federal government to decline prosecution when the state takes first jurisdiction. This is based on a directive to U.S. attorneys by the U.S. Attorney General's Office which came out during the Eisenhower administration. However, that directive is not mandatory; dual prosecutions sometimes happen.[12]

Once a sovereign has exercised its power, it cannot retry the defendant if he or she does not appeal the decision. In the *Waller* case the city had convicted the defendant of property destruction.[13] Then the state attempted to prosecute Waller for the very same act, as a violation of state law. The Supreme Court held that the state had already used its sovereignty. Cities are creatures of the legislature and therefore have no independent sovereignty. A city's power to enact ordinances comes from the state's power and not from the people governed.

The more difficult question arises when several offenses occur in one criminal transaction. Suppose a larceny takes place during a burglary. Can the state try the defendant for the burglary if proof of the larceny is used to prove the intent for the breaking and entering and then try the defendant for the larceny as an independent crime? To prove burglary the state must show breaking and entering with the intent to commit a crime therein. Suppose the defendant is acquitted because he entered without breaking. Can he be tried for the larceny alone? Yes. But if the burglary acquittal came as a result of the failure to prove the larceny as the intent, he may be tried on the larceny. The crimes of larceny and burglary do not merge.

However, if the major crime was robbery, which is larceny by force or threat of force, there is only one possible crime. The larceny would not be offered as merely proof of intent but as the intent itself—taking and carrying away of the property.

The more perplexing problem is that of lesser and greater included offenses. Suppose a defendant is indicted for murder and convicted of the lesser included offense of manslaughter. Assume further that the verdict is appealed and the defendant wins a reversal. Can the state retry the defendant on the murder, the greater included offense, or are they limited to a retrial of the manslaughter? The U.S. Supreme Court faced this issue in *Price* v. *Georgia*. The court said: "To be charged and to be subjected to a second trial for first-degree murder is an ordeal not to be viewed lightly."[14] They rejected the Georgia argument and held that an acquittal of a greater included offense precluded a retrial on that greater offense.

Consider an even more complex problem. Almost all states have the year-and-a-day rule. Basically the rule means that if a person dies of injuries sustained in an assault within a year and a day from the date of the assault, the perpetrator can be convicted of murder if the felonious intent can be established. Assume that Jones is injured in an assault in January. His family convinces him to press assault charges while in the hospital. The charges are tried before a lower court of limited jurisdiction. Suppose, too, that the defendant is acquitted in a February trial. Jones dies in March as a direct result of the injuries inflicted. The prosecutor obtains an indictment for murder. Since assault is the lesser included offense of murder, can this second trial stand constitutional muster?

Because a court has resolved the issue of assault (one of the major elements of murder) the second trial would be double jeopardy. Would the result be the same had the first court convicted the defendant?

At the time of the first trial the murder had not been completed. Would this make a difference? Would the fact that at a second trial the court could find the defendant guilty of the same assault as a lesser included offense have an effect on the answer? Yes. This is exactly what happened in *Diaz* v. *U.S.*[15] The court upheld the second trial on the murder charge.

In *Ashe* v. *Swensen* the U.S. Supreme Court has added a new twist to the double-jeopardy problem. This involves the use of *collateral estoppel* (an issue of fact has been determined by a valid and final judgment and cannot be litigated again). In the case before the Court, a defendant was charged with robbing six poker players. He was tried on robbery of one of the six victims and was acquitted. He was then tried on a second robbery charge of another victim and was found guilty. The defendant claimed double jeopardy and the Court agreed. Saying that *collateral estoppel* applied, the Court held that a name change of victim had no bearing on the issue of whether the defendant was one of the robbers.[16]

Can a person who is retried be constitutionally given a more severe sentence at the conclusion of the second trial? This was answered in *North Carolina* v. *Pearce*.[17] There is no absolute bar to a more severe sentence upon reconviction. However, there is always a due-process question. Vindictiveness must play no part in the new sentence. The judge must show valid reasons for imposing the tougher sentence.

On the subject of vindictiveness, consider the case of *Blackledge* v. *Perry*. The defendant had been convicted of a misdemeanor and chose to seek an appeal by *trial de novo*. At the time he did this, the prosecutor obtained a felony indictment based upon the same incident. Claiming double jeopardy, the defendant appealed. The Court felt that the opportunities for vindictiveness were great. They held that it was not constitutionally permissible for the state to bring a more serious charge against him at the *trial de novo*.[18]

Incriminating Statements   The next division of the Fifth Amendment requires that a citizen should not be compelled in any criminal case to be a witness against himself. To be a witness is to give testimony or testimonial evidence. However, a defendant can be made to give a voice exemplar so that a witness may identify the voice. A defendant, after lawful arrest, can be compelled to give fingerprints, handwriting exemplars, and even blood samples as long as humane conditions are observed and due process followed.

The crux of this division is that incriminating statements cannot be compelled. Thus they are a waivable right. The waiver will be good as long as it was freely, intelligently, and voluntarily given without force, threat of force, or promise of reward. That one's will can be overborne does not require much exposition. That intelligently waived rights require knowledge of the rights (and thus require pre-warning) is the subject of *Miranda*.[19]

Courts uniformly have been holding that any person can waive a right as long as he or she has reasonable intelligence and is not suffering from drug withdrawal, delirium tremens, or the like. Lack of normal intelligence, particularly an I.Q. under 60, can destroy a waiver, but lack of education cannot. Youth, as a single factor, is not sufficient to destroy a waiver. The circumstances of each case must be taken into account.

Courts are practical despite criticisms to the contrary. Defendants can voluntarily incriminate themselves through spontaneous statements before the warnings can be given. Officers are allowed two or three preliminary questions at the scene of the crime before they give the warnings. An officer is not expected to encounter a murder scene where the defendant holds the bloody knife and not ask the obvious question: "Did you do this?"

"I stand on my Fifth Amendment rights" became a dirty phrase during the McCarthy and Kefauver days. People were angered that obviously guilty individuals were hiding behind the Constitution. The angry people may have disregarded the fundamental reason for the right to remain silent. The state has the burden of proving guilt and of doing it without the defendant's help. If the defendant wants to help the state, fine; if not, they cannot compel him or her to help them.

Due-Process Provision   The final provision of the Fifth Amendment dealing with criminal procedure is the due-process provision. The framers of the amendment chose a very nebulous phrase that defies exact definition. Due process means fair play if it means anything at all, but fair play does not mean perfect play. The defendant is entitled to a fair trial, not a perfectly error-free trial. Therefore, harmless error, error that did not materially shape the outcome of the trial, is permitted.

Due process requires notice, a right to be heard, and a right to challenge those making the accusation. When due process is applied to the states it means the defendant is entitled to the protection of the Bill of Rights of the U.S. Constitution. Though some disparities exist between the treatment of a defendant in a federal court and in a state court, the real meaning of due process is a rough sense of uniformity in treatment from state to state and between the state and federal courts. Absolute uniformity is not required.

Sixth Amendment

The Sixth Amendment sets the guidelines for trials. Already discussed is the right to a speedy trial. The defendant is also entitled to a public trial. There can be no secret trials and no secret verdicts. Is this always true? Under what circumstances can a trial court close the proceedings?

Closed Courtroom   Except in notorious cases, few people bother to go to a courtroom and watch a trial. It is the notorious case that causes the problem. Reporters, thrill seekers, and even lawyers show up. A carnival atmosphere abounds. This very notoriety places the court in the position of having to lock the jury up even when the defendant is free to come and go on bail.

Battle lines have been drawn along the fair-trial–free-press border rather than on the public-trial–secret-trial border. Television has been banned from the courtroom. The U.S. Supreme Court listed four major reasons for denying coverage: impact on the jury, the witnesses, the judge, and the defendant.[20] Therefore a trial is public in a firsthand sense only for those who can get to the courthouse. The rest of the public will have to get their information secondhand.

ABA standards relating to the function of the trial judge deal with the misconduct of spectators and others. The language is fairly strong.

> The right of the defendant to a public trial does not
> give particular members of the general public or of the
> news media a right to enter the courtroom or to remain
> there. Any person who engages in conduct which disturbs
> the orderly process of the trial may be admonished or
> excluded and, if his conduct is intentional, may be pun-
> ished for contempt. Any person whose conduct tends to
> menace a defendant, an attorney, a witness, a juror, a court

officer, or the judge in a criminal proceeding may be removed from the courtroom.

The official comment to this section makes it clear that a public trial is not "infringed by excluding unruly persons."[21] The court is reminded that the unruliness may be due to a lack of knowledge by the public as to how to behave. Therefore, the court is not to jump to any conclusions but is urged first to gently correct unruly persons.

Pretrial Publicity   A recent public-trial problem has arisen involving attempts by courts to keep the pretrial publicity to a minimum. Court orders requiring nondisclosure of known information have been called "gag orders." The Supreme Court met this issue head-on in *Nebraska Press Association* v. *Stuart*.[22]

Gag orders, in themselves, were not prohibited. However, the Court required that there be more than mere speculation that pretrial publicity would have an impact on prospective jurors. There was no proof in *Nebraska Press Association* v. *Stuart* that normal measures such as continuances, sequestration of the jury, or change of venue would have failed in providing the defendant a fair public trial.

An Impartial Jury   The publicity problem cuts into the next section of the Sixth Amendment, which is to assure the defendant an impartial jury. How impartial is impartial? Is there anything such as an impartial jury? Where can an absolutely unbiased mind be found? In reality it would be better to acknowledge that all people come to the jury with preconceived ideas and biases. The best that can be expected is a jury that honestly acknowledges these biases and has the integrity to put these aside for the period of the trial.

Attorneys do not want impartial juries. What they really seek are partial jurors leaning their way. No secret is being revealed here; it is a fact of life. They know that this will not be allowed by the opposition, so they seek the best jury they can, under the circumstances.

For this reason the jury system has been heavily criticized. The critics, most of whom have not served as jurors, do not realize that jurors, for the most part, take their burden seriously. They realize the power that is theirs and generally are careful in its exercise. This the Constitution demands; this is an impartial jury.

The primary purpose of the jury is to prevent the possibility of oppression by the government. The defendant can waive his right to a trial by jury, but can the defendant insist upon having the case tried to the jury alone? This was the issue in *Singer* v. *U.S.*[23] The Court skipped the issue and said that the defendant's reason, to save time, was not enough. They indicated there could be a case where passion, prejudice, or some other factor might cause them to reconsider.

It had long been thought that an impartial jury required a unanimous verdict. In *Apodaca* v. *Oregon*,[24] however, the Court said:

> We perceive no difference between juries required to act unanimously and those permitted to convict by votes of ten to two or eleven to one. Requiring unanimity would obviously produce hung juries in some situations where nonunanimous juries will convict or acquit. But in either case, the interest of the defendant in having the judgment of his peers interposed between himself and the officers of the state who prosecute and judge him is equally well served.[25]

Jury panels must reflect a cross-section of the community. Every distinct voice in the community does not have a right to be on every jury. All the Constitution forbids is the systematic exclusion of identifiable segments of the community from jury panels and from the juries ultimately drawn from those panels. A defendant may not challenge the makeup of the jury merely because no members of his race are on the jury. In order to change this jury, a defendant must prove that people of his race have been systematically excluded.[26]

Is there any magic in the number twelve? Can a defendant be convicted by a six-person jury? The Court has held that a twelve-person jury is not an indispensable component of the Sixth Amendment.[27]

The process of selecting jurors is based on the question-and-answer period called *voir dire*. It is during *voir dire* that the basis for accepting or challenging jurors is formed. The judge is responsible for the *voir dire* examination and must ask questions to determine the qualifications of the jurors to serve. The court can permit additional questions by the attorneys in the case.[28]

Once the jury is sworn, the judge must take appropriate steps to ensure that the jurors will not be exposed to sources of information or opinion or be subject to influences which might tend to affect their ability to render an impartial verdict on the evidence.[29] The judge has to indoctrinate, admonish, and even sequester them to ensure impartiality. If this security is not maintained, the verdict can be impeached.[30]

How the defendant appears to the jury is very important. Defense counsel have known this for years. Every effort is usually made to straighten out a defendant before trial. The state cannot require the defendant to appear at trial in prison clothes, but the defendant has to object to such attire in time for other clothes to be provided before the trial starts.[31]

The more difficult problem is what to do with the disruptive defendant. Recently defendants have been heard screaming obscenities in court, attacking witnesses, and generally acting with disrespect. What can the court do? The ABA standards deal with the problem in this manner:

> 5.3(b) The trial judge should not permit a defendant or witness to be subjected to physical restraint unless the judge has found such restraint to be reasonably necessary to maintain order or provide for the safety of persons. If the judge orders such restraint,
>
> (i) he should enter into the record the reasons therefor, and
>
> (ii) he should instruct the jurors that such restraint is not to be considered in weighing evidence or determining the issue of guilt.[32]

The Right to Be Informed of Charges   The venue matter of the Sixth Amendment has already been discussed. The next section deals with the right to be informed of the nature and cause of the accusation. Little could be more unfair than being tried and not knowing why. Indictments and other charging instruments must specify the crime charged. They will be strictly construed against the state. The indictment must do more than simply repeat the language of the statute offended.[33]

The defendant is entitled to be confronted with witnesses against him. The defendant has the right to a full cross-examination of witnesses against him. Cross-examination is the main way of testing believability. The ABA standards set out the legitimate limits of cross-examination.[34] Undue harassment, repetition, and irrelevant matters are to be avoided. A court cannot, however, issue protective orders to prevent inquiry into past conduct, not even a prior juvenile record.[35]

Whether a prior statement made by a witness can be used if the witness is not physically present depends on whether there was an opportunity to cross-examine the witness at the time the pretrial statement was made. If the statement bears that indication of reliability, the statement can be admitted even if the witness is not present. This was the situation in *Mancusi* v. *Stubbs,* where the prior statement was made at an earlier trial upon full cross-examination.[36] In *Pointer* v. *Texas* the prior statement was made at a preliminary hearing when the defendant did not have a lawyer and did not fully cross-examine the witness.[37]

When codefendants are tried together and the confession of one implicates the other, several problems can arise. *Bruton* v. *U.S.* found that if the codefendant whose confession is admitted refuses to take the stand, the other codefendant has been denied the right to confrontation.[38]

198

The defendant can invoke the government's power to compel the attendance of witnesses on his behalf. When a person is accused of a crime there are not always a lot of people willing to speak on his behalf. Some people do not like to get involved. For any number of reasons the defendant might have a hard time getting his witnesses to the trial.

The Right to Counsel   The final right of the Sixth Amendment is the right to counsel. That this is a fundamental right was established in *Gideon* v. *Wainwright*.[39] The Court then and there required appointed counsel for those who could not afford hired counsel of their own.

However, *Gideon* was a felony case. Would counsel be required on lesser charges? In *Argesinger* v. *Hamlin* the U.S. Supreme Court struck a Florida rule allowing counsel in only those cases where the punishment could exceed six-months imprisonment.[40] The Court held that without a knowing and intelligent waiver, no person may be imprisoned for any offense, whether classified as petty, misdemeanor, or felony, unless he was represented by counsel at his trial.

If there is a right to counsel, is there also a right to represent oneself? The problem of *pro se* representation was raised in *Faretta* v. *California*.[41] The Court upheld the right despite the fact that the defendant forgoes the benefits derived from having a lawyer. The Court said the defendant should be aware of the dangers. Once it is recorded that the defendant knows what he or she is doing, the trial court can accept the waiver.

Does the right to counsel give one the right to a good lawyer? About the most that can be said is that the defendant can have competent counsel. Definite standards of conduct have come more from the bar than from the bench. In looking at case law one sees broad generalizations such as that counsel should not make a mockery of justice. Between the lines, however, one gets the impression that more could have been done. The ABA *Standards, Defense Function* (1971) is a legitimate guide for defense counsel and spells out counsel's responsibilities.

The right to counsel attaches at the precharging stages whenever the right to remain silent comes into play but is not pertinent to lineups or fingerprinting. The right to counsel applies to all stages once the charge is formally set and until sentence is imposed. This last part is significant. If a defendant was put on probation with sentencing reserved, the right to counsel stays with him at a probation-revocation hearing where a sentence will be passed.[42] But, if the defendant received a sentence and was then put on probation, the defendant does not have a right to counsel at a probation-revocation hearing.[43]

About the time that everyone thought they understood right to counsel, the Supreme Court of the United States dropped a minor bombshell. A defendant had been arrested in county A for the murder of a child. He there obtained counsel. The defendant was then to be transported to county B, where the crime took place and where he would meet with his other lawyer. The lawyer in county A told the defendant not to say anything to the police and cautioned the police that they were not to ask any questions of the defendant.

On the trip from county A to county B the following events took place as excerpted from the opinion in *Brewer* v. *Williams.*

> "We both know that you're being represented here by Mr. Kelly and you're being represented by Mr. McKnight in Des Moines, and . . . I want you to remember this because we'll be visiting between here and Des Moines." Williams then conferred again with Kelly alone, and after this conference Kelly reiterated to Detective Leaming that Williams was not to be questioned about the disappearance of Pamela Powers until after he had consulted with McKnight back in Des Moines. When Leaming expressed some reservations, Kelly firmly stated that the agreement with McKnight was to be carried out—that there was to be no interrogation of Williams during the automobile journey to Des Moines. Kelly was denied permission to ride in the police car back to Des Moines with Williams and the two officers.
>
> The two detectives, with Williams in their charge, then set out on the 160-mile drive. At no time during the trip did Williams express a willingness to be interrogated in the absence of an attorney. Instead, he stated several times that "[w]hen I get to Des Moines, and see Mr. McKnight, I am going to tell you the whole story." Detective Leaming knew that Williams was a former mental patient, and knew also that he was deeply religious.
>
> The detective and his prisoner soon embarked on a wide-ranging conversation covering a variety of topics, including the subject of religion. Then, not long after leaving Davenport and reaching the interstate highway, Detective Leaming delivered what has been referred to in the briefs and oral arguments as the "Christian burial speech." Addressing Williams as "Reverend," the detective said: "I want to give you something to think about while we're traveling down the road. . . . Number one, I want you to observe the weather conditions, it's raining, it's sleeting, it's freezing, driving is very treacherous, visibility is poor, it's going to be dark early this evening. They are predicting

200

several inches of snow for tonight, and I feel that you yourself are the only person that knows where this little girl's
body is, that you yourself have only been there once, and if
you get a snow on top of it you yourself may be unable to
find it. And, since we will be going right past the area on
the way into Des Moines, I feel that we could stop and locate the body, that the parents of this little girl should be
entitled to a Christian burial for the little girl who was
snatched away from them on Christmas Eve and murdered.
And I feel we should stop and locate it on the way in rather
than waiting until morning and trying to come back out
after a snow storm and possibly not being able to find it at
all."

Williams asked Detective Leaming why he thought
their route to Des Moines would be taking them past the
girl's body, and Leaming responded that he knew the body
was in the area of Mitchellville—a town they would be
passing on the way to Des Moines. Leaming then stated: "I
do not want you to answer me. I don't want to discuss it
further. Just think about it as we're riding down the road."

As the car approached Grinnell, a town approximately
100 miles west of Davenport, Williams asked whether the
police had found the victim's shoes. When Detective Leaming replied that he was unsure, Williams directed the
officers to a service station where he said he had left the
shoes; a search for them proved unsuccessful. As they continued toward Des Moines, Williams asked whether the
police had found the blanket, and directed the officers to a
rest area where he said he had disposed of the blanket.
Nothing was found. The car continued toward Des Moines,
and as it approached Mitchellville, Williams said that he
would show the officers where the body was. He then directed the police to the body of Pamela Powers.

The defendant was convicted and appealed his conviction. The
U.S. Supreme Court said:

We conclude, finally, that the Court of Appeals was correct in holding that, judged by these standards, the record in this case falls far short of sustaining the state's
burden. It is true that Williams had been informed of and
appeared to understand his right to counsel. But waiver requires not merely comprehension but relinquishment, and
Williams' consistent reliance upon the advice of counsel in
dealing with the authorities refutes any suggestion that he

waived that right. He consulted McKnight by long-distance telephone before turning himself in. He spoke with McKnight by telephone again shortly after being booked. After he was arraigned, Williams sought out and obtained legal advice from Kelly. Williams again consulted with Kelly after Detective Leaming and his fellow officer arrived in Davenport. Throughout, Williams was advised not to make any statements before seeing McKnight in Des Moines, and was assured that the police had agreed not to question him. His statements while in the car that he would tell the whole story *after* seeing McKnight in Des Moines were the clearest expressions by Williams himself that he desired the presence of an attorney before any interrogation took place. But even before making these statements, Williams had effectively asserted his right to counsel by having secured attorneys at both ends of the automobile trip, both of whom, acting as his agents, had made clear to the police that no interrogation was to occur during the journey. Williams knew of that agreement and, particularly in view of his consistent reliance on counsel, there is no basis for concluding that he disavowed it.

Despite Williams' express and implicit assertions of his right to counsel, Detective Leaming proceeded to elicit incriminating statements from Williams. Leaming did not preface this effort by telling Williams that he had a right to the presence of a lawyer, and made no effort at all to ascertain whether Williams wished to relinquish that right. The circumstances of record in this case thus provide no reasonable basis for finding that Williams waived his right to the assistance of counsel.

The Court of Appeals did not hold, nor do we, that under the circumstances of this case Williams *could not,* without notice to counsel, have waived his rights under the Sixth and Fourteenth Amendments. It only held, as do we, that he did not.[44]

Eighth Amendment

The right to freedom, inherent in this nation's ideology, is of no less importance to the individual who has been arrested than to any other citizen. In this country, a person charged with a crime is not ordinarily imprisoned until after a judgment of guilt; incarceration may even be avoided during the time between conviction and appeal, unless the appeal is frivolous. This basic right to freedom must, however, be squared with the possibility that a defendant may avoid the processes of the court. The right to bail represents the compromise between freedom and the possibility of flight.[45]

The Right to Bail   The right to bail is protected by the Eighth Amendment which prohibits the imposition of *excessive* bail. This constitutional provision does not, however, guarantee a pretrial release in all cases. For example, some state constitutions deny the right to bail where a capital offense is involved, others allow bail in such cases unless the presumption of guilt is great. Moreover, a pretrial release may be denied where the court finds that the defendant poses a grave threat to the community.

Since these limited instances do not represent the bulk of cases which confront the courts, setting bail is a typical problem for a judicial officer. One very serious problem in regard to the fundamental nature of the right to bail concerns the inability of the defendant to make any bail whatsoever. In cases involving financially crippled defendants, the court has the option of releasing an individual on his own recognizance—his promise to appear in court at the time of trial. The matter of releasing a defendant on his own recognizance, like that of setting a certain monetary value for bail, is usually left to the sound discretion of the court. The court's judgment will not be disturbed without proof of manifest error or abuse of discretion. The factors considered by a judge deciding the pretrial release issue are discussed in greater detail in the following chapter.

Cruel and Unusual Punishment; Capital Punishment   The Eighth Amendment not only prevents the imposition of excessive bail but also invalidates cruel and unusual punishments and excessive fines. Cruel and unusual punishments are not permitted. There is no way to list all such punishments. Much depends on the sophistication of the court, as well as its sensitivity and its humaneness.

The major issue of the 1970s has been and continues to be (despite a series of 1976 decisions) capital punishment. Confusion followed the plurality decision in *Furman* v. *Georgia,* which appeared to hold that great discretion as to who received the death penalty made such discretionary practice cruel and unusual.[47] States responded. Many enacted mandatory penalties for specified homicides. Others allowed some limited discretion.

In 1976 the Court announced *Gregg* v. *Georgia* and companion cases.[48] The Court held that capital punishment is not cruel and unusual per se. However, discretion (at least some) was apparently made a requirement and the mandatory sentences were held to violate the Eighth Amendment.

There are two guidelines for determining whether a punishment is cruel and unusual. First, the punishment must not involve the unnecessary and wanton infliction of pain. Second, the punishment must not be grossly out of proportion with the severity of the crime.[49]

STUDY QUESTIONS

1. What is the purpose of criminal law?
2. What are the two elements of the crime?
3. How are *mala in se* and *mala prohibita* crimes different?
4. Identify and briefly discuss three jurisdictional safeguards.
5. What is probable cause?
6. What proof is required for conviction of a criminal charge?
7. Identify and briefly discuss the heart of constitutional rights.

NOTES

1. *Gustafson* v. *Florida*, 414 U.S. 260 (1973) and *U.S.* v. *Robinson*, 414 U.S. 218 (1973).
2. *South Dakota* v. *Opperman* 428 U.S. 364, 96 S.Ct. 3092, 49 L. Ed. 2d 1000 (1976).
3. *Ker* v. *Illinois*, 119 U.S. 436 (1886) and *Frisbie* v. *Collins*, 342 U.S. 519 (1952).
4. *U.S.* v. *Gross*, 159 F. Supp. 316 (D. Nev. 1958).
5. *Commonwealth* v. *Sunneck*, 32 Pa. D.&C. 2d 257 (1963).
6. *People* v. *Sowers*, 22 Cal. Rep. 401 (Cal. App. 1962); *Taylor* v. *U.S.*, 238 F. 2d 259 (C.A.D.C. 1956); and *State* v. *Lupino*, 129 N.W. 2d 294 (Minn. 1964).
7. For a full discussion see *Annot.*, 47 ALR 2d 887 (1956).
8. ABA, *Standards Relating to Speedy Trial* (1968).
9. *U.S.* v. *Marion*, 404 U.S. 307 (1971).
10. For a discussion of the historical background see *U.S.* v. *Jenkins*, 490 F. 2d 868 (C.A. 2d 1973).
11. *Benton* v. *Maryland*, 395 U.S. 784 (1969).
12. *Bartkus* v. *Illinois*, 359 U.S. 121 (1959) and *Abbate* v. *U.S.*, 359 U.S. 187 (1959).
13. *Waller* v. *Florida*, 397 U.S. 387 (1970).
14. *Price* v. *Georgia*, 398 U.S. 323 (1970).
15. *Diaz* v. *U.S.*, 223 U.S. 442 (1912).
16. *Ashe* v. *Swenson*, 397 U.S. 436 (1970).
17. *North Carolina* v. *Pearce*, 395 U.S. 711 (1969).
18. *Blackledge* v. *Perry*, 417 U.S. 21 (1974).
19. *Miranda* v. *Arizona*, 384 U.S. 436 (1966).
20. *Estes* v. *Texas*, 381 U.S. 532 (1965).
21. ABA, *Standards, Function of the Trial Judge* 91 (1972).
22. *Nebraska Press Ass'n* v. *Stuart*, 423 U.S. 1319, 96 S.Ct. 237, 46. L. Ed. 2d 199 (1976).
23. *Singer* v. *U.S.*, 380 U.S. 24 (1965).
24. *Apodaca* v. *Oregon*, 406 U.S. 404 (1972).
25. Ibid., 404, 411.
26. *Swain* v. *Alabama*, 380 U.S. 202 (1965).
27. *Williams* v. *Florida*, 399 U.S. 78 (1970).
28. ABA, *Standards, Function of the Trial Judge* § 5.1 (1972) and ABA, *Standards, Trial by Jury* § 2.4 (1968).
29. ABA, *Standards, Function of the Trial Judge* § 5.2 (1972).
30. ABA, *Standards, Trial by Jury* § 5.7 (1968).

31. *Estelle* v. *Williams,* 19 Crim. L. Rep. 3061 (U.S. S. Ct. #74–676 May 3, 1976).
32. ABA, *Standards, Function of the Trial Judge* § 5.3(b) (1972).
33. For a full discussion of the problem see *Russell* v. *U.S.,* 369 U.S. 749 (1961).
34. ABA, *Standards, Function of the Trial Judge* §§ 5.4 and 5.5 (1972).
35 *Davis* v. *Alaska,* 415 U.S. 308 (1974).
36. *Mancusi* v. *Stubbs,* 408 U.S. 204 (1972).
37. *Pointer* v. *Texas,* 380 U.S. 400 (1965).
38. *Bruton* v. *U.S.,* 391 U.S. 123 (1968).
39. *Gideon* v. *Wainwright,* 372 U.S. 335 (1963).
40. *Argesinger* v. *Hamlin,* 407 U.S. 25 (1972).
41. *Faretta* v. *California,* 422 U.S. 806 (1975).
42. *Mempha* v. *Ray,* 389 U.S. 128 (1967).
43. *Gagnon* v. *Scarpelli,* 411 U.S. 778 (1973).
44. *Brewer* v. *Williams,* U.S. 387, 51 L. Ed. 2d 424 (1977).
45. *Bandy* v. *U.S.,* 82 S. Ct. 11, 7 L. Ed. 2d 9 (1960).
46. ABA, *Standards, Pretrial Release* §§ 5.1–5.12 (1968).
47. *Furman* v. *Georgia,* 408 U.S. 238 (1972).
48. *Gregg* v. *Georgia,* 19 Crim. L. Rep. 3250 (U.S. S. Ct. #74–6257 June 30, 1976).
49. *Id.* at 3256.

chapter eight
Moving Through the Court System

Although no two courts use identical procedures, there is enough uniformity among the different types of courts to generalize about the formal hearing stages that exist. In the United States there is an underlying fear that the wrong person will be convicted. This concern creates a need for certain pretrial processes to give reasonable assurance that state action is not arbitrary or capricious.

During some of these stages the defendant is not present. However, the court is physically present during most of these processes. For example, before a search can be made under a warrant or an arrest made by warrant, the Constitution requires a neutral and detached magistrate to examine the underlying facts and circumstances. The court is also required to judge the legitimacy and freshness of the relevant information and its source. If the court is satisfied that the defendant probably committed the crime in question, a warrant will be issued. This is the function of probable cause.

When a defendant is arrested without a warrant based upon either a warrantless search or on-the-scene activity, the defendant is taken as soon as possible before a judicial officer to determine the issue of probable cause. For many years this was called a "preliminary hearing." More modern usage labels this stage a "first appearance."

THE FIRST APPEARANCE: PRELIMINARY HEARING

Having the defendant appear before a judicial officer at this early stage in the process serves several purposes. One function, as stated above, is to ensure that all warrantless police activity was conducted with probable cause. The presiding judicial officer can, at this point, reopen the question of probable cause where the arresting officer was executing a warrant. If the judge decides that the police officer did not have sufficient reason for conducting the search or making the arrest, the defendant may, at that point, go free. If, however, probable cause is found, the judge informs the defendant of the nature of the charges brought against him and of the constitutional rights he enjoys but may wish to waive. Generally, the arresting officer has already communicated such matters to the defendant, but the repetition ensures that the defendant is fully cognizant of his situation.

At this point the court decides whether the defendant will be released until further court proceedings require his attendance or whether he shall be detained. When releasing a defendant, the court has three options, with some variations on each.

The defendant may be released on his own recognizance, that is, his promise to appear at trial. According to the American Bar Association (ABA) Standards, a defendant should have a presumption that he is entitled to a release on such a promise. If the prosecution objects on the grounds that the defendant may not appear at a later date, the court conducts an inquiry into the defendant's personal background to determine if the fear is well grounded. This investigation should include matters relating to defendant's social, familial, and employment situations, his position in the community, his reputation and length of residence, his past criminal record, and the offense charged in the case at hand. If the court decides against release on recognizance, it should include in the record the factors leading to that decision and then decide on the least onerous means of ensuring that the defendant will not flee. One such way is to release the defendant to the supervision of a parole officer or some other responsible figure in the community.

Upon finding that either of these devices would be ineffective, the court can require the defendant to pay a money bail to the court. If bail is set, the court stipulates the means of payment, ranging from the simple execution of an unsecured bond to deposit of the full amount in cash. In setting the amount to be paid, the court should consider again the personal background of the defendant and set the sum no higher than necessary.

If the judge decides that the risk of nonappearance is so great that neither release on recognizance nor money bail will ensure the defendant's return to court, or that there is a substantial possibility that the defendant will engage in further criminal conduct or will intimidate witnesses, the judge may require that the defendant remain in custody. The ABA recommends that the judge use a little imagination about when an individual is held in custody so that, if possible, the defendant may be released during working hours or may simply be restricted in his mobility.

207

A TWO-EDGED DRAMA
IN SANTA MONICA

The Victim: "If This Typifies Criminal Justice, We're in Big Trouble . . ."

Police officers, judges, and politicians frequently claim that the ultimate deterrent to crime is an involved citizenry—a public that actively helps to put criminals behind bars. Recently I became an involved citizen who attempted to do my duty, and now I doubt the effort was worth it.

One morning earlier this year, I drove my two-and-one-half-year-old daughter to her nursery school in Santa Monica. I was just maneuvering her through the school's front door when I spotted a young man about six feet tall standing astride his bicycle next to my car. As I watched, he quickly reached through the open car window, grabbed the purse I'd left on the front seat, then rode off. Since the handbag contained almost $60 and many personal papers and credit cards, I immediately turned my child over to a teacher, ran back to my car, and began to give chase, impelled by blind outrage.

The thief apparently realized his bicycle was no match for a car, because only a few blocks from the school he stopped in front of a house, jumped off the bike, and ran inside.

I wrote the address down on a slip of paper, then drove back to my daughter's school and used a phone to call the Santa Monica police. As I was telling my story to a department operator, I heard a footstep close by. Through the open doorway I could see the same young man who had stolen my purse—and, more important, *he* could see *me*. My anger turned to fear as, any moment, I expected to see him draw a knife or gun.

"Don't call the police," the man said, stepping inside the school foyer.

"It's too late. I've already called," I managed to blurt out.

The police operator, overhearing the exchange, quickly asked if I was being confronted by the thief. "Yes," I said, trying to control my terror.

"We'll have a car right there," the operator assured me.

As calmly and firmly as I could, I told my nemesis the police were on their way. Without another word, he dropped my handbag on a table and fled.

Still trembling, I waited anxiously for the officers, thinking they would arrive any moment since they knew a lone woman might be in grave danger. A full ten minutes later two patrolmen finally appeared, offering no explanation for their delay.

One officer asked if I could identify the thief and whether I'd be willing to press charges if he were apprehended.

208

I hesitated. The thief knew where my child went to school and what time in the morning I drove her there. Suppose he sought revenge, or resorted to violence to "silence" me?

When I phoned my husband for advice, we decided that, despite our personal concerns, we weren't about to let a thief get away with his crime. If he stole from me, we reasoned, what had he done, or what might he do, to others? So I told the police, yes, I'd press charges.

Eventually the suspect was found and arrested. Then the courtroom process began, and over the next six months trial dates were set and postponed, over and over again. For each trial date I was on call to appear as a witness, meaning that I had to rearrange my private life and work to suit the court calendar. Meanwhile, each trial was postponed because the suspect's lawyer needed more time, or the suspect, who was out on bail, failed to appear, and so forth.

Finally one morning, Stuart Barasch, a deputy city attorney for Santa Monica, phoned me at home to say that the trial would at last take place. Our conversation continued something like this:

"I have to tell you," he said, "that we aren't charging the suspect with theft."

"Why not?" I asked. "He stole my handbag."

"But you didn't lose any money. You got it all back."

"What does that have to do with it?"

"He returned your bag. That shows remorse."

"It shows nothing of the kind," I said, shocked. "He brought it back because of fear I was reporting him to the police."

"Even so, you didn't lose any money, so we'll have to go for a lesser charge. What he did was like someone taking a car for a joyride, then bringing it back."

"I've never heard of a grown man joyriding a handbag," I said coldly.

The deputy city attorney obviously saw justice differently from the way I did, and I began to feel I might have risked my life merely to see a court slap a criminal's wrist and send him off with a lecture. Still, I was willing to testify and asked when I should appear. He told me the date.

"I'm sorry," I replied, "but in addition to being a wife and a mother, I have a job. I already have an all-day business meeting scheduled then. It's the most important meeting of the year, so please make it another day." (I'm a clothing designer and at this companywide annual conference, all my budgets, designs, and production schedules for the next season would be decided. My absence was inconceivable.)

"We can't put it off," he said. "The trial's set."

"It's been put off for months for everyone else's convenience . . . why can't it be put off for mine? I'd be perfectly willing to appear on any other day."

"If you're unwilling to testify . . . "

"But I *am* willing to testify."

"Then it has to be then. Otherwise we'll have to let him go."

"If you do, he might go out and commit another crime, maybe more serious."

"Then it's your duty to . . . "

"I've already done my duty," I said. "I chased him. I identified him. I've had to take my child out of the school in his area because I'm afraid for her and for me. I've been on call to testify for six months."

Soon after this exchange, I hung up, and I never heard from Barasch again.

But a couple of weeks ago, my husband called the Santa Monica city attorney's office to find out what happened in the case. A secretary consulted her records, then read Barasch's note that the charges had been "dismissed due to failure of victim . . . to appear. (Victim) stated that she was unwilling to appear. . . . "

I look back on all this with disgust and disbelief. First the police were apparently in no big hurry to come to my aid. Then the court was in no hurry to bring the suspect to trial, and the prosecuting attorney was evidently willing to settle the matter with gentle chastisement on a minor charge. Firmness and urgency only came into play at the end, and these were directed against me when proceeding with the case finally suited the court schedule and the convenience of lawyers and the judge.

If this is typical of criminal justice in America, then let me say this from the victim's point of view: We are in big trouble.

By Alleen Morris

Los Angeles Times, 11 December 1977, VI-5. Reprinted by permission of the Times-Mirror Syndicate.

Due to the variety of issues decided at the initial appearance, the courts are urged to ensure that the defendant is adequately represented by counsel at this stage. In any event, counsel should be retained or appointed no later than the initial appearance.

THE CHARGING PROCESS

Assuming that the defendant was arrested without a formal charge, the next stage involves the charging process. Under the common-law system, all felonies had to be charged upon an indictment or true bill returned by the grand jury. This system still prevails in some states today, while other states use the grand jury for capital offenses only. In these latter states, other felonies are charged through a device called a "direct information" which is issued by the prosecutor's office. Regardless of which device is used, the decision to advance the state's case is the responsibility of the prosecutor, who must take the infor-

210

mation to the grand jury if it is necessary for that body to issue the formal charge.

The grand-jury proceeding, although an old and established part of the court system, is still hotly debated. In spite of the many recent developments designed to protect an individual charged with a crime, a defendant still has no right to appear before the grand jury. Nor can the defendant's lawyer take part in the proceeding. Thus the grand jury hears only one side of the problem, the prosecution's, in an *ex parte* proceeding.

This secrecy that clothes the grand jury's activity has been challenged, but as yet remains virtually unchanged. The justification for this condition is that grand juries do not determine guilt; they only determine probable cause.

In an effort to protect the defendant's interests, the ABA has issued standards requiring the prosecutor to present only admissible evidence to the grand jury. In the same vein, the prosecutor is not to make arguments or statements he could not make before a trial jury. Unfortunately, in practice the rules do not offer as much protection as the defendant might hope. In *U.S.* v. *Calandra* the court, refusing to allow a witness to invoke the exclusionary rule of the Fourth Amendment, said that the grand jury should be allowed to act "unimpeded by the evidentiary and procedural restrictions applicable to a criminal trial."[1] This simple statement directly contravenes the ABA's admonition to the prosecutor to present only evidence that would be admissible at a trial.

Even if the *Calandra* case does not completely destroy the effectiveness of the "admissible-evidence" rule, the defendant has virtually no recourse against a prosecutor's misconduct. Just because the grand jury was presented with inadmissible evidence does not mean that the defendant might have the indictment discharged. Rather, the rule is that the grand jury must have heard *only* inadmissible evidence for the indictment to be discharged.

The defendant cannot challenge the grand jury's racial or ethnic makeup. At trial, the defendant could challenge such an impropriety as a violation of his guarantees to a fair trial, but the Supreme Court has decided that the due-process requirements of the Fifth Amendment do not extend to the grand-jury hearing. Thus the states are not compelled to ensure that the grand jury represents a cross-section of the community where the defendant is being charged.

OTHER PRETRIAL PROCEEDINGS

Introduction

It is at this point that the nomenclature of all pretrial proceedings becomes confusing. In the traditional states there are two possible pretrial hearings: (1) the preliminary hearing, which merely

211

determines probable cause and sets bail but does not require a plea to the charge; and (2) the arraignment, where the defendant is asked to plead to the charge. At the arraignment, discovery motions are made and constitutional questions are raised for the record.

The new format substitutes the first appearance for the preliminary hearing and labels the plea-taking hearing a "preliminary hearing." Then a third hearing, the omnibus hearing, is held for determining whether the plea should be changed and for other matters such as constitutional issues, discovery motions, and need for a pretrial conference.

Discovery

The word "discovery" has been used in connection with the discussion of pretrial hearings. The ability to find out what evidence the other side has is what discovery is all about.

Before the twentieth century pretrial discovery was almost unheard of in civil and criminal trials. The trial was the place of discovery. Other lawyers did not know which witnesses to expect, much less what those witnesses were going to say. Trial was a guessing game.

To bring more openness to the scene and to take out some of the game-playing, discovery was created. This innovation came first to civil cases. Some states still do not allow discovery in criminal cases. Others allow only limited discovery to witness lists or to the physical evidence that will be produced at trial.

The philosophy of the ABA *Standards, Discovery and Procedure Before Trial* (sections 1.1 through 4.7 [1970]) requires that discovery be encouraged to:

1. minimize surprise
2. expedite trials
3. provide a base for better cross-examination
4. give a better basis for informed pleas and
5. meet the requirements of due process; i.e., the effective assistance of counsel.[2]

Failure to follow the discovery procedures can bring sanctions to the offending attorneys.

Some states tried to bring about discovery through a *quid pro quo* rule. In order to get discovery the defense had to let the state know whether certain defenses such as alibi or insanity were to be used. This type of discovery was challenged twice in recent years. The first test came in *Williams* v. *Florida*.[3] The Court found the Florida position very liberal in providing discovery by the defendant. They upheld the Florida provisions. The next challenge came in *Wardius* v.

212

Oregon.[4] The Court began by reminding everyone that the Florida law provided the defense reciprocal discovery against the state. The Oregon statute did not provide this. The Court held that discovery must be a two-way street and therefore struck down the less-liberal discovery scheme of Oregon.

Pretrial Conference

For many years there was no such thing as a pretrial conference in civil cases let alone in criminal ones. With the revision of the Federal Rules of Civil Procedure in the 1930s the pretrial conference was born. Its purpose is to encourage the lawyers to reach certain agreements upon some noncontested features of the case so that the trial will run more smoothly. The subject matter of a pretrial conference may cover a vast number of topics, ranging from the most ministerial, such as seating arrangements for counsel, to crucial decisions concerning the separation of codefendants, discovery, and the order of presentation of evidence. At this time, counsel can also make stipulations (or agreements) that certain facts are not disputed so that trial time will not be wasted on matters where the parties are already in accord.

Unfortunately, this useful tool is not always used. Some judges are opposed to them and even some prosecutors and defense attorneys object to them, although their reasons are not always logical.

THE TRIAL

Once the pretrial stages have been completed, the next step is the trial itself. There are three basic protections to which the defendant is entitled at the trial.

The defendant has the right to counsel, the right to an impartial jury, and the right to confront witnesses against him. Other trial rights, such as speedy trial and public trial, have been discussed already.

Right to Counsel

The basic question is: "Does the defendant have to have a lawyer?" In 1975 the U.S. Supreme Court answered the question in *Faretta* v. *California*.[5] The Court said a defendant could represent himself. He may lose the traditional benefits that go with having a lawyer but that does not prevent self-representation. The defendant can give up the right to counsel only after a full explanation of the dangers and disadvantages. The Court even went so far as to rule that the defendant cannot be forced to have an attorney.

213

If the defendant does not want to represent himself, he is entitled to an attorney. There is an entire set of ABA standards on providing defense services. At the outset the standards call for some system of assuring competent lawyers for those needing defense services. The standards give a nod of approval to either the appointive system or to an organized public-defender system. Both systems are supposed to have adequate funding and investigative services. The general result is that defender systems usually get more money for investigative services.

A constant debate rages about whether the appointment system provides the best in professional services. It is true that many established lawyers avoid such duty, thereby allowing the defense system to fall upon less-experienced trial attorneys. This is not supposed to happen, yet the realities are that, like jury duty for citizens, lawyers can get out of appointive duties.

This brings up the problem of competency of counsel. Everything in print suggests that a defendant is entitled to competent counsel. However, the courts have provided only very broad definitions of incompetency. If the lawyer did not make a mockery of the trial or make the trial a farce, the defendant is said to have had effective or competent counsel. This definition is so broad that even a tax lawyer could give competent assistance.

Right to Jury Trial

The next trial right is that of a jury trial. While the common belief is that every criminal defendant has a right to a jury trial and that the jurors must be unanimous in their decision, these rights have been restricted in some few cases. For example, if the applicable state constitution permits, a state may deny a jury trial where the defendant is charged with a petty offense, if the state also provides the defendant with a right of appeal for a new trial with a jury. Furthermore, as seen in the preceding chapter, in *Apodaca* v. *Oregon* it was decided that a defendant is no longer necessarily entitled to a unanimous verdict.[6]

Are twelve-person juries required? Certainly the ABA standards show such a preference.[7] This issue was raised in *Williams* v. *Florida*.[8] Florida law allowed six-person juries in noncapital cases. Calling the twelve-person jury a historical accident the Court said the number has no relation to the true purpose of a jury. A jury is to stand as a buffer between the state and the defendant. Thus the six-person jury was upheld.

The jury-selection process is still the battleground for an impartial jury. Minorities cannot be systematically excluded from the group from which the jury is drawn. That group, the jury panel, must reflect a cross-section of the community. But choosing the jury panel is not completed simply by ensuring that the group in fact represents the racial and ethnic makeup of the area. Prospective jurors must also be screened to determine whether they can render efficient jury service. During *voir dire,* the judge briefly outlines the nature of the case and identifies all the parties for the benefit of the jurors. Then the judge and counsel ask the jurors a myriad of questions designed to determine a juror's capacity to render effective service.

On the basis of knowledge gained through *voir dire,* counsel may ask that a prospective juror be excused. The attorneys are armed with two means of preventing a person from being seated on the jury. The first is the challenge for cause. *Voir dire* may have exposed the fact that the prospective juror did not understand the English language, that he suffered from some mental or physical infirmity, or that he had some interest in the case to be tried. For these and other reasons, counsel may request that a juror be excused; if the judge agrees, the juror is dismissed. The second method of preventing a person from becoming a juror is to use a peremptory challenge. No reason has to be given for this challenge. Normally, by statute, each side is given a certain number of peremptory challenges. The question has arisen as to whether a prosecutor who does not like a minority can use his peremptory challenges on members of that group. If so, will this destroy the impartiality that a random selection of the community ostensibly creates? These questions came up in *Swain v. Alabama.*[9] There the Court skirted the issue, saying that the defendant had not shown that the prosecutor was bent on striking blacks from the jury regardless of trial-related considerations.

In order for the defendant to be assured that the jury remains impartial after it is selected, it is essential for the court to prevent undue influence being exerted by those responsible for caring for the jury during the trial. In *Turner v. Louisiana,* the deputies kept up a close and constant association with the jurors.[10] Conversations between the jurors and deputies were unrestricted. These deputies were also key witnesses. The Court said that "it would be blinding reality not to recognize the extreme prejudice inherent in this continued association throughout the trial between the jurors and these two key witnesses for the prosecution."[11]

Right to Confrontation

The final trial right is the right to confront witnesses. A defendant cannot be tried upon hearsay or affidavits, not because they are unreliable alone but because they cannot be challenged by careful cross-examination. Cross-examination is confrontation.

Perhaps the leading case is *Davis v. Alaska.*[12] In *Davis* the star witness had a juvenile record which would certainly be used to attack the witness's credibility. The prosecutor asked for and got an order

215

protecting the witness from such attack. The Court laid out the meaning of cross-examination in this language:

> The Sixth Amendment to the Constitution guarantees the right of an accused in a criminal prosecution "to be confronted with the witnesses against him." This right is secured for defendants in state as well as federal criminal proceedings under *Pointer* v. *Texas,* 380 U.S. 400, 85 S.Ct. 1065, 13 L.Ed.2d 923 (1965). Confrontation means more than being allowed to confront the witness physically. "Our cases construing the [confrontation] clause hold that a primary interest secured by it is the right of cross-examination." *Douglas* v. *Alabama,* 380 U.S. 415, 418, 85 S.Ct. 1074, 1076, 13 L.Ed.2d 934 (1965). Professor Wigmore stated: "The main and essential purpose of confrontation is *to secure for the opponent the opportunity of cross-examination.* The opponent demands confrontation, not for the idle purpose of gazing upon the witness, or of being gazed upon by him, but for the purpose of cross-examination, which cannot be had except by the direct and personal putting of questions and obtaining immediate answers." (Emphasis in original. 5 Wigmore, Evidence § 1395, at 123 [3d ed. 1940].)
>
> Cross-examination is the principal means by which the believability of a witness and the truth of his testimony are tested. Subject always to the broad discretion of a trial judge to preclude repetitive and unduly harassing interrogation, the cross-examiner is not only permitted to delve into the witness's story to test the witness's perceptions and memory, but the cross-examiner has traditionally been allowed to impeach, i.e., discredit, the witness. One way of discrediting the witness is to introduce evidence of a prior criminal conviction of that witness. By so doing the cross-examiner intends to afford the jury a basis to infer that the witness's character is such that he would be less likely than the average trustworthy citizen to be truthful in his testimony. The introduction of evidence of a prior crime is thus a general attack on the credibility of the witness. A more particular attack on the witness's credibility is effected by means of cross-examination directed toward revealing possible biases, prejudices, or ulterior motives of the witness as they may relate directly to issues or personalities in the case at hand. The partiality of a witness is subject to exploration at trial, and is "always relevant as discrediting the witness and affecting the weight of his testimony." 3A Wigmore, Evidence § 940, at 775 (Chadbourn rev. 1970).

We have recognized that the exposure of a witness's motivation in testifying is a proper and important function of the constitutionally protected right of cross-examination. Greene v. McElroy, 360 U.S. 474, 496, 79 S.Ct. 1400, 1413, 3 L.Ed.2d 1377 (1959).

    The state's policy interest in protecting the confidentiality of a juvenile offender's record cannot require yielding of so vital a constitutional right as the effective cross-examination for bias of an adverse witness. The state could have protected Green from exposure of his juvenile adjudication in these circumstances by refraining from using him to make out its case; the state cannot, consistent with right of confrontation, require the petitioner to bear the full burden of vindicating the state's interest in the secrecy of juvenile criminal records. The judgment affirming petitioner's convictions of burglary and grand larceny is reversed and the case is remanded for further proceedings not inconsistent with this opinion.

    It is so ordered.

At one time, a defendant was convicted largely on the basis of a transcript of testimony given by another person at a preliminary hearing. The defense argued this was a denial of the right of confrontation since the witness was not present at the trial for cross-examination. The Court held in *Pointer* v. *Texas,* that the use of the transcript denied the defendant a constitutional right.[13]

    However, where the defendant had the full opportunity to cross-examine the previously recorded testimony and in fact had conducted such a cross-examination, a different rule results. In *Mancusi* v. *Stubbs* the missing witness, a Swedish citizen, was in Sweden during the second trial. The Court permitted the use of the testimony from the first trial in the second trial.[14]

Arguments by Counsel to the Jury

    In any trial both the prosecutor and the defense counsel have an opportunity to make opening and closing arguments to the jury. These arguments are often the segments of a trial that are portrayed on television. The importance of these statements is often greatly exaggerated, but they do provide a great service by encapsulating the evidence that is drawn out during the long and tedious process of the trial.

    Because the arguments give a preview of what will be disclosed during the trial and then sum up what actually happened, the respective attorneys must abide by the many restrictions imposed on their presentations. In opening statements, counsel, for both the prosecution and the defense, must confine his statements to evidence he intends to offer, evidence which he, in good faith, believes will be admissable. He may also state the basic issues of the case, but if he makes comments that will not be supported by the evidence he will be subject to disciplinary action.

Similarly, in closing, counsel may argue all reasonable inferences from the evidence disclosed at trial, but he should not express his opinion about the weight or credibility of the evidence, nor the guilt or innocence of the defendant. Nor should counsel use arguments calculated to inflame the passions or prejudices of the jurors.

This last admonition is the most difficult to regulate. Counsel, after many hours of preparation, are often deeply involved in the case and sometimes have a tendency to get carried away. More emotion is tolerated of the defense attorney. Prosecutors, however, are not supposed to get as emotional. Yet actual cases reveal more handslapping than reversals for prosecutorial misconduct. For example, in *Frazier v. Cupp* the prosecutor read a statement in opening argument that could not be put in evidence.[15] It was objected to and sustained. In *Donnelly* v. *DeChristofora,* the prosecutor expressed his personal belief in the defendant's guilt.[16] This the Court saw as a response to personal comments in the defense's statement. A second comment, suggesting that the defense had tried to plea bargain, was made. The Court found that since this statement was a quick reference in the midst of a long closing argument it was not grounds for reversal. Thus it can be concluded that the statements must incite the jury before being found prejudicial. As long as the court trying the case issues cautionary instructions to the effect that statements in counsel's argument are not evidence and to disregard erroneous statements, the trial decisions will be upheld.

There is an area of prosecutorial misconduct that cannot be tolerated. Prosecutors are not to fabricate or use fabricated evidence. This is illustrated by *Miller* v. *Pate*.[17] The prosecutor had used so-called blood-stained shorts that were really paint-stained shorts. The prosecutor knew this. The Court said that "the Fourteenth Amendment cannot tolerate a state criminal conviction obtained by the knowing use of false evidence. . . . There can be no retreat from that principle here."[18]

Any prosecutor using such evidence should be disbarred. Such conduct represents the worst possible behavior. However, can the defendant receive monetary damages from a prosecutor who uses fabricated evidence? Not according to *Imbler* v. *Pachtman*.[19] The Court held that the prosecutor had absolute immunity from civil-rights action. In this case the prosecutor apparently used both false testimony and suppressed material evidence. However, prosecutors cannot escape criminal liability for such actions.

218

The Trial of Codefendants

Dockets are overcrowded. Systems are being modified to speed the adjudication process. Efficiencies are sought. All agree that where two or more defendants are tried simultaneously for a crime committed by all of them the time of the court is more efficiently used. Yet there are inherent constitutional and practical problems in joint trials.

One of those problems came out in *Bruton* v. *U.S.*[20] Bruton's codefendant had made a confession that inculpated Bruton. This confession was read to the jury. The jury was instructed to disregard the statement involving Bruton. They were not to consider it as evidence of Bruton's guilt. The Court held such a procedure unconstitutional. They found that a jury cannot segregate evidence into separate intellectual boxes. The Court said constitutional rights cannot be sacrificed merely for efficiency.

Thus most states as well as the federal system provide for separate trials for codefendants. As was pointed out in *Schaffer* v. *U.S.*, the defendant makes the severance motion.[21] The defendant is required to prove prejudice. If prejudice occurs after the trial begins, the defendant can renew the motion, or the court, on its own motion, can order a severance and a new trial for the prejudiced codefendant.

The problem of joining offenses raises the possibility of double jeopardy if such offenses are not joined for one trial. This was the question raised in *Ashe* v. *Swenson*.[22] The defendant was charged with robbing six poker players. The first trial involved the conduct against only one poker player. The defendant was acquitted on that charge. The second trial involved the same activity against the second poker player. The defendant was convicted. Rather than call this conduct by the state double jeopardy, the Court characterized it as a collateral-estoppel problem. Since the same witnesses were used in the second trial the Court said the state was estopped (stopped) from pursuing the prosecution. The Court said collateral estoppel is part of the double-jeopardy doctrine.

Charging the Jury

The charging process of the trial occurs after all the evidence has been presented and after closing arguments by the attorneys. The charges, or jury instructions, are the rules of law that the jury must apply to the case.

The judge is responsible for charging, or instructing, the jury. Usually counsel for each side submits a list of instructions they would like to have used. The judge decides which ones he or she will use. This is a matter of record, that is, part of the official transcript. If either attorney objects to the instructions listed he or she makes it known and thus preserves the right to appeal the judge's decision. If justice requires, however, substantial defects or omissions in jury instructions may provide a basis for appeal even though no objection was made at the appropriate time.

After instructions the jury retires to deliberate and to arrive at a verdict. Their first order of business is usually the selection of a foreman. After that the jury begins considering the case.

When the jury leaves the courtroom, the court may allow them to take with them a copy of the charges against the defendant and exhibits and writings (except depositions) which have been received in evidence. In exercising this discretion, the court should consider whether such materials will assist the jury in its deliberations and weigh that fact against the risk that the material may be used improperly by the jury.

If the jurors, during their deliberations, decide that there is confusion about some testimony or evidence disclosed during trial or about the instructions received from the judge, they may request a review of the evidence or further instructions. In these rare instances, the court may grant the request, but it should take special precautions to avoid giving a one-sided view of the facts or the law. The court, on its own motion, can also recall the jury to correct any erroneous or ambiguous instructions originally given to the panel.

The most significant problem arises when the jury appears to be "hung." There is no magic point at which this determination can be made. What can the court do to move the jury to a decision?

This is where the "Allen charge" comes into play. The charge in that case was as follows:

> Although the verdict must be the verdict of each individual juror, and not a mere acquiescence in the conclusion of his fellows, yet they should examine the question submitted with candor, and with a proper regard and deference to the opinions of each other; that it was their duty to decide the case if they could conscientiously do so; that they should listen, with a disposition to be convinced, to each other's arguments; that, if much the larger number were for conviction, a dissenting juror should consider whether his doubt was a reasonable one which made no impression upon the minds of so many men, equally honest, equally intelligent with himself. If, upon the other hand, the majority were for acquittal, the minority ought to ask themselves whether they might not reasonably doubt the correctness of a judgment which was not concurred in by the majority.[23]

This charge has been criticized but has not been overruled since its acceptance by the U.S. Supreme Court in *Allen* v. *U.S.*

The dilemma comes to this: When can the judge know that the jury is hopelessly deadlocked? There is no answer. Neither is it known how many times the jury can be sent back for one more try. Perhaps no better reason can be advanced for the less-than-unanimous verdict as upheld in *Apodaca* v. *Oregon*.[24]

After the jury returns with a verdict, it is read in open court. If either attorney or the court has a feeling that the verdict does not represent each juror, a poll can be made. Each juror is asked whether the announced verdict is his or her verdict. There are only two responses allowed: yes or no. Reasons are not sought nor can they be. If there is no unanimity the judge can either send them back for further deliberations or he or she can discharge them.

After the verdict the jury is excused. Often television shows portray the judge as being very happy with the verdict or expressing great dissatisfaction. The judge is not supposed to do either. The only thing the judge should do is thank the jury for their public service.[25]

Can the verdict be impeached? Yes, if matters not in evidence were considered that would violate the defendant's constitutional right of confrontation. The answer is also yes if some other misconduct occurred, such as bribing a juror.

SENTENCING

Following a verdict of guilty comes the sentencing stage. As the introduction to the ABA standards states, the "consequences of a sentence are of the highest order."[26] A wrong sentence, either too long or too short, can have bad results for both society and the offender. The sentence must take into account the nature of the crime as well as the psychological makeup of the offender.

Because each case is unique and therefore requires experience, both the ABA and the National Advisory Commission on Criminal Justice Standards and Goals require that the judge do the sentencing. The commission says that jury sentencing (practiced in some states) is more likely to be "arbitrary and based on emotions rather than the needs of the offender or society."[27]

The general philosophy of sentencing is best summed up by the ABA.

The sentence imposed in each case should call for the minimum amount of custody or confinement which is consistent with the protection of the public, the gravity of the offense, and the rehabilitative needs of the defendant.[28]

Balancing these three criteria is something that cannot be done on the spur of the moment. The best tool yet devised for helping the court set the proper balance is the presentence report. The presentence report is the responsibility, usually, of the probation and parole officer attached to the court. The presentence report should, ideally, contain a complete description of the offense and the circumstances surrounding its commission; a thorough study of the defendant's background, including his prior criminal record, his education, employment, family relationships, and medical history; and a study of the environment to which a defendant would return if probation should be granted. With the information gathered, the court should be able to make a rational sentencing decision.

Heated debate has surrounded the advisability of the disclosure of the presentence report. Fair play would dictate that defendant and his or her counsel should see the report. With some minor exceptions this is the position taken by the ABA.[29] Sometimes information is given that is quite reliable yet to reveal its source would jeopardize the informant. Thus the court can, as long as it states its reasons, except some material from the defendant's eyes.

The defendant can challenge the report in a presentence conference. It is here that the factual basis can be attacked. The defense attorney will try to make sure that only relevant information will be used in the report.

After the presentence report conference comes the actual sentencing. There is considerable debate about whether the same judge who conducted the trial should sentence the offender. The National Advisory Commission and the ABA recommend that the trial judge do the sentencing.[30]

One of the big problems is a lack of uniformity. This problem becomes acute when inmates get together and begin comparing sentences. However, there can be no uniformity when three criteria are used. The inmates understand this to some degree. The bone of contention is that some judges do not use any criteria. Some judges always give the maximum sentence, while others give the minimum. Inmates know this and harbor a grudge—that they may have committed their crime in the wrong county or were tried by the wrong judge.

To remedy this, the ABA calls for a sentencing institute for judges.[31] This program would entail holding seminars where judges, both experienced and inexperienced, could discuss the techniques and criteria used for the imposition of sentences. Ideally, the institute would provide a forum for all persons involved in the criminal process, from the attorneys to the corrections authorities, where the exchange of ideas would develop a better understanding of the sentencing process and greater uniformity in the results. The ABA suggests also that judges regularly visit incarceration facilities and receive information on the status of those whom they have sentenced.[32]

Not all offenders deserve confinement. Some would be properly punished if they were partially confined. Some would be better off if they were released on probation. The trial judge is supposed to have enough flexibility to do some innovative things. Perhaps a man who only gets in trouble on weekends should be incarcerated for his latest spree on weekends. The rest of the week he lives at home, maintains his job, and supports his family.

Innovation is limited by the imagination of the trial judge and the cooperation of local law enforcement. It is no secret that some law-enforcement officers abhor any apparent softness in the treatment of offenders. Some reports reveal that some officers go out of their way to find a probationer in violation of his probation status.

This state of affairs is considered one of the great ironies of the legal system. The vast network of safeguards designed to protect the defendant at trial vanishes at the sentencing phase. Yet the majority of defendants plead guilty without trial and, thus, their only concern is with the sentence imposed. In those cases, the entire responsibility for the defendant is vested in the single personage of the sentencing judge. Such discretion naturally lends itself to abuse and results in irrational and excessive punishments.

Knowing that a defendant has no access to a formal sentence review, appellate judges often ferret out mere technical errors in the conduct of the trial in order to reverse a decision made unjust by too severe a sentence. This process, as well as general dissatisfaction with the inequity of an improper sentence, undermines the public respect for the court system and should be corrected. The ABA's Advisory Committee on Sentencing and Review has suggested that groups of trial judges be impaneled to hear such appeals.[33] To facilitate the review, the lower court should include in the record the factors which precipitated the decision. If the reviewing panel should decide the punishment was improper, it could modify the decision or remand the case for resentencing. The opposition to this innovation argues that the new process would annihilate the trial judge's discretion and would swamp the already overworked appellate courts. Despite these objections, the system obviously needs to be revamped to ensure the proper disposition of each and every case.

STUDY QUESTIONS

1. What is the function of the first appearance?
2. What is the function of the omnibus hearing?
3. Why is pretrial discovery essential to the orderly administration of justice?

4. If you were on trial for a crime would it bother you to be convicted by a ten-to-two vote rather than by a unanimous vote?

5. What are the elements of a pre-sentence report?

NOTES

1. *U.S.* v. *Calandra*, 414 U.S. 338 (1974).
2. ABA, *Standards, Discovery and Procedure Before Trial* sec. 1.2 (1970).
3. *Williams* v. *Florida*, 399 U.S. 78 (1970).
4. *Wardius* v. *Oregon*, 412, U.S. 470 (1973).
5. *Faretta* v. *California*, U.S. (1975).
6. *Apodaca* v. *Oregon*, 406 U.S. 404 (1972).
7. ABA, *Standards, Trial by Jury* sec.1.1 (1968).
8. *Williams* v. *Florida*, 399 U.S. 78 (1970).
9. *Swain* v. *Alabama*, 380 U.S. 202 (1965).
10. *Turner* v. *Louisiana*, 379 U.S. 466 (1965).
11. *Turner* v. *Louisiana*, 379 U.S. 473 (1965).
12. *Davis* v. *Alaska*, 415 U.S. 308 (1974).
13. *Pointer* v. *Texas*, 380 U.S. 400 (1965).
14. *Mancusi* v. *Stubbs*, 408 U.S. 204 (1972).
15. *Frazier* v. *Cupp*, 394 U.S. 731 (1969).
16. *Donnelly* v. *DeChristofora*, 416 U.S. 637 (1974).
17. *Miller* v. *Pate*, 386 U.S. 1 (1967).
18. *Miller* v. *Pate*, 386 U.S. 7 (1967).
19. *Imbler* v: *Pachtman*, U.S. (1976).
20. *Bruton* v. *U.S.*, 391 U.S. 123 (1968).
21. *Schaffer* v. *U.S.*, 362 U.S. 511 (1960).
22. *Ashe* v. *Swenson*, 397 U.S. 436 (1970).
23. *Allen* v. *U.S.*, 164 U.S. 492 (1896).
24. *Apodaca* v. *Oregon*, 406 U.S. 404 (1972).
25. ABA, *Standards, Trial by Jury* sec. 5.6 (1968).
26. ABA, *Standards, Sentencing Alternatives and Procedures* (1968).
27. National Advisory Commission on Criminal Justice Standards and Goals, *Courts*, 110 (1973).
28. ABA, *Standards, Sentencing Alternatives and Procedures* sec. 2.2 (1968).
29. ABA, *Standards, Sentencing Alternatives and Procedures* sec. 4.4 (1968).
30. Op cit note 27. and ABA, *Standards, Sentencing Alternatives and Procedures* sec. 1.1 (1968).
31. ABA, *Standards, Sentencing Alternatives and Procedures* sec. 7.2 (1968).
32. Ibid., sec. 7.4 and 7.5.
33. ABA, *Standards, Appellate Review of Sentences*, Introduction (1968).

ILLUSTRATIVE CAREERS IN THE JUDICIAL PROCESS

Seventy percent of the personnel employed in the judicial process are judges, clerks, bailiffs, and kindred workers. Almost 25 percent are prosecutors, and the balance are public defenders. Employment in the judicial process is strikingly a feature of local government where some 75 percent of all courts are situated; the federal government accounts for only 5 percent of all courts.

MANPOWER NEEDS

Courts

Employment in state and local courts is projected to increase by 54 percent in the next ten years. Rates of growth are likely to be greatest in the appellate level courts and trial courts of general jurisdiction. This reflects a trend toward the consolidation of county and municipal courts of limited jurisdiction. The overall growth in court employment is likely to be accompanied by growth in the number of support personnel such as law clerks and others. There is likely to be slower growth in judgeships than in the support personnel associated with the courts themselves.

Prosecution and Legal Services

Employment in state and local prosecutorial agencies is expected to increase by 71 percent by 1985. A more rapid growth is projected at the state level than at the local level. State prosecution agencies are expected to increase at a more rapid rate than local agencies because of the increase of civil litigation such as consumer protection and the like, which is concentrated at the state level. In the prosecutors' offices there is expected to be a more rapid growth rate among attorneys than among support personnel.

Public Defenders

Public defender agencies have the greatest growth potential for employment opportunities. It is projected that there will be a growth rate of something like 91 percent in public defender personnel over the next ten years. By 1985, it is projected that there will be approximately 10,000 full-time public defenders and another 11,000 individuals working in public defense by contract. The high turnover rate combined with continued employment growth has resulted in a rather low experience level in these agencies.

ILLUSTRATIVE CAREERS

Court Administrator

There are at least 455 court administrators in the United States. As the name implies, the court administrator serves to manage the court's calendar and caseload. A partial listing of his duties includes the following tasks:

1. Establishes and maintains effective procedures for calendar management and control for the court in both civil and criminal areas.
2. Establishes procedures for the selection, calling, management, and coordination of trial juries and grand juries.
3. Manages the space and facilities utilized for operation of the courts.
4. Prepares and administers the court budget.
5. Assists the judge in establishing and administering an adequate system for determination of indigency and assignment of counsel for indigent defendants.
6. Serves as secretariat for meeting of the judges of the court he serves.

The court administrator is an appointed official. He is usually appointed by a legislative body, such as a county commission, or by a judicial body such as a court. Court administrators are found at all levels of government, though it is in the federal court system that they are concentrated. State governments are establishing court administration offices that are state-wide in scope and reflect standards that are uniform throughout the state. Eleven percent of the court administrators work under the direction of a central court administrator. Salaries for administrators vary; in the Southeastern United States the average starting salary for a court administrator is around $18,500 a year. The position of court administrator requires a strong background in public administration. Bachelor's and Master's degrees provide the essential academic preparation for the job of court administrator.

U.S. Attorneys

Federal law places upon the Attorney General responsibility for the conduct of all litigation affecting the interests of the United States. This responsibility is carried out by delegating, to officers throughout the country, authority to handle such litigation and to appear in court as the government's advocates. These field officers are the U. S. Attorneys. U. S. Attorneys are presidential appointees and serve terms of four years. Some of the larger U. S. Attorneys' offices, such as those in New York and Los Angeles, employ more than seventy Assistant U. S. Attorneys. U. S. Attorneys must have good undergraduate and legal education. There is also a requirement for experience in trial practice. Candidates must have a minimum of five years trial experience with significant exposure to federal trial and appellate practice in the judicial district for which he or she would be a candidate. They are often hired in the first few years after law school. The starting salary for an Assistant U. S. Attorney depends upon one's level of experience. For those just beginning to practice (as attorneys with no significant experience, but who are deemed specially qualified) the starting salary is $18,300 as of the October 1977 salary schedule. Normally, assistants are eligible for their first promotion one year after their entrance. Assistant attorneys may receive an increase each year in any amount up to $3,100 until they reach a salary of $24,800, thereafter they may receive an increase each year in any amount up to $1,900 until they reach $31,000 annually.

Trial Court Judge

In examining the role and function of the trial court judge, one sees that the judge is both a jurist and an administrator. Judicial decision making is most apparent where it is done in the courtroom setting. We are all familiar with the judge in his robes who presides at trials, conducts hearings, sets bail, and imposes sentence. These acts of decision making form the public image of the judge. There is another side of judicial decision making that the public rarely sees. As there are fewer than 500 court administrators, most judges are, by necessity, administrators. As such, they have responsibility for the operation of the courts. They must manage caseload, calendar, budget, and all the administrative necessities that are part of court operations. Of the more than 31,000 judges in America, 21,600 are found in local courts of limited jurisdiction. Judges in these courts are often part-time officials who may continue in private practice or follow an altogether different occupation. There are some 5,400 judges in courts of general jurisdiction. At the federal level, these courts of general jurisdiction are referred to as Federal District Courts. At the state level, they are referred to as Superior Courts. Judges here are full-time personnel rather than part-time, as in the lower courts. In addition, there are some 800 appellate court judges in the United States. Judges for both the appellate courts and the general trial courts are usually either elected or appointed. The political element in judicial selection has been often criticized but remains still. Indeed, an old saying has it that a judge is "a lawyer who knows a politician." Even where the judicial office is elective, there is such a tradition of incumbency that, barring out-and-out scandal in the courts, the sitting judge is usually reelected.

Judges' offices are increasingly being supported by paralegal personnel, that is, those who do not have formal law degrees. Presently there are something like 4,400 paralegals who perform such functions as legal assistants. Paralegals almost invariably possess a baccalaureate degree. They work as aides to the trial court judge.

chapter nine
The Court System: Its Dilemma Today

Why are the state and federal court systems facing possible destruction? What factors got them there? What can be done to solve the problems? The balance of this chapter deals with these matters.

PUBLIC ATTITUDES ON COURTS
Expectations High, Performance-Ratings Low

Americans have extraordinarily high expectations of their courts, but they are generally disappointed with the courts' performance, according to the first national survey of public attitudes toward courts in the United States.

Although the survey shows that U.S. citizens have limited experience and relatively meager knowledge of their courts, it also reveals that they are prepared to see more of their tax dollars go toward improving the fairness and efficiency of their courts.

Funded by a grant from LEAA's National Institute of Law Enforcement and Criminal Justice to the National Center for State Courts, the survey was conducted by the nationally known firm of Yankelovich, Skelly, and White.

It was released at the dedication of the new National Center for State Courts in Williamsburg, Va. The Center is a private nonprofit organization devoted to improving the operation of the courts at state and local levels.

The survey sampled a statistically valid cross section of the American public through nearly 2,000 in-person interviews averaging over an hour each in length. In addition, special sampling was done among community leaders, lawyers, and judges to compare their views with those of the general public.

229

The Yankelovich study points to a number of "major conclusions," as follows:

- There is no profound difference in view between the general public and community leaders on the one hand, and judges and lawyers on the other hand, with respect to what the courts do and should do in our society. For example, 43 percent of the public see courts that do not decrease the amount of crime as a major problem; only 13 percent of judges and 28 percent of lawyers share this view.

- The general public and community leaders are dissatisfied with the performance of state and local courts, ranking them lower than many other major institutions, including local police, public schools, the U.S. Supreme Court, organized religion, the news media, and American business. Fewer than one out of four Americans are "very confident" about the performance of state courts.

- The general public's knowledge of and direct experience with courts is low. More than four out of ten Americans report at least some experience with courts, one-fourth of these in traffic court, 40 percent as defendants, and only 6 percent as jurors. But 30 percent of Americans incorrectly believe that a district attorney's job is to defend an accused criminal who cannot afford a lawyer, 37 percent incorrectly think a person accused of a crime must prove his innocence, and 72 percent incorrectly believe the U.S. Supreme Court can review and reverse any decision made by a state court.

- It is "a very sobering fact" that outside of judges and lawyers people having the most knowledge of and experience with courts voice the greatest dissatisfaction. Of those having most extensive knowledge, 55 percent see a significant need for reform. This is 10 percentage points higher than those with average knowledge and some 20 points higher than those with only limited knowledge.

- There is "impressive support" for reforming and improving courts, even at significant cost in tax dollars. The study sees this as a reflection of the high expectations the people have for their courts. Three out of four Americans think it would be "extremely or very useful" to spend tax dollars to get the best possible people to serve as judges. Seven out of ten are prepared to commit tax dollars to make good lawyers available to anyone who needs one.

Source: *LEAA Newsletter* 7 (April 1978): 1 and 9.

APPELLATE COURTS AND THE ROLE
OF PRECEDENT

One reason for the situation the courts are in is that the system allows people to appeal lower-court decisions. Although everyone has a right to his or her day in court, the system gives a person at least two, sometimes three, and many times seven days in court.

For example, a defendant is tried on a misdemeanor in a lower court in Massachusetts and is found guilty. He appeals. By statute he gets a *trial de novo* in the general trial court and is again convicted. He appeals to the next level and the next until his state-court remedies (and the courts) are exhausted. Until recently he could then seek relief through the federal district court by habeas corpus, alleging a violation of some constitutional right. If he were to lose there, he could appeal to the Court of Appeals. Losing there, he could petition the U.S. Supreme Court by writ of *certiorari;* even if he were turned down, someone would have to take the time to deny the writ.

The Constitution of the United States guarantees only a right to a trial.[1] No right of appeal is guaranteed there. The state constitutions, however, create constitutional appellate courts and by statute make at least one appeal a matter of right. If one defendant successfully appeals, his case is often retried and the cycle begins again.

What solutions can be offered? Some are very simple but will not be accepted. First, require that all judges of trial courts be certified educationally and psychologically before taking the bench. Then eliminate the appellate system and allow just one supervisory court to review only those criminal cases where life imprisonment or the death penalty is involved. If not that, consider assigning an appellate judge to each trial court. The appellate judge could sit in a booth observing the trial. As motions are made or objections offered the appellate judge rules after the trial judge as to whether an error has been made simply by pressing a button lighting either a green or red light. When the red light comes on the trial judge corrects himself and the trial goes on.

As Madison Avenue would say, these ideas will not "fly." All proposals for change that are "flying" do not look to the re-creation of the system but only to its modification. The more legitimate proposals for change are offered in the latter sections of this chapter.

The doctrine of precedent or *stare decisis,* also clogs the system. The importance of precedent is that it lends predictability and thus stability to the system. However, because each factual situation is unique, there are no cases exactly alike and it is therefore very difficult to apply precedents. The heart of most arguments on appeal is the similarity or difference to precedent-setting cases. This leads to a certain amount of nitpicking; the modern-day equivalent of the debate about how many angels fit on a pinhead.

Although all appellate rules prohibit frivolous appeals, the articulate and well-trained lawyer can demonstrate enough uniqueness about his or her case to avoid the frivolous label. The decision to appeal is the client's. Even when an attorney advises against appeal, if the client decides to go ahead the lawyer owes the client every reasonable, ethical argument.

The concept of precedent incorporates the idea of "bindingness." *Stare decisis* means that the inferior court must pay attention to and follow the decisions of the superior courts directly above it. This rule raises two questions. First, are there any decisions by a directly superior court on a case like this one? Second, what superior courts are directly above this court?

The first problem has been discussed. A lawyer who is apparently confronted unfavorably with a precedent will argue that that case was not really like the case before the court.

The second problem is more complex. Consider the federal system. The trial courts are the district courts. The district courts are bound by the decisions of the U.S. Supreme Court. However, they are bound also by the decisions of the court of appeals for the circuit in which the district court lies. Thus a Florida district court would be bound by a fifth-circuit decision but not by a sixth-circuit decision. The courts of appeals can be inconsistent one with the other because they are on the same level and are neither superior nor inferior to each other. The U.S. Supreme Court then becomes the vehicle for resolving these differences—but only if it wants to do so.

Similarly organized state systems face the same problem. Instead of speeding justice such systems often bog it down. Before action can be taken, each court must determine what actions were taken by which other courts and whether such actions are binding on it.

REFORM PROPOSALS

Besides general trial courts there are probate courts, traffic courts, divorce courts, and on and on. In some jurisdictions the probate judge could work three days a week while the trial judge worked six. Some judicial talent goes to waste while other judges are truly overworked. Likewise, a general trial judge in a rural area of the state could have more leisure time than the judge sitting on the urban or suburban bench. The simple solution to this condition is to assign idle judges to help busy judges. By what authority can this be done? Nowhere was it written that judges could be moved around. Nowhere was it written that a probate judge could hear a criminal case. Nowhere was the money provided for travel expenses for such moves.

232

INHERENT POWER

The concept of inherent power could be characterized as filling in the blanks. No system created by humans could ever foresee all exigencies. If a court system is to work it must be able to do all the things necessary to accomplish its goals, so long as those things are within the law. In situations such as those discussed above, it would be necessary to determine what could be done and then find out if the necessary action is prohibited. If it is not prohibited, the proper authority should make the change.

By coupling the concept of inherent power with judicial review, a state court system can prevent a legislature from overriding the nonmonetary rules. Judicial review allows the court to declare void any statute which violates the state constitution. All state governments provide for three independent branches of government with a system of checks and balances. Judicial review prevents the legislature from unduly restricting the independence of the judicial branch.

Therefore a state supreme court could assume its role as the leader of the state judiciary. It could order that underworked judges aid overworked judges by permitting the special appointment of general trial judges on a temporary basis. Unless something in the state's constitution prohibited this, the appointments would be valid.

Although such appointments would temporarily alleviate some problems, something more permanent is needed. To accomplish such changes drastic reform of the system is needed.

Court Reorganization Models: The Unified System

The use of inherent powers is at best a stopgap measure. It would be better if the system were reformed and properly funded to achieve the goals of justice and efficiency.

The need for reform was recognized by the President's Commission on Law Enforcement and Administration of Justice. Their Task Force Report stated that "the complex problems of court administration will not yield to any one simple solution, but a well-structured and efficiently organized system is a condition precedent to further change."[2] The task force recognized the need for a "unified, simplified court structure within a state."[3] Six years later the National Advisory Commission on Criminal Justice Standards and Goals echoed the same recommendation. They called for all trial courts to be consolidated into a single court of general trial jurisdiction.[4] When they said all, they meant all. This system would include municipal courts as well as all state trial courts.

The most complete statement on the subject of unification comes from the American Bar Association in its standards relating to court organization.

233

The aims of court organization can be most fully realized in a court system that is unified in its structure and administration, staffed by competent judges, judicial officers, and other personnel, and that has uniform rules and policies, clear lines of administrative authority, and a unified budget.

The structure of the court system should be simple, preferably consisting of a trial court and an appellate court, each having divisions and departments as needed. The trial court should have jurisdiction of all cases and proceedings. It should have specialized procedures and divisions to accommodate the various types of criminal and civil matters within its jurisdiction. The judicial functions of the trial court should be performed by a single class of judges, assisted by legally trained judicial officers (commissioners, associate judges, magistrates, and similar officers) assigned to such matters as preliminary hearings, non-criminal traffic cases, small claims, and responsibilities usually discharged by lower court judges, referees, or hearing officers. The appellate court should have general appellate jurisdiction and should be divided into levels or tiers when a single appellate court level cannot adequately handle the appellate caseload.

All judges should be selected on the basis of professional competence and experience through a merit system of appointment. They should have substantially secure tenure in office, subject to periodic referral of their record to the electorate and to a requirement of compulsory retirement at a designated age. Their fitness to serve in office should be subject to investigation by a board of judicial inquiry acting subject to the final authority of the state's highest court. Judges and judicial officers should receive adequate compensation, provision for their retirement, and opportunity for continuing training and education for their professional functions.

The administrative policy of the court system should be established by the judiciary and administered under the direction of judges through clear and distinct lines of administrative authority. Judges throughout a court system should participate in court policy-making by means of judicial councils, consisting of a limited number of judges representative of the various courts of the system, and judicial conferences, consisting of the entire membership of the judiciary. The courts should have authority to prescribe

234

rules of procedure according to arrangements that include opportunity for the public and the bar to participate. The courts should be provided with an adequate and competent staff of auxiliary personnel acting under the supervisory authority of the judiciary and the management of a court administrative office. The financial operations of the courts, including salaries of personnel and operating and capital expenditures, should be managed through a unified budget that includes all courts in the system.

A unified court system has a structure with the following characteristics:

(a) Uniform jurisdiction. The jurisdictional authority of the courts in the system should be defined in a uniform way, such that all courts at each level in the system have identical jurisdiction.

(b) Simple jurisdictional divisions. The jurisdictional divisions between courts in a system should be simple. The basic division should be between courts of original proceedings and appellate courts.

(c) Uniform standards of justice. The procedures by which the court system administers justice should be based on principles applicable throughout the system, and, so far as practicable, should be uniform in their particulars. The court system should have:

(i) Uniform rules of procedure, promulgated by a common authority;

(ii) Rules of court administration that are uniform so far as possible and have local variations only as approved by an appropriate central authority in the court system;

(iii) A continuous program of professional education and training for judges and auxiliary court personnel;

(iv) A program of conferences and consultations for judicial and auxiliary personnel, the bar, and the public, on problems and needed improvements in administering justice;

(v) Consistent administration of policy.

(d) Clearly vested policy-making authority. Responsibility for making policy, including regulations concerning court administration and participation in making procedural rules, should be vested in the state's highest court or in a council made up of judges.

(e) Clearly established administrative authority. Administrative supervision of the court system as a whole

235

should be exercised by a chief justice, chosen as recommended in Section 1.33. The policy-making body referred to
in paragraph (d) should serve in an advisory capacity to the
chief justice in his performance of administrative responsibilities. Responsibility for administrative supervision of
subordinate units within the court system should be vested
in presiding justices or judges chosen as recommended in
Section 1.33, and acting in consultation with advisory
groups where appropriate. The administrative duties and
powers of such officials should be specified, together with
those to whom they are responsible and who in turn are
responsible to them.[5]

Although there is a recognized need for reorganization it has
been slow in coming. The major opponents are the judges themselves.
The ABA calls for patience and flexibility.[6] The ABA goes on to say
that without reorganization none of the other goals (uniform rules,
administration, uniform records, etc.) can be accomplished.[7] Thus
reorganization is the most important goal.

The Court Administrator

Central to total reform is the fact that nonjudicial duties take up
too much of a judge's time. The answer to this problem is to have an
administrator to care for the housekeeping chores such as hiring
court personnel, maintaining the court building, managing people
hired by the court, and providing supplies.[8] The people who are often
least qualified to perform these tasks are the judges themselves. Despite that fact, most judges waste their time on such tasks. The National Advisory Commission is one of several groups that has recommended creating the post of court administrator for state and local
courts.[9] The state court administrator's duties would be as follows.[10]

An office of State court administrator should be established in each State. The State court administrator should
be selected by the chief justice or presiding judge of the
State's highest appellate court, and he should be subject to
removal by the same authority. The performance of the
State court administrator should be evaluated periodically
by performance standards adopted by the State's highest
appellate court.

The State court administrator should, subject to the
control of the State's highest appellate court, establish
policies for the administration of the State's courts. He also
should establish and implement guidelines for the execution of these policies, and for monitoring and reporting

their execution. Specifically, the State court administrator should establish policies and guidelines dealing with the following:

1. Budgets. A budget for the operation of the entire court system of the State should be prepared by the State court administrator and submitted to the appropriate legislative body.

2. Personnel Policies. The State court administrator should establish uniform personnel policies and procedures governing recruitment, hiring, removal, compensation, and training of all nonjudicial employees of the courts.

3. Information Compilation and Dissemination. The State court administrator should develop a statewide information system. This system should include both statistics and narrative regarding the operation of the entire State court system. At least yearly, the State court administrator should issue an official report to the public and the legislature, containing information regarding the operation of the courts.

4. Control of Fiscal Operations. The State court administrator should be responsible for policies and guidelines relating to accounting and auditing, as well as procurement and disbursement for the entire statewide court system.

5. Liaison Duties. The State court administrator should maintain liaison with government and private organizations, labor and management, and should handle public relations.

6. Continual Evaluation and Recommendation. The State court administrator should continually evaluate the effectiveness of the court system and recommend needed changes.

7. Assignment of Judges. The State court administrator, under the direction of the presiding or chief justice, should assign judges on a statewide basis when required.

The local court administrator's duties would be somewhat different.[11]

Each trial court with five or more judges (and where justified by caseload, courts with fewer judges) should have a full-time local trial court administrator. Trial courts with caseloads too small to justify a full-time trial court administrator should combine into administrative regions and have a regional court administrator. Local trial court administrators and regional court administrators should be appointed by the State court administrator.

The functions of local and regional court administrators should include the following:

1. Implementation of policies set by the State court administrator;

2. Assistance to the State court administrator in setting statewide policies;

3. Preparation and submission of the budget for the court or courts with which he is concerned;

4. Recruiting, hiring, training, evaluating, and monitoring personnel of the court or courts with which he is concerned;

5. Management of space, equipment, and facilities of the court or courts with which he is concerned;

6. Dissemination of information concerning the court or courts with which he is concerned;

7. Procurement of supplies and services for the court or courts with which he is concerned;

8. Custody and disbursement of funds for the court or courts with which he is concerned;

9. Preparation of reports concerning the court or courts with which he is concerned;

10. Juror management;

11. Study and improvement of caseflow, time standards, and calendaring; and

12. Research and development of effective methods of court functioning, especially the mechanization and computerization of court operations.

The local and regional court administrators should discharge their functions within the guidelines set by the State court administrator.

In conjunction with the recommendations for court administrators, the National Advisory Commission on Criminal Justice Standards and Goals has made certain recommendations for court information systems.[12]

The Commission noted that information is the cornerstone of good management. An information system must provide facts for decisions and for management.[13] To this end the following standards were proposed.

1. Decision Making in Individual Cases

A court information system should provide information unique to the defendant and to the case. Required information includes:

1. Defendant background data and other characteristics needed in decision making such as defendant's family status, employment, residence, education, past history, indigency information relative to appointment of counsel, and such data as might be determined by a bail agency interview.

2. Current case history stating the proceedings already completed, the length of time between proceedings, continuances (by reason and source), representation, and other participants.

2. Calendar Management in the Courts

Criminal courts should be provided with sufficient information on case flow to permit efficient calendar management. Basic data to support this activity include the following:

1. Periodic disposition rates by proceeding; these statistics can be used to formulate and adjust calendar caseload limits;

2. An attorney and police witness schedule which can be used to minimize scheduling conflicts;

3. Judge and courtroom schedule;

4. Range of time which proceedings consume;

5. An age index of all cases in pretrial or awaiting trial (by type of trial requested) to determine if special attention is required or the speedy trial rule endangered;

6. An index relating scheduled cases to whether the defendant is confined, released, rearrested, at large, or undergoing adjudication on a separate offense;

7. A recapitulation of offenders booked in jail but not released, to determine if special attention is required;

8. An index of multiple cases pending against individual defendants, to permit consolidation;

9. An index of information on possible or existing case consolidations; and

10. An index of defendants whose existing probation or parole status may be affected by the outcome of current court action.

3. Court Management Data

For effective court administration, criminal courts must have the capability to determine monthly case flow and

239

judicial personnel workload patterns. This capability requires the following statistical data for both in misdemeanors and felonies:

1. Filing and dispositions—number of cases filed and the number of defendants disposed of by offense categories;
2. Monthly backlog—cases in pretrial or preliminary hearing stage; cases scheduled for trial (by type of trial) or preliminary hearing; and cases scheduled for sentencing, with delay since previous step in adjudication;
3. Status of cases on pretrial, settlement, or trial calendars—number and percent of cases sent to judges; continued (listed by reason and source), settled, placed off-calendar; *nolle prosequi;* bench warrants; terminated by trial (according to type of trial);
4. Time periods between major steps in adjudication, including length of trial proceedings by type of trial;
5. Judges' weighted workload—number of cases disposed of by type of disposition and number of cases heard per judge by type of proceeding or calendar;
6. Prosecutor/defense counsel workload—number of cases disposed of by type of disposition and type of proceeding or calendar according to prosecutor, appointed defense counsel, or private defense counsel representation;
7. Jury utilization—number of individuals called, placed on panels, excused, and seated on criminal or civil juries;
8. Number of defendants admitted to bail, released on their own recognizance, or retained in custody, listed by most serious offense charged;
9. Number of witnesses called at hearings on serious felonies, other felonies, and misdemeanors; and
10. Courtroom utilization record.

4. Case Management for Prosecutors

For the purpose of case management, prosecutors shall be provided with the data and statistics to support charge determination and case handling. This capability shall include, as appropriate, the following:

1. A means of weighting cases according to prosecution priority, policy, and the probability of success;
2. Time periods between major steps in adjudication;
3. Daily calendar workloads and dispositions;

240

4. Age of cases in pretrial or awaiting trial (by type of trial) to determine in part whether the right to a speedy trial is enforced;

5. Case-schedule index listing police witnesses, expert witnesses; defense counsel, assigned prosecutor, and type of hearing;

6. Record of continuances by case, number, and party requesting;

7. Selection criteria for witnesses at court hearings; and

8. Criteria for rating adequacy of investigation and legality of procedure by each police unit.

5. Case Counting

Transactional and Event Data Elements shall be recorded for counting purposes as follows:

1. Data elements using individual defendants as the basic statistical unit shall record action taken in regard to one individual and one distinct offense. The term "distinct offense" refers to those sets of related criminal activities for which, under state law, only one conviction is possible, plus conspiracy.

Under this standard, if two men are charged for the same criminal activities, this is reported as two defendant cases. If two charges for which an individual might receive two separate convictions are consolidated at one trial, it is to be reported as two trials. If a jury trial is held for three men on the same crime, the event should be reported as three jury trials.

2. Data elements that describe events occurring in the criminal-justice system shall record the number of events, regardless of the number of defendant transactions involved. Those data elements may report the number of individual transactions as an additional explanatory item.

Under this standard, if two men are charged for the same criminal activities, this is reported as one charge or one charge with two defendants. If two charges are consolidated at one trial, it is to be reported as one trial or one trial on two charges. If a jury trial is held for three men for the same crime, the event should be reported as one jury trial or one jury trial for three defendants.[14]

Parajudges: A Way of Speeding Justice

For several years courts have employed people who help in the decision-making process. Whether they are called commissioners, refferees, or masters, all are used to conduct hearings and report their findings to the judge who makes the final decision. The court does not have to accept the parajudge's report; however, it is rare for the judge to reject it.

In the federal system the parajudge is the magistrate. According to one report, as long as the final decision is made by the court, the magistrate may "hold evidentiary hearings on actions other than habeas corpus petitions and may submit reports dealing with findings of fact, conclusions of law, and proposed orders."[15]

The National Center for State Courts indicates that twenty-six states use parajudges in general jurisdiction courts and twenty-four use them in limited jurisdiction courts.[16] Some appellate courts use them as well.

Does a parajudge have to be a lawyer? No two states agree. Some say no, but a majority of states do require legal training (although that has not been defined).[17]

Should parajudges be used or should the states simply create more judgeships? Consider these comments from the National Center for State Courts.

> There has always been some controversy connected with the use of parajudges. On the one hand, the American Bar Association has advocated the use of parajudicial personnel ("judicial officers") to assist judges, and Standard 1.26 of its *Standards Relating to Court Organization* seeks to provide guidelines that would ensure their efficient and effective participation in the court system.
>
> On the other hand, the National Advisory Commission on Criminal Justice Standards and Goals rejects the use of parajudges, despite the Commission's Courts Task Force recommendation that a standard for judicial officers, other than judges, be provided. Rather, the Commission felt that a system of parajudges would "tend to preserve disadvantages found in some systems of magistrates or lower court judges. . . ."
>
> In the last five or six years, there has been a good deal of attention focused on parajudicial officers. There appears to be a trend to restricting or reducing use of parajudicial personnel. Ohio, for example, repealed its statutory provisions for parajudicial officers, except probate and juvenile courts, in 1971. Hawaii repealed all provisions for subordinate judicial personnel in 1973. Oklahoma followed suit in 1975, retaining only its provisions for juvenile court referees. Virginia repealed its provisions for referees in juvenile court in 1973, but kept those authorizing commissioners in chancery.

In California, over the past few years, there has been considerable discussion about the need, authority, and duties of commissioners. Many of the California courts, especially those in metropolitan areas, rely heavily upon the use of the commissioner system to deal with their high caseloads. In Los Angeles, the use of commissioners as judges pro tem (thereby removing restrictions on the kinds of judicial decisions they can make) has expanded dramatically. . . .

Throughout its long history, the office of the parajudge has changed very little. The locus of employment of the parajudge has altered from appellate courts to trial courts, but his purpose is the same: to assist the court in dealing with its caseload. He has become a fixture in many court systems, one with whom some courts have become uncomfortable. Several states have reevaluated the position of the parajudge and a few have abandoned his use in some or all of the state's courts.

Abandoning the use of subordinate judicial officers and replacing them with judges, aside from the issue of the quality of justice, is a luxury many jurisdictions simply cannot afford in view of both economics and rising caseloads. It is doubtful, for example, that the federal courts will call for the repeal of the Magistrates Act, because of the great assistance these officers have provided to U.S. district court judges.

In the states, too, the parajudges have been of immeasurable help to many courts. After analyzing the use of these officers in the various states, it becomes apparent that they are most frequently and probably the most effectively used in trial courts where they are assigned to hear cases in one specific area. Because the parajudges are responsible for probate, or traffic, or domestic relations, or small claims, or juvenile cases, they are able to develop an area of expertise in which the judges trust their performance. As a result, the judges are free to deal with the more complicated civil cases and the criminal caseload, which was the primary reason for the employment of these subordinate judicial officers.

Another effective use of parajudges is in counties without a resident judge, where a commissioner can be responsible for actions that must be undertaken immediately, e.g., the custody or detention of delinquent and dependent children. . . .

There are many approaches a state can take with regard to parajudicial personnel. One, of course, is to reject their use entirely. Another is to restrict or to modify their activities. Other courts might profit by expanding the authority of their parajudges. Each court must make its own decision in this regard based upon its own unique circumstances and procedures.[18]

Defusing the Bomb: Cutback of Jurisdiction

One way for a court to cut back on its caseload is to determine that particular types of relief are not appropriate. Some states will not allow a challenge to a conviction by way of habeas corpus. This limits the defendant to one review, by appeal only, rather than the two that would be allowed by both habeas corpus and appeal.

The most recent illustration of cutting back the workload of a court came from the United States Supreme Court in 1976. Prior to the decision in *Stone* v. *Powell*,[19] defendants convicted by state courts could challenge that conviction in a federal district court as long as the defendant alleged a violation of his or her constitutional rights. This was allowed even if the defendant had a full and fair hearing on those rights in the state courts. The rule announced in *Stone* v. *Powell* is as follows.

> Where the state has provided an opportunity for full and fair litigation of a Fourth Amendment claim, a state prisoner may not be granted federal habeas corpus relief on the ground that evidence obtained in an unconstitutional search or seizure was introduced at his trial.[20]

This rule effectively stops wholesale petitions for habeas corpus. The appeals that would follow from such petitions are also thwarted.

Lay Justice in America

Despite the fact that many states have moved to a unified court system, some have not. Some states have unified on some levels but not all. Thus there is left a lower court system variously known as "magistrate courts," "justice courts," or "justice-of-the-peace courts." In most states that retain these courts there is no requirement that the judges have legal training. Ever since the days of the infamous Roy Bean, lay justice has been looked upon with suspicion.

The lay justice system came under heavy attack by the President's Commission on Law Enforcement and Administration of Justice. That commission recommended the abolition of lay justice altogether; if that was not possible they recommended abolishing the fee system. Judges of these courts should be on a salary. It was recommended that legal training be required.[21] Another commission

244

labeled these courts the stepchild of the judicial system. They too called for the abolition of the lay justice system.[22] The ABA standards, in the section on selecting judges, makes no provision for lay judges.

> Persons should be selected as judges on the basis of their personal and professional qualifications for judicial office. Their concept of judicial office and views as to the role of the judiciary may be pertinent to their qualification as judges, but selection should not be made on the basis of partisan affiliation.
>
> Personal and professional qualifications: All persons selected as judges should be of good moral character, emotionally stable and mature, in good physical health, patient, courteous, and capable of deliberation and decisiveness when required to act on their own reasoned judgment. They should have a broad general and legal education and should have been admitted to the bar. They should have had substantial experience in the practice, administration, or teaching of law for a term of years commensurate with the judicial office to which they are appointed.[23]

Against this background the Supreme Court was asked to declare lay judges unconstitutional. In *North* v. *Russell*[24] they held that as long as there was a *trial de novo* right before a legally trained judge there is no violation of the Constitution. It is ironic that the case involved Kentucky, whose new constitution provides for a court system with no lay judges.

FEDERAL REFORM PROPOSALS

Earlier in this chapter it was mentioned that the federal system was itself in trouble due to the increased caseload. Several suggestions have been made to improve the situation. One step, the practical elimination of federal habeas corpus review of state court action, will help some.

In 1972 the Congress created the Commission on Revision of the Federal Court Appellate System of the United States.[25] That commission was limited only to the study of appellate courts and what needed to be done. It made its final report in June of 1975.

I. A National Court of Appeals

1. The Commission recommends that Congress establish a National Court of Appeals, consisting of seven judges

245

appointed by the President with the advice and consent of the Senate.

2. The National Court of Appeals would have jurisdiction to hear cases (a) referred to it by the Supreme Court (reference jurisdiction), or (b) transferred to it from the regional courts of appeals, the Court of Claims, and the Court of Customs and Patent Appeals (transfer jurisdiction).

(a) *Reference jurisdiction.* With respect to any case before it on petition for *certiorari,* the Supreme Court would be authorized:

(1) to retain the case and render a decision on the merits;

(2) to deny *certiorari* without more, thus terminating the litigation;

(3) to deny *certiorari* and refer the case to the National Court of Appeals for that court to decide on the merits;

(4) to deny *certiorari* and refer the case to the National Court, giving that court discretion either to decide the case on the merits or to deny review and thus terminate the litigation.

The Supreme Court would also be authorized to refer cases within its obligatory jurisdiction, excepting only those which the Constitution requires it to accept. Referral in such cases would always be for decision on the merits.

(b) *Transfer jurisdiction.* If a case filed in a court of appeals, the Court of Claims, or the Court of Customs and Patent Appeals is one in which an immediate decision by the National Court of Appeals is in the public interest, it may be transferred to the National Court provided it falls within one of the following categories:

(1) the case turns on a rule of federal law and federal courts have reached inconsistent conclusions with respect to it; or

(2) the case turns on a rule of federal law applicable to a recurring factual situation, and a showing is made that the advantages of a prompt and definitive determination of that rule by the National Court of Appeals outweigh any potential disadvantages of transfer; or

(3) the case turns on a rule of federal law which has theretofore been announced by the National Court of Appeals, and there is a substantial question about the proper interpretation or application of that rule in the pending case.

The National Court would be empowered to decline to accept the transfer of any case. Decisions granting or denying transfer, and decisions by the National Court accepting or rejecting cases, would not be reviewable under any circumstances, by extraordinary writ or otherwise.

3. Any case decided by the National Court of Appeals, whether upon reference or after transfer, would be subject to review by the Supreme Court upon petition for *certiorari*.

II. Internal Operating Procedures

4. *Mechanism for circuit procedures.* Each circuit court of appeals should establish a mechanism for formulating, implementing, monitoring, and revising circuit procedures. The mechanism should include three essential elements:

(a) publication of the court's internal operating procedures;

(b) notice-and-comment rule making as the normal instrument of procedural change; and

(c) an advisory committee, representative of bench and bar.

5. *Oral argument.* Standards for the grant or denial of oral argument, and the procedures by which those standards are implemented, are appropriately dealt with through the rule-making process. We recommend the following as an appropriate minimum national standard for inclusion in the Federal Rules of Appellate Procedure:

(a) In any appeal in a civil or criminal case, the appellant should be entitled as a matter of right to present oral argument, unless:

(1) the appeal is frivolous;

(2) the dispositive issue or set of issues has been recently authoritatively decided; or

(3) the facts are simple, the determination of the appeal rests on the application of settled rules of law, and no useful purpose could be served by oral argument.

(b) Oral argument is appropriately shortened in cases in which the dispositive points can be adequately presented in less than the usual time allowable.

Because conditions vary substantially from circuit to circuit, each court of appeals should have the authority to establish its own standards, so long as the national minimum is satisfied, and to provide procedures for implementation which are particularly suited to local needs.

6. *Opinion writing and publication.* The Commission recommends that the Federal Rules of Appellate Procedure require that in every case there be some record, however brief and whatever the form, of the reasoning which underlies the decision.

247

The Commission strongly encourages a program of selective publication of opinions.

III. Accommodating Mounting Caseloads: Judgeships, Judges, and Structure

7. *Creation of needed judgeships.* The creation of additional appellate judgeships is the only method of accommodating mounting caseloads without introducing undesirable structural change or impairing the appellate process. Accordingly, the Commission recommends that Congress create new appellate judgeships wherever caseloads require them.

A. Assuring Judges of Superior Quality in Adequate Numbers

8. *Filling of vacancies.* The executive and legislative branches should act expeditiously to fill all judicial vacancies.

9. *Intercircuit assignments.* The procedure for making intercircuit assignments of active judges should be simplified. Specifically, the judiciary should return to the simple procedure established by Congress: certification of necessity by the borrowing court, consent by the lending court, and designation by the chief justice.

10. *Easing of senior status requirements.* The requirements for taking senior status should be eased; a judge should be eligible for retirement when the number of years he has served on the bench, added to his age, equals eighty, as long as the judge has served a minimum period of ten years and has attained age sixty.

11. *Adequate judicial salaries.* Federal judicial salaries should be raised to a level that will make it possible for outstanding individuals to accept appointment to the bench and adequately compensate those now serving.

IV. Other Recommendations

12. *Commission on the federal judicial system.* The Commission recommends that Congress consider the desirability of creating a standing commission to study and to make recommendations with respect to problems of the federal courts.

13. *District court judges of high quality in adequate numbers.* The Commission recommends that the Congress assure to each of the districts courts judges of superior

quality in sufficient numbers and with adequate support facilities, not only because of the importance of their function, but because of the resultant significant impact on the work of the appellate courts.

14. *Tenure of chief judges.* The judicial code should be amended to provide for a maximum term of seven years for the chief judge of a circuit, who would continue to be selected on the basis of seniority.

15. *Selection of the presiding judge of a panel.* Congress should provide that the presiding judge on a panel shall be the active judge of the circuit who is senior in commission.

16. *Adequate staffing and support.* Congress should provide adequate staff and support facilities for each of the courts of appeals as well as for all of the judges.

17. *Discipline of judges.* The Commission recognizes that a mechanism for handling allegations of judicial misconduct and incapacity is an important matter and recommends that Congress turn its attention to this subject.

18. *Availability of court of appeals documents.* The Library of Congress should serve as a national depository for briefs and other appropriate documents in cases in the federal intermediate appellate courts. The Library of Congress should micro-copy such materials and make them available to the public at cost.

A substantial majority of the Commission supports each of the recommendations set forth above. . . . We are, moreover, unanimous in our recognition of the serious problems presently besetting the federal courts and of the need for sustained concern to the end that appropriate and enduring solutions be achieved.[26]

In addition to these recommendations by the Commission it has been suggested that diversity jurisdiction of the federal courts be eliminated. Diversity jurisdiction is that power to try cases between citizens of two states. It is used by the citizen of one state where he feels he cannot get a fair trial in the court system of the defendant's home state. This would require an amendment of Article III § 2 of the U.S. Constitution.

It has been suggested also that provisions for three-judge courts be eliminated. Three-judge courts are used primarily for challenging state statutes and for issuing injunctions to prevent the operation of those statutes. There is considerable confusion as to which matters can be tried before a three-judge court. This has created a heavy appellate caseload with numerous reversals, thereby requiring a new beginning for the litigation. In response Congress passed Public Law 94-351. This statute effectively limits the use of the three-judge court to reapportionment cases only.

EPILOGUE

There are no easy solutions for the reform of our court systems. These problems directly affect the future of every citizen. The issues involve more than the pocketbook. A serious question of satisfaction with government arises. Can a system designed for the nineteenth century survive into the twenty-first century?

> "Only by the adoption of sound administrative practices will the courts be able to meet the increased and increasing burdens placed on them. The time has passed when the court system will carry its load 'if each judge does his job.' There must also be organization and system so as to leave the judge to his job of judging."
>
> *Chief Justice Warren E. Burger*[27]

STUDY QUESTIONS

1. Discuss the doctrine of *stare decisis*.
2. What are the characteristics of a unified court system?
3. What is the importance of the role of court administrator?
4. What are parajudges and how are they used?
5. What is the purpose of the National Center for State Courts?
6. Identify the findings appearing in the first national survey of public attitudes toward courts in the United States.
7. What is the major dilemma facing the court system today?
8. What is meant by efficient calendar management in the courts?
9. What was the impact of *Stone v. Powell*?

NOTES

1. U.S., *Constitution,* Amend. 6.
2. President's Commission on Law Enforcement and Administration of Justice, *Task Force Report: The Courts* (Washington, D.C.: Government Printing Office, 1967), p. 82.
3. Ibid.
4. Ibid., p. 83.

5. ABA, *Standards Relating to Court Organization* (1974), pp. 1–4.
6. Ibid., p. 6.
7. Ibid.
8. President's Commission on Law Enforcement, *The Courts,* p. 81.
9. National Advisory Commission on Criminal Justice Standards and Goals, *Courts* (1973), pp. 176–186.
10. Ibid., p. 176.
11. Ibid., p. 183.
12. National Advisory Commission on Criminal Justice Standards and Goals, *Criminal Justice System* (1973), pp. 68–80.
13. Ibid., p. 69.
14. Ibid., pp. 70–79.
15. National Center for State Courts, *Parajudges: Their Role in Today's Court System* (1976), p. 3.
16. Ibid., p. 5.
17. Ibid., p. 6.
18. Ibid., pp. 8 and 11.
19. *Stone* v. *Powell,* 422 U.S. 1055 (1976).
20. Ibid.
21. President's Commission on Law Enforcement, *The Courts,* pp. 34–36.
22. National Advisory Commission, *Courts,* pp. 161–162.
23. ABA, *Court Organization,* pp. 40–42.
24. President's Commission on Law Enforcement, *The Courts,* p. 36.
25. Public Law 92-489 (Oct. 13, 1972).
26. Commission on Revision of the Federal Court Appellate System, *Structure and Internal Procedures: Recommendations for Change* (June 1975), pp. vii–xi.
27. Institute for Court Management, *1976 Education Programs* (Denver, Colorado: The Institute, 1976), p. 2.

chapter ten
Judicial Behavior

"The quality of justice depends in large measure on the quality of judges." Thus begins Chapter 6 of the *Task Force Report: The Courts* prepared by the President's Commission on Law Enforcement and Administration of Justice.[1] This report, along with the ABA *Canons of Judicial Ethics*, the ABA *Standards, The Function of the Trial Judge,* [2] the *Task Force Report on Courts* by the National Advisory Commission on Criminal Justice Standards and Goals,[3] and *The State Trial Judge's Book,*[4] will be the basis of the discussion in this chapter.

How important is a judge? The *Task Force Report: The Courts* summarizes it best.[5] Since the trial judge is at the center of the criminal process, he or she exerts an influence that determines decisions by police, prosecutors, and defense counsel. How is this influence felt?

Consider a police department and prosecutor faced with an outbreak of pornography shops and an irate citizenry. If the local judge is known to favor unlimited exercise of the First Amendment's freedom-of-the-press provision, the police and prosecutor know very well that the judge will probably not issue warrants to arrest the shop owners. Even if such warrants were issued and served, the judge would grant the defense dismissal motions or motions to quash the charges. Given these conditions, the police do not even try to close down the shops.

Even the way a judge issues sentences on certain crimes and offenses will shape police and prosecutor behavior. An example was given in the *Task Force Report: The Courts*. Arrests for prostitution and solicitation had dropped off for a six-month period in a major city because a judge who routinely dismissed such cases was sitting in the misdemeanor division.[6] Should judges allow personal preferences, biases, and prejudices to have such a telling effect on the entire system? If the judge has such an influential role, how should that role be played?

Responding to these questions the ABA promulgated the *Standards Relating to the Function of the Trial Judge*,[7] the *Canons of Judicial Ethics*,[8] and the current *Code of Judicial Conduct*.[9] Responding to the needs for a better-trained judiciary, organizations such as the National College of the State Judiciary (an arm of the ABA) and the American Academy of Judicial Education (an arm of the American Judicature Society) were created. Additional state and local judicial-training groups, such as the Mississippi Judicial College or the state bar's continuing legal-education arm, are filling the training needs on a local level. The goal is a better-informed judiciary that knows the purpose of judging and therefore better understands its role. Nowhere in law school are students taught to be judges. The *Standards, Canons,* and training groups fill that void.

THE FUNCTION OF THE TRIAL JUDGE: GENERAL PRINCIPLES

More is required of a judge than merely knowing substantive and procedural law. The judge needs to know and follow the canons of ethics governing judicial and attorney behavior.

Can a judge reflect the dignity of the office and enhance public confidence in the administration of justice by wearing a robe? The ABA thinks so.[10] The robe is a commitment to impartiality. It adds dignity to the courtroom. More important, however, is judicial behavior. The judge should not send out, even unconsciously, messages of partiality, lack of respect, or disbelief in what has been said. Facial expressions, rolled eyes, and head shaking have an effect, one that is not recorded in the transcript.[11]

More than refraining from negative behavior is required. The judicial canons require judges to avoid both impropriety and the appearance of impropriety.[12] Judges are expected to conduct their personal lives in a manner beyond reproach. Some judges seem more interested in golf or tennis than in the courtroom and their other judicial duties. This is discouraged by both the *Canons* and *Standards*.[13]

The judge has an obligation to use judicial time effectively. Lawyers, police officers, and witnesses should know that the judge means business when court appearance times are set.[14]

"War" stories of arbitrary and capricious judges abound in every jurisdiction. The old saying that judges forget that they were appointed (or elected) and not anointed is sometimes true. Some judges refer to the courtroom as "my" courtroom, "my" patience, "my" time, and on and on. Egos can become overinflated. The *Canons* speak to this subject several times.

A judge is supposed to be temperate and patient.[15] A judge is supposed to be considerate.[16] *Canon* 10 (1967) requires the judge to practice courtesy and civility. He or she is expected to require the staff to do likewise. The judge is to avoid a controversial manner or tone.[17] A judge is to remember that he or she is not a depository of arbitrary power.[18]

One of the more interesting 1967 canons is number 21. It is entitled "Idiosyncrasies and Inconsistencies." The judge's conduct is not to be "extreme or peculiar," "spectacular or sensational." The judge is not to "humiliate" anyone. This conduct is also covered by *Canon* 3 (1972).

Perhaps the most difficult mental attitude for any human is that of impartiality. If the judge allows family, social, or other relationships to influence his judicial conduct or judgment, he destroys public confidence in the integrity of the system. The judge is not part of the prosecution team. The judge is not an advocate.

Must a judge abandon all his former friends? Of course not. However, there may be times when the judge will have to disqualify himself from a case because of past friendships. *Canon* 33, "Social Relations," says that a judge does not have to be a recluse. It encourages mingling as long as it does not interfere with his work.

> He should, however, in pending or prospective litigation before him be particularly careful to avoid such action as may reasonably tend to awaken the suspicion that his social or business relations or friendships constitute an element in influencing his judicial conduct.[19]

From time to time lawyers, whether prosecutors or defense attorneys, and some law-enforcement officers like to drop in on a judge and discuss, generally of course, a pending case. This is taboo. Both the *Canons* and *Standards* prohibit this type of conduct.[20]

If a judge has any doubt about his ability to remain impartial, he should remove himself from the case. What are the situations in which a judge should excuse himself? One example is where the judge has blood relationships or marital kinships with the accused, witnesses, or other key figures in a trial. A new judge who had helped prepare the case, either as a prosecutor or as defense counsel, should excuse himself. The key to less obvious situations is whether the public impression will be favorable. The standards are quick to point out, however, that self-removal should not be used to avoid unpopular cases or unpleasant ones.[21]

JUDICIAL BEHAVIOR: PRETRIAL DUTIES

When it comes to issuing search and arrest warrants, the judge has to be the leading example of compliance with constitutional safeguards. The law requires a neutral and detached judicial personality. The judge cannot be a rubber stamp for law enforcement. How can law-enforcement officers have respect for the law if the judge is "one of the boys"? At one time, judges who did not want to be bothered on the weekends or during evening hours signed blank warrants and left them at the station house. This is prohibited today. Judges can now be required to testify at the probable-cause hearing on the warrant.[22] If a judge were to sign a blank warrant today, he might have to perjure himself and say that he did conduct a full hearing on the affidavit and warrant. Most judges obey the law; they understand that when a judge "winks," others close their eyes to justice.

Judges have a duty to inspect jails to make sure no one is being detained illegally. In one state, in one of the larger cities of that state, the prosecutor and sheriff had made a deal. They incarcerated people, without hearings, arraignments, and the like, whom they felt could not be convicted. They did this because they were sure these defendants were guilty of something. A judge inspected the county jail and found fourteen or fifteen inmates who had been in jail for over a year without having a single charge filed against them. There is no doubt that many of those incarcerated deserved their lot. Yet even the guilty have rights. There was no explanation as to why other judges had not exercised their responsibility in this matter.[23]

The judge has a duty to keep prosecutors, law-enforcement officials, and defense counsel from trying the case in the public media. Not everything that the police know has been put in the public record. Much of the police record is highly prejudicial. The court should prevent leaks.

The subject of a fair trial and the freedom of the press was discussed briefly in the earlier chapter on individual rights. However, the judge has a duty to see that news is managed to assure a just trial. It is in this context that members of the media must zealously protect their rights.

Can the two principles, fair trial and free press, be accommodated? The ABA thinks so and has produced a series of standards which they think will protect both constitutional rights.[24] Their statement of principles is as follows.

> (a) *General.* Freedom of speech and of the press are fundamental liberties guaranteed by the United States Constitution. They must be zealously preserved, but at the same time must be exercised with an awareness of the potential impact of public statements on other fundamental

rights, including the right of a person accused of crime, and of his accusers, to a fair trial by an impartial jury.

(b) *The need to inform the public.* It is important both to the community and to the criminal process that the public be informed of the commission of crime, that corruption and misconduct, including the improper failure to arraign or to prosecute, be exposed whenever they are found, and that those accused of crime be apprehended. If, however, public statements and reporting with respect to these matters assume the truth of what may be only a belief or a suspicion, they may destroy the reputation of one who is innocent and may seriously endanger the right to a fair trial in the event that formal charges are filed.

(c) *From the time of arrest or the filing of charges to the beginning of trial.* A man who has been arrested, for whom an arrest warrant has been issued, or against whom a criminal complaint, information, or indictment has been filed, has only been charged with the commission of crime. He is entitled under the Constitution to a fair and impartial trial, in which he is presumed innocent until proved guilty by competent evidence. Thus during the period prior to trial, public statements originating from officials, attorneys, or the news media that assume the guilt of the person charged, that include inaccurate or inadmissible information, or that serve to inflame the community, may undermine the judicial process by making unobtainable a jury satisfying the requisite standard of impartiality. . . . The right to a fair trial may thus be substantially endangered by public statements or by reporting prior to trial going beyond a factual description of the person arrested and of the crime charged and a factual statement of the arrest and surrounding circumstances. . . .

(d) *During the trial.* The public should be adequately informed of the administration of justice in our criminal courts. But if a criminal trial takes place before a jury, and if the jury is not isolated during the course of the trial, the dangers of potentially prejudicial material coming to a juror's attention are particularly great, even when the jury is warned not to read or listen to news reports. Moreover, public statements or reports of a sensational or inflammatory character may adversely affect the atmosphere in which the case is tried, thus impeding the administration of justice, and may permanently scar even those who are innocent. . . .

(e) *After trial or disposition without trial.* After a criminal case has been tried or disposed of without trial, criticism of the outcome or of the conduct of the court, attorneys, law-enforcement officers, or others who were involved in the case is essential to the improvement of the criminal process. Moreover, since appeals from convictions, as well as the exhaustion of other remedies, may take an extended time, comment and criticism might be of little or no value if postponed further than the completion of trial or disposition without trial. Although the possibility of prejudice is substantially reduced once the verdict has been rendered, such prejudice may result (1) from comment on the sentence if sentence has not yet been imposed, and (2) from comment on the case if a new trial is ordered by a trial or appellate court or is required because the jury has been unable to reach a verdict.[25]

The whole idea of promulgating standards for this area stemmed from the problems concerning the arrest and death of Lee Harvey Oswald. The importance of and need for these standards was reemphasized in the 1977 "Son of Sam" case in New York City. The standards offer some solutions. Only time will tell whether they have been successful. They are as follows.

Part I. Recommendations Relating to the Conduct of Attorneys in Criminal Cases

1.1 Revision of the Canons of Professional Ethics.

It is recommended that the Canons of Professional Ethics be revised to contain the following standards relating to public discussion of pending or imminent criminal litigation:

It is the duty of the lawyer not to release or authorize the release of information or opinion for dissemination by any means of public communication, in connection with pending or imminent criminal litigation with which he is associated, if there is a reasonable likelihood that such dissemination will interfere with a fair trial or otherwise prejudice the due administration of justice. . . .

From the time of arrest, issuance of an arrest warrant, or the filing of a complaint, information, or indictment in any criminal matter until the commencement of trial or disposition without trial, a lawyer associated with the prosecution or defense shall not release or authorize the release of any extrajudicial statement, for dissemination by any means of public communication, relating to that matter and concerning:

(1) The prior criminal record (including arrests, indict-

257

ments, or other charges of crime), or the character or reputation of the defendant, except that the lawyer may make a factual statement of the defendant's name, age, residence, occupation, and family status . . . ;

(2) The existence or contents of any confession, admission, or statement given by the defendant, or the refusal or failure of the defendant to make any statement;

(3) The performance of any examinations or tests or the defendant's refusal or failure to submit to an examination or test;

(4) The identity, testimony, or credibility of prospective witnesses, except that the lawyer may announce the identity of the victim if the announcement is not otherwise prohibited by law;

(5) The possibility of a plea of guilty to the offense charged or a lesser offense;

(6) The defendant's guilt or innocence or other matters relating to the merits of the case or the evidence in the case, except that the lawyer may announce the circumstances of arrest, including time and place of arrest, resistance, pursuit, and use of weapons; may announce the identity of the investigating and arresting officer or agency and the length of the investigation; may make an announcement, at the time of the seizure, describing any evidence seized; may disclose the nature, substance, or text of the charge, including a brief description of the offense charged; may quote from or refer without comment to public records of the court in the case; may announce the scheduling or result of any stage in the judicial process; may request assistance in obtaining evidence; and, on behalf of his client, may announce without further comment that the client denies the charges made against him. . . .

Part II. Recommendations Relating to the Conduct of Law-Enforcement Officers and Judicial Employees in Criminal Cases

2.1 Rule of court relating to disclosures by law-enforcement officers.

It is recommended that the following rule be promulgated in each jurisdiction by the appropriate court:

Release of information by law-enforcement officers.

From the time of arrest, issuance of an arrest warrant, or the filing of any complaint, information, or indictment in any criminal matter within the jurisdiction of this court, until the completion of trial or disposition without trial, no law-enforcement officer subject to the jurisdiction of this court shall release or authorize the release of any extrajudicial statement, for dissemination by any means of public communication, relating to that matter and concerning:

(1) The prior criminal record (including arrests, indictments, or other charges of crime), or the character or reputation of the defendant, except that the officer may make a factual statement of the defendant's name, age, residence, occupation, and family status, and if the defendant has not been apprehended, may release any information necessary to aid in his apprehension or to warn the public of any dangers he may present;

(2) The existence or contents of any confession, admission, or statement given by the defendant, or the refusal or failure of the defendant to make any statement;

(3) The performance of any examinations or tests or the defendant's refusal or failure to submit to an examination or test;

(4) The identity, testimony, or credibility of prospective witnesses, except that the officer may announce the identity of the victim if the announcement is not otherwise prohibited by law;

(5) The possibility of a plea of guilty to the offense charged or a lesser offense;

(6) The defendant's guilt or innocence, or other matters relating to the merits of the case or the evidence in the case, except that the officer may announce the circumstances of arrest, including the time and place of arrest, resistance, pursuit, and use of weapons; may announce the identity of the investigating and arresting officer or agency and the length of the investigation; may make an announcement, at the time of the seizure, describing any evidence seized; may disclose the nature, substance, or text of the charge, including a brief description of the offense charged; may quote from or refer without comment to public records of the court in the case; may announce the scheduling or result of any stage in the judicial process; and may request assistance in obtaining evidence. . . .

2.2 Rule of court relating to disclosures by judicial employees.

It is recommended that a rule of court be adopted in each jurisdiction prohibiting any judicial employee from disclosing, to any unauthorized person, information relating to a pending criminal case that is not part of the public records of the court and that may tend to interfere with the right of the people or of the defendant to a fair trial. . . .

Part III. Recommendations Relating to the Conduct of Judicial Proceedings in Criminal Cases

3.1 Pretrial hearings.

It is recommended that the following rule be adopted in each jurisdiction by the appropriate court:

Motion to exclude public from all or part of pretrial hearing.

In any preliminary hearing, bail hearing, or other pretrial hearing in a criminal case, including a motion to suppress evidence, the defendant may move that all or part of the hearing be held in chambers or otherwise closed to the public on the ground that dissemination of evidence or argument adduced at the hearing may disclose matters that will be inadmissible in evidence at the trial and is therefore likely to interfere with his right to a fair trial by an impartial jury. The motion shall be granted unless the presiding officer determines that there is no substantial likelihood of such interference. . . .

3.2 Change of venue or continuance.

It is recommended that the following standards be adopted in each jurisdiction to govern the consideration and disposition of a motion in a criminal case for change of venue or continuance based on a claim of threatened interference with the right to a fair trial.

(a) Who may request.

Except as federal or state constitutional provisions otherwise require, a change of venue or continuance may be granted on motion of either the prosecution or the defense.

(b) Methods of proof.

In addition to the testimony or affidavits of individuals in the community, which shall not be required as a condition to the granting of a motion for change of venue or continuance, qualified public-opinion surveys shall be admissible as well as other materials having probative value.

(c) Standards for granting motion.

A motion for change of venue or continuance shall be

granted whenever it is determined that because of the dissemination of potentially prejudicial material, there is a reasonable likelihood that in the absence of such relief, a fair trial cannot be had. This determination may be based on such evidence as qualified public-opinion surveys or opinion testimony offered by individuals, or on the court's own evaluation of the nature, frequency, and timing of the material involved. A showing of actual prejudice shall not be required. . . .

3.3 Waiver of jury.

In those jurisdictions in which the defendant does not have an absolute right to waive a jury in a criminal case, it is recommended that the defendant be permitted to waive whenever it is determined that (1) the waiver has been knowingly and voluntarily made, and (2) there is reason to believe that, as a result of the dissemination of potentially prejudicial material, the waiver is required to increase the likelihood of a fair trial.

3.4 Selecting the jury.

It is recommended that the following standards be adopted in each jurisdiction to govern the selection of a jury in those criminal cases in which questions of possible prejudice are raised.

(a) Method of examination.

Whenever there is believed to be a significant possibility that individual talesmen will be ineligible to serve because of exposure to potentially prejudicial material, the examination of each juror with respect to his exposure shall take place outside the presence of other chosen and prospective jurors. . . .

(b) Standard of acceptability.

Both the degree of exposure and the prospective juror's testimony as to his state of mind are relevant to the determination of acceptability. A prospective juror who states that he will be unable to overcome his preconceptions shall be subject to challenge for cause no matter how slight his exposure. . . .

(c) Source of the panel.

Whenever it is determined that potentially prejudicial news coverage of a given criminal matter has been intense and has been concentrated primarily in a given locality in a state (or federal district), the court shall have authority to draw jurors from other localities in that state (or district).

3.5 Conduct of the trial.

It is recommended that the following standards be adopted in each jurisdiction to govern the conduct of a criminal trial when problems relating to the dissemination of potentially prejudicial material are raised.

(a) Use of the courtroom.

Whenever appropriate in view of the notoriety of the case or the number or conduct of news media representatives present at any judicial proceeding, the court shall ensure the preservation of decorum by instructing those representatives and others as to the permissible use of the courtroom, the assignment of seats, and other matters that may affect the conduct of the proceeding. . . .

(b) Cautioning parties and witnesses; insulating witnesses.

Whenever appropriate in light of the issues in the case or the notoriety of the case, the court shall instruct parties and witnesses not to make extrajudicial statements, relating to the case or the issues in the case, for dissemination by any means of public communication during the course of the trial. . . .

(c) Exclusion of the public from hearings or arguments outside the presence of the jury.

If the jury is not sequestered, the defendant shall be permitted to move that the public be excluded from any portion of the trial that takes place outside the presence of the jury on the ground that dissemination of evidence or argument adduced at the hearing is likely to interfere with the defendant's right to a fair trial by an impartial jury. The motion shall be granted unless it is determined that there is no substantial likelihood of such interference. . . .

(d) Cautioning jurors.

In any case that appears likely to be of significant public interest, an admonition in substantially the following form shall be given before the end of the first day if the jury is not sequestered.

During the time you serve on this jury, there may appear in the newspapers or on radio or television reports concerning this case, and you may be tempted to read, listen to, or watch them. Please do *not* do so. Due process of law requires that the evidence to be considered by you in reaching your verdict meet certain standards—for example, a witness may testify about events he himself has seen or heard but not about matters of which he was told by others.

262

Also, witnesses must be sworn to tell the truth and must be subject to cross-examination. News reports about the case are not subject to these standards, and if you read, listen to, or watch these reports, you may be exposed to misleading or inaccurate information which unduly favors one side and to which the other side is unable to respond. In fairness to both sides, therefore, it is essential that you comply with this instruction. . . .

3.6 Setting aside the verdict.

It is recommended that, on motion of the defendant, a verdict of guilty in any criminal case be set aside and a new trial granted whenever, on the basis of competent evidence, the court finds a substantial likelihood that the vote of one or more jurors was influenced by exposure to an extrajudicial communication of any matter relating to the defendant or to the case itself that was not part of the trial record on which the case was submitted to the jury. . . .

Part IV. Recommendations Relating to the Exercise of the Contempt Power

4.1 Limited use of the contempt power.

The use of the contempt power against persons who disseminate information by means of public communication, or who make statements for dissemination, can in certain circumstances raise grave constitutional questions. . . .

4.2 Reimbursement of defendant.

In the event that a mistrial or change of venue is granted or a conviction set aside, as a result of an extrajudicial statement held to be in contempt of court, it is recommended that the court have the authority to require that all or part of the proceeds of any fine be used to reimburse the defendant for the additional legal fees and other expenses fairly attributable to the order that the case be tried in a different venue or tried again in the same venue.[26]

In addition to these standards, the judge should remain silent about a pending case. Too often, though, judges are impressed with reporters and are eager for publicity that may accelerate their judicial careers. Judges must not speak too freely. Whether in historical perspective the Watergate people were guilty of more than political misdeeds is not ours to say. However, the Watergate judge spoke very freely to the press, indicating his obvious bias against the purported wrongdoers. There is no room in the ABA *Standards* and *Canons* for such conduct.[27]

Plea negotiation (a nice phrase for plea bargaining), although heavily criticized, is part of most systems. The judge cannot be involved in the preagreement discussions except to remind the lawyers that they may explore the possibility of disposition without trial. Before the judge can accept a plea of guilty or nolo contendere (no contest), he or she must determine if there has been an agreement. If there has been one, the judge requires it to be put into the record.[28]

However, the attorneys cannot bargain away the judge's sentencing power. Therefore, any concessions that the judge is supposed to make are void unless the judge independently agrees to the concessions. The judge can permit the defendant to withdraw his plea.

The *Standards* require that the judge not accept a plea of guilty or nolo contendere until he or she is satisfied that the defendant understands (1) the nature of the charge, and (2) that he is waiving valuable rights. The judge must be satisfied that the plea is voluntary.

A recent case illustrates the problem of a defendant who does not understand the nature of the charge to which he pleads guilty. The defendant was charged with first-degree murder. A plea was negotiated and defendant made a plea of guilty to second-degree murder. Defendant was not told that second-degree murder was an intent-to-kill crime. He claimed his plea was involuntary. The court, in reversing his plea, said that a defendant must be given real notice of the true nature of the charge against him. It must be explained that a plea would be an admission of a fact. This case is unique because the Court found as a fact that the element of intent was not explained to the defendant.[29]

As was stated in *Boykin* v. *Alabama,* a plea of guilty is more than a confession.[30] It is a conviction. The judge must make sure that the accused has a full understanding of the consequences of such a plea.

JUDICIAL BEHAVIOR: TRIAL DUTIES

The judge's control of *voir dire* and of the jury have already been discussed in Chapter 7. The judge's function with regard to the physical appearance of the defendant was also discussed there. The same rules apply to a witness. The witness should not appear in distinctive attire. The judge can deal with disruptive witnesses in the same manner as he can with a disruptive defendant.

There are other problems witnesses face. The judge is there to prevent unnecessary intimidation and humiliation. Where the line is drawn is difficult to say. Some of this behavior can be prevented by keeping the attorney in his or her place. Judges are supposed to require counsel to stay at the counsel table or at a lectern to conduct the examination or cross-examination.[31] This rule may be observed more in its breach, however. It is the court's duty to keep the cross-examination or examination-in-chief within certain boundaries. Needless repetition is to be avoided.[32] Irrelevant lines of questions are taboo.

Just because the judge must not allow his preferences to show does not mean that the judge must be totally aloof during the trial. The *Standards* say:

> When necessary to the juror's proper understanding of the proceedings, the judge may intervene during the taking of evidence to instruct on a principle of law or the applicability of the evidence to the issues. This should be done only when the jurors could not be effectively advised by postponing the explanation to the time of giving final instructions.[33]

There are times when a judge has to intervene to prevent a mistrial. In a recent case involving Watergate defendants, the prosecutor made an improper statement during the opening argument. The prosecutor said that "a grand jury thought they were guilty and indicted them." This was objected to. The court sustained the objection, but denied a defense motion for mistrial. The court then instructed the jury to disregard the comment and explained briefly that a grand-jury indictment was not proof of guilt and gave a little information about the role of the grand jury. The jury did not let the statement affect them, as is shown by the fact that they acquitted the defendants.

As indicated, a judge may interrupt to expedite matters. He is there to prevent wasting time unnecessarily and also to clear up obscurities. The judge must guard against a tone or inflection that might indicate a bias or that might terrify an already-upset witness.[34]

Judges should take notes during the proceedings and pay close attention to the questioning of witnesses. If it is obvious that a question is unclear, the judge should see that it is clarified. There are times when a key question has not been asked. The judge can ask it, but he or she should wait until all examination is complete to ask any remaining questions.[35]

Judges can be a little arbitrary. They sometimes prevent attorneys from making objections or, if allowed, they will not let the attorneys argue their merits. Judges are required to respect the obligations of attorneys to do their job. Every now and then, arguments become irrelevant or long-winded. The judge can and must stop these.[36]

Attorneys often badger each other. This is referred to as colloquy between attorneys.

Colloquy or argument between attorneys serves no proper purpose in the trial. Sometimes it is highly inflammatory or prejudicial, and invariably detracts immeasurably from the order and dignity of the proceeding. The judge must not hesitate to stop it and should apply sanctions upon repetitions.[37]

The judge is to respect the attorney-client relationship. The court should not put the attorney in the position where he has to reveal privileged matters.[38] The respect for the attorney-client relationship goes further than this, as is illustrated in a recent United States Supreme Court opinion.

In *Geders* v. *U.S.*, the defendant had taken the stand as a witness on his own behalf when an overnight recess was called. It is normal procedure for a judge to admonish a witness that he should not speak to anyone until the trial resumes and his examination is complete. In this case the prosecutor asked the judge not to allow the defendant to discuss the case with anyone. The court agreed and forbade the defendant from having more than a brief meeting with his attorney immediately after the day's session. Defense counsel strenuously objected. The Supreme Court said that although the judge has legitimate powers to sequester witnesses, the defendant is not a mere witness. Recesses are times of intensive work for counsel and client. They said there are other ways to deal with the problem of coaching. Any doubts in this instance have to be resolved in favor of allowing consultation between attorney and client.[39]

Children get frustrated when they are constantly sent from the room because of grown-up talk. Jurors get much the same feeling every time they are herded from the courtroom so that the judge and the attorneys can have a conference. The judge should keep these interruptions to a minimum and hold them during recesses whenever possible.[40]

The judge's final trial duty (besides those discussed in Chapter 9) is to thank the jurors. Instead, television often portrays, as does the movies, an angry judge who is disgusted with the verdict. He berates the jury in no uncertain terms. Such behavior is not advisable. The *Standards* say that "while it is appropriate for the trial judge to thank jurors at the conclusion of a trial for their public service, such comments should not include praise or criticism of their verdict."[41]

The Contempt Power

The judge is in charge. He sets the tone of the proceedings. He must practice self-restraint. Even when he must discipline someone, he should do it in a firm, dignified, and restrained manner. Respect disappears when the judge gets into a shouting match with someone in the courtroom.

What is the court to do when an attorney misconducts himself? The *Standards* list five appropriate sanctions. They are: (1) censure or reprimand; (2) citation or punishment for contempt; (3) removal from the courtroom; (4) suspension for a limited time of the right to practice in the court where the misconduct occurred (if permitted by law); and (5) informing the appropriate disciplinary bodies in every jurisdiction where the attorney is admitted to practice of the misconduct and of any sanction imposed.[42]

The single most effective power is the contempt power and it can be used against anyone. It is one of the inherent powers of the court. Unless the misconduct is outrageous, a warning should be given by the judge before imposing the contempt sanction. It is best for the court to postpone contempt hearings until after the trial unless prompt punishment is imperative. Notice and at least a brief opportunity to be heard should be afforded as a matter of course, but a full trial is not required.[43]

The Judge and Sentencing

The Task Force on the Administration of Justice looked into the problems of the exercise of court sentencing authority and made several observations. First, sentencing requires experience. The judge should know all the alternatives and the utility of each. The judge should be skilled in interpreting presentence and psychiatric evaluations. The second point made concerns disparity in sentencing between judges.[44] There is, of course, a certain lack of uniformity in sentencing that is justifiable. The key word is justifiable. If there is no reasonable basis for unequal sentences for the same conduct, the criticism of disparity is justified. There are tough judges; there are lenient judges. If the personality of the judge is the reason for disparity, this does injustice to the concept of equal justice. It also causes attorneys to shop around for a more lenient judge. For this reason the ABA recommends that the judge who tried the case not sentence the offender.[45]

The actual imposition of the sentence is an interesting matter. After giving the defendant the right to speak his or her mind, the judge states the sentence. All judges differ in their approach. Some judges deliver sentence in a tirade, others sweet talk the defendant in an almost apologetic way. Some appear bored with the whole ordeal and anxious to have the matter at an end. As the National Conference of State Judges states, there is no more difficult or awesome duty. A judge should "pronounce the sentence in a careful and understandable way and . . . give the reason for it."[46] In imposing the sentence the judge should try to conform to a reasonable standard of punishment and should not seek popularity or publicity by either exceptional severity or undue leniency.

HOLDING JUDGES ACCOUNTABLE

What is to be done with a senile judge or one whose physical illnesses prevent regular attendance to duties? What of the attorney who just does not make the transition to judging? These and other reasons for judicial removal were the subjects of the Task Force on Courts of the National Advisory Commission on Criminal Justice Standards and Goals. Their study, entitled *Courts,* found that there are several ways to remove judges. Among them are impeachment and recall. These were found to be cumbersome and expensive systems.[47] As an alternative, they recommended the creation of a judicial-conduct commission composed of judges, lawyers, and laypersons. Such a system exists in California and Texas. The ABA has also recommended the creation of such commissions.[48]

The Task Force on the Administration of Justice of the President's Commission on Law Enforcement and Administration of Justice found a hitch in the California plan. "The vast majority of California attorneys interviewed had never heard of the Commission . . . or were acquainted only with the name, believing that the Commission was concerned with approving the governor's judicial appointments."[49] A secret body whose function is not known cannot be expected to do much in removing bad judges, sick judges, or unethical judges.

One of the greatest problems faced by many systems is what to do with the aged judge who constantly sleeps on the bench or otherwise has become disabled. He is not misconducting himself; he merely cannot function. The ABA, as well as the others, recommends an equitable, prompt, retirement system.[50] Without such a system, judicial commissions are not going to remove a judge only to have him become a member of the poverty group.

STUDY QUESTIONS

1. Of what influence is a judge on the process of criminal justice?
2. Give two examples of when it would be appropriate for a judge to remove himself or herself from a case.
3. What is the ABA position on the principles of a fair trial and a free press?

4. Compare the effects of a confession and a plea of guilty.
5. What sanctions may a court impose for an attorney's misconduct?
6. Why was the National College of the State Judiciary established?
7. When should a judge use the contempt power?
8. What is a judicial conduct commission?

NOTES

1. President's Commission on Law Enforcement and Administration of Justice, *Task Force Report: The Courts* (Washington, D.C.: Government Printing Office, 1967).
2. ABA, *Standards Relating to the Function of the Trial Judge* (Chicago, Ill.: American Bar Association, 1972).
3. National Advisory Commission on Criminal Justice Standards and Goals, Task Force on Courts, *Report on Courts* (Washington, D.C.: Government Printing Office, 1973).
4. National Conference of State Trial Judges, *The State Trial Judge's Book*, 2d ed. (St. Paul, Minn.: West Publishing, 1969).
5. President's Commission, *The Courts*, pp. 65–66.
6. Ibid., p. 65.
7. Op cit note 2.
8. ABA, *The Code of Professional Responsibility—Judicial Ethics* (Chicago, Ill.: ABA, 1967), hereafter cited as the *Canons* (1967).
9. ABA, *Code of Judicial Conduct* (1972). This version is shorter than the 1967 version, yet the intent is the same. It will be cited as *Canons* (1972).
10. ABA, *Standards, Function of the Trial Judge* §1.3 (1972).
11. Ibid. §1.3, p. 31.
12. *Canon* 4 (1967) and *Canon* 2 (1972).
13. ABA, *Standards, Function of the Trial Judge* §1.4, and *Canons* 6 and 7 (1967) and *Canon* 3 (1972).
14. ABA, *Standards, Function of the Trial Judge* §1.4.
15. *Canon* 5 (1967) and *Canon* 3 (1972).
16. *Canon* 9 (1967) and *Canon* 3 (1972).
17. *Canon* 15 (1967) and *Canon* 3 (1972).
18. *Canon* 20 (1967) and *Canon* 3 (1972).
19. *Canon* 33 (1967) and *Canon* 3 (1972).
20. *Canon* 17 (1967) and *Canon* 3 (1972) and ABA, *Standards, Function of the Trial Judge* §1.6.
21. ABA, *Standards, Function of the Trial Judge* §1.7.
22. *Aguilar* v. *Texas*, 378 U.S. 108 (1964).
23. ABA, *Standards, Function of the Trial Judge* §3.2.
24. ABA, *Standards, Fair Trial and Free Press* (1968).
25. Ibid., pp. 16–18.
26. Ibid., pp. 2–15.
27. *Canon* 35 (1967), *Canon* 3 (1972), and ABA, *Standards, Function of the Trial Judge* §3.7.
28. ABA, *Standards, Function of the Trial Judge* §§4.1 and 4.2.
29. 19 Crim. L. Rep. 3133 (U.S. Sup. Ct. #74–1529 June 17, 1976).
30. *Boykin* v. *Alabama*, 395 U.S. 238 (1969).
31. ABA, *Standards, Function of the Trial Judge* §5.4.
32. Ibid. §5.5.

33. Ibid. §5.6(b).
34. *Canon* 15 (1967) and *Canon* 3 (1972).
35. National Conference, *State Trial Judge's Handbook*, pp. 119–120.
36. ABA, *Standards, Function of the Trial Judge* §5.7.
37. National Conference, *State Trial Judge's Handbook*, p. 113.
38. ABA, *Standards, Function of the Trial Judge* §5.8.
39. 18 Crim. L. Rep. 3157 (U.S. Sup. Ct. #74–5968 March 30, 1976).
40. ABA, *Standards, Function of the Trial Judge* §5.9.
41. Ibid. §5.13 and ABA, *Standards, Trial by Jury* §5.6 (1968).
42. ABA, *Standards, Function of the Trial Judge* §6.5.
43. Ibid. §§7.1–7.4.
44. President's Commission, *The Courts*, pp. 22–24.
45. ABA, *Standards, Function of the Trial Judge* §8.1.
46. National Advisory Commission, *Report on Courts*, p. 296.
47. Ibid., p. 153.
48. ABA, *Standards, Function of the Trial Judge* §9.1.
49. President's Commission, *The Courts*, p. 71.
50. ABA, *Standards, Function of the Trial Judge* §9.2.

chapter eleven
Evidentiary Problems in Criminal Proceedings

In most instances the rules of evidence are the same for both civil and criminal trials; the major difference is the burden of proof. In criminal trials the state must prove the defendant guilty beyond a reasonable doubt. In the civil case the plaintiff must, to win, prove his allegations with a preponderance of the evidence. Thus in a civil trial, if the jury feels the plaintiff's proof is a little stronger than the defendant's, they can find in favor of the plaintiff, while in a criminal case the state must convince the jury that there is no other plausible course than to find the defendant guilty.

Certain types of evidence are used only in criminal trials and not in civil cases. In other instances the type of evidence is the same, such as opinion evidence, but the rules governing its admission in criminal trials are more strictly construed. Such strict rules conform with the heavy burden of proof required in criminal proceedings.

This chapter treats eyewitness identifications, confessions, character evidence, opinion evidence, and *res gestae*. While this is only a partial survey of the field of evidence, it will serve to introduce some of the key concepts and problems faced by prosecutors, defense counsel, and judges.

EYEWITNESS IDENTIFICATION PROCEDURES

There are several opportunities in the processing of a criminal defendant where he, or his likeness, may be viewed by the witnesses. These identification procedures, both extra and intrajudicial, are the subject of this section.

No discussion of identification procedures is complete without briefly covering certain significant United States Supreme Court decisions. Although much has been written about *U.S.* v. *Wade* and *Gilbert* v. *California,*[1] it appears that the cases of *Stovall* v. *Denno*[2] and *Kirby* v. *Illinois*[3] have emerged as the most important of the identification cases because they involved preindictment identification procedures.

In the *Stovall* case a face-to-face confrontation was arranged in the victim's hospital room between her and the suspected perpetrator. The Court held that the hospital confrontation was essential because of the possibility that the victim, who had been stabbed eleven times by her assailant, might die. The Court stated that "a claimed violation of due process of law in the conduct of a confrontation depends on the totality of the circumstances surrounding it."[4]

Kirby, which also involved a preindictment identification, held in a five-to-four decision that the exclusionary rule does not apply to identification of a suspect at a police-station showup after he has been arrested but before he has been indicted or otherwise formally charged with any criminal offense.[5] It was pointed out in a separate concurring opinion, however, that where the police abuse identification procedures during the course of a criminal investigation such abuses, even if they occur prior to the initiation of judicial criminal proceedings, are not beyond the reach of the Constitution. The due-process clause of the Fifth and Fourteenth Amendments still forbids a lineup which is unnecessarily suggestive and conducive to irreparable mistaken identification.

Therefore, in any identification procedure it is essential to distinguish between postindictment and preindictment identifications and to look at the surrounding circumstances regarding the necessity and fairness of these procedures. The police have a choice of three identification procedures: face-to-face confrontation, photographic identification, and lineup.

Face-to-Face Confrontations

Several federal decisions have bearing on what is permissible in face-to-face confrontations (or showups). Perhaps the most significant case is *Bates* v. *United States.*[6] Two women were attacked in their apartment. One of the women had a fairly good look at the attacker because of a streetlight shining into the bedroom window. The women gave the police a description of the man. Both had observed that their assailant had a bandage wrapped around his hand. Within thirty minutes of the attack a suspect was arrested, placed in a patrol wagon, and taken to the victims' apartment. The women were asked to come downstairs and look at the man confined in the vehicle. One of the women could not positively identify the man, although she said he had the same general appearance as the intruder. The other woman, the one who had a much better view of the assailant, identified him as the attacker. The Court said that there is no rule against the viewing of a suspect alone in what is called a "one-man showup" when this occurs near the time of the alleged crime. For its authority it cited *Biggers* v. *Tennessee*,[7] where Justice Douglas pointed out that due process is not always violated when the police, instead of conducting a lineup, conduct a one-man showup. The *Bates* case added that such a course of action does not necessarily tend to bring about misidentification but tends instead, under some circumstances, to ensure accuracy. Of course the existence of certain infirmities, such as hysteria of the witness, as well as the presence of other factors that might taint the intrajudicial identification testimony of a witness can be explored on cross-examination and alluded to during argument.

Bates concluded by saying that prudent police work should confine these on-the-spot identifications to situations where possible doubts as to identification need to be promptly resolved. Without such a need, the conventional lineup is the appropriate procedure. Police action in returning the suspect to the vicinity of the crime for immediate identification fosters the desirable objectives of fresh and accurate identification. In some circumstances this procedure may lead to the immediate release of an innocent suspect and at the same time enable the police to resume the search for the actual culprit while the trail is still fresh.

A more recent federal decision illustrates the problem of the one-man showup where the defendant does not know he is being viewed by a witness. *Hastings* v. *Cardwell* held that, where the police act promptly and a lineup would have been difficult or impossible, there is no violation of the due-process clause of the Fourteenth Amendment in a one-man showup.[8] The showup in this case, unlike *Bates,* was not a face-to-face confrontation. The witness viewed the defendant through a one-way mirror while the defendant was being fingerprinted.

A number of cases have dealt with the problem of a showup conducted during certain courtroom proceedings. In a majority of these cases the defendant, who is either on trial for another charge or is in the court for a preliminary hearing, is unaware that he is being observed. A witness is brought into the courtroom and asked if he can identify the person who perpetrated the crime. The first decision on this question came in *United States* v. *Roth*.[9]

In *Roth* the witness on two occasions walked into the courtroom during court recesses to see if he could identify the man who had conned him. The first walk-through occurred several days before he was to testify in court. Roth, the accused, was not in the courtroom at that time and the witness did not identify anyone. The second walk-through occurred shortly before the witness was to testify. He entered the courtroom and observed four people, one of whom resembled the perpetrator of the crime. The witness, however, was not sure of his identification. The prosecutor did not press the witness for a more positive identification. The court was not overly impressed with this identification procedure. It said that the more informal the viewing procedure, the greater the possibility of subtle suggestiveness. When a walk-through occurs, the prevailing conditions are beyond the control of the government and, more likely than not, the defendant will be sitting at the counsel table, the very place the witness would look and expect to find him. A defendant is acutely aware of what is happening when a lineup takes place and gains some impression of the surrounding circumstances. This is not the case in a *Roth* situation, where there is no compelling reason for the attorney or his client to focus on their surroundings and to remember them. They are both unaware of what is occurring. Reconstruction of the confrontation at the trial may be difficult or impossible. Furthermore, the government itself cannot justify a need for identification at this stage of the case. The court in *Bates,* however, found that the identification procedure did not taint the case because one witness made no positive identification, and the preponderance of the other evidence clearly indicated guilt.

The supreme court of Wisconsin recently upheld a courtroom identification in a judicial decision meriting some discussion. In the case of *Dozie* v. *State* the defendant was identified from a photograph.[10] Following this identification, the witness was requested to appear in the county courtroom at 2:00 P.M. The witness was not told the defendant's name or that the defendant was in custody on another criminal charge. The witness was seated in the courtroom with instructions to approach a certain police officer and tap his shoulder if he observed anyone he could identify as the person who had committed the crime. An hour and a half passed without incident. The courtroom was very busy with about 150 persons present. When the defendant appeared with his attorney, the witness tapped the police officer on the shoulder. The court upheld this identification procedure. They found nothing illegal because the witness sat alone and was not influenced by the presence or comments of anyone. He made a prompt and positive identification. The court said there was simply no element of suggestiveness in the procedure followed.

Two recent cases confirm the point that, where a witness is present at a preliminary hearing to testify against the accused, an identification of the defendant which takes place prior to the witness's taking the stand is permissible and does not violate due process.[11]

Photographic Identification

"Reliance by the victim upon what someone else has told him about the identity of the perpetrator, rather than upon his own independent recollection of the offender, has always been the concern to police, prosecutor, and defense counsel alike."[12] The major concern is that the seeds of suggestion will be planted in such a manner that the eyewitness or victim will identify the person the police want to prosecute.

The two leading cases on photographic identification are *Simmons* v. *United States* and *United States* v. *Ash*. The *Simmons* case involved a prosecution for bank robbery. The day following the crime photographs were shown to the five bank employees who were present during the robbery. Each identified Simmons as one of the culprits. A week or two later three of these employees identified photographs of Garrett as the other man. Two employees said they did not get a clear view of the second man. During the trial all five employees identified Simmons; three of them picked Garrett as his cohort.

The Court said that each case must be considered on its own set of facts. There was little chance for misidentification here because the robbery took place in a well-lighted area, and the robbers wore no masks. The witnesses were shown six photographs the day following the crime. Each witness was alone when viewing the pictures. There was no evidence that the witnesses were told anything about the progress of the investigation. Nor was there any suggestion that the witnesses were told which of the people in the photographs were suspects. The Court said that the procedure complied with constitutional standards and could only have been more ideal

> by allowing only one or two of the five eyewitnesses to view the pictures of Simmons. If thus identified, Simmons could later have been displayed in a lineup, thus permitting the photographic identification to be supplemented by a corporeal identification which is normally more accurate.[13]

The more recent case involving identification by photographs is *United States* v. *Ash*.[14] The Court articulated the issue as follows: Does the Sixth Amendment grant to the accused the right to have counsel present whenever the government conducts a postindictment photographic display containing a picture of the accused, for the purpose of allowing a witness to attempt an identification of the offender?

In this robbery the perpetrators all wore stocking masks. About six months after the robbery four witnesses were shown five black and white photographs of black males with the same general physical characteristics. The four witnesses made uncertain identifications of the defendant's picture. Two months later Ash was indicted, and two years later the case was set for trial. Just prior to trial the witnesses were shown five color photographs. Three of the witnesses identified Ash. One witness was unable to make a selection. Nobody selected Bailey, who was charged as an accomplice and whose photograph was one of the original five shown to the witnesses.

The Court noted that adversary problems are not present in photographic identification situations. The defendant is not present, and no possibility arises that the accused might be misled by his lack of familiarity with the law or overpowered by his professional adversary. The traditional counterbalance in the American adversary system for prosecutorial interviews arises from the equal ability of defense counsel to seek and interview witnesses himself. "We are not persuaded that the risks inherent in the use of photographic displays are so pernicious that an extraordinary system of safeguards is required."[15]

Therefore, it appears that the burden is on the defense to attack the identification procedure. However, one writer has suggested that certain procedures be followed:

1. A series of at least ten photographs, only one of which is the suspect, shall be presented to the witness. If there are two or more suspects, no two shall be presented together in a single group of photographs.

2. Insofar as practicable, all photographs shall be unmarked and of the same size. The photographs should be of persons of approximately the same weight, height, age, and color of hair and skin.

3. When there are two or more witnesses, each should be required to view the photographs separately, and to make identification separately, out of the presence and hearing of one another. After the first witness has made a photographic identification, it would be better practice to require all other witnesses to view the suspect in a corporeal lineup only.

4. It is essential that the police personnel involved in conducting such procedures keep an accurate record of photographs identified, as well as noting all remarks made by any witness upon identification of a photograph. Failure to make an identification or a mistake in identification also should be noted. All photographs exhibited to the witnesses should be preserved and appropriately identified for further use in court.

5. Finally, whenever a subject is exhibited to an eyewitness in a corporeal lineup, a large color photograph of the lineup (at least 8″ × 10″), exactly as viewed by such witness, should be made and preserved for in-court use. The presentation of such photographs in court enables the trial judge, and later the jury, to better determine whether or not such lineup was unfairly conducted.[16]

The defense attorney will be looking for chinks or weak spots in identification procedures. Wall warns that the prosecutor and police should be aware of certain danger signals. The existence of one or two of these factors, in itself, is usually insufficient to render the identification invalid, but in combination their effect can be dangerous. Wall lists twelve danger signals.

1. Where the witness originally states that he would be unable to identify anyone;
2. Where the identifying witness knows the defendant prior to the crime, but makes no accusation against him when questioned by the police;
3. Where a serious discrepancy exists between the identifying witness's original description of the perpetrator of the crime and the actual description of the defendant;
4. Where the witness erroneously identifies some other person before identifying the defendant at the trial;
5. Where other witnesses to the crime fail to identify the defendant;
6. Where, prior to trial, the witness sees the defendant but fails to identify him;
7. Where the witness had a very limited opportunity to observe the defendant;
8. Where the witness and the person identified are of different racial groups;
9. Where, during his original observation of the perpetrator of the crime, the witness is unaware that a crime situation is involved;
10. Where a considerable period of time elapses between the witness's view of the criminal and a subsequent identification of the defendant;
11. Where the crime is committed by a number of persons;
12. Where the witness fails to make a positive identification.[17]

Lineups

In the case of *Kirby* v. *Ellis* the United States Supreme Court held that the defendant is not entitled to counsel before he has been indicted or otherwise formally charged with any criminal offense.[18] Thus *Wade* and *Gilbert* are limited only to postindictment situations.

The primary concern of the courts focuses on the fairness of the lineup and the treatment of the identifying witnesses. Wall's twelve danger signals should be kept in mind when testing the validity of lineup procedures. For a lineup to be fair the defendant must not stick out like a sore thumb. Moreover, the police should not harass, beg, or cajole the witness. If there is more than one witness, they should not view the lineup together. However, if a lineup or other identification procedure is tainted, the taint can be overcome by the presence of an independent source of identification.

CONFESSIONS: *MIRANDA AND THE OUT-OF-COURT STATEMENT*

The question concerning the admissibility of confessions took on new dimensions with the decision in *Miranda* v. *Arizona*.[19] Rather than merely judging the voluntariness of a confession, the Supreme Court held that "the prosecution may not use statements, whether exculpatory or inculpatory, stemming from custodial interrogation of the defendant unless it demonstrates the use of procedural safeguards effective to secure the privilege against self-incrimination." From that date forward the police have been required, except in limited circumstances, to give a defendant certain basic warnings. We will discuss the use of *Miranda,* attempt to show those exceptional circumstances where warnings are not necessary, and demonstrate what warnings are adequate.

Custody

The *Miranda* requirements do not come into play unless the person in question is in custody. This requirement put to rest the issue of "focus" that was discussed in the *Escobedo* case. As a matter of fact, the United States Supreme Court in *Miranda* said that what is meant by "focus" is the combination of custody and interrogation. Therefore, the threshold question should be whether the questioning by police officers or other state officials took place under custodial circumstances.

Custody means that the accused has been deprived of his freedom of action in a significant way. In *Evans* v. *State* the defendant was under investigation for embezzlement.[20] The record did not disclose where the FBI agents questioned her, but it was clear that the questioning was not done in a building housing law-enforcement personnel. The Court said that the defendant had not been taken into custody, nor had she been deprived of her freedom of action in any way. Therefore, the custodial-interrogation safeguards of *Miranda* were inapplicable to this situation. The same result was reached where agents interviewed a defendant at her place of business while her husband was present.[21]

The point as to where general investigation becomes custodial interrogation is very important. If there has been custodial interrogation, at trial the prosecution must show that the defendant was given the *Miranda* warnings before custodial interrogation began, that the defendant had the opportunity to exercise those rights, and that he or she knowingly and intelligently waived these rights before answering questions or making a statement. If these procedures are not followed, any evidence obtained as a result of the custodial interrogation is inadmissible. On the other hand, if the interrogation was not custodial, then failure to give the *Miranda* warnings will not require suppression of the evidence obtained from the investigation.[22]

In these cases the courts look to the atmosphere surrounding the questioning to determine if the interrogation was custodial. If they find no coercive or compelling atmosphere, they will find that the defendant was not in custody.[23]

Sometimes, during the general investigation of a crime, a suspect will voluntarily go to the police department for questioning. Although the suspect may feel free to leave, care should be taken to ensure that the proper constitutional warnings are given. Such circumstances are suspect, thus placing a higher burden of proof on the prosecution to show the noncustodial atmosphere. A state case in this area is *Brunson* v. *State*.[24] Police officers discovered some footprints at the scene of the crime and identified them as having been made by the defendant. The police found the defendant at the home of a friend and asked him if he had any objection to coming down to city hall. He had none and went there in his own car. He consented to being fingerprinted. After a little "folksy" exchange, the police told the defendant that his footprints were found at the scene and asked him when he was last there. He said that he had been there that morning to pick up his check. The police said the print was exceptionally sharp to last until early the next morning, especially since several cars had been in and out of the parking lot. They then asked, "Billy, what about that track?" Billy confessed. The defendant had not been given his warnings; therefore the court considered the defendant under arrest or in custody at the time of this confession.

When police officers take victims of a crime to a cafe and have them confront certain suspects and where the police ask certain on-the-scene questions, it has been held that the individuals suspected of the crime were not in custody.[25]

On-the-Scene Exception

When the police come to the scene of a crime, it is natural for them to be inquisitive. They are not always expected to begin reading the *Miranda* warnings as they approach the scene of the crime.

Therefore, when certain investigative questions are asked before any formal arrest is made, the Court allows the questioning without the requirement of the *Miranda* warnings. In *McMillian* v. *U.S.* federal agents told the defendants that they were investigating an unregistered still.[26] Before anything else was said one defendant replied, "Our land don't go down to the still," and another declared, "I don't know anything about that moonshine still." The agents already knew that the still was on the defendants' property. The defendants were arrested. The court held their statement admissible as part of an on-the-scene investigation. In *U.S.* v. *Robertson* a title clerk referred the police to a suspicious motor-vehicle-title application.[27] The police searched for the car and found it. As the defendant approached the car, the police told him that there were some irregularities regarding the papers he had presented at the title office. He was asked about the new auto tags he had in his hand, and he said they were for another car. The defendant also told them the car was owned by his company. These statements, which proved to be false, were used against him at his trial; they were upheld under the on-the-scene exception.

A few states have had occasion to consider the on-the-scene exception. Perhaps the leading case is *Nevels* v. *State.*[28] A Mississippi highway patrolman observed a heavily loaded car weaving across the center line. The car came to a stop in a driveway and the occupants got out and ran. The highway patrolman called for help and the deputy sheriff arrived with bloodhounds. Without opening the car, the patrolman could see rolls of barbed wire in the car and in the open trunk. The dogs barked and Nevels came out of the bushes, stating, "Mr. Langford, I was going to give myself up anyway." Then the patrolman asked the following questions. "Jerry, is this your car?" Jerry said, "No sir, I stole the car." "What about the wire?" Jerry replied, "I stole it." "Where did you get the wire from?" Again Jerry replied, "I think International Paper Company owned it." The Court said that these statements were within the on-the-scene exception. Another pertinent case is *Ford* v. *State* where, at the scene, the defendant told the patrolman that he had been drinking.[29] The court found this within the on-the-scene exception as customary questioning in regard to the attendant facts of a crime.

Another case which illustrates this point is *Amos* v. *State.*[30] While at a dance the defendant asked two officers to help him find his lost or misplaced coat. He later left the dance without the coat. Later a coat fitting the description given by Tommy Amos was handed to the officers by someone and, seeing no name tag, they went through the jacket to determine its owner. They found some matchboxes, one of which was open and revealed something that looked like marijuana. Tommy Amos was brought back to the dance so he could identify the coat. The police asked him if the coat was his and Amos said it was. They then asked him to check to see if everything was there, and he said, "Everything is here." He started to leave. The police then arrested him and gave him the *Miranda* warnings. Since the police did not know that the coat belonged to the defendant, they had a duty to question him about the coat and were permitted to do so under the on-the-scene-interrogation exception to the *Miranda* rule.

Amos also demonstrates the closeness between noncustodial interrogation and the on-the-scene-interrogation exception. The court could also have found that the defendant was not in custody, because Amos felt free to leave after identifying his coat.

Voluntary and Spontaneous Statements

Spontaneous statements and voluntary comments are admissible even though the defendant was in custody when they were made. The court looks at the circumstances and, if it finds a lack of compulsion, the statements will be admitted.

In *U.S.* v. *Welsh* the police were called to a motel by a clerk who became suspicious when Welsh incorrectly described his car when registering.[31] The police arrested Welsh at the motel for automobile theft when he incorrectly identified his car to them as a "1963 Chevy II" when it was actually a 1966 Chevy II and could not perform basic operations, such as raising the hood. Before the warnings were given, the defendant said his friends were in the room with sawed-off shotguns and might use them since they were high on narcotics. As there was no interrogation, the court admitted this statement as voluntary.

In a different case, a FBI agent read the defendant his rights in his cell, but the defendant refused to sign a waiver. As the agent got up to leave, the defendant began to talk, in an attempt to exculpate himself. This was deemed by the court to be a voluntary statement. The court further determined that the agent was entitled to pursue the line of inquiry begun by the defendant. The ensuing discussion was found to resemble one where the accused voluntarily confesses prior to questioning.[32]

An example of a voluntary admission is found in *Boyles* v. *State,* where the defendant, upon voluntarily surrendering, handed the sheriff a pistol and said that he had shot a man.[33] Although Boyles was not warned of his constitutional rights before his admission, the court held that the "statement of an arrested person freely and voluntarily given, without compelling influences, is a recognized exception set out specifically under the *Miranda* rule."

In *Wash* v. *State* the deputy sheriff was allowed to testify to statements made by the appellant when arrested, but before he advised her of her *Miranda* rights.[34] The deputy testified: "I said, 'Leida, you are under arrest.' She said, 'It's about Temmie J., ain't it?' I said, 'Yeah.' She said, 'I hope he's dead.' I said, 'Well, you've got your hope for he's sure dead.' " The court said these statements were voluntarily and spontaneously made by the appellant. "The deputy was making no effort to examine her or to obtain any information from her. She spoke so quickly, he did not have time to give her the warning."[35]

In another case, the defendant requested a deputy to come to the jail. Once there, the deputy was told where he might find some pistols. The deputy addressed no questions to the defendant. The court held that the defendant gave the deputy the information extemporaneously and without any compelling influences.[36]

In *Chinn* v. *State* the only question asked by the police was not about the crime, but about the reason for the defendant's voluntary surrender.[37] The court held it was not an error to admit the statement the defendant made at the time of his surrender.

Waiver of Right to Remain Silent   Waiver cannot be presumed from silence. If a defendant says he understands his rights, wants to make a statement, and then makes a statement there may be a valid waiver. The surrounding facts and circumstances must be looked at to determine whether the waiver was obtained by compulsion and whether the person could intelligently waive his rights.

To be able to waive his rights he must understand his rights. In *U.S.* v. *Trabucco* the defense argued that the warnings given were insufficient for an "ignorant Chilean seaman who knew nothing about our laws and customs, much less our Constitution."[38] The court held that, since the warnings were given in Spanish by a Spanish-speaking police officer, a valid waiver could be given.

In *U.S.* v. *Martin* the court held that even though under the influence of alcohol a person may still have enough mental presence to knowingly confess and intelligently waive his rights.[39] Along these lines consider the Mississippi case of *State* v. *Williams*.[40] In a period of about eight hours the defendant confessed to a judge, who said he was drunk, and later to the D.A., who said he was not intoxicated. But since the defendant had been drinking solidly for weeks the court found that a knowing or intelligent waiver could not have been made; his intoxication and other factors produced a mania.

As a waiver must be intelligently made, the person making the waiver must be intelligent enough to understand what he is doing. In *Dover* v. *State* an examination revealed that the defendant had an I.Q. of sixty and moderate mental retardation.[41] The doctor testified that such a person does not exercise good judgment under periods of stress. The court was unable to say that his confession was voluntary beyond a reasonable doubt. The court was of the opinion that a mentally deficient person of the caliber shown here cannot knowingly and effectively waive his constitutional rights. The same result obtained in *Harvey* v. *State*[42] and in *Cooper* v. *Griffin*.[43]

Should educational level be a factor? Consider *Harris* v. *State*.[44] The defendant was arrested at his home and the interrogation began the next day. After the warnings were given, the defendant told the officers that he did not need a lawyer because he was not guilty. He talked and talked quite freely. He later claimed that since he had only gone through the fourth grade in public school, and the tenth grade in G.I. school, his waiver was invalid. The court found ample evidence of the rights having been read and explained and affirmed the conviction. In *Stewart* v. *State* the court said that the extent of education is only one factor to be taken into account.[45] Any person with reasonable intelligence could understand these warnings; no specialized erudition was required to comprehend them. Therefore, even though the defendant had only a second-grade education, he was held to have voluntarily waived his rights.

The fact that a defendant cannot read or write does not necessarily mean that he is incapable of waiving his constitutional rights. This is true even if he signs the waiver and confession by using his mark, an X. The jury is entitled to consider whether the waiver and confession were freely and voluntarily given, but only after the court determines as a matter of law the issues of a knowing and voluntary confession. Where the state offers the testimony of all of the officers present at the time of the questioning, this is sufficient to show that the defendant freely and voluntarily made the confession.[46]

Is a confession admissible as a matter of law if it is freely and voluntarily given while the defendant is in custody under an unlawful arrest? As long as the defendant is fully apprised of his rights, the fact of detention is only one fact to be weighed when determining voluntariness and not controlling.[47]

Coercion   The primary issue concerning a confession is whether or not it was obtained by coercion. For many courts this has become the only issue of merit involving a *Miranda* question. Coercion can take many forms. The threat to the defendant does not have to come directly from the police or prosecutor, as was pointed out in *Armstrong* v. *State*.[48] The defendant in this case made several confessions. The first had been given without *Miranda* warnings. The second confession was made at the scene of the crime. There was a large crowd gathered at the scene and the defendant said that he was scared because the crowd seemed bent on vengeance. These two confessions were not admitted into evidence. However, the third and fourth confessions, which were made the next day, were allowed by the trial judge. The Mississippi Supreme Court reached the following conclusions. First, where a subsequent confession is not the result of a prior invalid confession the subsequent confession may be introduced. However, prior threats or compulsion continues unless it is clearly shown that the compulsion has ceased. The court then stated that this ruling was not contrary to the decision of the United States Supreme Court in *Clewis* v. *Texas*.[49] *Clewis* was tried before the date of the *Miranda* decision and, although the requirements of *Miranda* were not directly applicable to *Clewis,* the Court determined that *Miranda's* requirements are relevant on the issue of voluntariness. The *Clewis* case points out that very often there is a stream of events from the arrest of a defendant until he confesses. The court must look at this stream and determine, from the totality of the circumstances, whether the statements of the defendant are truly voluntary. The Court stated that there was no break in the stream of events, from the arrest of Clewis until he confessed, sufficient to insulate the statement from the prior illegalities.

In *Reid* v. *State* the defendant claimed that his confession was coerced.[50] He was in custody from 6:30 A.M. until 4:30 P.M. Some of the time was spent in a car going from the town where he was arrested to another town for testing. The defendant admitted that he voluntarily made the trip to submit to a polygraph test. He said he felt free to leave up until the point when the sheriff called the testing center to say that a cohort had confessed and implicated the defendant. The defendant says that the officers told him it would be better for him to confess, but he also stated that there was no prolonged questioning. No questions were asked of him on the trip back to jail. It was not until he had talked to his cohort that he made the disputed confession. The court held that this confession was free and voluntary and not the result of any promises of leniency.

The *Reid* case also points out that where the accused offers testimony that offers of reward, promises of leniency, or force induced the confession, the state must offer all the officers who were present when the accused was questioned or else give satisfactory reasons for their absence.

Adequacy and Form of Warnings

There would be no problem in this area if every law-enforcement officer gave the warnings exactly as spelled out in *Miranda*. However, sometimes these warnings, as given in the field, are different and the courts have been called upon to determine if the changes have substantially affected their meaning.

For example, in *Windsor* v. *U.S.* the defendant was told that he could speak with an attorney or anyone else before he said anything.[51] The court held that this warning was inadequate because the defendant was not informed that he was entitled to the presence of an attorney during interrogation and that one would be appointed if he could not afford one.

Perhaps the most confusing problem in this area involves language which indicates to the defendant that he is entitled to an attorney at trial. In *Mayzak* v. *U.S.* the FBI told Mayzak that they could not furnish an attorney until federal charges had been brought against him.[52] Rather than specifically approving this language, the court found that Mayzak understood his right to remain silent and thus upheld the admission of his damaging statements. The issue came up again in *Gilpen* v. *U.S.*[53] Gilpen was told, "We have no way of giving you a lawyer but one will be appointed for you if you wish, if you go to court." The fifth circuit said that this was an inadequate warning and held that the failure of interrogating officers to give all of the "*Miranda* bundle of warnings" will destroy the voluntariness of the confession.

The following form, approved in *Hodge* v. *U.S.*, complies with all of the *Miranda* requirements.

Your Rights   Before we ask you any questions, you must understand your rights. You have a right to remain silent. Anything you say can be used against you in court. You have a right to talk to a lawyer for advice before we ask you any questions and to have him with you during questioning. If you cannot afford a lawyer, one will be appointed for you before any questioning, if you wish. If you decide to answer questions now, without a lawyer present, you will still have the right to stop answering at any time. You also have the right to stop answering at any time until you talk to a lawyer.

Waiver of Rights   I have read this statement of my rights and I understand what my rights are. I am willing to make a statement and answer questions. I do not want a lawyer at this time. I understand and know what I am doing. No promises or threats have been made to me and no pressure or coercion of any kind has been used against me.[54]

Merely saying that the rights were read from such a card, without proof of what was on the card, is not considered to be adequate assurance that the proper rights were given.[55]

It appears that one of the most important parts of the warning is for the interrogators to make it clear that the defendant can have an attorney present during interrogation.[56] Of course, the duty of furnishing an attorney applies only upon the representation by an individual that he is indigent and that he wishes an attorney.[57]

285

The Right to Remain Silent

Miranda makes it clear that once the defendant says he wants a lawyer and wishes to remain silent all interrogation should cease. This was made clear in *U.S.* v. *Ramos.*[58] In 1969 a state court was presented with a right-to-remain-silent problem.[59] The defendant was arrested for criminal homicide and given the *Miranda* warnings by one police officer. He was not interrogated at this time. Later a deputy sheriff and two patrolmen arrived, took custody of Spurlin, and asked him if he had had his rights explained to him and if he understood them. He said that he did. The defendant and the officers got into a car; after a while Spurlin asked if he could get a lawyer. One of the officers told him that he could have one as soon as they got to their destination and that he did not have to say anything if he did not want to. The officer then asked Spurlin where the gun was. He told them it was at his home and offered to take them to it. They went to his home and found the gun. The trial court held that this statement and the evidence seized as a result were admissible. The Mississippi Supreme Court based its opinion on the fact that the statement was made freely and voluntarily without compelling influence. They barely mentioned the fact that he had asked for an attorney. Some courts in other jurisdictions have held that when the defendant asks for an attorney he is exercising his right to remain silent. However, most states hold that a person who says he would like an attorney in the future but answers questions without counsel has waived his right to counsel. Caution should be exercised, however, to make sure that, as the *Spurlin* case infers, the will of the defendant has not been overcome by compelling influences. If the defendant requests an attorney and the police continue to press the defendant for answers to questions through intensive interrogation, any statement made by the defendant will be inadmissible.

The refusal to sign a waiver does not mean that the defendant is necessarily exercising his right to remain silent. This is especially true where the defendant says he does not want an attorney present.[60] The fifth circuit has held that where the defendant shows a reluctance to talk and refuses to sign a waiver any future conversation with him must be initiated by him.[61] The fifth circuit has also held, however, that when all of the circumstances indicate that an accused knew of his right to remain silent, and knowingly waived that right, his refusal to sign a written waiver does not render the confession inadmissible.[62]

The fact that a defendant has told one set of police officers that he does not want to speak to them does not mean that another officer can initiate interrogation. There are exceptions to this, however. In

Jennings v. *U.S.* the defendant was arrested by local police, given his warnings, and questioned for an hour.[63] He refused to talk. An FBI agent came in later and did not know of the previous refusal. The agent gave the defendant his warnings; this time the defendant did not show the same reluctance to speak. His statements to the FBI agent were held admissible.

In *U.S.* v. *Brown,* the defendant had been interviewed several times by the Secret Service.[64] She refused to talk to the agents at these interviews. Later she had a session with an attorney—one of her own choosing. She confessed at the next interview following the conversation with her attorney. At this interview she did not request an attorney. The court held that this confession was admissible.

Miranda Today

The Supreme Court has recently reexamined the constitutional requirements of *Miranda* in *Michigan* v. *Tucker.*[65] In that case, Tucker was arrested for rape and questioned by the police. He was advised of his right to remain silent and his right to counsel, but he was not advised of his right to appointed counsel. During the interrogation, Tucker named an alibi witness; the police later elicited information from the alibi witness that incriminated Tucker. At defendant's post-*Miranda* trial, the court excluded Tucker's own statements taken during the interrogation, but allowed the testimony of the witness, and Tucker was convicted.

Following affirmance on appeal, Tucker sought habeas corpus relief, which the district court granted on the ground that the witness's testimony was inadmissible because of *Miranda* violations. The court of appeals affirmed that decision.

The issue, as the Supreme Court saw it, was whether the witness's testimony must be excluded because the police had learned of his identity through the in-custody questioning of Tucker, at which time Tucker was not informed of his right to appointed counsel.

The Supreme Court refused to exclude the evidence derived from the interrogation, stating that the police conduct did not directly infringe upon Tucker's right against self-incrimination but merely violated the prophylactic rules developed to protect that right. The Court further stated that a failure to give an interrogated suspect the full *Miranda* warnings does not exclude the suspect's statements in every situation. Quoting *Harris* v. *New York,* the Court affirmed the principle that *Miranda* bars the prosecution from making its case with statements by an accused while in custody prior to waiving his rights.[66] While such evidence is inadmissible from the prosecutor's case in chief, the statements may be admissible to impeach the defendant's testimony.

The majority of the justices determined that the reasoning of *Harris* was applicable to *Michigan* v. *Tucker*. The respondent was able to block admission of his own statements, but *Miranda* does not require the prosecution to refrain from use of all Tucker's statements. Therefore, the testimony of the alibi witness was properly admitted.

CONFESSIONS: THE NON-MIRANDA PROBLEMS

A confession is admissible when it is properly qualified. A properly qualified confession is one that was not induced by promises, threats, or violence. The defendant is entitled to a hearing on this issue in the absence of the jury before the confession is admitted in evidence. Failing this, it is an error to admit the confession.

It is the judge's duty to determine whether a confession is admissible. The judge should not permit the jury to hear the confession if the proof tends to show that the alleged confession was made involuntarily. The burden of proof is upon the state to prove beyond a reasonable doubt that a confession was freely and voluntarily made. The defendant has the right to testify as to its voluntariness without being subjected to cross-examination as to its truthfulness. There must be corroborating evidence independent of the confession to avoid convicting a person solely on the basis of his own testimony. The general rule is that the prosecution should submit evidence tending to prove the existence of a crime before introducing into evidence a confession.

Some actions which would render a confession inadmissible on the basis of involuntariness are: promises of any kind; force or coercion; being held incommunicado; and not being allowed to speak to a close relative or spouse. Obviously force or coercion by a state officer cannot be tolerated. But what about a threat by a simultaneously jailed coindictee? One defendant said that a prior confession was involuntarily made because he was threatened by a coindictee. The court said there was insufficient evidence on this point but it did not rule out that possibility.[67]

The mere illegal detention of a defendant does not make a confession involuntary. The key is whether, in conjunction with this illegal detention, the defendant was given his constitutional rights. The fact of the illegal detention is but one factor the trial judge must weigh. A confession should not be rejected because it was made under a fear produced, not by extraneous pressure, by apprehension due to the situation in which the accused finds himself merely by being in jail. The circumstances surrounding the arrest and detention must be examined to determine what effect they had upon the giving of the confession. Mental coercion may be as strong as physical coercion.[68]

The state has the burden of showing that the confession was voluntary. At the beginning of the suppression hearing the state must make a prima facie case of voluntariness. The state must show the surrounding circumstances leading up to the confession. When a defendant denies the voluntariness of a confession, it is usually necessary for everyone present at the time of the confession to testify. If all of them cannot be there, good cause must be shown why they are absent.

All persons present means not only the officers present but anyone else who acted as part of the interrogation team. Generally, when the accused claims "foul" on a confession, the state should recall the officers present to deny the charge. Not to do so causes concern. The error will be judged harmless if there was a sufficient interval between the alleged threat and the confession, during which the defendant had his rights explained and signed a statement that he understood them. More important would be a statement in court that he was not scared.[69]

What is an adequate excuse for an officer who acted as part of the interrogation team not to be present? Certainly, "His dad said he was in Vicksburg in the oil field" was not good enough in *Evans* v. *State*.[70] Most courts have held that an officer being in another state testifying under subpoena is justification enough for an absence at the suppression hearing.

Where a second confession is said to be based on an earlier involuntary confession the unlawful influences of the first are presumed to have continued through the second confession. The state, when offering the second confession or any subsequent confession, must overcome the presumptions of the first if it has been found involuntary.

A first confession must be considered even if it is not offered if the defendant says his second confession was based upon fear or promises involved in the first. A passage of time, admitted to by the defendant, can obviate this requirement if it is a long enough interval. In *State* v. *Fabian*, the second confession was made three months after the one made to Tennessee officers. The evidence showed that no promises or threats were made by the Mississippi police officers.[71]

If a defendant alleges that an offer of leniency or reward was made by the district attorney or other officer, the confession is inadmissible unless that district attorney or officer testifies. An unsworn statement will not substitute for the testimony required.

If the defendant does not complain that the confession was involuntary he cannot have it excluded just because all the witnesses to his confession were not put on the stand while the state was making its case. This is especially true where the defendant's testimony and that of the interrogating officers establish its voluntariness.

289

If a person is arrested, detained all day, and signs a confession that day while going through drug withdrawal, that confession is not voluntary. The same rule would apply to someone suffering from the delirium tremens. Being a little drunk would probably not invalidate an otherwise good confession.

If the defendant's past record is good and other factors such as age warrant it, a statement like, "It would be better to tell the truth, as it would go lighter with you," may render a confession inadmissible. A leading case in this area is *Agee* v. *State*.[72] In *Agee* the sheriff's testimony showed that violence was inflicted on the defendant two hours before the confession was signed. This made it inadmissible. An additional reason for ruling the confession inadmissible was that the sheriff had called the defendant's teacher to come down and talk to the defendant about telling the truth. *Agee* thus reinforces earlier case law that promises made by individuals while a defendant is in custody have the same effect as those made by officers if the individual makes the offer on behalf of the state.

CONFESSIONS AND JOINT TRIALS: THE PROBLEM

Most of the fifty state jurisdictions have long recognized that the confession of a codefendant implicating a separately tried defendant is not admissible as evidence in the trial of the second defendant if the codefendant's confession was not made in the presence of the implicated defendant. Likewise, if the implicating confession is made in the presence of the defendant but was denied by him at the time, the confession of the codefendant is inadmissible as hearsay as it relates to the other defendant. However, if a codefendant makes an implicating confession in the presence of another defendant, the veracity of which is not then denied, that confession is always admissible against the other defendant as an exception to the hearsay rule.

Whether a statement is admissible against another defendant or not, a competent and voluntary confession made by a codefendant who has been properly advised of his rights is normally admissible as proof of his own guilt.

Where codefendants are tried jointly it is quite possible that the extrajudicial confession of a codefendant who chooses not to testify in his own defense may not be introduced into evidence at all, even though the confession is clearly admissible under the rules of evidence as proof of guilt. Under these circumstances, allowing such a confession to be placed in evidence may well operate to deny another codefendant his Sixth Amendment right of confrontation. Where such a confession is placed in evidence the second codefendant has no way of cross-examining the party who made the statement and thereby loses a valuable constitutional right. Thus such confessions are normally excluded altogether in joint trials.

The Old Law: State and Federal Practice

At one time, most courts followed the procedure that was used in virtually every state and allowed the confession of one codefendant to be placed in evidence in joint trials of two or more defendants provided that the jury was instructed to regard the confession as probative only of the guilt of the person who made the confession and to completely disregard the confession in determining the guilt or innocence of the other codefendants. In holding that such a confession was admissible, the Mississippi Supreme Court used the following language.

> The voluntary confession of a codefendant cannot be admitted against the other defendants when such confession was not made in their presence and assented to by them, even though the several defendants are being tried jointly. However, the confession of one such defendant can be admitted against that defendant, with instruction by the court to the jury that it is only admitted against that one defendant and is not to be considered as evidence against his codefendants.[73]

Only two years later the United States Supreme Court handed down an identical ruling in *Delli Pooli* v. *United States.*

The New Law: The Bruton Rule

In 1968 the United States Supreme Court reversed its holding in *Delli Pooli* in the case of *Bruton* v. *United States.* The circumstances surrounding the *Bruton* case were quite unusual. Bruton and a codefendant named Evans were tried jointly in federal district court in the eastern district of Missouri. Testimony was introduced at the trial to the effect that Evans had confessed to a witness that he and Bruton had committed an armed robbery together. Evans himself exercised his privilege and did not testify. The jury was instructed that it could not consider Evans's confession in regard to Bruton's guilt or innocence; the confession applied only to the guilt of Evans. Nevertheless, both defendants were convicted, and both appealed to the Eighth Circuit Court of Appeals. The eighth circuit reversed Evans's conviction because he had not been advised of his rights under *Miranda* v. *Arizona* prior to making his confession. Therefore Evans's confession was inadmissible. However, the eighth circuit affirmed Bruton's conviction since the jury had been instructed to disregard the evidence of Evans's confession in their determination of Bruton's guilt or innocence.

In overruling *Delli Pooli* the *Bruton* court said the following.

> We hold that, because of the substantial risk that the jury, despite instructions to the contrary, looked to the incriminating extrajudicial statements in determining petitioner's guilt, admission of Evans' confession in this joint trial violated petitioner's right of cross-examination secured by the Confrontation Clause of the Sixth Amendment. We therefore overrule *Delli Pooli* and reverse.

The rule which emerged from the *Bruton* case is as follows

> The introduction at a joint trial of a nontestifying defendant's extrajudicial confession, which confession inculpates a codefendant, violates a codefendant's right of confrontation guaranteed by the Sixth Amendment, despite specific limiting instructions by the trial judge as to the restricted use the jury might make of such a confession.[75]

Later that same year the United States Supreme Court expanded the scope of the *Bruton* rule by making it fully retroactive and by extending its application to trials in state courts. This ruling was given in *Roberts* v. *Russell.*[76]

It must be noted that the scope of the *Bruton* ruling has been narrowed somewhat since the original decision. In 1967, in *Chapman* v. *Calif.,* the United States Supreme Court recognized that errors of a constitutional nature may, under some circumstances, be harmless, and may, therefore, be insufficient grounds for reversal.[77] Applying the *Chapman* rule, the Supreme Court in 1969 held in *Harrington* v. *California* that the introduction of statements of nontestifying codefendants to demonstrate another defendant's presence at the scene of a crime was harmless error and merely a part of the cumulative evidence where the defendant himself admitted being present.[78]

More recently the Burger court has applied the harmless-constitutional-error doctrine of *Chapman* in a case where the erroneously admitted evidence was not so innocuous as in *Harrington.*

The testimony, the admission of which the United States Supreme Court held to be harmless error, was to the effect that Schneble's nontestifying codefendant had admitted that he and Schneble had murdered a third party. The Court noted that "the independent evidence of guilt ... [was] overwhelming"; indeed, Schneble himself had admitted strangling the victim. In explaining the Court's finding, Justice Rehnquist used the following language.

> In some cases the properly admitted evidence of guilt is so overwhelming, and the prejudicial effect of the codefendant's admission is so insignificant by comparison, that it is clear beyond a reasonable doubt that the improper use of the admission was harmless error.[79]

Alternatives Available to the Prosecutor

The lesson to be learned from *Bruton* and its attendant cases is that joint trial of codefendants should be avoided where one or more of the codefendants has made an extrajudicial confession of guilt. Although introduction of a nontestifying codefendant's implicating confession in a joint trial may, in some circumstances, be harmless, it is nevertheless always error. In knowingly attempting to introduce such a confession into evidence a prosecutor would be exceeding his own authority, usurping a judicial function, violating his professional ethics, and running the risk of reversal. Thus a joint trial under certain circumstances may completely prevent the introduction of a confession into evidence and might well result in a patently guilty person going free through a prosecutorial blunder.

A joint trial should be avoided where implicating extrajudicial confessions or admissions have been made unless the prosecutor feels that he has sufficient evidence aside from these confessions or admissions to assure conviction of the defendant or defendants who made them. If a prosecutor should proceed to joint trial in the belief that he has enough evidence to convict aside from these confessions or admissions, he should scrupulously avoid placing the confessions or admissions into evidence in the event that the codefendant or codefendants who made them should fail to testify.

In addition to separate trials of codefendants and joint trial without use of a codefendant's confession, there is a third possible course of action open to the prosecutor. It may be possible to edit a confession, admission, or statement of a codefendant and delete all references to other defendants, thereby making the confession nonimplicating with regard to other defendants when placed in evidence at a joint trial. Neither the United States Supreme Court nor most of the state courts have spoken to the propriety of using such a confession in a joint trial, but the Fifth Circuit Court of Appeals has repeatedly held that a codefendant's confession is admissible in a joint trial if references to other defendants are deleted. Thus if a prosecutor believes the confession or admission of a codefendant can be successfully edited so as to render it nonimplicating to the other defendants, he might proceed to a joint trial and attempt to use the edited confession to prove the guilt of the party who made it.

In recognition of the *Bruton* decision and its effect on the requirements of joinder and severance, the American Bar Association Special Committee on Standards for the Administration of Criminal Justice has adopted the following policy.

(a) When a defendant moves for a severance because an out-of-court statement of a codefendant makes reference to him but is not admissible against him, the court should determine whether the prosecution intends to offer the statement in evidence at the trial. If so, the court should require the prosecuting attorney to elect one of the following courses:

   (i) a joint trial at which the statement is not admitted into evidence;

   (ii) a joint trial at which the statement is admitted into evidence only after all references to the moving defendant have been effectively deleted; or

   (iii) severance of the moving defendant.[80]

Crimes committed by two or more persons in league are extremely common. And in many instances joint trials of these persons are advisable as efforts to save time and money. However, joint trials may prove to be pitfalls to the unwary prosecutor. Only by being familiar with *Bruton* and its attendant cases can a prosecutor make an intelligent decision as to whether to seek severances or joinders in the trials of codefendants.

CHARACTER OF THE ACCUSED

Testimony regarding the character of the accused is strictly limited in order to protect the defendant's rights. Although several noted authors suggest certain guidelines to the permissible introduction by the state of testimony about the defendant's character, it does not appear that most courts will allow any such extensions; the courts respect the very real possibility of prejudice which such testimony brings to the courtroom. It was stated in *Hassell* v. *State* that "it must be borne in mind that an accused cannot be convicted of a crime simply because of his bad character or reputation, or because in the past he has been convicted of other crimes. The particular offense must be charged and proved."[81]

294

Thus character evidence cannot be initiated by the prosecution. Courts will not uphold a decision by a lower court permitting evidence of an earlier unrelated quarrel between the accused and another where the accused had not placed his character in issue. A lower court had permitted that evidence on the theory that the earlier, unrelated quarrel tended to show that the accused was of an aggressive, quarrelsome, and vicious disposition and, therefore, would shed light upon who was the aggressor in the subsequent conduct.[82]

Simply because the accused takes the stand does not mean he has opened his character to attack. In those instances where the accused has not put his character in issue, the exact limits of cross-examination by the prosecution have been carefully spelled out by the Mississippi Supreme Court. Considerable latitude should be allowed in the cross-examination of the accused. A defendant who takes the stand in his own behalf waives his constitutional privilege of silence. The prosecution has the right to cross-examine him upon his evidence in chief as to the circumstances connected with the crime with the same latitude as would be exercised in the case of an ordinary witness. The accused does not, however, by offering himself as a witness in his own behalf, waive his right to object to improper cross-examination designed to elicit incompetent evidence.

Sometimes it is difficult to know just when the accused puts his character in issue. One such case is *McGee* v. *State*.[83] The accused testified in his own behalf and was asked by his counsel whether he had ever been convicted of any offense. His reply was that he had, but only for trespass in driving a horse across the school grounds; he did not offer any evidence as to his general reputation for peace or violence. Based solely on the answer to that one question, defense counsel said in his closing argument, "If the reputation of defendant was not good, then why didn't the state bring in proof of his bad reputation?" The state objected to this and the court sustained it. The state, in closing, pointed out that reputation was not in issue. The defense objection to this was overruled. The court viewed the original question about prior crimes not as a character issue but as a factor in determining the credibility of the defendant as a witness; therefore the state's comment was permissible.

Not all subtle surprises are cause for reversal, however. In *Pope* v. *State* the defense complained that the sheriff's testimony should have not been admitted because it presented to the jury the reputation of the accused.[84] The court said that if it was error it was harmless error because, when set against the other facts in the case, it "pales into insignificance." Thus the rule is that if there is enough evidence to convict without the questionable character testimony, admission of such testimony is a harmless error.

Sometimes it may appear that the accused has put his character in issue when he really has not. For example, if defense counsel asks one of the defense witnesses if he knows of the accused's general reputation for being a law-abiding citizen, the character of the accused has not been put into issue if the witness says he knows nothing about it. The witness's answer proved nothing. If nothing is proved there is nothing to rebut.

The accused can open the issue of character by cross-examination of a state witness. In one such case the defense opened the question of good character by asking a state witness on cross-examination if the defendant had a reputation for telling the truth. The court said the prosecution may introduce evidence in rebuttal and, within limits, may elicit evidence of the accused's bad character by cross-examination of the witness who testified as to his good character.

Although no case explains the permissible limits of rebuttal evidence, McCormick gives some guidance.

> The rule permitting the cross-examination to ask the character witness whether he has "heard" or knows of other particular crimes of accused involving the same trait is pregnant with possibilities of destructive prejudice. The mere asking by a respected official of such a question, however answered, may well suggest to the jury that the imputation is true. The courts agree that propounding such a question in bad faith may be ground for reversal.[85]

The courts have said that it is manifest error on the part of the judge to exclude testimony offered to show the good character of the accused as related to the particular crime charged. Proof of good character is admissible as a matter of right. In *Ridgeway* v. *State* the lower court sustained objections to a series of questions asked by appellant's counsel regarding Ridgeway's general reputation for peace in his community.[86] (Based on these objections, the defense had declined to offer other character witnesses.) The defense's questions lacked perfect form but contained the substance of a proper character examination. The lower court, without explanation, refused to admit this evidence, but the Supreme Court held that the trial judge should have told the defense why the objections were sustained so that the defense counsel could have corrected the form of his questions.

Evidence of good character is admissible, but it should be confined to the particular trait involved in the type of crime charged against the defendant. The defense attorney must limit his questions accordingly. Therefore each crime must be categorized as one involving violence, honesty, or some other trait.

Sometimes, however, a crime relates to two traits; in that case the accused is allowed to present evidence about each trait. For example one court said that since robbery involves not only violence but also honesty the defendant should not have been limited to character evidence concerning his reputation for peace or violence.

At times courts have allowed evidence of habit as character evidence. The defendant in one action was involved in a case where the issue concerned reckless use of an auto. He offered the testimony of four qualified witnesses that he had a general reputation in his community for being a careful driver. The lower court refused to admit this testimony. The higher court reversed that decision, saying the testimony was extremely relevant and that it is the jury's responsibility to weigh its value.

Neither the accused nor the state can resort to just particular facts to establish or refute the character thus put in issue. The reputation of the person, or what particular witnesses believe of him from his course of life, defines the limit of the rule. One court said, "We think the court erred in allowing several character witnesses to be examined with respect, not to the general reputation of the defendant, but minutely with respect to a number of independent transactions, fights, etc."

OPINION EVIDENCE

There are two key principles that must be kept in mind when considering the admissibility of opinion evidence. First, if the opinion tends to take away from the jury its fact-finding function, the evidence should not be admitted. Second, if the persons giving the evidence do not have sufficient basis for forming an opinion, their evidence should be disregarded. These conditions apply whether the evidence is given by nonexpert or expert witnesses.

Nonexpert Opinion

That the opinion of a layperson is, under some circumstances, admissible is recognized by all courts. The courts indicate that the form of the question and answer dialogue has a lot to do with whether or not lay opinion can be admitted. The courts recognize that there is no exact rule regarding the amount of knowledge a witness must possess. They make clear, however, that any opinion given must depend on the facts and circumstances within the knowledge of the witness. The court must instruct the witness to detail only the relevant facts as known to him or her.

The value of such testimony will depend largely on the opportunities of the witness for correct observation. Without a specific statement of specific facts on which an opinion is based, the evidence will be inadmissible.

Laymen are permitted to testify as to appearances where it is demonstrated that the witness had the power to observe the incident. For example, the courts have allowed lay opinion regarding the issue as to whether a defendant was intoxicated.

However, not all appearances and conduct of the defendant can be testified to in this manner. The demeanor, acts, and conduct of an accused, both at the time of and subsequent to the crime, are admissible. But such testimony should be limited to a statement of the facts by the witness, leaving the jury free to form its own conclusions.

In the same vein the courts say that there should be no opinion allowed as to what a person means by what he says. This is a jury question; the witness should only detail the statements. Therefore the court has ruled that it is a reversible error if a witness testifies regarding his or her understanding of a conversation. The witness should have been required to detail the statements of the defendant, or at least the substance thereof, from which the jury could draw its own conclusions or inferences.

Where the jury can easily reach a given conclusion without the aid of an opinion, the witness should be prevented from giving an opinion. For example, in the case of *Cumberland* v. *State* the court said that the witness should not have been allowed to express his opinion that it "looked like there had been a crap game there."[87] The court said that the witness should have stated the facts and let the jury draw the conclusion.

To overcome the problem raised by the *Cumberland* case, a method of questioning should be developed that will prevent opinion evidence that invades the function of the jury. A 1949 case demonstrates this method. Officers were testifying to certain observable facts regarding tracks left in the soil. By the use of extensive detailed examination the prosecutor's evidence was presented in such a way that the jury could come to only one conclusion. Upon reflection there is no way that the jury could have been absolutely sure that the defendant's feet were in the shoes when the tracks were made. But, by establishing ownership and by giving detailed analysis, it was left to the jury to draw the conclusion that the prosecutor wanted.

Obviously, if a fact is not in issue no opinion, whether lay or expert, is allowed. This is illustrated by *Johnson* v. *State*.[88] In that case appellant's counsel asked a witness his opinion of appellant's mental age and about any peculiarities appellant displayed. The court ruled that since appellant was not pleading insanity, opinion on the issue of sanity was not proper.

In regard to demonstrative evidence, whether testimony of laypersons is admissible or not depends on how far the testimony goes. If the testimony relates to matters of common experience the testimony will be allowed. However, if the testimony is such that the jury can reach the same conclusion as the witness with regard to the physical evidence, the opinion will not be allowed. Finally, if the evidence concerns that which is normally a subject of expert testimony, the court will usually hold such testimony inadmissible simply because the jury is as capable of reaching an opinion as is the nonexpert witness.

Expert Opinion

Expert opinion is, of course, allowable under certain circumstances. The two major conditions are that the questions must be based on the area of the witness's expertise, and that the witness must have a proper basis in fact for reaching his or her conclusion. These two questions, plus the use of the hypothetical question, have been before the courts more often than other questions involving expert opinion. The problem of qualifying a witness as an expert has come up, but much less frequently.

To qualify as expert testimony the subject matter must be within the area of the witness's expertise. An expert witness need not be infallible or possess the highest degree of skill. It is sufficient that the expert possess peculiar knowledge respecting a matter not likely to be possessed by the ordinary layperson. But if a purported expert admits, on the stand, that the area of questioning is not something on which he is up-to-date, the trial court must exclude his testimony. In such an instance his testimony would be pure opinion and is no better than lay opinion. If it is to be admitted at all, it must meet the test required for lay opinion. In another case a doctor was allowed to testify that people who are insane do not kill people for money. The court found this judgment to be outside the area of an expert physician.

In addition to the requirement that the expert be qualified, it is also essential that the expert have some basis for his conclusions. The foundation on which the expert bases his observation is subject to attack. For example, in *Freeman* v. *State,* the issue of the bank's solvency arose.[89] An expert accountant testified as to his opinion on its solvency, but it was shown that the bank records he used to arrive at this conclusion were not adequate for supporting an opinion. While the value of property can be established by experts, the accountant in the *Freeman* case could not determine, by looking at numerical entries in the books, the value of certain loans secured by collateral.

In yet another case a doctor, who had known the accused murderer in the past but had not observed his behavior for a considerable length of time before the killing, was not permitted to give his opinion since he had not had recent opportunity to observe the defendant's conduct.

The jury is entitled to know on what facts the witness bases his opinion in order that they may judge the value of the expert's evidence. Therefore, after the trial court determines the competency of the witness, the weight to be given such opinion belongs solely to the jury. The reason for this rule is best summed up in *Foster* v. *State*. In matters of common knowledge and experience—and when scientific opinions are not required or even possible—it is error "to fling the weight of a distinguished expert's opinion into the scale, with a view to having the jury adopt and act upon it, instead of forming and acting upon its own conclusions drawn from the established facts."[90]

A corollary to the *Foster* rule is that where expert evidence is needed to overcome a legitimate assumption, failure to produce an expert means that the assumption must be believed.

Experts do not have to be trained in college. They can get their experience through formal schooling, but they can also gain expertise through experience on the job. In one case it was argued that the sheriff should not have been questioned on his knowledge of stills although the foundation was established that he had extensive experience in the field. A person's expertise is to be determined through the sound discretion of the court, which makes this determination after hearing the witness's qualifications. This court said it must clearly appear that an expert was not qualified before it will overturn the trial court's decision to permit an expert to testify. This is the general rule.

The final problem involving expert witnesses concerns the use of hypothetical questions.

> The opinion of expert witnesses is best presented to the jury by means of a hypothetical question. . . . Each party to an issue may submit hypothetical questions to expert witnesses, assuming facts therein reasonably consistent with the facts in evidence and which accord with his theory of the case. It is not imperative that hypothetical questions cover all the undisputed facts in evidence; but a hypothetical question may be asked a medical expert embracing practically all the evidence on the question of the homicide. The form of the hypothetical question is a matter within the sound discretion of the court. Hypothetical questions should be based on facts disclosed by the evidence, or facts fairly inferable from the evidence or which the evidence tends to prove. Hypothetical questions are improper when there is no evidence to sustain the facts assumed.[91]

The courts are very strict with regard to the asking of hypothetical questions. It has been said that in a criminal case where life, liberty, and reputation are the issue the prosecuting officer, in examining an expert, should lay before such expert fairly and fully every undisputed material fact that can have a possible bearing upon the opinion of that witness. In a hypothetical question all facts should be excluded which the jury can interpret as well as the expert. The question must include all the undisputed facts related to the subject within the expert's field. To permit a culling of the facts to suit the purposes of conviction and to propound a hypothesis to the experts and then instruct the jury that the only way to contradict the opinion of the experts is by the opinion of other experts is to deny a fair trial. Obviously, prosecutors cannot use imaginary facts either.

The jury does not have to pay attention to any opinion evidence by either expert or nonexpert witnesses. The jury is not deprived of the right to use common sense in resolving the question of whether or not a defendant appreciated the nature and consequence of his act or whether he knew it was wrong. Expert opinion on these matters is not conclusive.

RES GESTAE AND THE RIGHT OF CONFRONTATION

Latin terms often hide ambiguities. *Res gestae* is no exception. It means "things done." At every event in life there are things going on: people saying things, people reacting to things, and so forth. In order for a jury to get a feeling for things as they were at the time of the crime, courts often admit evidence about these surrounding sounds and actions.

There are two branches of *res gestae*. There is the nonhearsay branch, such as when an eyewitness reports hearing the defendant say, "I wish I had not run that red light." There is the hearsay branch, where an eyewitness hears another eyewitness say, "They are going to kill someone driving that fast," and the person who made the statement is not present to testify.

The nonhearsay branch allows also a description of surrounding circumstances. This sounds fine until it is examined in regard to concrete facts. Assume A is on trial for the possession of narcotics. Suppose A's house was constitutionally searched and several illegally held weapons were found at that time. Should the officer be able to describe those weapons at the trial for narcotics possession? Theoretically the answer should be no because weapon possession is not relevant or material to the charge of narcotics possession. Additionally, such testimony would be an attack upon the character of the defendant and, unless he had opened that to attack, the description fails to meet that admissibility criterion. Despite this logic, many courts would allow the description of the house as part of the *res gestae*.

301

The more serious problems of *res gestae* involve the hearsay branch. Allowing any form of hearsay creates a conflict with the Sixth Amendment to the Constitution. That amendment guarantees a defendant a right to confront the witnesses against him. As explained in Chapter 8 the right of confrontation includes the very valuable right of cross-examination.

It is true that the testifying witness can be cross-examined but. the absent witness who purportedly made the out-of-court assertion cannot be; the testifying witness can merely repeat what the absent witness was supposed to have said. Nothing can be learned about the prejudices or shortcomings of the absent witness. Yet such evidence is permitted under the *res gestae* banner. Among the hearsay evidence that may be admitted are dying declarations, confessions, spontaneous exclamations, and conversations in the defendant's presence. The admission of these categories of evidence is subject to strict tests that must be met in order to minimize the likelihood of error or deceit.

STUDY QUESTIONS

1. What guidelines are suggested for regulating the use of photographs by the police to establish the identity of a perpetrator?
2. What are the danger signals of a weakness in an identification procedure?
3. What warnings comply with the Miranda Requirements?
4. Of what effect is an illegally obtained confession if a second and legally valid confession is obtained?
5. Can character evidence be initiated by the prosecutor?
6. What is *res gestae*?

NOTES

1. *U.S.* v. *Wade,* 388 U.S. 218, 87 S.Ct. 1926, 18 L.Ed. 2d 1149 (1967); *Gilbert* v. *Calif.,* 388 U.S. 263, 87 S.Ct. 1951, 18 L.Ed. 2d 1178 (1967).
2. *Stovall* v. *Denno,* 388 U.S. 293, 87 S.Ct. 1967, 18 L.Ed. 2d 1199 (1967).
3. *Kirby* v. *Illinois,* 406 U.S. 682, 92 S.Ct. 1877, 32 L.Ed. 2d 411 (1972).
4. *Stovall* v. *Denno,* p. 1206.
5. See *Kirby* v. *Illinois.*
6. *Bates* v. *U.S.,* 405 F. 2d 1104 (D.C. Cir. 1968).
7. *Biggers* v. *Tennessee,* 390 U.S. 404, 88 S. Ct. 979, 19 L.Ed. 2d 1267 (1968).
8. *Hastings* v. *Cardwell,* 480 F. 2d 1202 (6th Cir. 1973).
9. *U.S.* v. *Roth,* 430 F. 2d 1137 (1970).
10. *Dozie* v. *State,* 49 Wisc. 2d 209, 181 N.W. 2d 369 (1970).
11. *U.S. ex rel Riffert* v. *Rundle,* 464 F. 2d 1348 (3d Cir. 1972); *U.S.* v. *Cole,* 449 F. 2d 194 (8th Cir. 1971); and *State* v. *Ruggiero,* 279 A. 2d 128 (N.J. 1971).
12. Allison M. Rouse, *Are We in Focus on Photo Identification,* 7 *University of San Francisco Law Review* (1973) p. 419.

13. *Simmons* v. *U.S.*, 390 U.S. 377, 88 S. Ct. 967, 19 L.Ed. 2d 1247 (1968).
14. *U.S.* v. *Ash*, 37 L.Ed. 2d 619 (1973).
15. Ibid., p. 633.
16. Rouse, *Are We in Focus*, p. 434.
17. From Patrick Wall, *Eye-Witness Identification in Criminal Cases*, 1975, pp. 90–130. Courtesy of Charles C. Thomas, Publisher, Springfield, Illinois.
18. *Kirby* v. *Ellis*, 406 U.S. 682, 92 S. Ct. 1877, 32 L.Ed. 2d 411 (1972).
19. *Miranda* v. *Arizona*, 384 U.S. 436 (1966).
20. *Evans* v. *State*, 377 F. 2d 535 (5th Cir. 1967).
21. *Archer* v. *U.S.*, 393 F. 2d 124 (5th Cir. 1968).
22. *U.S.* v. *Montos*, 421 F. 2d 215 (5th Cir. 1970).
23. *U.S.* v. *Littlepage*, 435 F. 2d 498 (5th Cir. 1970).
24. *Brunson* v. *State*, 264 So. 2d 817 (Miss. 1972).
25. *Williams* v. *State*, 232 So. 2d 366 (Miss. 1970).
26. *McMillian* v. *U.S.*, 399 F. 2d 478 (5th Cir. 1968).
27. *U.S.* v. *Robertson*, 425 F. 2d 1386 (5th Cir. 1970).
28. *Nevels* v. *State*, 216 So. 2d 529 (Miss. 1968).
29. *Ford* v. *State*, 226 So. 2d 378 (Miss. 1968).
30. *Amos* v. *State*, 234 So. 2d 630 (Miss. 1970).
31. *U.S.* v. *Welsh*, 417 F. 2d 361 (5th Cir. 1969).
32. *U.S.* v. *Hopkins*, 433 F. 2d 1041 (5th Cir. 1970).
33. *Boyles* v. *State*, 223 So. 2d 651 (Miss. 1969).
34. *Wash* v. *State*, 241 So. 2d 155 (Miss. 1969).
35. Ibid., p. 158.
36. *Fabian* v. *State*, 267 So. 2d 294 (Miss. 1972).
37. *Chinn* v. *State*, 276 So. 2d 456 (Miss. 1973).
38. *U.S.* v. *Trabucco*, 424 F. 2d 1311 (5th Cir. 1970).
39. *U.S.* v. *Martin*, 434 F. 2d 275 (5th Cir. 1970).
40. *State* v. *Williams*, 208 So. 2d 172 (Miss. 1968).
41. *Dover* v. *State*, 227 So. 2d 296 (Miss. 1969).
42. *Harvey* v. *State*, 207 So. 2d 108 (Miss. 1968).
43. *Cooper* v. *Griffin*, 455 F. 2d 1142 (5th Cir. 1972).
44. *Harris* v. *State*, 226 So. 2d 760 (Miss. 1969).
45. *Stewart* v. *State*, 273 So. 2d 167 (Miss. 1973).
46. *Viverett* v. *State*, 269 So. 2d 862 (Miss. 1972).
47. *Bell* v. *State*, 274 So. 2d 371 (Miss. 1973).
48. *Armstrong* v. *State*, 214 So. 2d 589 (Miss. 1968).
49. *Clewis* v. *Texas*, 386 U.S. 707 (1967).
50. *Reid* v. *State*, 266 So. 2d 21 (Miss. 1972).
51. *Windsor* v. *U.S.*, 389 F. 2d 530 (5th Cir. 1968).
52. *Mayzak* v. *U.S.*, 402 F. 2d 152 (5th Cir. 1968).
53. *Gilpen* v. *U.S.*, 415 F. 2d 638 (5th Cir. 1969).
54. *Hodge* v. *U.S.*, 392 F. 2d 522, 524 (5th Cir. 1968).
55. *Moll* v. *U.S.*, 413 F. 2d 1233 (5th Cir. 1969).
56. *Tathers* v. *U.S.*, 396 F. 2d 524 (5th Cir. 1968).
57. *DeLa Fe* v. *U.S.*, 413 F. 2d 543 (5th Cir. 1969).
58. *U.S.* v. *Ramos*, 448 F. 2d 398 (5th Cir. 1971).
59. *Spurlin* v. *State*, 218 So. 2d 876 (Miss. 1969).
60. *U.S.* v. *Phelps*, 443 F. 2d 246 (5th Cir. 1971).
61. Ibid.
62. *U.S.* v. *Johnson*, 455 F. 2d 311 (5th Cir. 1972).
63. *Jennings* v. *U.S.*, 391 F. 2d 512 (5th Cir. 1968).
64. *U.S.* v. *Brown*, 459 F. 2d 319 (5th Cir. 1971).
65. *Michigan* v. *Tucker*, 41 L.Ed. 2d 182, 94 S.Ct. 2357 (1974).
66. *Harris* v. *New York*, 401 U.S. 422, 28 L.Ed. 2d 1, 91 S.Ct. 643 (1971).
67. *Rollins* v. *State*, 300 So. 2d 145 (Miss. 1974).
68. *Garrity* v. *New Jersey*, 385 U.S. 493, 87 S.Ct. 616, 17 L.Ed. 2d 562 (1967).
69. *Fitzgerald* v. *State*, 275 So. 2d 390 (Miss. 1973).
70. *Evans* v. *State*, 285 So. 2d 786 (Miss. 1973).
71. *State* v. *Fabian*, 263 So. 2d 773 (Miss. 1972).

72. *Agee* v. *State,* 185 So. 2d 671 (Miss. 1966).
73. *Dueitt* v. *State,* 225 Miss. 254, 83 So. 2d 91 (1955).
74. *Delli Pooli* v. *U.S.,* 352 U.S. 232 (1957).
75. *Bruton* v. *U.S.,* 391 U.S. 123 (1968).
76. *Roberts* v. *Russell,* 392 U.S. 293 (1968).
77. *Chapman* v. *Calif.,* 386 U.S. 18 (1967).
78. *Harrington* v. *Calif.,* 395 U.S. 250 (1969).
79. *Schneble* v. *Fla.,* 405 U.S. 427 (1972).
80. ABA, *Standards, Joinder and Severance,* pp. 34–35.
81. *Hassell* v. *State,* 229 Miss. 824, 92 So. 2d 194 (1957).
82. *Kehoe* v. *State,* 194 Miss. 339, 12 S. 2d 149 (1943).
83. *McGee* v. *State,* 50 So. 2d 394 (Miss. 1951).
84. *Pope* v. *State,* 242 Miss. 362, 135 So. 2d 818 (1962).
85. McCormick, *Evidence,* 2d ed. (St. Paul: West Publishing Co., 1972), p. 457.
86. *Ridgeway* v. *State,* 245 Miss. 506, 148 So. 2d 513 (1963).
87. *Cumberland* v. *State,* 110 Miss. 521, 70 So. 695 (1915).
88. *Johnson* v. *State,* 223 Miss. 56, 76 So. 2d 841 (1955).
89. *Freeman* v. *State,* 108 Miss. 818, 67 So. 460 (1914).
90. *Foster* v. *State,* 70 Miss. 755 (1893).
91. Harry Clay Underhill, *A Treatise on the Law of Criminal Evidence,* 4th ed. (Indianapolis: The Bobbs-Merrill Company, 1935).

chapter twelve
Probation and Parole

The criminal-justice system exists to protect society. The practical application of this responsibility is in the hands of the police, courts, and corrections. Each of these subsystems administers and enforces criminal law. The function of each agency is clearly defined: police identify and arrest suspects who have allegedly violated existing laws; courts determine guilt or innocence and sentence the guilty; and corrections punishes and, hopefully, rehabilitates the guilty.

Corrections has two aspects: field agencies and institutions. Field agencies supervise the offender in the community. They are known as probation or parole departments. Two-thirds of all correctional clients are in these community-based programs at any one time.[1] The others clients are confined in local, state, or federal institutions. Probation is really a substitute for imprisonment. It is agency supervision with revocation as the implied threat. Parole is community management after a partial sentence has been served. Incarceration is the second most severe sanction, after capital punishment. Prisons are expensive. Their function is intended to be temporary, with the majority of inmates being released eventually. Although institutions hold only one-third of the clients referred at any given time, they require over three-fourths of the money allocated by the state to corrections.

The fragmentation of corrections seriously limits its effectiveness. Probation departments are administered by either the county or the state. Within the state different agencies may control institutions and parole. In turn, the local jail facilities may be under the jurisdiction of the sheriff or of a state agency. The federal government operates a probation service and maintains its own correctional institutions. Some states have separate departments for juvenile probation, training schools, and parole. Agency autonomy continues to impede progress. The attempt to unify corrections and avoid this duplication of effort has so far been unsuccessful.

PROBATION

The American Bar Association defines probation as "a sentence not involving confinement which imposes conditions and retains authority in the sentencing court to modify the conditions of the sentence or to resentence the offender if he violates the conditions."[2] Probation is a type of suspended sentence granted to those who do not require imprisonment as a form of punishment. Probation may be granted after conviction or before adjudication. The decision to grant probation is based upon the presentence report prepared for the court. The report investigates past behavior, family circumstances, and the personality of the offender in order to assist the court in determining the most appropriate sentence. A presentence investigation report corresponds to the juvenile predisposition report which is outlined in Chapter 15. Probation is a form of treatment which stresses community supervision by a probation officer. If the offender does not make a satisfactory adjustment in the community, probation is revoked and the original sentence is imposed by the court.

The advantages of probation have made it the most popular service. It has been available in all states since 1956. A federal probation law was passed by Congress in 1925. The first state to introduce probation was Massachusetts. Its legislation was enacted in 1878 and within two years every community in the state was employing probation officers. A sensitive Bostonian, John Augustus, was the father of probation. He saw that local jails were doing great harm while making no progress toward reforming those people serving time. It was in the year 1841 that he offered to take offenders into his home after paying their bail himself. The court honored his request. He agreed to report to the judge the progress made by his house guest. The judge often released the prisoner. Thus John Augustus developed the service which is now granted to more than 50 percent of the offenders sentenced by the courts.

The administrative structure of probation varies from state to state. It may take one or both of the following forms: (1) state-level probation department with offices in various cities; (2) county control which in turn may be administered by the court or a separate probation department under the direction of a chief probation officer appointed by the judges or other members of local government. The pattern of organization used in adult probation may not be the same for juvenile probation. The department may be very large with thousands of probation officers or a single-room office with only one worker. Diversity in the administration of probation seriously limits the development of minimum standards for personnel and services. However, it is the actual supervision which determines success on probation.

Probation has proven less expensive than confinement. It offers advantages for the offender motivated to end his criminal career. He can live where there are supportive family relationships and friends. There can be continuous employment. He avoids the reentry problems associated with incarceration. Social services of the probation department and other local agencies are available if needed. All of these benefits are possible where departments are really innovative. But two conditions are absolutely necessary in all departments: (1) screening of offenders assigned to probation; and (2) continous supervision, which includes providing various services.

The probation department has two functions. The staff prepares presentence reports for the court and supervises clients. Neglect of either of these aspects presages an ineffective program.

The Presentence Investigation

The presentence report relieves the impersonality of the justice system and helps the court and probation officer get to know the offender. The presentence investigation is made by the probation officer at court request. This written report attempts to evaluate the defendant awaiting sentence and determine whether he would benefit from probation or some other alternative to confinement. The method used in preparing the evaluation is borrowed from social work because it is a social evaluation of the client. It differs from other social investigations in that it must deal with both the current offense and the prior criminal history of the subject. In addition to this information, the report tells us something about the following areas in the offender's background: (1) relationship with parents, siblings, marital partner, children, and relatives; (2) work history, including an inventory of skills; (3) educational attainment; (4) military service; (5) health-related physical and emotional problems; (6) current living condition and financial capacity; and, (7) specific needs. This report serves several purposes, the chief one being to guide the judge when making a disposition of the case. It may also serve as an aid to the institution where the defendant is committed, or to help the staff if probation is granted. These reports are important also as research documents.[3] We should not hope for too much from the presentence investigation. After all, the probationer is an involuntary client who knows that his officer represents the court. Carter, in his study of these reports, identifies the factors usually cited in recommending probation. They have to do with the offense and the prior criminal record.[4] So the traditional philosophy of criminal justice, centering on the individual and his offense, continues to govern the probation decision. The usefulness of this paperwork must be weighed against the probation officer's duty to supervise his clients. Some states allow the

307

judge to decide whether a presentence report is necessary. Judges accept the recommendation of the probation officer in 95 percent of their cases.[5] This high ratio of cooperation speaks well for relations between the court and the probation staff.

Conditions of Probation

The decision to grant probation depends upon more than a satisfactory presentence investigation and a recommendation for this form of disposition. Approximately 70 percent of the states set some statutory restrictions on the use of probation. The type of offense is very important. Probation may not be granted for murder, rape, or crimes in which the death penalty is applicable. The increasing incidence of violent behavior will certainly move legislators to expand the list of crimes for which probation cannot be used. Sometimes there are additional restrictions. For example, if a defendant shows a repetitive pattern of similar serious offenses; if he was armed when committing the crime; or if the statutes set an unusually high minimum sentence. California requires its judges to explain why they have chosen probation when imposing a sentence.

The judge may attach certain conditions to probation when granting it to a defendant. The most important prerequisite is that the person obey all laws. Additional rules are often imposed. These might be that the probationer will: (1) cooperate with the probation officer in fulfilling the program of supervision; (2) maintain employment; (3) refrain from working in certain occupations, professions, and settings which provide contact with criminal activity; (4) reside in areas approved by the agency; (5) enroll in educational institutions or vocational-training programs if these are required to enhance existing work skills; (6) undergo recommended medical or psychiatric care; (7) meet routine family responsibilities; (8) abstain from association with certain types of people where it might lead to criminal activity; (9) make restitution if the crime resulted in financial profit, property was destroyed, or others were injured; or (10) serve a portion of the sentence in the county jail. The person who successfully meets the conditions of probation spends an average of three years under supervision. If a probationer returns to criminal activity, the judge may modify probation. This is accomplished by adding new conditions, imposing jail time, or revoking probation and imposing the initial prison sentence.

Probation Supervision

The supervision of clients can be a rewarding experience. It requires an ongoing, positive relationship between the probationer and the worker. Sometimes the officer writing the presentence report goes on to supervise the same client. The investigative report should include a careful assessment of the problems which led to the commission of the crime. Good supervision will direct the client to services which will minimize this earlier propensity for illegal conduct.

The probation staff are assigned large caseloads. Each one may be asked to supervise from 35 to 100 people. The time each probationer is allowed to spend with his supervisor is limited. The probation officer should see himself as a community-resource manager but not the only source of help. He must know how to utilize community services. Being close to the client, the probation officer is his primary resource. The probation officer, in his role as community-resource manager, will have to

> assess the situation, know available resources, contact the appropriate resource, assist the probationer to obtain the services, and follow up the case. When the probationer encounters difficulty in obtaining the service he needs, the probation officer will have to explore the reasons for the difficulty and take appropriate steps to see that the service is delivered. The probation officer also will have to monitor and evaluate the services to which the probationer is referred.[6]

Effective supervision can be measured by how well the individual adjusts to the temporary conditions of probation. The stigma of arrest need not defeat the person who wants to end his or her criminal career. However, the probationer needs a pilot to lead him or her away from the lawless element. For this reason we should consider probation the appropriate sentence for first offenders. Of course, this may not be possible in the case of certain violent crimes which cause the public to be afraid. Probation should, in most cases, be granted only once, although unusual circumstances may warrant more frequent use of conditional freedom by the courts. There is resistance to this form of sentence because crimes are sometimes committed during the probationary period. Everyone deserves a chance. Convicted felons have the right to services which, while utilizing their capacities, obviate the need for criminal activity. It is *not* the right sentence when its comparative freedom is misused.

A correctional system should evaluate its services so that convicted offenders are given opportunities to reorder their lives. This requires carefully prepared presentence investigations and supervision by someone who cares about the individual. The probation officer needs knowledge dealing with casework methods, interviewing techniques, and community resources for referral. He or she does not require information dealing with interrogation techniques, surveillance techniques, or appropriate use of firearms. Although probation is the least expensive correctional service, it can be effective if the agency is willing to mobilize community services to aid the offender. The advocates of probation claim a success rate of 75 percent. That figure seems to be correct, unless a particular agency fails to provide vocational training or adequate services for drug abuse, alcoholism, or emotional problems.

PAROLE

The most frequent method employed in releasing a prisoner from a state or federal prison is parole. This usually occurs after a portion of the sentence has been served. The decision is made by an administrative board and not by the court. Parole is accompanied by supervision of the parolee, who can be returned to prison if certain conditions are not observed.

The use of parole varies. Some states parole 100 percent of their released prisoners while others parole as few as 60 percent. Of the 84,225 sentenced prisoners departing state institutions and receiving conditional release in 1976, approximately 88 percent were granted a parole.[7] Thirteen states, the District of Columbia, and the federal prison system use either parole or supervised mandatory release. Both are considered to be conditional releases. However, mandatory release is automatic after a portion of the maximum sentence is served. It requires no parole-board action and depends on the accumulation of good-time credits by the prisoner. Mandatory release resembles parole because those granted it are subject to brief supervision and must abide by conditions similar to those imposed on parolees.

Parole is the safety valve of corrections. It requires selection of prisoners for conditional release. Prison critics claim, with some justification, that 25 to 50 percent of all ex-offenders return to prison. Yet crowded institutions demand the routine release of part of the inmate population. Several states have had to delay acceptance of prisoners because of crowded institutions. These people have to remain in local county jails until space is available. Serious crises have been the result. Prison records hold few clues upon which to base the decision to release a prisoner. Additional information must be made available; the parole-board hearing provides an opportunity for assembling those data. This is especially important with violent offenders who may resume criminal behavior if paroled too soon. Correctional authorities are severely criticized when a parolee commits a crime of violence.

Parole is a useful device in spite of the number who violate its conditions and return to prison. It keeps the prisoner under the control of the system. The parolee needs help in his adjustment to a less restrictive life. The released prisoner encounters both real and imagined suspicion. His self-doubt complicates the everyday problems he has to face. The prison creates dependency but the urban environment demands independence. Therein lies the problem. For the parolee, then, the kind and quality of supervision is crucial. When President Jimmy Carter was governor of Georgia he started a work-release program which placed selected prisoners in the employ of the governor's mansion. This is how Mary Fitzpatrick was hired as Amy Carter's nurse from 1971 to 1974. This young woman was paroled from the Women's Work Release Center in Atlanta in early 1977. Her employer once more is Jimmy Carter and her residence is the White House.

PRESIDENT'S DAUGHTER GETS UNIQUE BABYSITTER

ATLANTA (AP)—Mary Fitzpatrick, sentenced to life in prison seven years ago for murder, put on "just one of my old blue dresses" today and went off to work in the White House for the president's family.

"I'm nervous, really nervous," Amy Carter's nurse said as she emerged from her room at the Georgia Women's Early Release Center to the glare of television lights and reporters' questions.

Mrs. Fitzpatrick, 31, was Amy's nurse while Jimmy Carter was governor of Georgia, from 1971 through 1974, under a program by which the state corrections department supplies trusty prisoners as kitchen help, maids, gardeners, and other workers at the governor's mansion.

The Carters asked her to take her old job in a new city. And for that she was given a reprieve to allow her to leave the minimum security two months ahead of her scheduled parole eligibility.

Mrs. Fitzpatrick, who has been at the center for two years, said she heard about her early release on Wednesday "and I haven't been able to sleep since."

She was granted the reprieve by the Georgia Board of Pardons and Paroles two months before she becomes eligible for parole from her sentence of life in prison for the murder of Johnny Bynum.

The reprieve came after the pardons board received a written request from the White House, said Rob Haworth, executive officer of the board. He would not say who signed the request.

Mrs. Fitzpatrick was convicted of shooting Bynum in 1970 by a Supreme Court jury in Stewart County.

Stewart County Sheriff Bob Mitchell said Mrs. Fitzpatrick had been visiting friends in Lumpkin, Ga., the county seat, and was with a girlfriend when the shooting occurred.

Mitchell said that when the two women encountered Bynum with another woman, Mrs. Fitzpatrick's friend—who had dated Bynum—threatened to shoot him. It was then, he said, that Mrs. Fitzpatrick took the gun and shot Bynum.

The sheriff said the four apparently had been drinking. Mitchell, a Lumpkin police officer at the time of the shooting, took Mrs. Fitzpatrick into custody.

Officials at the Atlanta Women's Work Release Center had given Mrs. Fitzpatrick a three-day pass last month to attend President Carter's inauguration and visit with nine-year-old Amy, whom she tended while a prison trusty from 1971 to 1974.

Mrs. Fitzpatrick, described as a model prisoner, saw the inaugural parade and babysat for Amy while her parents attended inaugural parties. Amy said then they were "having a good time" together.

Parole board rules allow convicts with exemplary prison records to be paroled within ninety days of the eligibility date, Haworth said.

"The unusual opportunity for employment also was important" in Mrs. Fitzpatrick's case, he said.

Under Georgia law she will be eligible for parole after seven years, on April 1, Haworth said.

Source: *The Sacramento Bee,* 4 February 1977, pp. A1 and A24. Reprinted by permission.

Unfortunately, inmates discharged at the expiration of their sentences (i.e., unconditional release) are not eligible for parole-office services. If recidivism—the return to prison—is to be reduced, a program to identify prisoners needing such services is essential. Also, new ways must be found to minimize the stress associated with reentry. We need parole supervisors who understand the needs of inmates but are aware of their enforcement obligations. The goal is community protection. The parole staff should not overlook the potential for criminality in their clients. Some parolees return to crime because of their failure to resolve everyday problems which seem hopeless. Others are career criminals who had always planned to resume their illegal activity as soon as possible. Recidivism is generally higher among prisoners whose crimes are identified with economic gain, such as burglary, forgery, larceny, and robbery. Recidivism is lower for those who committed crimes resulting from situational factors which may not reoccur, as in murder, rape, and embezzlement. The low recidivism rate does not hold where the offender selects strangers as victims and systematically plans the commission of the crime.

History of Parole

The origin of parole is traced to several penal reformers who believed prisoners should be rewarded for good behavior while confined. Captain Alexander Maconochie was the administrator of a small prison colony on the island of Norfolk in Australia for four years beginning in 1840. He introduced a system of rewards based upon a point system which permitted prisoners to obtain their release and eventually return to their homes in England. This program received much notoriety in Great Britain. Sir Walter Crofton, an administrator in the Irish prison system, introduced a similar program in 1846. He modified the earlier program and made supervision upon release from prison a condition of the reward for accrued good time. The police in Ireland were selected to supervise ex-prisoners. Crofton was praised for his program at Mountjoy Prison in Ireland and was an invited guest in 1870 at the first meeting of the American Prison Association in Cincinnati. A prison warden, Zebulon Brockway, also attended this prison congress. He was to become the superintendent of the Elmira Reformatory in New York when it was opened in 1876. Brockway introduced parole into this country. His inmates, who were the younger offenders, were released before completing the fixed prison sentence. This new concept, known as the indeterminate sentence, allowed prisoners to complete a portion of their confinement outside of the institution under supervision. The decision to release was made not by the prison itself but by a parole board. Legislation implementing this form of conditional release has existed in every state since 1945.

Since 1976 a number of states have enacted determinate sentencing laws which replace existing indeterminate sentencing legislation. Under the indeterminate system the parole board decides when to release a prisoner based on such items as the nature of the offense, the offender's propensity for further violence, and whether or not he or she has been rehabilitated. The determinate or fixed-term system is one in which the judge decides how long the sentence will be, based on legislative guidelines. The emphasis is punishment rather than rehabilitation. Modern determinate sentencing has been called the "just desserts" approach to punishment because the sanctions are adjusted to match the seriousness of the particular offense. The punishment of crime, not the offender, becomes the focus of sentence fixing. The new system is not a simple procedure under which a robber, for example, gets so many years in prison. A number of factors, known

313

as enhancements, enter into computing the term. Did the person have a firearm? Did he or she use it? How much money was taken in the robbery? Does he or she have a record of prior felonies or prison terms? Were there mitigating circumstances? More states are expected to follow California, Indiana, Illinois, Maine, Minnesota, and Washington in proposing and passing such laws. The move from indeterminate to determinate sentencing has led to the abolishment of parole in Maine and a limiting of its function in California.

The Parole Board

The administrative structure of the parole board varies among the states. In its most popular form it operates autonomously within the state correctional system. Known as the consolidation model, it operates in thirty states. The alternative model, operating in twenty states, is the independent parole board.[8] The consolidation model is considered more successful for many reasons. It is sensitive to institutional programs and attempts to consider the recommendation of the prison staff in formulating a decision. A parole board which is a part of a larger state agency is more likely to balance successfully several considerations when determining parole—the protection of society and the possibility that parole can be successful with adequate supervision. The consolidation model favors the selection of career personnel in corrections as parole-board members with fewer political appointees who have no insight into the problem. In addition, the consolidation model presupposes a concern with the supervision and control of parolees after the decision to release is made.

The board determines parole policy and meets regularly to decide which prisoners are eligible for release. It also handles the paperwork when violators are returned to prison. There are additional responsibilities although these vary in each state. The other duties can include: (1) clemency hearings; (2) commuting sentences; (3) appointing parole supervision staff; (4) administering parole services; (5) granting or withholding "good time" in states where mandatory release is used; and (6) supervising parolees released from county correctional facilities.

There are fifty-three agencies with parole jurisdiction over felony offenders sentenced to adult institutions for one year or longer. These include one parole authority in each state, a separate parole board for women in Indiana, the District of Columbia Parole Board, and the United States Parole Commission. Appointment of parole-board members varies between the jurisdictions; the governor has the power of appointment in forty states, the power is shared by the governor and other state officials in three jurisdictions, appointment is through the civil service in three states, and in four states the decision is made by other state departments. Parole-board size is usually three or five members but there may be as many as twelve including the chairperson. The term of office ranges from three to seven years, with four or six average.[9] It is a handicap to the board that in many jurisdictions its members serve only part time. Hearing examiners with correctional experience should be hired to help them. There should also be uniform qualifications for appointment to these boards as recommended by the National Advisory Commission on Criminal Justice Standards and Goals.

Each state should specify by statute the qualifications and conditions of appointment of parole-board members.

1. Parole boards for adult and juvenile offenders should consist of full-time members.

2. Members should possess academic training in fields such as criminology, education, psychology, psychiatry, law, social work, or sociology.

3. Members should have a high degree of skill in comprehending legal issues and statistical information and an ability to develop and promulgate policy.

4. Members should be appointed by the governor for six-year terms from a panel of nominees selected by an advisory group broadly representative of the community. Besides being representative of relevant professional organizations, the advisory group should include all important ethnic and socioeconomic groups.

5. Parole boards in the small states should consist of no less than three full-time members. In most states, they should not exceed five members.

6. Parole-board members should be compensated at a rate equal to that of a judge of a court of general jurisdiction.

7. Hearing examiners should have backgrounds similar to that of members but need not be as specialized. Their education and experiential qualifications should allow them to understand programs, to relate to people, and to make sound and reasonable decisions.

8. Parole-board members should participate in continuing training on a national basis. The exchange of parole-board members and hearing examiners between states for training purposes should be supported and encouraged.[10]

Parole Decision Making

Release from prison depends on many factors. It would be gratifying if the decision to parole were to coincide with the prisoner's ability to benefit from it. But circumstances make that ideal condition impossible. The statutes determine the sentence for a specific crime and usually set the minimum time that must be served before parole can be considered. For instance, the law might impose a penalty of six months to fourteen years, and also specify a five-month period before the initial parole hearing. In this case, the first interview would be a month before the earliest legal parole date. So, within boundaries, the parole board has the discretion to set conditions for release and supervision. Those states using mandatory release reduce the maximum sentence by the amount of time accrued for good behavior and follow the policy regarding minimum time to be served in prison before release. Eligibility for parole does not mean, of course, that parole will be granted in all cases. In fact, the revised Model Sentencing Act, prepared by the National Council on Crime and Delinquency, recommends the abolition of all minimum sentences in the statutes.[11] This would give the parole board discretion at any point short of the maximum sentence.

The decision to parole is affected by the various legal restrictions and the obvious vagaries of an eclectic board. Practically, parole dates are set keeping two things in mind: the protection of the public, and the probability of inmate adjustment on the outside. The imponderables of assessing motive assure a measure of error for even the best board. To the extent that it is impossible to predict future criminal behavior, the parole board can be excused for its failures.

Parole hearings take place regularly in the institutions within the jurisdiction of the board. Panels, composed of board members or representatives, rotate visits. The inmate is present during the hearing in all states except Georgia, Hawaii, and Texas. Four states grant interviews only to inmates who merit parole consideration and screen the files of the other prisoners. Progress reports, prepared by institutional parole officers, are available before the hearings. Ideally, these are prepared at least one month before the scheduled meetings. The preparole summary is a staff assessment of inmate progress. A recommendation supporting or rejecting parole is included. The preparole report becomes a summary sheet in the institutional inmate file which is made available to the board.

A glance through the file shows these things: disciplinary infractions, work patterns, participation in education and vocational programs, relationships with personnel and other prisoners, contacts with correspondents or visitors, involvement in therapy or counseling sessions, and his or her changing attitudes about the offense. If the inmate requests specific programs while at the prison, this is noted. Any program request denied the prisoner should be included together with the reasons for the decision. The good behavior of the inmate

316

should be recognized and encouraged. Prisoners often voluntarily participate in experimental programs, record books for the blind, or even risk their lives by being injected with germs to test the effectiveness of new disease-fighting drugs. During prison disturbances many inmates have been instrumental in protecting threatened staff members.

The parole board reviews the severity of the offense and takes into account any known opposition to release. Letters received from the victim, his or her family, police officials, the district attorney, or the sentencing judge are reviewed. In turn, the parole prognosis is carefully considered. Prison adjustment is not necessarily an indication of behavior after release. For this reason, some boards are using parole prediction tables in order to obtain more information about prisoners. The most useful instrument intended to measure the probability of favorable parole adjustment was developed in California, although that state discontinued its use in 1976. It is called the base-expectancy scale; scores are calculated for each offender using twelve characteristics found in the earlier criminal career. Points are assigned if the following characteristics are present.

1. Arrest-free period of five or more consecutive years (12 points);
2. No history of any opiate use (9 points);
3. Few jail commitments—none, one, or two (8 points);
4. No checks, forgery, or burglary—most recent court commitment (7 points);
5. No family criminal record (6 points);
6. No alcohol involvement (6 points);
7. Not first arrested for auto theft (5 points);
8. Six or more consecutive months for one employer (5 points);
9. No aliases (5 points);
10. First imprisonment under this serial number (5 points);
11. Favorable living arrangement (4 points); and
12. Few prior arrests—none, one, or two (4 points).[12]

Favorable parole outcome is related to the scores received on the base-expectancy scale. Of those paroled in 1967, the percentage of those with a favorable parole outcome after two years was directly related to their cumulative BE score. The data are as follows: BE score 69–76, 97 percent successful; BE score 53–68, 73 percent successful; BE score 46–52, 56 percent successful; BE score 33–45, 50 percent; BE score 27–32, 41 percent; BE score 17–26, 34 percent; and BE score 00–16, 23 percent.[13] The use of statistical information such as the base expectancy or any other experience table can provide a parole board with additional input and reduce the possibility of subjective bias. Many states oppose the use of such tables, claiming the method identifies groups of prisoners with a potential for favorable adjustment while overlooking critical information in special cases. Perhaps this is true, but the base expectancy can prove helpful when board members are uncertain about a decision using only more subjective criteria.

Most states allow the inmate to participate in the board hearing at the institution. Parole representatives usually question the prisoner directly. Often the questioners tend to reflect their own professional biases. Some common approaches involve: (1) testing the offender's response to provocative questions; (2) probing for the prisoner's subjective view of his or her criminal act; (3) assessing the benefit derived from specific institutional programs; and (4) evaluating the offender's plans for his or her future outside of prison. The inmate should be treated respectfully during this hearing. He or she should be allowed to express his or her feelings about parole and confinement. The board hearing is the most important interview experienced by the prisoner, who approaches it with some anxiety since the board determines whether he or she will be released. Norman Hayner, late professor emeritus of sociology at the University of Washington, and former chairman of the Washington State Board of Prison Terms and Paroles, describes a typical parole-board hearing.

> A special room is set aside at each institution for use by the board. The room contains a long table behind which the three board members sit. A representative of the institution, usually the associate superintendent in charge of treatment, is at one end of the table. Occasionally, a visitor, who takes no part in the interviews, is at the opposite end. The board has found it very helpful to have a judge, prosecutor, police chief, or sheriff sit in on the hearings. Nothing seemed to develop better cooperation than to let them see how the board operated.
>
> There was a time when a telephone was located in each board room, and hearings could be interrupted or confused by the ring of the bell or extraneous conversation. These phones were taken out, accordingly, as no such interruptions were wanted. No one was permitted to enter the board room during a hearing—only between hearings. The inmate was not being tried. The judge had done that, and the man had either pleaded guilty or been found guilty.

The board's purpose was simply to determine the length of time he would spend in prison. It wanted to concentrate on his story and give him every opportunity to speak freely.

With a buzz from the chairman, an inmate would come in and sit down. The institution representative introduced him to each board member as Mr. _____. Although not common practice in prison, it was felt that the designation "Mister" gave him more recognition as a person. The name of each member appeared also on a plaque, clearly visible to the inmate, immediately in front of the member. This helped the inmate to orient himself with reference to the different personalities on the board.

The member to whom the case had been assigned usually commenced by trying to put the prisoner at ease. He might comment on some athletic facility the inmate had exhibited, make some pleasant remark about the man's home town, or just inquire about his age. The man was usually nervous. If it was summer, he had great wet patches under the arms from perspiration. A human approach made him feel that the members were, after all, not such ogres as he may have thought and that he could relax and talk freely.

There are weaknesses that a board of this type has to watch. All members must know the salient facts of the case. No member should be permitted to dominate the proceeding. It is easy to preach or moralize, but this should be kept at a minimum. A certain amount of levity is desirable to relieve the tension of such sessions, but it should never be at the expense of the inmate. Jokes about inmates must be reserved for times when they are not present. If there is a coffee break, time out should be taken for it. Munching cookies and sipping coffee while trying to talk to a prisoner is inappropriate. In brief, the session should be conducted in quiet dignity with ample opportunity for statements or questions by the man being sentenced. Since the average inmate's educational achievement is less than eighth grade, explanations should be in simple words.

Another aspect of board hearings to remember is that prisoners have time. Many of them use this time thinking about the personalities of the board and figuring out what "line" would be most effective. The more intelligent may try their best to "con" the board. For a preacher member, they have gotten religion, are attending Bible class, or perhaps plan to go into religious work when they are paroled. For a lawyer, they purposely play up legal points

319

to draw him out. For a sociologist, it is surprising how many correspondence courses they have taken in that field and how often they are planning to attend college. One should not be too critical, however. It is better to be "conned" occasionally than to discourage a man with an honest story.

The member to whom the case had been assigned asked questions about the past record, the present crime, and about the future. All members were quick to note the man's attitude toward his crime. Did he accept responsibility for what he has done or project the blame onto others. Did he attempt to conceal or minimize the importance of his offenses? What were his feelings about the plan which the reception and guidance staff have worked out with him? Was he going to make constructive use of his time in the institution? For such a hearing, ten or twelve minutes were usually enough, but sometimes it took more than sixty.[14]

Parole hearings are too brief, usually only five to fifteen minutes, although Hayner recalls some deliberations lasting as long as an hour. The National Advisory Commission on Criminal Justice Standards and Goals recommends that the board hear no more than twenty cases each day.[15] O'Leary and Hanrahan found that twenty parole boards were conducting an average of thirty or more hearings each day.[16]

The method used to inform the prisoner of the parole-board decision has changed in recent years. In the past, the results were not reported to the prisoner immediately. He or she received the decision through a representative of the board or a member of the prison staff. Sometimes the delay was several weeks. And even after the board decided to grant or deny a parole it was not obliged to specify the reasons for its decision. This action resulted in low prisoner morale and frequent disciplinary problems. Now, however, twenty-two jurisdictions excuse the inmate for a few minutes while the board deliberates. Then the inmate is recalled and given the decision and the reasons for it. To be denied parole is unsettling because another interview can be six months or a year away. The prisoner often needs help so he can present himself to the board in the best possible light next time. If he is paroled, preparations should begin in prison since he may have to wait several months to actually be released.

Conditions of Parole

When the prisoner is released on parole he agrees to limit his activities in certain ways and to report regularly to the parole officer.

Certain conditions are imposed by the agency; if these are violated the parole may be revoked. Each state authorizes its own set of conditions. There are over fifty different rules governing parolee behavior; however, the majority of states consider less than twenty to be sufficient. The usual conditions of parole include the following.

1. Use of alcoholic beverages is prohibited.
2. Change of employment or residence requires prior permission.
3. Association with undesirable persons or groups is prohibited.
4. The parolee must report in person to the parole office as soon as possible after leaving the institution.
5. Written reports must be submitted regularly to the parole officer.
6. Approval of marriage or divorce requires prior permission.
7. Driving or owning an automobile requires consent of the parole officer.
8. Travel outside the county or state demands prior approval.
9. Dependents must be supported adequately.
10. Compliance with the law is compulsory.

The parolee who violates any condition of parole can be returned to prison. The commission of a new offense is only one reason for revoking parole. The other conditions are equally binding and failure to obey them is considered a technical violation. The parole officer may return a parolee to prison on a technical violation. The list of parole conditions should be flexible enough to be tailored to the individual parolee. The discretion of the parole officer and philosophy of the agency will determine how often minor violations lead to revocation. The purpose of parole conditions is to prevent crime. Perhaps only one rule is necessary and that is that compliance with the law is compulsory. Fair and effective conditions will be possible if the following recommendation is implemented.

Each state should take immediate action to reduce parole rules to an absolute minimum, retaining only those critical in the individual case, and to provide for effective means of enforcing the conditions established.

1. After considering suggestions from correctional staff and preferences of the individual, parole boards should establish in each case the specific parole conditions appropriate for the individual offender.

2. Parole staff should be able to request the board to amend rules to fit the needs of each case and should be

empowered to require the parolee to obey any such rule when put in writing, pending the final action of the parole board.

3. Special caseloads for intensive supervision should be established and staffed by personnel of suitable skill and temperament. Careful review procedures should be established to determine which offenders should be assigned or removed from such caseloads.

4. Parole officers should develop close liaison with police agencies, so that any formal arrests necessary can be made by police. Parole officers, therefore, would not need to be armed.[17]

Parole supervision

Surveillance and treatment are the two objectives of parole. The returning parolee can scarcely hide the fact that he has been in prison. He has to explain himself to employers, neighbors, and would-be intimates. If he denies his status he has to construct a frustrating cover-up and then wonder when he will be found out. Leaving prison the ex-offender faces his first condition of parole, that he report to his parole officer immediately. The parole experience should be more than surveillance, that is, adherence to the conditions imposed by the agency under fear of revocation. The diligence of supervision should be more than the discovery of violations by the parole agent. Supervision requires a parole officer who is concerned about the problems confronting former prisoners. He must realize that the parolee, more than the probationer, has problems that defy easy adjustment. This is especially evident in the ex-offender's everyday peer relationships. Supportive counseling will be helpful in reducing worry about employment, housing, how to meet routine expenditures, and personal morale. Only a parole officer with a reputation for fairness can expect to influence a man or woman with such difficulties.

The parole agent should supervise no more than fifty clients if he is to respond to the needs of the ex-offender. Most agencies are understaffed and overworked. Caseloads may range in size from less than 50 to more than 200. Whatever the number of cases supervised by the officer he serves as a vital link between the ex-offender and groups organized to help him. The first sixty to ninety days are the most difficult for the paroled offender. Without careful supervision and community help he may violate one of the technical conditions, commit a new crime, or abscond. Individual treatment requires community services to meet the problems faced by the ex-prisoner on parole. The National Advisory Commission on Criminal Justice Standards and Goals recommends the following policy.

322

Each state should begin immediately to develop a diverse range of programs to meet the needs of parolees. These services should be drawn to the greatest extent possible from community programs available to all citizens, with parole staff providing linkage between services and the parolees needing or desiring them.

     1. Stringent review procedures should be adopted, so that parolees not requiring supervision are released from supervision immediately and those requiring minimal attention are placed in minimum supervision caseloads.

     2. Parole officers should be selected and trained to fulfill the role of community resource manager.

     3. Parole staff should participate fully in developing coordinated delivery systems of human services.

     4. Funds should be made available for parolees without interest charge. Parole staff should have authority to waive repayment to fit the individual case.

     5. State funds should be available to offenders, so that some mechanism similar to unemployment benefits may be available to inmates at the time of their release, in order to tide them over until they find a job.

     6. All states should use, as much as possible, a requirement that offenders have a visible means of support, rather than a promise of a specific job, before authorizing their release on parole.

     7. Parole and state employment staffs should develop effective communication systems at the local level. Joint meetings and training sessions should be undertaken.

     8. Each parole agency should have one or more persons attached to the central office to act as liaison with major program agencies, such as the Office of Economic Opportunity, Office of Vocational Rehabilitation, and Department of Labor.

     9. Institutional vocational training tied directly to specific subsequent job placements should be supported.

     10. Parole boards should encourage institutions to maintain effective quality control over programs.

     11. Small community-based group homes should be available to parole staff for prerelease programs, for crises, and as a substitute to recommitment to an institution in appropriately reviewed cases of parole violation.

     12. Funds should be made available to parole staffs to purchase needed community resources for parolees.

13. Special caseloads should be established for offenders with specific types of problems, such as drug abuse.[18]

Parole Revocation

The most severe sanction available to the parole officer is the power to recommend revocation of parole. It is invoked when the parolee fails to observe the conditions governing parole. A representative of the parole board reviews the recommendation before final action is taken. Controversy rages over the use of the revocation power. The "conman" parolee complains when his return to crime is discovered by representatives of the justice system. The inadequate ex-prisoner often denies his inability to follow the conditions of parole, conditions which are a measure of his conformity in the community. Whatever the reason for the violation the parolee has a right to know why he is being recommended for revocation.

Too often in the past parolees were detained for parole violation without knowing the charges. The broad discretion given parole officers was not always accompanied by procedural safeguards for the parolee. In 1972 the U.S. Supreme Court handed down its landmark decision, *Morrissey* v. *Brewer,* in which it stated "fair treatment in parole revocations will enhance the chance of rehabilitation by avoiding reactions to arbitrariness."[19] The Court ruled that the parolee is entitled to due-process protections throughout the revocation proceedings. These are conducted in two stages: the preliminary hearing following arrest, carried out while the parolee is in detention; and the second hearing which actually revokes parole. The preliminary hearing should be conducted by an impartial officer who is not connected with the case. It ought to be scheduled promptly in or near the place of the violation. The parolee should receive prior notice of the inquiry, its purpose, and the list of alleged violations. The hearing decides whether there are reasonable grounds to believe that the parolee committed acts which violate his parole. The hearing officer rules on whether charges should be dropped or whether a revocation hearing should be held. He summarizes the meeting and decides whether the parolee should be confined until a final parole decision is made. The parolee is allowed to answer the allegations and to present evidence and witnesses to support his position.

The revocation hearing should be held as soon as possible after the preliminary hearing. It is the purpose of this final hearing to decide, based on the facts in the case, whether parole will be revoked. The parolee is entitled to: (1) a written notice of the alleged infractions of parole conditions; (2) disclosure of the evidence against him; (3) an opportunity to be heard in person and to present witnesses and documentary evidence; (4) the right to confront and cross-examine adverse witnesses unless the hearing officer finds good cause for not allowing it; (5) a neutral and detached hearing body or traditional parole board, members of which need not be judicial officers or lawyers; and (6) a written statement by the fact finders about the evidence relied on and the reasons for revoking parole. The action of the U.S. Supreme Court has removed the secrecy which once surrounded revocation proceedings. This is a step toward fairness and justice. Openness about accusations could motivate more parole officers to consider alternatives to revocation, especially in the case of technical violations. Parolees can be handled short of revocation by employing intensive supervision, fines, short-term local confinement, or referral to other community agencies. The parole officer can focus on rules whose intent is the prevention of new offenses. Surveillance activity should not intrude on the privacy of the parolee except in cases where illegal activity is known.

MANDATORY RELEASE

Some adult offenders are released automatically after serving a portion of their prison sentences. Mandatory-release legislation exists in New York, Wisconsin, and is part of the federal probation and parole system. This form of conditional release is not to be confused with parole; it is the result of accumulated credit for good behavior in prison. The period given for good behavior, usually six months, is subtracted from the sentence expiration date and does not need approval by the parole board. However, there is a short period of release supervision. The regulations governing parole apply to it.

DISCHARGE FROM PRISON

Many prisoners are unconditionally released after having served their full sentences. There is neither supervision nor support from state or federal agencies. Many of these prisoners would be considered poor parole risks. But they have served the maximum term and must be freed. A total of 22,703 prisoners received an unconditional release from state institutions in 1976. This is in addition to the previously mentioned 84,225 inmates granted a conditional release during the same year.[20] Louisiana, Oklahoma, South Carolina, and Wyoming discharge at least 50 percent of their prisoners without any follow-up services.

325

PARDONS

The exercise of mercy and the mitigation of punishment is reflected in the pardon. This form of clemency is the prerogative of the executive branch of government; it is granted by the governor or the president of the United States. Sometimes the recommendations of a pardon board are solicited. The pardon is used to remedy an injustice, as in the case of a prisoner who is later found to be innocent. A pardon was recently granted to Clarence Norris by the state of Alabama. He was found innocent of the offense for which he was sentenced to die at the highly publicized "Scottsboro Boys" trial held forty-six years ago.

"SCOTTSBORO BOY" GETS FULL ALABAMA PARDON

MONTGOMERY, ALA.—Yesterday, forty-five years after it began, "Scottsboro Boy" Clarence Norris won a full pardon from the state of Alabama.

He had spent five years on death row, years more behind bars, and decades living as a fugitive, all for a crime he always insisted he did not commit.

"It's great to be free. There's nothing like being free," Norris said in New York, where he now lives.

First the Alabama Pardon-Parole Board and then Governor George Wallace signed a pardon for the sixty-four-year-old laborer who, with eight other young black men, was accused of raping two white women aboard a freight train in Alabama in 1931.

The case became one of the most controversial in the South. Because the alleged rape occurred near Scottsboro in north Alabama and the trial was held there, the defendants became known throughout the world as the "Scottsboro Boys."

Norris, the last of the nine defendants known to be still alive, is working now as a laborer for the city of New York. He fled from Alabama after being paroled in 1946, and the state continued to list him as a parole violator.

The pardon-parole board not only pardoned Norris but in effect also recognized his innocence. By law, the board could pardon him only if it felt there was proof of his innocence.

Now that he is free to do so, Norris said he would go back to Ala-

326

bama. "I'll go to any state because I'm free," he said. "I was born and raised in the South. It's one of the most beautiful places in the world."

At a news conference at the New York headquarters of the NAACP, which represented him in pursuing the pardon, Norris said there is a lesson for black people in his pardon.

"Don't ever give up hope," he said. "Always fight for your rights. That's what I believe in. Even if it kills you, stand up for your rights."

"I feel different because I'm free," he said. "Being free means a whole lot to you. You can speak your mind about what you think."

When Norris first inquired last summer about a pardon, he ran into stern resistance from the pardon-parole board. The chairman of the board, Norman Ussery, said Norris was still a fugitive and would have to return to prison in Alabama before the request could be considered.

Norris said repeatedly he did not want to go back to an Alabama jail.

Ussery ultimately changed his mind, and in a statement yesterday he explained why.

At first, he said, "We did not have any information as to where he was living, where he worked, or what his behavior had been since he left Alabama."

But the official application gave the board "the necessary information to investigate this case," the chairman said, and "after verifying this information, I no longer felt that he was a fugitive from justice."

Norris is married now, and has two daughters, twenty and sixteen years old. Mayor Abraham Beame of New York supported his request for pardon.

Source: *San Francisco Chronicle*, 26 October 1976, p. 1. Reprinted by permission of The Associated Press.

Shortening an existing sentence is the most frequently employed form of clemency. This occurs when a governor commutes (that is, reduces) a sentence of death to life imprisonment, or life without possibility of parole to a specific number of years in prison.

Amnesty is another form of general pardon. It may be extended to certain groups after a war or insurrection. Sometimes governors are sensitive to the rehabilitative efforts of former prisoners. They can restore the civil rights of ex-offenders after a reasonable time. Certainly decisions involving the restriction or deprivation of civil rights should be reviewed. These disabilities ought to be eliminated when the probationer or parolee proves satisfactory. It is unfortunate that the executive branch of government has to step in where punishments have been excessively harsh and burdensome. The courts and corrections should have the power to correct some of these inequities themselves.

CONCLUSION

Probation and parole are the assistance services of corrections. Effective probation reduces the need to employ incarceration when punishing offenders. Parole provides supervision and services which are responsive to the critical problems of community reentry for the ex-prisoner. Greater emphasis on more thorough and careful procedures for selecting offenders for these treatment measures can enhance the role of corrections in preventing and controlling crime. The recently formed American Probation and Parole Association is endeavoring to: (1) advance progressive probation and parole practices throughout the United States; (2) stimulate high standards of training and the professionalization of personnel; (3) promote international communication and exchange of ideas; (4) encourage public awareness and acceptance of probation and parole as an effective means to deal with prevention, control, and correction of crime and delinquency; and (5) encourage the development of innovative services, research design, and program evaluation.

STUDY QUESTIONS

1. Define probation.
2. Identify the administrative structure of probation in your state.
3. What information should you find in the presentence investigation report? How is the report used by the judge and probation department?
4. How do you determine effective probation supervision of the correctional client?
5. Define parole, mandatory release, commutation of sentence, and pardon.
6. Differentiate the probation client from the parole client.
7. What are the responsibilities of the parole board?
8. What is the average length of the parole hearing in your state? How many cases will the board review each working day?
9. Identify the conditions of parole imposed in your state. Would you add more conditions or reduce the current number? Explain.
10. Why are some prisoners paroled and others discharged from the correctional institution?

NOTES

1. National Advisory Commission on Criminal Justice Standards and Goals, *A National Strategy to Reduce Crime* (Washington, D.C.: Government Printing Office, 1973), p. 121.

2. American Bar Association, *Standards Relating to Probation* (1970), p. 9.
3. John A. Wallace, "Probation Administration," in *Handbook of Criminology,* ed. Daniel Glaser (Chicago: Rand McNally, 1974), p. 951.
4. Robert M. Carter, "The Presentence Report and the Decision-Making Process," in *Probation, Parole, and Community Corrections,* 2d ed., eds. Robert M. Carter and Leslie T. Wilkins (New York: John Wiley, 1976), pp. 201–210.
5. James Robison, *The California Prison, Parole, and Probation System,* Technical Supplement No. 2 (Sacramento: California Assembly, 1969), p. 23.
6. National Advisory Commission on Criminal Justice Standards and Goals, *Report on Corrections* (Washington, D.C.: Government Printing Office, 1973), p. 323.
7. U.S. Department of Justice, Law Enforcement Assistance Administration, *Prisoners in State and Federal Institutions on December 31, 1976* (Washington, D.C.: Government Printing Office, 1978), pp. 8 and 28.
8. National Advisory Commission, *Report on Corrections,* pp. 396–397.
9. Vincent O'Leary and Kathleen J. Hanrahan, *Parole Systems in the United States,* 3rd ed. (Hackensack, N.J.: National Council on Crime and Delinquency, 1976), pp. 12–24.
10. National Advisory Commission, *Report on Corrections,* p. 420.
11. Council of Judges, National Council on Crime and Delinquency, "Model Sentencing Act—Second Edition," *Crime and Delinquency* 18 (Oct. 1972): 365.
12. California Department of Corrections, *The Base Expectancy Scale BE61A* (Sacramento: California Department of Corrections, Research Measurement Unit, 1970), p. 1.
13. Ibid., p. iv.
14. Norman S. Hayner, "Sentencing by an Administrative Board," *Law and Contemporary Problems* 23 (Summer 1958): 489–490.
15. National Advisory Commission, *Report on Corrections,* p. 422.
16. O'Leary and Hanrahan, *Parole Systems,* p. 35.
17. National Advisory Commission, *Report on Corrections,* p. 433.
18. Ibid., p. 430.
19. *Morrissey* v. *Brewer,* 408 U.S. 471, 92 S.Ct. 2593, 33 L.Ed. 2d 484 (1972).
20. Department of Justice, *Prisoners in State and Federal Institutions,* p. 28.

AN ILLUSTRATIVE CAREER IN PROBATION AND PAROLE
The Federal Probation Service

The Federal Probation Service supervises those who are released to the community on parole or probation. The basic tasks of the probation officer include supervision and investigation. Supervising offenders who are in the community is an important part of the probation officer's daily endeavors. In encouraging the person to live a lawful life, the probation officer must help him or her learn how to get along with others, obtain and maintain employment, use leisure time constructively, and learn the necessary skills to keep up with the demands of fast-paced modern life. In addition to work in the supervision of offenders, the probation officer plays a vital role in the sentencing process. In almost all criminal cases, presentence reports are prepared by the probation officer for the district court judge. These reports review the defendant's social history and provide insight relating to his or her character and background. The work of the parole officer is significant, difficult, and challenging. It is important to recognize that the relationship between the probation officer and the client is such that the officer is involved with a reluctant client who has been forced into the relationship. In this work the probation officer must exercise skills demanding independence, judgment, and problem-solving ability. The role of the probation officer is critical to the operations of both the corrections and the courts processes.

Entry Requirements

Probation officers are appointed by the district courts which they serve. Probation officers must be college graduates with a bachelor's degree from a college of recognized standing and have two years of work experience being responsible for the welfare of others or they must have a master's degree awarded for two years of specialized training in a professional course in counseling, welfare, or other related areas.

Career Development

A career with the U. S. Probation Service reflects all the challenges and opportunities of delivering social services. Probation officers enter the service at GS-9, which has a starting salary of $15,090, with the possibility of advancement through GS-12 upon the recommendation of superiors. There are opportunities for advancement to supervising, deputy chief, and chief probation officer in each of the field offices of the U. S. Probation Service. The probation service provides generous leave, retirement, and health policies.

chapter thirteen
Correctional Institutions

Probation is granted the offender considered likely to benefit from programs existing in the community. Parole and other forms of conditional release are available to those prisoners no longer requiring imprisonment. The correctional institution is used for the incarceration of those deemed to be dangerous and in need of restraint. During the late 1960s a prison-reform movement emerged which spoke of the cruel and inhumane punishment of the prison. There was discussion of forbidding the construction of more institutions. People who subscribed to this approach believed that most prisoners are not in need of banishment and incarceration. This trend was premature and erroneous; there was overcrowding in the penal institutions because greater numbers of criminals were requiring incarceration. Louisiana was considering turning a mothballed Navy ship into a floating prison. Florida was putting prisoners in tents. Missouri was considering converting an empty seminary into a prison. Prison populations are increasing at an alarming rate. More individuals are committing serious offenses, the severity of these crimes prohibits the use of probation, and new mandatory sentencing laws demand incarceration for the convicted felon.

An inmate in a state or federal correctional institution is one who has been sentenced as an adult or youthful offender and whose maximum sentence length is a year and a day or longer. A number of other offenders are serving sentences of one year or less in local jails where modern penal practices are often overlooked. A short discussion of the jail will precede our inquiry into the role of the correctional institution in controlling crime.

The abolition of prisons, in short, always seems to be located, even by its most enthusiastic proponents, at some point in space or time removed from the distasteful realities of the world in which we live. Somewhere, sometime, the walls will come down, the morning stars will sing together, and all the decarcerated sons of God will shout for joy and become "morally autonomous, self-disciplined people"; but not here, not now. Here, now and for the forseeable future, that frequently deplored, rarely defended, but "deeply-rooted" institution we call prison is seen by the majority of citizens as, in some form or other, a necessary, or at least inevitable, feature of society.

Source: Gordon Hawkins, *The Prison: Policy and Practice* (Chicago: University of Chicago Press, 1976), p. 40.

JAILS—JUSTICE OR INJUSTICE?

The local jail is the intake facility for the criminal-justice system and the skid row of American corrections. It is a national disgrace. The jail system has defied a long history of criticism. The slum areas of our cities, with their dreary flophouses, rescue missions, and soup kitchens, are home for the unemployed and forgotten. When their serious problems are further exacerbated by criminal conduct, a jail sentence ensues. Local jail populations are representative of the social problems which the justice system is asked to correct.

But the long history of jail criticism has failed to improve the structure or administration of the local jail. In our early history jails were the only form of confinement for offenders. The early settlers adopted the English administration which placed jails under the control of a sheriff or town marshal. For this reason the confinement of prisoners, both those sentenced and those awaiting pretrial processing, was left to the local facility. Further correctional reforms, under the leadership of the Society of Friends, brought the penitentiary system, which was the basis for more humane treatment of convicted felons. These prisoners were sentenced to institutions operated by the state or federal government. The field of penology evolved a body of knowledge for classifying, detaining, and providing services for prisoners. Staff members received training and the field of corrections

333

came to be considered a profession. Despite all these changes, the local jail was overlooked and allowed to keep its power while rejecting advanced penological theories. Instead of the modern approach of the prisons it substituted county control by the elected sheriff pursuing a system unchanged since colonial times. The typical jail is not the multipurpose facility of our larger cities. It is the small building located in the county seat anywhere in America and constructed over fifty years ago. It may house less than twenty inmates on an average day and employ two or three jail officers. The facilities are overcrowded and understaffed. Record keeping is poor and frequent attempts to conduct a national jail census have been handicapped by the disinterest of jailers.

The Law Enforcement Assistance Administration has conducted a number of jail surveys since 1970. A recent report by that agency shows 141,588 inmates housed in 3,921 jails operated by local units of government throughout the United States.[1] These are facilities that have the authority to detain for forty-eight hours or more. The jail has a variety of inmates. Some are there for pretrial processing, others are serving sentences imposed by the court. The classification of prisoners is difficult because of the small capacity of jails and the many processing categories for those confined. For example, only 113 of the 3,921 jails in the recent census are equipped to handle 250 or more inmates.

Jails house many kinds of prisoners: (1) persons awaiting arraignment; (2) those detained for further court action, final sentencing, or hearing on an appeal; (3) individuals being held for other authorities; (4) convicted prisoners serving jail sentences; and (5) persons sentenced to state prison but detained in the local jail until transportation can be arranged or space becomes available. The largest jails sometimes provide separate facilities for offenders serving one-year sentences in the county, but this is impossible in most jurisdictions. It has been estimated that 3 million persons are confined in jails yearly. It is the first contact with corrections for those who violate the law. Those eligible for bail may spend only a few hours in jail before release. For others, as Ronald Goldfarb tells us, the jail is the ultimate ghetto and the poorhouse of the twentieth century.[2]

Jail administrators are poor record keepers. Accurate profiles of inmate populations are seldom available. However, that population always reflects the environment of the city in which all social problems emerge to create disorder and a feeling of discomfort for those who move through the area. The jail houses the misdemeanant offender whose pattern of recidivism involves alcoholism, prostitution, petty thievery, and other offenses which are related to personal fail-

JAIL COSTS ARE HIGH

Booking a person into jail costs about $24. Keeping him there costs almost $12 a day. Annual jail operating expenditures are approaching the $1 billion level nationwide.

Source: U.S. Department of Justice, Law Enforcement Assistance Administration, *Instead of Jail: Pre- and Post-trial Alternatives to Jail Incarceration*, vol. 1 (Washington, D.C.: Government Printing Office, 1977), p. 1.

ure. The inmate profile in the *Survey of Inmates of Local Jails* supports the traditional view that they are male, uneducated, unemployable, and without family members. Members of minority groups are overrepresented in the population. For example, 23 percent had not continued in school beyond the eighth grade, only 43 percent had completed one to three years of high school, 95 percent were male, and 76 percent were never married. Their employment history was sporadic; part-time work was more common than a full-time position. The average yearly income before arrest was less than $2,000 per year for 44 percent of them.[3]

The jail confines its prisoners in facilities which are overcrowded and understaffed and which lack social-service programs. The usual complaints mention bad food, filthy sanitation, sexual attacks on prisoners, inadequate visiting arrangements, and excessive control by inmate trustees. Attempts by some jail administrators and county sheriffs to pass bond issues for improvement usually meet with apathy from a disinterested voting public. Some excellent jail facilities exist and these should be noted. They are the San Mateo County Jail in California; Multnomah County Jail in Portland, Oregon; Suffolk County Jail in Boston, Massachusetts; and the San Diego County Jail in California.

Statewide studies of the jail system have been conducted in California, Connecticut, Illinois, Iowa, Kentucky, Minnesota, Missouri, Nebraska, North Carolina, South Dakota, Texas, and Wisconsin. Each study found that programs for inmates are inadequate or nonexistent. Enforced idleness replaces activities which could explore and reduce the personal and social liabilities of the jail population.

335

This goal is not reflected in the local rehabilitative services and programs found in the nation's jails. Church missions are found in skid row and, therefore, religious services are the most frequent program in the local jail. This service is found in 58.5 percent of jails. There is a dramatic drop in other programs although treatment programs dealing with alcoholism or drug addiction are fairly frequent. The public inebriate receives consideration, if only to dry out, in 35.3 percent of the facilities. Drug-addiction programs will be found in 26.2 percent of the jails. Unfortunately, there is a lessened concern with the problems which are identified routinely with the inmate population of jails. Nearly three out of every four prisoners serving a sentence in a jail have completed one or more previous prison sentences. It is for this reason that the jail system is called the revolving door of corrections. Group counseling which could deal with the problems of this offender group is found in only 17.3 percent of the jails. The problem of chronic unemployment and the absence of work skills is overlooked. Vocational training is available in only 13.8 percent of the facilities, and this is supplemented with job development and placement services in 12.5 percent of the institutions. The assessment of vocational potentials and prevocational training is found in less than 9 percent of the jails. Remedial education for those with less than an eighth-grade education is found in only 10.7 percent of the facilities housing these prisoners. These percentages are for all jails surveyed in the LEAA study and do not reflect the greater availability of such programs in jails housing 250 or more inmates.[4] However, even in these institutions there is a dramatic drop in program availability except for religious services. Some church-related groups, especially the Salvation Army, have excelled in providing social services to the population which is identified with the jail system. It is hoped that new programs offering aid to this prisoner group will use the input available to them from members of the Salvation Army so that they might avoid the pitfalls present when middle-class treatment strategies are applied to the culture of skid row.

A promising program combining prevocational instruction, remedial education, tutoring, and vocational counseling is that operated by PACE in the Cook County Jail in Chicago. PACE (Programmed Activities for Correctional Education) occupies two buildings built between the cell blocks of the jail. Inmates are eligible for the program if they have at least four months remaining on their jail sentences. Trainees use individual instructional materials and teaching machines in order to prepare them for grade- or high-school equivalency examinations. Prevocational training and counseling permits the offender to receive job-related training in fields such as television repair, automobile mechanics, machine shop, electronics, refrigerator repair, and welding. Vocational counselors assess the prisoners' motivation for employment after release, refer them to a job or vocational training, or assist them in returning to school. PACE has attempted to maintain follow-up communication with the trainees. In spite of their efforts, they were unable to locate 28.1 percent of the trainees. Of those located, 13.2 percent were in jail at the time of the follow-up; 6.0 percent had been sent to prison; 19.2 percent were employed; and 22.4 percent were unemployed, but employable. There were 469 alumni who had been trained and released at the time of the follow-up study.[5] Such programs and activities exist only in the larger jails and evaluation of their results are seldom available. Therefore, the success of the PACE program is promising.

Work-release programs in prisons have lagged behind those instituted for inmates sentenced to jail. The first such program was instituted in Wisconsin in 1913. The Huber law allowed prisoners to be used as farm laborers for ten to twelve hours per day while serving time. Frankly, this was retribution and a form of punishment but the law was revised in later years to be more fair. The Wisconsin courts were then allowed to sentence misdemeanants to ordinary jail confinement or to confinement only when their normal workday was completed. Thus a prisoner would continue his employment and report to the jail in the evening. This form of day parole did not require a large number of jail personnel to administer. The prisoner maintained his earning capacity, which was helpful to his family. The problem of unemployment during and immediately following completion of the jail sentence was avoided. The daytime jail population was reduced. Approximately 42.5 percent of the jails reported in the national jail survey use the work-release program. At the time of the survey, some 8 percent of all sentenced inmates were participating in such a program. A related program, the weekend sentence, exists in 46.4 percent of the jails. This innovation allows the prisoner an opportunity to serve his time on weekends. Only a few prisoners, approximately 900, are completing their jail terms in this manner.[6] The jail system in this country resists change within the jail itself but it is willing to initiate programs which remove selected prisoners from the jail setting. Work release, weekend sentences, and pretrial diversion are growing in popularity.

Prearrest screening is one procedure which can reduce the size of the jail population and avoid confining individuals who have committed minor offenses and are not considered a danger to the community. San Jose, California, operates such a program. It is the Custody Classification Preprocessing Center. The center operates twenty-four hours each day and is staffed by a supervising sergeant from the local police department, a deputy district attorney, and a specialist in crisis

337

intervention from the Department of Social Services. The center is sponsored by the Santa Clara County District Attorney's Office. It processes all adult arrests except those involving drunk driving, public intoxication, and warrant arrests. The program operates out of a large trailer located near the entrance to the pretrial jail. Within fifteen minutes the suspect goes through a series of screenings to determine whether a charge will be filed and whether the person is eligible for release on his own recognizance if the determination is made to book him. At the same time, the crisis-intervention worker will determine if referral or diversion to other services such as mental health might be appropriate. The same concept, pretrial release for those offenders who may be unable to afford cash bail, has been used successfully in Des Moines, Iowa. The comprehensive community-based corrections program in that city is operated by the Polk County Department of Court Services. It is designed to reduce the population of the Polk county jail. The prerelease trial program allows arrested persons with previously good records to be released prior to trial without money bond. About 1,300 such people are released annually; only 1.8 percent have failed to show up for trial.[7]

Jail reform is an immediate concern for those interested in the administration of justice. Overcrowding and idleness must be reduced. Reduced jail populations are possible and at the same time public safety can be maintained. Pretrial and posttrial diversion is occurring more frequently and with more success. Existing social-service agencies should be utilized when programs are established in community correctional centers. Duplication of staff is expensive. Jails should develop more extensive classification programs in order to identify the requirements of special population groups such as alcoholic, mentally ill, juvenile, and violent offenders. The use of diversion will increase the number of prisoners who will present serious behavior problems during pretrial detention and when completing a jail sentence. Jail budgets should reflect the added costs required for improved staffing and programming when there is a relative increase in the proportion of violent offenders to nonviolent offenders.

In-service training for jail personnel is required. The majority of institutions are staffed by sworn sheriff's deputies whose training in the academy did not prepare them for correctional duties. It is true that a new deputy will understand the administration of justice more adequately if he or she is required to spend one or two years in a custodial setting. This experience will allow superiors to observe the officer in moments of stress. It is likely to reveal the manner in which the officer will interact with individuals he meets when working patrol. The advantage of the jail setting is that behavior, which cannot be observed on the streets, can be observed by supervisors; this should create better patrol officers. However, it is important that new deputies receive training in the academy which prepares them emotionally for a corrections assignment. Jail improvements will not succeed if law-enforcement personnel continue to be assigned to the jail as punishment by their superiors. This still occurs and it violates and contradicts other sheriff-department directives which attempt to inform new staff that every sworn officer is required to work in the jail setting for a specific period of time following graduation from the law-enforcement academy.

Minimum jail standards, which have been provided in at least twenty-four states, should be enforced. Some have advocated state control of jails in order to upgrade personnel and programs. The state operates the jails in Alaska, Connecticut, Delaware, Rhode Island, and Vermont. However, it is unlikely that many other states will take over control of jails. Three of the five states operating local jails are in the northeastern region of the country. Jails are least prevalent in that region. State control of jails exists in Alaska but it operates only seven jails and six of them are small and hold fewer than twenty-one inmates each. The largest number of jails are located in the South. All are under local control except for Delaware. States with the largest number of jails are Texas (318), Georgia (239), and Florida (164). The largest number of inmates are found in jails located in the South and the West. It is unlikely that these regions will abolish local control, which is a pattern that has continued in this country since its founding. Upgrading personnel and diverting offenders is a more realistic solution to the perennial jail problem. The National Institute of Corrections has established a National Jail Center in Boulder, Colorado, to serve as the coordinator for state, federal, and local efforts to improve jail operations and programs. The NIC Jail Center, established in 1977, uses the Boulder county jail as a training resource for the center.

PRISONS AND PRISONERS

Correctional institutions operated by the state or federal government receive from the courts offenders given maximum sentences of more than one year. Imprisonment is punishment, but it also implies community protection and prisoner rehabilitation. Punishment means loss of freedom. The community is protected by banishing the offender from free society. Treatment programs provide the potential for possible rehabilitation. The effectiveness of these programs in reducing future criminality has been questioned. But no one denies that the prison is effective as a temporary restraining force. For this reason, prison populations expand as anxiety about crime continues.

339

NIC JAIL CENTER FUNCTIONS

The NIC Jail Center will provide training, technical assistance, and information for the jail community on:

- Jail organization and management
- Legal/constitutional issues for jail management
- Jail programs and services
- Alternatives to jail incarceration
- Volunteer training and programs
- Development and utilization of community resources
- Jail standards and inspection systems
- Intake diagnostic services.

TRAINING

The jail center will conduct training programs in a variety of areas for persons in jail-related professions. Training will be done both at the center and on-site at jails requesting assistance.

- Jail Center Training will focus on sheriffs, jail administrators, jail trainers (persons who will return to their respective jails and train others), jail inspectors, and elected officials.
- On-Site Training will be available, on a limited basis, for line officers at the requesting jail.

In addition, the NIC staff will keep abreast of specialized, high-quality services and programs operating in jails across the nation and will consider establishing some of them as training models.

Specific training opportunities at the center will be announced as they are scheduled. To achieve a representative cross-section of individuals, program participants will be selected by review of applications submitted.

TECHNICAL ASSISTANCE

The NIC Jail Center will provide on-site technical assistance to: (1) jail agencies requesting guidance in addressing specific problems and needs, (2) persons who have completed NIC training and are attempting to design and/or implement particular programs, policies, or procedures as a result of that training, and (3) elected officials, courts, and professional groups.

In addition, the NIC Jail Center will sponsor the exchange of information, programs, and experiences among jail administrators. The center will support this interchange in various ways, ranging from merely providing information on innovative programs at other jails to sponsoring an individual's short internship at another agency to enable firsthand experience with a particular program or operation.

INFORMATION SERVICES

NIC staff will utilize all existing information and clearinghouse services to serve jail leaders. The NIC Jail Center will also maintain a library of soft-cover, jail-related materials and will accumulate information on progressive and innovative programs operating in jails across the nation. The latter function will enable the center to serve as a referral service and respond directly to inquiries about particular programs, services, training, etc.

Source: U.S. Department of Justice, Bureau of Prisons, *NIC Jail Center: Opening the Jail Door to Progress* (Washington, D.C.: National Institute of Corrections, 1977), p. 1.

At the end of 1977 there were 292,325 inmates confined in prisons. This was an increase of 5 percent over the preceding year. Males predominated in the prison population.[8] Although that fact has been true for a long time, recently there has been an alarming increase in women prisoners. Reasons for the increase in prison sentences for women are unknown. The question of whether female criminality differs significantly from that of males has not been answered satisfactorily. Much of the earlier research is moralistic and written by males. A renewed interest in the criminality of women and the training of more female criminologists should provide additional answers in the future. Hoffman-Bustamante, in her study of the nature of female criminality, suggests that the kinds of crimes committed by women are the outcome of one or more of the following factors.

Differential role expectations for men and women; sex differences in socialization patterns and application of social control; structurally determined differences in opportunities to commit particular offenses; differential access or pressures toward criminally oriented subcultures and

341

careers; and sex differences built into the crime categories themselves.[9]

Between 1976 and 1977 the proportion of women prisoners increased 10.1 percent. There were 12,055 women in custody on December 31, 1977, compared with 10,946 in state and federal institutions on the last day of 1976.[10] Ruth Glick, in a study of 1,607 women surveyed in fifteen state prisons and forty-two local jails, found that most women prisoners rate high in self-esteem and are optimistic about their future. The women accepted blame for what they had done and felt they could benefit from educational programs in the institution. The study provides the following profile of the woman prisoner: (1) the typical woman prisoner is black and under age 30; (2) more than two-fifths of women offenders surveyed had jobs in the two months before imprisonment and nearly all had worked at some time in their lives; (3) only a small percentage of women are incarcerated for prostitution; (4) murder and robbery were the most frequent offenses committed by the small number of women (6.5 percent) sentenced for a violent crime; (5) forgery or fraud were the leading property offenses for women serving prison or jail terms; and (6) the misdemeanant prisoners serving jail time were usually arrested for such offenses as drunkenness, drunk driving, disorderly conduct, and vagrancy.[11]

Some states imprison more often than others. The following incarcerate the largest number of prisoners per 100,000 persons in the general state population: South Carolina, Georgia, North Carolina, Florida, Maryland, Texas, Nevada, Michigan, Oklahoma, and Virginia.[12] The types of institutions are directly related to the state population. Larger jurisdictions have a variety of facilities for adults and juveniles. There are approximately 350 state-operated adult correctional institutions and 200 more for juveniles. Thirty-four states have separate facilities for women offenders.[13] The Federal Bureau of Prisons, established in 1930, administers forty-four institutions ranging from penitentiaries to halfway houses.

Correctional institutions are differentiated according to the security provided. There are maximum, close, medium, and minimum-security structures. The federal government operated the best-known maximum security prison—Alcatraz. Notorious federal prisoners were housed there who never escaped. Alcatraz was closed some years ago and the remaining prisoners were transferred to a new maximum-security facility located at Marion, Illinois. It houses career criminals who are serious escape risks or endanger other prisoners. The prison at Marion is not escape-proof and several inmates got away in 1975. States which do not have separate maximum-security facilities must rely upon adjustment centers or inner-prisons with increased custody and security. Most states have multipurpose institutions which provide the above-mentioned custody levels—close, medium, and minimum. Close custody refers to the most secure housing units, usually inside cellblocks located on tiers or separate floors. Ideally, the cells accommodate only one person. The inmate is allowed out of the cell during the day to work within the building while under constant supervision. Prisoners in medium-custody sections live in the traditional cell, which may have a window. They may be allowed to live in a dormitory and to work within the prison boundaries, provided there is continuous supervision. Minimum-security prisoners are allowed to work outside the prison under general supervision in forestry camps or in prison industries. Minimum security allows a humane environment for the offender who is not an escape risk. The fundamental responsibility of prison management is secure custody and control of prisoners. Historically, the prison physical plant reflects this concern.

Prisons are too large and too old. They are located far from the urban centers where the majority of offenders are sentenced. America pioneered in the development of prisons in the last century. Bastilles were constructed for thousands of prisoners. Prison architecture reflected two philosophies which were popular at the time. One group represented the principle that prisoners should be housed in solitary confinement in order to avoid contact with other criminals. This approach, known as the Pennsylvania system, was doomed to fail. Isolated living may appear to be contemplative, but it produced two undesirable side effects. Prisoners became mentally ill and even psychotic. In addition, separate housing proved to be expensive. Thereafter, those interested in prisons decided upon another approach known as the Auburn system. This plan relegated segregation to nighttime hours. The prisoners worked together in prison industries during the day and returned to their separate cells in the evening. Silence was invoked during the day when prisoners were together. This rule was later rescinded when the importance of verbal communication was understood. Some of the prisons constructed prior to 1870 are still used for maximum security. Construction in the last fifty years has been multipurpose, allowing for the needs of prisoners in each custodial category. These prisons use double cyclone fences, guard towers, and electronic equipment to secure their parameters. Some of the earlier maximum-security buildings were surrounded by stone walls that cost more than the prison itself. Constructional reform is due in large part to the establishment of the National Clearinghouse for Correctional Programming and Architecture at the University of Illinois. It now seems obvious that security can be incorporated into building plans while keeping them pleasant and livable. New guidelines for prison construction are concerned with building something more than warehouses. They seek prison sites near urban centers rather than in the country. Correctional facilities in rural areas have many limitations: (1) community agencies and professional personnel cannot be fully utilized; (2) correctional staff cannot be recruited in outlying areas and, when they are, they may not be aware of current trends in the field; (3) visiting is more difficult for families of prisoners; and (4) preparole planning programs and work-release activities are seriously curtailed.

Many new institutions reflect a concern for security while respecting the incarcerated offender. Prisons are being constructed in areas close to cities, universities, and business firms. Single occupancy cells are replacing dormitories because group housing created numerous problems such as sexual activity, group pressure to use narcotics, and lack of privacy for the individual. Security equipment figures inconspicuously in the building design, which in turn blends with its surroundings. High-rise buildings are replacing traditional low construction which utilized land space poorly. Two coeducational institutions were developed by the U.S. Bureau of Prisons in 1974. They housed young adults and were located at Terminal Island and Pleasanton, California. Twenty-three women prisoners became pregnant at the two facilities before the coeducational concept was abolished in late 1977. The Bureau claims the pregnancies did not lead to the phasing out of the male-female prisons. Rather, the increasing number of women being sentenced to prison required a separate institution for women. The Federal Youth Center at Pleasanton is now receiving only female offenders. In spite of the policy change in the federal system, a number of state institutions for males continue to set aside housing units for overnight conjugal visits. This humane development has been welcomed by prisoners and their families on the outside.

An attempt is being made to place the prisoner in the facility which best suits his or her needs. Prison architecture can create places which offer privacy and informality to confined inmates along with the necessary control. Men and women should be assigned to a specific prison on the basis of age, severity of offense, length of sentence, past record, and place of residence. Some of the best new models for prison design include the Robert F. Kennedy Youth Center in Morgantown, West Virginia; the South Carolina Women's Institute at Columbia; St. Albans Correctional Facility in Vermont; Leesburg Medium-Security Prison in New Jersey; Purdy Treatment Center for Women near Gig Harbor, Washington; and the Eagle River Correctional Center in Alaska.

CLASSIFICATION AND TREATMENT

The history of corrections is characterized by two philosophies: the classical school with its focus on a uniform system of penalties in order to correct existent irregularities in criminal law and procedural

Purdy Treatment Center for Women—located near Gig Harbor, Washington.

matters; and the positive school which has provided a scientific basis for controlling crime by differential treatment of the offender in accordance with his or her presenting problems. Modern penology emphasizes different treatment programs for different offenders. This philosophy assumes that all offenders, while incarcerated, ought to have the opportunity for involvement in self-betterment programs. They should be allowed to increase their skills in an academic area, to undergo vocational training for easier placement in the labor force, and to participate in the various group treatment programs which aim for better understanding of self. Every prison has some form of program in vocational, academic, and work-assignment areas. Fewer prisons offer group psychotherapy or transactional analysis because such programs require the presence of certain professionals who are not easily recruited by social-control agencies.

Therefore, selection for treatment in the correctional community might be viewed as a two-step inmate management process: (1) transfer to a specific institution within the statewide organization and (2) assignment to specific activities or programs within the individual correctional institution. These functions are carried out by the reception center clinical staff when formulating the offender prison-transfer recommendation and by the classifications committee at the receiving institution.

It is possible to differentiate the programs and activities subsumed under treatment into those which are carried out by clinical staff and those which are not. Thus the activities delegated to mental health practitioners are reduced to (1) diagnostic procedures in reception centers; (2) evaluative studies on individual offenders when requested by the administration; (3) ongoing group treatment in institutions which emphasize such activities; and (4) preparole reports.

The individual case summary is the principal source of information the correctional agency uses as it processes the offender through

345

his or her prison stay and parole period. The correctional field has, at all times, been concerned with formal procedures for selecting and ordering recently incarcerated offenders into explicit activities within the various institutions comprising the state or federal prison system. These procedures are known as "classification."

The larger prison systems initiate the classification process in the reception center. States with fewer prisons evaluate new prisoners when they arrive at the existing multipurpose institution. The objective of classification has been met when there is an appropriate facility and individualized program for the male or female offender. This goal is seldom achieved where only one or two institutions exist. The field of classification is not recent; it is mentioned in a century-old report in which the British government

> determined to carry out a certain new classification of all convicts sentenced to transportation. In other words, felons were to suffer this punishment in different degrees, according to their condition and character. But to ascertain in which category offenders should be placed a time of probation and proof was needed, and this period should be passed at some general depot, where for nine or ten months the character of each convict might be tested.[14]

The individual treatment plan, prepared at the reception-guidance center, is advisory in nature. The implementation of the program is dependent upon the philosophy of the correctional institution receiving the offender. Most institutions do not have the clinical staff that is available in the separate reception-guidance centers. Geographical and professional isolation accompanies the acceptance of clinical positions in American prisons. Therefore, few will accept the challenge of correctional employment amid such risk.

It appears that the correctional agency is apologetic of the advisory nature of its guidance-center clinical summaries. Therefore, the literature mentions a second function for them—orienting the offender to the inmate prison world. The reception-guidance center does not orient the prison to the *specific* prison which will receive him or her in thirty to sixty days. It does not inform him or her of the differing philosophies of prison superintendents whose facilities are like monarchies—some are democratic and others are totalitarian. The center personnel are likely to describe an ideal prison community which does not exist. The work of the center has little worth beyond the uses to which it is put in actual treatment programs.

Most reception centers are located at existing prisons but are administered as autonomous units. The superintendent and staff are responsible to the director or deputy director of the state prison system. It is this autonomy which leads to isolation of the staff from both the personnel preparing the presentence investigation in the county of sentencing and the staff of those institutions which will receive the offender following the guidance-center period of evaluation.

The usual time needed for the preparation of reports on an offender is thirty to sixty days. It is traditional for the inmate to have one interview each with a social worker and a psychologist. In cases of violent crimes it is possible a psychiatric report will be prepared, based on one interview that may last fifteen minutes to one hour. It is extremely difficult to justify an observation period of thirty to sixty days when the inmate may be in conference with the clinical staff for only three hours during this total period. This time lapse, suffered by the offender, is due to several factors: (1) verification of social data necessitates much correspondence, which is a duplication of services performed in the preparation of the presentence report; (2) the clerical staff finds it impossible, without lengthy delays, to complete the work quota demands of a clinic serving a transit inmate population; and (3) there is a delay in transfer due to overcrowding at the recommended receiving institution.

The physical plant and the staffing pattern of the facility are oriented toward the fulfillment of the goal of the guidance center— the assignment of prisoners to the proper institution and the provision of an individualized treatment or training program. Unfortunately, the reception center detains an inmate population awaiting transfer to other correctional institutions. The inmate is tired from repeating the same information to clinical staff that he or she has related to the probation officer who prepared the earlier presentence report. The reception-center staff is overworked by the continuous demand for case production and an unending flow of offenders through the unit. The reception center and the reception area of the multipurpose prison are as regimented and drab as the county jail.

The individual case summary prepared at the time of admission to prison will include the following information: (1) description of the offense; (2) legal data relating to the crime; (3) arrest record; (4) personal history of the offender; (5) diagnostic evaluations by the clinical staff which are based upon interviews and examinations; (6) vocational and educational evaluation; (7) psychological evaluation; (8) psychiatric evaluation; (9) social evaluation; (10) medical and dental evaluation; (11) recreation evaluation; and (12) custodial evaluation. The clinical staff—usually consisting of a counselor, clinical psychologist, and psychiatrist—will determine the individual treatment needs of the prisoner. The recommendations formulated by the reception center or the institutional classification staff are usually thoughtful and certainly worthy of implementation. Unfortunately, transfer to a specific institution is based on other criteria, such as sex of the prisoner, age at time of commitment, recidivism history, and custody risk potential. Treatment recommendations which can be car-

347

ried out within settings adhering to the traditional control criteria are more likely to be implemented than more innovative recommendations. The resolution of conflict between the need for individualized programs for prisoners and the custodial demands of the prison confirms once more the main purpose of prisons. They exist to control, incapacitate, and punish. Perhaps, at times, they provide some services which redirect the lives of those within their walls.

Treatment Programs

The free community makes available to its members a number of programs such as education, vocational training, and mental-health clinics. Such resources are called "treatment programs" in the prison community. The American Correctional Association, in its declaration of principles, states the following goal.

> To assure the eventual restoration of the offender as an economically self-sustaining member of the community, the correctional program must make available to each inmate every opportunity to raise his educational level, improve his vocational competence and skills, and add to his information meaningful knowledge about the world and the society in which he must live.[15]

Prisoners consider confinement to be "dead time." Correctional programs are helpful in reducing idleness, boredom, and prison riots. Enrollment in treatment activities should be voluntary. The inmate should select an available program because it will minimize the negative aspects of congregate living in a coercive environment, or because it offers an opportunity for personal growth and self-improvement. It is unfortunate that institutional treatment has been acclaimed as a method of rehabilitation. Prisons have not been effective in changing criminal behavior.

Various institutional programs exist in a majority of the 592 state correctional facilities polled in a recent census. The following list gives the type of program and the percentage of institutions claiming to have it: religious services (96 percent); individual counseling (91 percent); remedial education (89 percent); job placement (84 percent); alcoholic treatment (83 percent); group counseling (82 percent); vocational training (81 percent); vocational counseling (80 percent); prevocational training (74 percent); drug treatment (74 percent); and college-degree courses (65 percent).[16] The existence of such programs does not assure the availability of qualified staff, adequate funding, or support for them by the administration. Participation in such programs should not influence the decision to release a prisoner. There is no available means for measuring the effectiveness of treatment activities in reducing recidivism.[17] Criminals are imprisoned for committing crimes whose punishment requires confinement. Programs for self-improvement should be available both in the institution and in the offender's community.

Individual prisoner counseling assumes greater importance when the subject is separated from family, friends, and relatives. Trained staff should answer questions and explore the problems inmates have with anxiety, which is often the cause of disciplinary problems. The "Dear John" letter, the death of a family member, and financial problems need attention. Crime occurs in prisons and the confined are the victims. Prisoners often request protective custody to avoid dangerous situations. Individual counseling, when requested, is important in resolving these problems. Group counseling consists of twelve to twenty inmates meeting regularly with a staff member in order to discuss inmate problems. Confidentiality of information cannot be protected in the group setting. Therefore, prisoners are unlikely to discuss matters which could create problems for them in the inmate community. The group is beneficial because it allows prisoners to ventilate feelings which might erupt in a more volatile manner at some other time. The counselor comes to know the members of the group intimately. The staff needs to know the inmates as well as possible—their moods, feelings, level of dangerousness, and relationships with each other and the staff. The group counseling session provides such an opportunity. Once again, enrollment in group counseling should be voluntary. Prisoners will gravitate to staff who have a reputation for fairness and understanding. A meaningful relationship with an authority figure can be important to the prisoner in confinement. The effective counselor will cultivate empathy, interpersonal awareness and sensitivity, an ability to listen, and a nonjudgmental attitude.

Education programs and vocational training are popular with prisoners. Remedial academic instruction allows prisoners to obtain grade-school and high-school diplomas. The local school district issues the graduation certificates, thereby avoiding the stigma of a prison diploma. Participation in vocational education requires greater planning. Prerequisites may include a certain grade placement, such as 8.0 (eighth grade), and a minimum number of hours for completing the program. For example, enrollment in an auto body and fender course might require 4,000 hours of instruction. The prisoner may not be able to score 8.0 on an academic achievement test and he will have to enroll in school until the minimum grade placement is achieved. Few prisoners wish to delay parole in order to obtain a certificate of competency in a vocational training program. Existing vocational courses in prisons sometimes fail to reflect current labor-market needs. Restrictions affecting the employment of ex-offenders in certain occupations should be considered in vocational counseling sessions. Job placement is critical for the released prisoner. A recent task force on prisoner rehabilitation concluded that only about one in four ex-inmates is working at a job he was trained for within six months after getting out of prison.[18] The introduction of college courses in prisons and the growth of college parolee programs on various campuses is promising. The convict's best hope for upward mobility is an improved knowledge base. The Association of Parolee Educational Programs was recently organized in California. Its purposes are (1) to facilitate communication between college ex-offender educational programs, social-service agencies, California Department of Corrections, and the Adult Authority (i.e., parole board); (2) to provide new and prospective ex-offender educational programs with resources and skills in developing this reentry service; and (3) to familiarize corrections agencies and the college administration with the concept of ex-offender educational programs and the needs of student ex-offenders.

Prison Life

The prison population is similar to the general population in mental functioning and intelligence. At the same time, the prison population is made up of individuals who have common characteristics which reflect troubled interpersonal relationships on the outside: (1) the juvenile years are characterized by delinquencies that are known to the police and that frequently terminate in placement in a correctional facility; (2) the adult criminal years reveal a pattern of arrests, jail sentences, and prison sentences; (3) the natural family situation of the offender is characterized by a large number of siblings and a family arrest history; (4) a particular marital status appears to be irrelevant, with an even distribution among the still married, the divorced or separated, and the unmarried; (5) the employment history is erratic, with less than full-time employment during the year preceding the present offense; and (6) the prisoner is at most a high-school drop-out.

Each new prisoner is assimilated into the prison culture. Clemmer calls this "prisonization" or "taking on in greater or less degree ... the folkways, mores, customs, and general culture of the penitentiary."[19] The inmate culture has been studied for thirty-five years and it has been found to exist in all institutions, both adult and juvenile. Its existence is separate from the world of the institutional staff. The personnel of the prison are concerned with order, an accurate population count four times each day, and the preparation of folders mapping inmate progress in programs. The inmates, in turn, are concerned with doing their time uneventfully, obtaining the earliest possible release from prison, and avoiding trouble while confined.

In the inmate world there are two broad labels. Prisoners perceive each other as either inmates or convicts. To the prisoners, an inmate is merely a person doing time. Basically, this is all the term means, and it has no emotional connotations. The term "convict," however, is more descriptive. A convict is sort of a modern-day Robin Hood. He lives by a code of honor. He resents all authority and comes into as little contact as possible with staff members. He has a great sense of loyalty to fellow convicts. He will risk danger to himself to protect a friend. In the minimum-security institution "convict" is a term that is still used to identify the prisoner who is all right, the person who can be trusted, as compared to the inmate, who is merely doing time. An often-used example is this: if a convict sees a man stabbed in a stairwell, he will walk in the opposite direction because it is not any of his business; an inmate will get excited and draw heat (attract attention); a snitch (informer) will run and tell the bulls (officers).

The newly arrived prisoner is stratified by fellow prisoners according to his offense and his identification with the staff. Excessive staff identification is suspect. By and large, the new man tends to identify with other prisoners convicted of similar offenses. This divides the social structure of the inmate world into a number of subcultural groups. Each subculture has its own frame of reference, its own way of evaluating situations characteristic of the particular group. In the subculture the new man finds acceptance, recognition, and the respect of other inmates within the group. Each member of the subculture might be said to be justifying his own overt mode of conduct by identification with men with similar modes of overt conduct. In some cases these groupings are well defined and clearly marked. In others, the dividing lines are vague and nearly indiscernible. Some support the prison administration, others manipulate it to their own advantage, and a few are both antiadministration and antiinmate. A small number of prisoners are loners and feel no identification with a particular group. They are accepted in the inmate world as loners and their desire to be left alone is respected.

The contemporary prison faces a new problem which disrupts the existing inmate-versus-staff world of the institution. The number of dangerous inmates has increased because of the practice of dealing with minor offenders on the local level. Violence has increased, along with the growth of gangs based on racial and ethnic divisions.

Prison Violence

Gang warfare is one of the major causes of prison violence. The California Department of Corrections has identified five distinct organizations within the prison system. There is the Mexican Mafia (EME), Nuestra Familia (NF), the Black Guerrilla Family (BGF), the Aryan Brotherhood (AB), and the Texas Syndicate. The existence of these gangs is changing the traditional inmate social system in prisons. The struggle between the two Mexican-American gangs has created the most difficulty for prison administrators. The war between the Mexican Mafia and Nuestra Familia began at San Quentin in 1968 when a fight over a pair of shoes led to the death of a gang member from each group. The violence has continued; the statistics in Figure 13–1 reveal the problem in California's prisons.

Prison gangs were once small groups that operated underground. They have become organized in recent years and their membership, both inside and outside correctional institutions, is more easily identified. The original La EME group was founded in the late 1930s in Mexican prisons. The first group in the United States was formed in one of the California institutions in 1957. La EME stands for El Mexicano Encarcerado or "The Incarcerated Mexican." The group is referred to also as the Mexican Mafia. Membership is for life. The orders given by the group leaders to other members must be carried out. The sanctions for disobeying an order are severe. A potential recruit is introduced to other members by someone who has known the person in his hometown. This accounts for the designation "home boy" for the person who is responsible for the actions of the new recruit for a period of not less than three months. In that time, the organization assesses the qualities of the potential member. Failure to meet the expectations of the group can result in death or a request

Figure 13-1 California Prison Violence: January 1970–June 1977

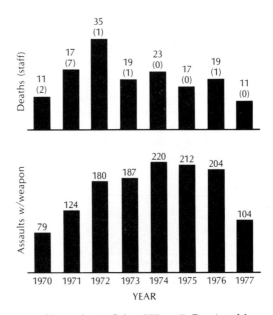

Source: *San Francisco Chronicle*, 31 July 1977, p. 5. Reprinted by permission.

for protective custody in prison. Membership in La EME appears to be restricted to those who have lived in the Southern California area, although this rule is sometimes lifted. Members are identified by a tattooed "EME" on the upper right arm in the area of the bicep.

Another prison gang, Nuestra Familia, was organized at San Quentin in 1967. Membership is made up mostly of prisoners sentenced from Northern California. It was formed to retaliate against La EME. Both groups are allegedly involved in the control of drugs and other contraband within the prisons. Struggles between the various gangs have led to some alliances for the maintenance of power. La EME and the Aryan Brotherhood (formed in 1966) appear to be united in continuous conflict against the Black Guerrilla Family (established in 1966) and Nuestra Familia. These groups tend to seek members among the younger inmates and seldom bother older prisoners. The newest prison gang is the Texas Syndicate. All the prisoners fear this group, which is composed of Mexican-American inmates who were born and reared in Texas but are presently incarcerated in one of the California prisons. Officials claim that the Texas Syndicate hopes to control the flow of narcotics within institutions.

Prison violence, created by the activities of prison gangs, can be controlled by the establishment of a gang surveillance unit at each institution. This unit will segregate known gang leaders and specific members in maximum-security areas and distribute others to different housing units. The surveillance team will maintain background information on gang membership and communicate this to staff during training sessions. Prison gangs have created more violence in our institutions than the prison riots which have received so much publicity. These groups are now operating in county jails, in juvenile institutions, and on the streets of many cities. More than 1,000 persons in California are allegedly members or associates of the Mexican Mafia. Nuestra Familia has an estimated membership of 200 to 500. The Black Guerrilla Family has 200 to 400 members. The Aryan Brotherhood is said to claim 200 to 500 members. The strength of the Texas Syndicate has been estimated to be 75 to 150 members. The gangs maintain elaborate lists of enemies and defectors, who are systematically eliminated while in prison or in the outside community. These groups are involved in numerous criminal activities such as drug trafficking, robbery, burglary, storage of illegal weapons, and murder.

Inmate Rights

The traditional attitude of the sentencing judge is that his responsibilities end with the imposition of sentence. Many criminal-court judges, often with great personal uneasiness, sentence offenders to confinement without fully recognizing what occurs after sentence is

YOUTHS GET A LESSON

Brutal Jail Life Taught by Inmates

RAHWAY, N.J.—Fourteen youngsters, grinning, joking, and gawking about, were led briskly through the iron-bar rotunda, the "hole," and into the shabby auditorium at Rahway State Prison.

A guard, Sergeant Alan August, ordered the juveniles—ranging in age from thirteen to fifteen years—onto a stage. Eight angry inmates scrutinized their every move.

August left and the heavy metal auditorium door was locked.

"Wipe those grins off your ——— faces," yelled Jerry Donnerstag, who is serving fifty-four years for armed robbery and murder.

"This ain't no sightseeing trip to the Bronx Zoo," he told the youngsters. "This is your next stop. This is your next home. Hollywood makes it all look so goddam glamorous. But this is real."

The youngsters, many already in trouble with juvenile authorities, came for an encounter session with members of Rahway's lifers' group.

Started a year ago by inmates serving life or terms of more than twenty-five years, it is the only juvenile crime-prevention program of its kind in the country.

Of the 1,001 teenagers who have gone through the two-and-one-half-hour sessions, only ten have been reported for new offenses. With news of the program's success spreading, sessions are booked through the middle of May.

What goes on behind the closed prison doors during a session is scary enough to make most of the youngsters think twice, according to counselors who have talked to the youths afterward.

The inmates talk about homosexual rape: "We ain't got no women in here, you see. So it's you we're goin' to ——, you know."

About escape: "One way to get out of here is to take a sheet, tie one end around your neck and hang yourself. That way, you don't owe the state no money, no time. And you don't get raped any more."

About prison life in general: "This isn't *On the Rocks* (a TV situation comedy about prison life). This is real. There was a guy in here stabbed nineteen times last week. His 'friends' didn't go help him. They stepped over the dumb bastard and went into his cell and took what little he had."

About crime: "If you think you can do it better than us, that we're dummies, then you're a bunch of fools. We know every trick in the book and we got caught.

354

"It's not like it is on the little color television, where you're going to keep going and never get caught. If you think that, you're full of it."

Source: *San Francisco Chronicle*, 28 March 1977, p. 3. Reprinted by permission of United Press, International.

imposed. In recent years, because of the growing number of lawsuits by prisoners, courts have become increasingly aware of the conditions of prison confinement. Continuing judicial supervision of correctional practices to ensure that the program applied is consistent with the court's sentence should result in increased interaction between courts and corrections. The courts did not become involved in prison reform and inmate rights until the early 1960s, when the civil-rights lawyers became concerned with the cruel and inhumane conditions in penitentiaries. Before that time, the courts were content to order the offender to prison and to avoid further involvement with the matter of imprisonment because they claimed to know very little about the field of corrections.

The new field of correctional law is attempting to ameliorate undesirable or unbearable prison conditions. Laws do not solve the problem, they only establish guidelines or safeguards. Prison administrators are presently faced with a new type of prisoner who defines himself as being (1) the victim of a system which tends to incarcerate the poor and powerless; (2) one who is generally imprisoned involuntarily; and (3) an individual with the right to request or reject treatment programs.

The problems facing correctional administrators cannot be solved without input from the courts, lawyers, legislators, informed citizens, ex-offenders, and personnel representing the criminal-justice system. Several obstacles are present in the current emphasis on the rights of prisoners: (1) a majority of prison-reform lawyers focus on the needs of inmates while overlooking the problems of correctional personnel; (2) the direction and interpretation of the courts is uncertain at this time; and (3) the recent movement of the courts into corrections has resulted in legal interpretations which have failed to reduce the operational problems of prison staff. The correctional institution can minimize the need for judicial intervention by introducing the following innovations.

1. Establish a disciplinary decision-making system which is fair and provides the prisoner with traditional procedural safeguards.

355

2. Prepare a rules and regulations handbook for both prisoners and staff outlining punishments for various infractions.

3. Formulate nonlegalistic means for handling grievance procedures and other internal problems.

4. Establish an ombudsman position. This person will investigate reported complaints from prisoners, report the findings to the administrators, and help to achieve equitable settlement of the grievance.

5. Set up courses in correctional law for institutional personnel in order to provide paraprofessional legal assistance.

6. Develop a research program which will explore the impact of judicial intervention on correctional administration and the inmate environment.

7. Create an advisory board of concerned laypersons and criminal-justice representatives who would review annually those policy procedures affecting both inmates and staff.

Such a policy would attempt to reduce the conflict existing between prisoners and staff in some institutions. It would emphasize the humane treatment of incarcerated offenders. Chief Justice Warren E. Burger articulated the urgent needs of corrections today when he indicated the need for:

1. Institutions that provide decent living conditions, in terms of an environment in which hope can be kept alive.

2. Personnel at every level who are carefully selected, properly trained, with an attitude of understanding and motivation such as we seek in teachers, and with compensation related to the high responsibility.

3. Improved classification procedures to insure separation of incorrigibles from others.

4. A balanced program of productive work, intensive basic education, vocational education, and recreation.

5. Communication with inmates.

6. A system of justice in which judges, prosecutors, and defense counsel recognize that prompt disposition of cases is imperative to any hope of success in the improvement of those convicted.[20]

STUDY QUESTIONS

1. Discuss the major concerns of the prison reform movement.

2. Why are prison populations growing? What are the populations in your various state correctional institutions?

3. Trace the history of the jail in America.

4. Identify the prisoner groups in a county jail. Are the needs of each group served adequately? Explain.

5. What is a work-release program? Is such a program operating in your local jail or statewide correctional system? If so, discuss the merits of the program.

6. Discuss needed jail reforms and determine the degree of community commitment to these changes.

7. What is the population of our state and federal prisons?

8. How did the Pennsylvania and Auburn systems influence prison architecture in America?

9. Has your state utilized a new model for prison design within the past ten years? If so, name the facility and compare it with older institutions in your area.

10. Define *classification*.

11. Describe the inmate social system.

12. Identify the sources of prison violence. How does the institutional staff control gang warfare?

NOTES

1. National Criminal Justice Information and Statistics Service, *The Nation's Jails* (Washington, D.C.: Government Printing Office, 1975), p. 1.
2. Ronald Goldfarb, *Jails: The Ultimate Ghetto of the Criminal Justice System* (Garden City, N.Y.: Anchor Press, 1975).
3. Law Enforcement Assistance Administration, National Criminal Justice Information and Statistics Service, *Survey of Inmates of Local Jails: Advance Report* (Washington, D.C.: Government Printing Office, 1974), pp. 3–6 and 15–16.
4. Ibid., p. 21.
5. *PACE Fact Sheet* (Chicago: PACE Institute, 1973), pp. 1–2.
6. Law Enforcement Assistance Administration, *Survey of Inmates,* p. 10.
7. Law Enforcement Assistance Administration, *A Handbook on Community Corrections in Des Moines* (Washington, D.C.: Government Printing Office, 1973) and Tully L. McCrea and Don M. Gottfredson, *A Guide to Improved Handling of Misdemeanant Offenders* (Washington, D.C.: Government Printing Office, 1974).
8. Law Enforcement Assistance Administration, *Prisoners in State and Federal Institutions on December 31, 1977: Advance Report* (Washington, D.C.: Government Printing Office, 1978), p. 1.
9. Dale Hoffman-Bustamante, "The Nature of Female Criminality," *Issues in Criminology* 8 (Fall 1973): 117.
10. Law Enforcement Assistance Administration, *Prisoners in State and Federal Institutions,* p. 2.
11. Ruth M. Glick, *National Study of Women's Correctional Programs* (Washington, D.C.: Government Printing Office, 1977).
12. Law Enforcement Assistance Administration, *Prisoners in State and Federal Institutions on December 31, 1976* (Washington, D.C.: Government Printing Office, 1978), pp. 4–5.
13. National Advisory Commission on Criminal Justice Standards and Goals, *Report on Corrections* (Washington, D.C.: Government Printing Office, 1973), pp. 341 and 379.

357

14. Arthur Griffiths, *Memorials of Millbank and Chapters in Prison History,* vol. 1 (London: Henry S. King, 1875), p. 307.
15. American Correctional Association, *Manual of Correctional Standards* (Washington, D.C.: American Correctional Association, 1966), p. xxii.
16. National Criminal Justice Information and Statistics Service, *Census of State Correctional Facilities, 1974* (Washington, D.C.: Government Printing Office, 1975), p. 30.
17. Douglas Lipton, Robert Martinson, and Judith Wilks, *Effectiveness of Correctional Treatment —A Survey of Treatment Evaluation Studies* (New York: Praeger, 1975).
18. *San Francisco Chronicle,* 30 January 1975, p. 3.
19. Donald Clemmer, *The Prison Community* (New York: Holt, Rinehart and Winston, 1958), p. 299.
20. Warren E. Burger, "Keynote Address" (National Conference on Corrections, Williamsburg, Va., Dec. 5–8, 1971), p. 10.

ILLUSTRATIVE CAREERS IN CORRECTIONAL INSTITUTIONS
The Federal Bureau of Prisons

The Federal Bureau of Prisons was established in 1930 to unify and integrate existing federal prisons. The mission of this bureau is to provide for institutional custody of offenders. Custody itself must be broadly defined to accurately describe the goals and objectives of the Federal Bureau of Prisons.

A report released in 1977 commented on the philosophy of the Federal Bureau of Prisons. The federal prison system has attempted to develop a balanced philosophy, one that recognizes that punishment, deterrence, incapacitation, and rehabilitation are all valid purposes of incarceration. Offenders are deprived of liberty by the courts as punishment, to prevent them from committing further crimes, and to deter others. Incarceration should be under humane conditions and offenders should have access to a wide variety of programs including education, vocational training, and counseling designed to help them change their patterns of criminal behavior. The mainstay of the federal prison system is the correctional officer. As a practical matter, the corrections officer is the person that has the most frequent contact with the individual offender. While a main focus of the corrections officer's role relates to security, he or she is a part of a corrections team that includes counselors and teachers. Officers are responsible for enforcing the rules and regulations governing the operation of correctional institutions, particularly as they concern the confinement, safety, health, and protection of inmates. They are further responsible for supervising the work assignments of inmates. Because of their frequent contact with inmates, officers are also involved with counseling them on personal and family problems.

Entry Requirements

The Federal Bureau of Prisons has established a clear-cut policy for employment qualifications that centers on the individual's own unique kind of experience and education.

For entry into the Federal Bureau of Prisons there is a general requirement that each applicant possess three-and-one-half years of supervisory experience in such interpersonal fields as teaching, enforcement, counseling, or sales work in which there was a high level of person-to-person contact. Education beyond the high-school level may be substituted for experience in the following manner:

(1) Two years beyond high school in a college program in social work, counseling, or a related field may be substituted for two years general experience.

(2) A four-year college degree may be substituted for three years of experience.

(3) One semester of graduate work in social work, criminology, or related fields may be substituted for six months general experience.

Additionally, applicants must be under age thirty-five and pass a physical examination. An important part of the application is the oral interview—a candidate must present himself to a board composed of experienced correctional officers. There is no written examination for this position.

Career Development

Work in the Bureau of Prisons begins with 160 hours of formal training during the first year of employment. In addition to this training, there is 80 hours of specialized training at residential training centers around the country. The entry level is a GS-6 which, according to the 1977 salary schedule, begins at $11,101. After one year of satisfactory service, a corrections officer may be advanced to the next highest grade level. The Bureau of Prisons maintains a strong internal merit promotion system which allows advancement to correctional treatment, specialists-teacher, and managerial positions within the bureau.

The Michigan Department of Corrections

State correctional officers work in facilities ranging from minimum-security conservation camps where inmates are housed in cottagelike settings to the traditional fortresslike surroundings of the maximum-security facility. The population of these institutions possesses one common attribute, they have all been convicted of crimes and are confined against their will. Employees in the state corrections system must be mindful of the fact that they deal with potentially dangerous and explosive situations. The Department of Corrections is more heavily staffed with custody officers than is any other department. Corrections Officer 06 is the most frequent entry level position. Officers may be assigned to maximum, medium, or minimum-custody facilities where they are concerned primarily with institutional security and control and surveillance of resident inmates. But, as in the federal prison system, corrections officers in Michigan are responsible for treating resident inmates in line with the department's general rehabilitative efforts. Although security and institutional control are important, it is only one aspect of the operation of a correctional facility. Efforts must be directed toward returning residents to society better prepared for normal community living than when they entered the institution.

Entry Requirements

Correctional officers in Michigan must possess the following minimum qualifications for employment: applicants must be at least twenty-one years of age; they must possess a high-school diploma or an equivalency certificate; they must be free from any organic or chronic illness or defect; and their height and weight must be in proportion to one another and to their age.

Like the federal prison system, the Michigan Department of Corrections does not require a written examination of the applicants for employment as correctional officers. It does, however, require a qualifying oral appraisal conducted by a committee of agency personnel. This oral examination is required of all applicants.

Career Development

Correctional officers enter the job at the 06 level. After one year of satisfactory service and with supervisors' recommendations, correctional officers may be promoted to the 07 corrections supervisors level. Advancement beyond the 07 level is by promotional examination as openings occur. The rank structure includes positions as Prison Sergeant 08, Prison Lieutenant 09, and Prison Captain 10, with responsibility increasing progressively.

chapter fourteen
Manpower
Development and
Corrections

The 1970s have seen progress in the administration of criminal justice. The concern for change is documented in the reports of the President's Commission on Law Enforcement and Administration of Justice (1967) and the National Advisory Commission on Criminal Justice Standards and Goals (1973).[1] The result was a comprehensive federal involvement in the struggle against crime, beginning in 1968 with the passage of the Omnibus Crime Control and Safe Streets Act (Public Law 90–351). This legislation established the Law Enforcement Assistance Administration within the United States Department of Justice. The agency began operations in the fall of 1968 with a mandate to revitalize the criminal-justice system by strengthening the police, modernizing the courts, and reforming corrections. Congress has approved legislation which allows the Law Enforcement Assistance Administration to continue operating through 1979.[2]

An important milestone in the activities of the Law Enforcement Assistance Administration was the creation of a National Advisory Commission on Criminal Justice Standards and Goals in October 1971. The Commission was composed of twenty-two members, who are local and state leaders in criminal justice or representatives from the private sector. There being no model, the Commission was asked to propose guidelines for a more effective criminal-justice system. In late 1973 the Commission released its summary volume entitled *A National Strategy To Reduce Crime*. It made important recommendations. Priority was given a plan to cut in half the rate of high-fear crimes over the next ten years. Aggravated assault, burglary committed by a stranger, murder, rape, and robbery are the offenses on which it will have to focus its activities. Corrections will have to share this responsibility with the police. The closed system so characteristic of corrections will have to begin to see outside itself. It is not only in the public mind that corrections has been isolated from the other branches of criminal justice. The compartmentalization of criminal justice into the distinct operations of the police, courts, and corrections has proven shortsighted. It has meant that the offender is more knowledgeable about the operations of the system than any of its personnel.

Public Opinion

Protection is sought through the various agencies representing the justice system. A recent Harris opinion poll asked a cross section of the public how they would rate the performance of law-enforcement officials. The poll found that a drastic decline in public confidence occurred over a three-year period. Satisfaction with local law-enforcement officials was highest with 58 percent of the public rating them as excellent or good; 51 percent of state law-enforcement officials got the same rating; and only 42 percent of federal law-enforcement officials were so rated. All these ratings are lower than those recorded in a poll conducted three years earlier. The poll indicates that the public is beginning to question the effectiveness of law-enforcement efforts.[3] This is a departure from earlier years when the fear of crime was the primary concern of the public.[4] The concern of the public for effective crime-control standards and goals has hastened the need for corrections to reform. Crime control requires rehabilitation in addition to mere confinement or supervision.

Public protection means the offender is apprehended, sanctions are imposed, and rehabilitation is sought. Corrections apart from confinement has to do with administering assigned penalties that look toward reforming the offender. Penalties do not reduce the incidence of crime. Knowledge of corrections as a system of operating agencies and an overview of the current issues are necessary to influence policies in the next few years.

The processing and programming of the prisoner are poorly understood by the public. The Joint Commission on Correctional Manpower and Training found that 72 percent of the public felt rehabilitation should be the major emphasis of the prison with only 48 percent agreed that this was the major concern currently.[5] The isolation of the prison from the community and other correctional agencies creates an inaccurate perception of prison life. The phrase "living behind bars" was used by 71 percent of those questioned in describing incarceration.[6] Lack of any real familiarity with corrections was reflected in the attitudes of respondents when asked if more money should be used for rehabilitation programs. Only 43 percent felt that more money should be spent on prison systems and rehabilitation programs; 33 percent were willing to see taxes raised to pay for these programs.[7] A number of teen-agers were among those questioned in the survey. They were asked about possible career choices, but only one percent considered corrections as a possibility.[8]

Careers in Corrections

Corrections will have to find manpower with the capacity to (1) isolate and identify the inner resources of the correctional client; (2) search for ways to reintegrate the ex-offender; and (3) evaluate the success of programs which have an impact on crime reduction and offender rehabilitation. The system has failed to utilize the potential manpower reserves available from 1,000 college and university programs. Personnel is the most important element in the correctional budget.

Interest in the corrections component of the criminal-justice curriculum was given added impetus in 1965 with the passage of the Correctional Rehabilitation Study Act (Public Law 89–178). This act provided for "an objective, thorough, and nationwide analysis and reevaluation of the extent and means of resolving the critical shortage of qualified manpower in the field of correctional rehabilitation."[9] The Joint Commission on Correctional Manpower and Training was partially funded through this legislation and produced a number of reports which, if implemented, could have mitigated the crime problem.[10] In 1969 Vernon Fox prepared guidelines for corrections programs in community and junior colleges.[11] At the same time the Law Enforcement Assistance Administration, through its Office of Educational and Manpower Assistance, began providing grants and loans to criminal-justice students enrolled in degree programs. This Law Enforcement Education Program (LEEP) has provided financial assistance to students who are employees of police, courts, and corrections agencies. Preservice students, preparing for careers in the field, have benefited from this program. However, the primary emphasis is on upgrading the skills of those already in the field. Among the 15,526 in-service LEEP recipients attending 105 educational institutions in California during a recent academic year, 63.3 percent were classified as police, 4.8 percent as judiciary, 28.2 percent as corrections, and 3.7 percent as other. The high enrollment of law-enforcement officers in criminal-justice programs reflects the recommendation of the National Advisory Commission on Criminal Justice Standards and Goals that new police officers obtain the baccalaureate degree.

Even though progress has been made in developing correctional programs in the schools, the field of corrections has not utilized them as readily as has law enforcement. In its study of the educational level of correctional personnel the Joint Commission on Correctional Manpower and Training found 41 percent of those in adult institutions have never attended college. This figure drops to 27 percent in juvenile institutions. At the same time the probation and parole officers in corrections represent a high educational level: 84 percent of those in adult field assignments have the baccalaureate degree or training beyond it; 91 percent of those in juvenile probation and parole have at least the undergraduate degree. This comparison is summarized in Table 14–1.

Studies of correctional manpower needs are limited but those available do support the premise that opportunities for preservice students exist. The President's Commission on Law Enforcement and Administration of Justice prepared projections for 1975; these are shown in Table 14–2. Unfortunately, later studies focus upon law enforcement rather than corrections. The personnel category reflecting the greatest growth in the ten-year period studied is that of case manager or probation and parole officer. The baccalaureate or graduate degree is recommended for the position of case manager. Many of the personnel in that position obtain the graduate degree while employed in the assignment. Other important assignments are in the group-supervisor and custodial-personnel categories. Correctional officers in the adult institution and cottage parents or group supervisors in juvenile institutions are included in this work description. The associate of arts degree should be required for this entry-level post. People entering the corrections field in the group-supervisor or line position have the opportunity for continuing their education while preparing to move into the case manager or field position. The experience gained in the line position, if it includes further education, can serve as a prerequisite for the field assignment. The

TABLE 14-1 Educational Level of Correctional Personnel, 1968, by Work Setting

| | WORK SETTING OF RESPONDENTS | | | |
| HIGHEST LEVEL OF EDUCATION ATTAINED | ADULT INSTITUTION | JUVENILE INSTITUTION | ADULT FIELD | JUVENILE FIELD |
		(PERCENTAGE DISTRIBUTION)		
Less than high-school graduate	10	7	*	0
High-school graduate	31	20	6	2
1–3 years of college	22	15	10	7
B.A. only	11	17	34	36
Some graduate study	13	14	29	25
M.A.	11	26	20	28
Ph.D.	2	1	1	2
TOTAL	100	100	100	100

Source: Joint Commission on Correctional Manpower and Training, *Perspectives on Correctional Manpower and Training* (Washington, D.C.: The Commission, 1970), p. 92.
*Less than 0.5 percent.

TABLE 14-2 United States Manpower Requirements for Corrections

PERSONNEL CATEGORY	NUMBER IN 1965	NEEDED IN 1965	SHORTAGE IN 1965	NEEDED IN 1975	% INCREASE 1965–75
Group Supervisors	63,184	89,600	29%	114,000	80%
Case Managers	17,416	55,000	69%	81,000	364%
Specialists	6,657	20,400	68%	28,000	321%
Technicians	33,906	60,300	44%	81,000	139%
Total	121,163	225,000	46%	304,000	152%

Source: Richard Myren, *Education in Criminal Justice* (Sacramento, Ca., Coordinating Council for Higher Education, 1970), p. II–11, adapted from President's Commission on Law Enforcement and Administration of Justice, *Task Force Report: Corrections* (Washington, D.C.: Government Printing Office, 1967), pp. 95 and 99.

staff members classified as specialists in Table 14–2 include personnel whose professional skills are needed in corrections. They include classroom teachers, clinical or vocational psychologists, and other personnel whose training in criminal justice may be limited. Another important manpower group in corrections is composed of the technicians and service personnel. These people operate the essential maintenance services of the institution as they would in any other community or large-scale organization. Criminal-justice majors tend to avoid this type of work. Students of business administration, agriculture, horticulture, and data processing should not overlook corrections when looking for a job.

It has been estimated that California alone will need at least three thousand new correctional employees annually.[12] A later study, conducted by the California Council on Intergovernmental Relations, indicates the greatest numerical growth projected for personnel in local government will occur in the following fields: criminal-justice activities, health services, and social welfare.[13] Although correctional manpower studies have not been compiled for many states, there is reason to believe that similar growth trends exist everywhere. A 1978 manpower study provides the following trends.

Hiring patterns are sometimes muted because of the traditional understaffing of corrections. Therefore, need may not be reflected in the number of positions available on the local and state level. For this reason it is important for the corrections applicant to systematically review potential resources in the field. A helpful source of information is the *National Criminal Justice Directory*.[14] A separate directory has been prepared for each LEAA region listing the addresses of probation and parole agencies, adult correctional institutions, and juvenile

THE EMPLOYMENT OUTLOOK

Overall employment growth in state and local law enforcement and criminal-justice agencies is expected to be considerably slower between 1974 and 1985 than during the early 1970s as the combined result of a projected slowdown in crime rates and of tighter state and local government budgets.

- The crime rate, as measured by the FBI index for Part I offenses, is expected to experience a relatively slow net growth between 1974 and 1980 and to decline significantly between 1980 and 1985 as a result of (1) a projected reduction in the youth population; (2) increased population decentralization; and (3) a projected reduction in unemployment rates.
- Criminal-justice expenditures and employment growth will also be checked by the more limited increase in state and local government expenditures projected for 1974–1980, as a result of the recent economic recession.
- Although "full-time equivalent" employment in criminal-justice activities is projected to grow by nearly 400,000 or 43 percent between 1974 and 1985, the projected annual growth rate, of about 3 percent, will thus be substantially below the average annual increase of about 5½ percent, experienced between 1971 and 1974.

Employment growth rates between 1974 and 1985 are projected to be substantially greater in the courts and correctional sectors than in law enforcement.

- Police protection agencies are expected to increase their staffs by about 180,000, or 33 percent, between 1974 and 1985, in full-time equivalents, but their share of total criminal-justice employment will decline from about 59 percent to 55 percent over this period. More rapid employment growth is projected for state and county agencies than for city police departments.
- Prosecution and public indigent defense agencies are expected to experience the most rapid growth rates—of 71 percent and 91 percent respectively.
- Total employment in state and local courts will increase by 54 percent with much more rapid growth for general jurisdiction courts than for courts of limited or special jurisdiction.

- Overall employment in corrections activities is projected to increase by 62 percent, but with very divergent growth trends for different agency categories. The most rapid employment growth is projected for probation and parole agencies and in locally based juvenile institutions in contrast to a projected employment decline in state juvenile institutions. Employment in adult correctional institutions is expected to increase by 58 percent as a result of a projected trend toward increased imprisonment of some categories of offenders.

Employment growth will be more rapid in the professional, technical, and administrative occupations than in the "line" law-enforcement occupations.

- In police agencies, the number of non-sworn personnel is expected to increase by 53 percent, as compared to a projected increase of 28 percent in sworn officer employment, as a result of the continued trend toward increased use of civilians in administrative and technical positions.
- Employment of non-judicial personnel in general jurisdiction and appellate courts is expected to grow more than twice as rapidly as judges, reflecting increased requirements for administrative and technical support personnel.
- Staff attorneys in prosecution and indigent defense agencies, and probation and parole officers, will also experience relatively rapid employment growth.
- Child-care workers in juvenile institutions are expected to experience very limited net employment growth, as a result of the projected continued trends toward deinstitutionalization and the use of community-based programs.

Analysis of a number of major recent trends or developments in the criminal-justice system indicates that they will have mixed impacts upon agency manpower requirements.

- The trend toward decriminalization of certain victimless offenses, such as public drunkenness, has apparently had limited impact upon police and prosecution manpower needs, based on executive responses.
- Formal pre-trial diversion programs were reported by about one-third of probation and parole agencies and about two-fifths of the prosecutors. Workload impacts were also reported to be limited. These programs may have contributed, however, to the declining trend in juvenile institutional populations.
- The impact of the trend toward determinate, and to mandatory minimum sentences, upon manpower needs cannot yet be determined,

but these trends are likely to entail more manpower for both correctional and courts agencies, with a probable reduction in parole-agency workloads.

Increased reliance upon community-based programs, primarily for juvenile offenders, is a significant factor contributing to a projected reduction in employment in state training institutions, and has also tended to shift some of the correctional employment from the public to the private sector.

The above manpower assessments and projections are necessarily subject to considerable margins of uncertainty because of the limited historical data base available and the need to make numerous assumptions concerning both future criminal-justice system trends and broader economic or social trends.

Source: *The National Manpower Survey of the Criminal Justice System: Executive Summary,* U.S. Department of Justice, Law Enforcement Assistance Administration (Washington, D.C.: U.S. Government Printing Office, 1978), pp. 5–7.

correctional institutions. The criminal-justice agencies are identified as state, county, or city units. In addition, the directory includes the names and addresses of enforcement agencies, courts, prosecutors, public defenders, and other agencies (for example, state planning agencies). According to the directory there are 57,575 public agencies in the criminal-justice system which are operated at the state or local government level: 5,468 of these are designated as corrections agencies. It is helpful to determine the geographical region in which one desires employment and then obtain the pertinent state directories in order to inquire about specific positions. Most correctional positions are covered by civil service. There are certain requirements that must be considered. The following are the most common: residency rules; unnecessarily long experience requirements; bars based upon age, sex, and physical characteristics (for example, height or weight); mandatory personality tests; barriers to hiring the physically handicapped; and legal or administrative barriers to hiring ex-offenders.

The National Advisory Commission on Criminal Justice Standards and Goals has sought to eliminate these practices in the hope of interesting qualified people in correctional work.[15] Recruitment has been inhibited by these restrictions, according to the Joint Commission on Correctional Manpower and Training.[16] In order to determine the requirements of a particular agency, consult the *National Criminal Justice Directory* for the address to contact for information. Residency requirements, usually six months to a year, are common.

There is little justification for this because it limits the employment of applicants from recognized schools in other jurisdictions. It restricts the hiring of personnel from outside corrections agencies who might want a lateral transfer to another state or agency in order to use already-developed skills. The growth of exciting new programs in this field has increased the need for personnel to move to nearby counties or distant states.

Another serious limitation is the requirement that experience precede hiring into an entry-level position. A few years ago it was possible to substitute years of education for experience. Now many agencies require experience plus the degree. One-year internships in correctional agencies during undergraduate years may satisfy this requirement. It is sometimes possible to obtain college credit for volunteer assignments in criminal-justice agencies. Some agencies will accept verified volunteer work conducted under the direction of qualified staff as partial fulfillment of the experience requirement. Part-time or on-call employment as a group supervisor in a juvenile hall is one way to gain approved experience. It is hoped that enrollment in and graduation from a criminal-justice program will soon be accepted as a substitute for experience at the time of initial employment in criminal justice. A recent study found "only 16 percent of those now employed in corrections came directly from classrooms."[17] It is no wonder the professionalization of corrections has been slow.

Age restrictions are being eased in this field. At one time it was felt that maturity, measured in chronological years alone, was a prerequisite for employment with offenders. Also, male institutions hired only men and probation and parole caseloads were assigned on the basis of sex. Some change is being effected with women being assigned caseloads with male as well as female offenders. Women correctional officers have been employed in the borstals or institutions for male offenders in Great Britain for many years. The plan has been successful but its implementation in this country has been slow. A recent survey of correctional personnel reveals the following age and sex profile. Of the total number of employees, 83 percent are male and 17 percent are female; 13 percent are twenty-nine years of age or less; 87 percent are white; and 20 percent have been employed in corrections for three years or less while 49 percent have been in the field for four through fifteen years.[18] This profile presents a pattern which is likely to be resistant to new ways of handling correctional clients. Such staff members will probably find the prison environment difficult since the prisoners are getting younger and the percentage belonging to racial minorities is increasing.

A usual prerequisite to employment is the entrance examination. This may be in the form of a written examination, oral interview, or both. The job announcement will define the subject areas to be covered in the written examination. Most of these are likely to include basic information from general subject areas to be found in the criminal-justice or corrections curriculum. A review of recent publications and journal articles in the field should serve as sufficient preparation.

Students should not fail to explore the emerging work categories in the field of corrections. A review of materials distributed by the National Criminal Justice Reference Service of the Law Enforcement Assistance Administration will alert the prospective professional to job descriptions which are overlooked in the usual surveys. The inquiring student can sometimes discover openings in regional and state planning agencies. There are agencies seeking interested applicants for youth service bureaus, halfway houses, and child advocacy programs. The body of recently published literature in corrections contains many clues to new job descriptions.

Greater interest in recruitment and the upgrading of existing correctional personnel has led to the establishment of the National Institute of Corrections. It operates under the joint sponsorship of the Law Enforcement Assistance Administration and the Federal Bureau of Prisons. The goals of the Institute are as follows:

- Receive and make grants;
- Serve as a clearinghouse and information center for corrections;
- Provide consultant services to federal, state, and local criminal-justice agencies;
- Assist federal, state, and local agencies and private organizations in developing and implementing improved corrections programs;
- Conduct seminars, workshops, and training programs for all types of criminal-justice personnel associated with the rehabilitation of offenders;
- Develop technical training teams to assist state and local agencies in organizing and conducting training programs;
- Conduct, encourage, and coordinate correctional research;
- Formulate and disseminate correctional policy, goals, and standards;
- Conduct programs evaluating the effectiveness of new correctional approaches, techniques, systems, programs, and devices;
- Use the statistics, data, program reports, and data of federal agencies;
- Use the assistance, services, records, and facilities of state and local governments or other public or private agencies; and

371

• Enter into contracts with public or private agencies, organizations, and individuals.[19]

Careers in corrections will be stimulated if the Institute moves forward with its proposals.

Priorities for Corrections

Three national commissions have focused upon the administration of criminal justice in the past fifty years. The earliest one, the National Commission on Law Observance and Enforcement, was formed in 1929 and is known as the Wickersham Commission. The chairman, appointed by President Herbert Hoover, was George W. Wickersham, a former United States attorney general. A number of reports of the Commission were published in 1931, including one entitled *Penal Institutions, Probation and Parole*.[20] The report on corrections offered detailed proposals for greater efficiency in the operation of the probation and parole system and of the correctional institutions.

It was not until thirty-six years later (1965) that the President's Commission on Law Enforcement and Administration of Justice was formed by Lyndon B. Johnson. The Commission was intended as a national response to the crime problem. A number of reports, including one on corrections, were issued in 1967. The emphasis was upon the development of community-based corrections. The Commission stated:

> Institutions tend to isolate offenders from society, both physically and psychologically, cutting them off from schools, jobs, families, and other supportive influences and increasing the probability that the label of criminal will be indelibly impressed upon them. The goal of reintegration is likely to be furthered much more readily by working with offenders in the community than by incarceration.[21]

The recommendations for the implementation of this new concept included the following:

1. Make parole and probation supervision available for all offenders.
2. Provide mandatory supervision of released offenders not paroled.
3. Increase number of probation and parole officers.
4. Use volunteers and subprofessional aides.
5. Develop new methods to reintegrate offenders by mobilizing community institutions.

6. Make funds available to purchase services otherwise unobtainable for offenders.

7. Vary caseload size and treatment according to offender needs.

8. Develop more intensive community treatment programs as alternatives to institutionalization.[22]

The acceptance of community-based corrections has been slow. Four years later only twenty-seven states, the Federal Bureau of Prisons, and the District of Columbia had developed these programs.[23] Why haven't more states implemented these concepts? The public's fear and misunderstanding about corrections and offenders are the most important reasons for resistance. The isolation of prisons goes hand in hand with public apathy toward their problems. The number of offenders actually in prison or being supervised by probation or parole agencies may exceed 1.8 million by 1982.[24] The concept of community corrections is not new. It has been a reality to most prison inmates: a majority of offenders are already on probation or parole, and 98 percent of those presently incarcerated will be released on parole at some future time.

There are critics of community corrections who say that institutions are necessary to control the crime problem. They assume incarceration means instant protection. They ignore the need for prison programs to help offenders. It is unfortunate that the law-and-order cabal never emphasizes rehabilitation. The demand for the prison to do more than serve as a holding facility has not been loud enough. Several years ago the Law Enforcement Assistance Administration, in its report *National Prisoner Statistics,* indicated that only thirty-three of the fifty states responded with sufficient information so that the agency could determine how many adult felons were admitted to and released from state correctional institutions during one year.[25] This also made it impossible to calculate the figures for adult felons incarcerated in institutions. The states gave the following reasons for their failure to provide this information: personnel shortages, inadequate budgets, and problems with internal operating procedures. If the administrators of our prisons cannot even keep track of their prisoners, it is doubtful that rehabilitation is being pursued rigorously. Those supporting crime control through incarceration are not demanding accountability for community protection in the future.

Several other reasons are given for the continuing resistance to community-based corrections. A number of states have indicated that the state legislature should modify existing legislation to create these programs. It is the responsibility of corrections administrators to inform lawmakers of this need. The few advocates of community programs are unfamiliar with the lobbying necessary to secure these programs. At the same time, prison-reform advocates are vocal and sometimes self-defeating in their goal to abolish all prisons. Incarceration will always be required for some offenders, especially those committing high-fear crimes or those who have a long history of criminal behavior. However, this does not diminish the fact that others can be served in the community if they do not threaten the citizenry and if the supervision of trained probation or parole officers is utilized. Even in cases of required confinement, the proximity of the prisoner to the home community can further his rehabilitation while protecting other citizens.

Ex-prisoners can be influential in determining the level of support mobilized in favor of community corrections. If one former offender commits a serious crime it can jeopardize these programs. However, many ex-offenders are able to take up an acceptable life style. The many offender-reentry organizations operating throughout the country should help to prevent these parolees from endangering useful programs. These groups can inform the public about inmates who have succeeded.

The President's Commission proposed further recommendations for the improvement of correctional institutions. These suggestions will be necessary regardless of new alternatives to actual incarceration. They are as follows:

1. Establish with state and federal funds small-unit institutions in cities for community-oriented treatment.
2. Operate institutions with joint responsibility of staff and inmates for rehabilitation.
3. Upgrade education and vocational training for inmates.
4. Establish state programs to recruit and train instructors.
5. Improve prison industries through joint state programs and federal assistance.
6. Expand graduated release and furlough programs.
7. Integrate local jails and misdemeanant institutions with state corrections.
8. Provide separate treatment to special offender groups, through pooling or sharing among jurisdictions.[26]

Progress in implementing these recommendations should be viewed in contrast to the traditional background. With its roots in the past, the prison system balks at community-oriented programs. Since these alternatives do exist the inmates excluded from them become bitter and alienated. This, in turn, leads to increased violence within the institution. It also increases antagonism toward the introduction of community programs. For those prisoners who would like to reform there is not much opportunity among armed robbers, thieves, and killers. In addition, racism is identified with the prison. Every institution has a disproportionately high number of minority prisoners and a disproportionately low number of minority staff members. Rehabilitation programs, when present in the confinement setting, are usually identified with the various counseling ideologies. Inmates are suspicious of the mental-health approach unless the clinical staff, artfully taking this into consideration, treat them accordingly. When staff fail to recognize these elementary facts about prisons the offenders control the program. The goal of prisoners is to obtain their release as soon as possible with the least personal inconvenience. Inmates who try to take part in institutional programs without manipulating the staff ought to be identified. Prisoners take their lives in their own hands when they decide to enter a rehabilitation program. The challenge of the prison is extraordinary. It must be met not only by the prisoners but also by the staff. The recommendations of the President's Commission are a response to this difficulty. There is a movement which recommends a moratorium on traditional prison construction so that an orderly transition can be made to community-based programs.[27] This transition requires increased research in order to evaluate the success of existing community programs. In addition, it is important that the moratorium on construction not reduce funds for the renovation of present structures that have progressive programs. The President's Commission dealt also with upgrading traditional correctional institutions, including local jails. It was suggested that standards for the operation of these facilities might be improved if jails were placed under the control of the statewide correctional system.

These ideals can hardly be met with mere rhetoric. There are many critical problems which must be explored if the correctional institution is to meet today's control and treatment standards. The major area of concern is that of manpower development—determining the impact of criminal-justice education on agency staffing and programming and establishing priorities for local and state government on the provision of adequate budgets for programs. For this reason the recommendations of the National Advisory Commission on Criminal Justice Standards and Goals (1973) serve to reiterate the earlier emphasis upon community corrections while pointing to priorities which influence change in a traditional field. The Commission has selected the following six priorities for corrections.

1. *Equity and justice in corrections.* Convicted offenders should retain all rights that citizens in general have, except those that must be limited to carry out the criminal sanction or to administer a correctional facility or agency.

2. *Exclusion of sociomedical problem cases from corrections.* It is beyond the competence and proper scope of corrections to deal effectively with the mentally ill, alcoholics, and drug addicts.

3. *Shifting of emphasis from institutions to community programs.*

4. *Unification of corrections and system planning.* Effective relationships among the various components of the criminal-justice system must be established and corrections must end its social and political isolation.

5. *Manpower development.* The commission recommends that corrections develop a comprehensive nationwide strategy to improve correctional manpower and that priority be given to implementation of a state-coordinated recruitment and development program.

6. *Increased involvement of the public in corrections.*

The recommendations of three national crime surveys emphasize the changing role of corrections in meeting the crime-control issues of the 1980s. Knowledge generated in the field can be utilized in seeking answers, although it has been overlooked in the past. This earlier resistance can be traced to the minimal receptivity of correctional administrators to education and training. The earliest crime survey, the Wickersham Report, suggested rejuvenation of some prison procedures which had been in use for 150 years. The second crime survey stressed the need for modernizing corrections and moving into the community. The most recent survey emphasizes an infusion of new personnel, cooperation with other agencies in the criminal-justice system, and a heightened respect for those confined. Change comes only when those who process convicted offenders believe firmly in their capacity to change. This is a good time for corrections and for those who select it as a career. The early social reformers held great hope for change; now the strategies for that change are here. Manpower development is defined as

> the process by which potentially qualified personnel and in-service personnel are selected and developed to their desired, fullest capabilities to better prepare them for their future, as well as present positions, in order to meet the individual, organizational program and system needs of criminal justice.[28]

The National Advisory Commission on Criminal Justice Standards and Goals stresses the "need for effective selection, placement, and evaluation of personnel."[29] The highest expenditure in a criminal-justice-agency budget is allocated to personnel. There is great concern for projecting future needs, but resources for determining these needs are being developed. Corrections has traditionally operated its programs with a smaller staff than it needs. Personnel in this field often express dissatisfaction with the effectiveness of corrections. The

376

prison-reform movement and heightened community fear of probationers, prisoners, and parolees adds a chilling validity to this response. The increase in urban violence and guerrilla tactics by those
who have had correctional care and processing points up the need for
new input.

STUDY QUESTIONS

1. Has the past decade been one of progress in the administration
   of justice? Explain.
2. Is corrections selected as a possible career goal by many teenagers? Conduct a survey in your own neighborhood to determine
   the answer.
3. What was the purpose of the Correctional Rehabilitation Study
   Act of 1965? Is this legislation in conflict with the goals of the
   National Institute of Corrections?
4. The educational level of correctional personnel is highest in
   which correctional work setting?
5. What are the future manpower needs for corrections? Has your
   state identified these needs? If so, summarize the current
   studies.
6. Is a baccalaureate degree required for the entry-level correctional positions in your community? Differentiate according
   to the following personnel categories: group supervisors, case
   managers, and field personnel.
7. Identify the source of information to be found in the *National
   Criminal Justice Directory.*
8. List the restrictions to employment found in the corrections job
   categories in your county and state. Has state legislation been
   proposed to remove these restrictions?
9. Describe the current age and sex profile of correctional personnel
   and explain its importance for dynamic rehabilitation programs
   in this decade.
10. Identify the recommendations of the President's Commission on
    Law Enforcement and Administration of Justice and the Na-
    tional Advisory Commission on Criminal Justice Standards and
    Goals. Were the recommendations implemented in your state? If
    so, which ones? If not, why not?
11. What is community-based corrections? Is there resistance to
    such programs in your locality?
12. Define manpower development.

NOTES

1. The summary volumes are the following: President's Commission on Law Enforcement and Administration of Justice, *The Challenge of Crime in a Free Society* (Washington, D.C.: Government Printing Office, 1967) and National Advisory Commission on Criminal Justice Standards and Goals, *A National Strategy To Reduce Crime* (Washington, D.C.: Government Printing Office, 1973).
2. *LEAA Newsletter* 6, (November 1976): 1.
3. Louis Harris, "Public Confidence in Work of Law Enforcement Officials Decline," *The Sacramento Bee,* 22 October 1973, p. B-8.
4. Vernon Fox, *Introduction to Corrections,* 2d ed. (Englewood Cliffs, N.J.: Prentice-Hall, 1977), pp. 42–43.
5. Joint Commission on Correctional Manpower and Training, *The Public Looks at Crime and Corrections* (Washington, D.C.: Joint Commission on Correctional Manpower and Training, 1968), p. 7.
6. Ibid., p. 8.
7. Ibid., p. 10.
8. Ibid., p. 22.
9. Correctional Rehabilitation Study Act of 1965 (Public Law 89–178), p. 1.
10. The final report of the Joint Commission on Correctional Manpower and Training, *A Time to Act* (Washington, D.C.: The Joint Commission on Correctional Manpower and Training, 1969). All Commission reports are available from the American Correctional Association, 4321 Hartwick Road, L-208, College Park, Maryland 20740.
11. Vernon Fox, *Guidelines for Corrections Programs in Community and Junior Colleges* (Washington, D.C.: American Association of Junior Colleges, 1969).
12. Eugene O. Sahs, *Mobilizing Correctional Manpower for California: Guidelines for Action* (Sacramento: California Youth and Adult Corrections Agency, 1968).
13. California Council on Intergovernmental Relations, *The California Governmental Manpower Needs Study,* vol. 1 (Sacramento: California Council on Intergovernmental Relations, 1971).
14. U.S. Department of Justice, Law Enforcement Assistance Administration, *Criminal Justice Agencies in Region . . .* (Washington, D.C.: Government Printing Office, 1975). Separate volumes are available for each LEAA region.
15. National Advisory Commission on Criminal Justice Standards and Goals, *Working Papers for the Operational Task Force for Corrections* (Washington, D.C.: National Conference on Criminal Justice, 1973), p. C-204.
16. Joint Commission on Correctional Manpower and Training, *Perspectives on Correctional Manpower and Training* (Washington, D.C.: Joint Commission on Correctional Manpower and Training, 1970), pp. 123–126.
17. Joint Commission, *A Time to Act,* p. 12.
18. Ibid., pp. 11–12.
19. Bureau of Prisons, *Questions and Answers About the National Institute of Corrections* (Marion, Ill.: Federal Prison Industries Printing Plant, 1976), p. 1.
20. The reports of the National Commission on Law Observance and Enforcement (1931) have been reprinted by the Patterson Smith Publishing Corporation, 23 Prospect Terrace, Montclair, New Jersey 07042.
21. President's Commission on Law Enforcement and Administration of Justice, *The Challenge of Crime in a Free Society* (Washington, D.C.: Government Printing Office, 1967), p. 165.
22. Ibid., p. 297.
23. Bertram S. Griggs and Gary R. McCune, "Community-Based Correctional Programs: A Survey and Analysis," *Federal Probation* 36 (June 1972): 7–13.
24. President's Commission, *Challenge of Crime,* p. 160.
25. Law Enforcement Assistance Administration, *National Prisoner Statistics. State Prisons: Admissions and Releases, 1970* (Washington, D.C.: Government Printing Office, 1973), p. 1.

378

26. President's Commission, *Challenge of Crime,* pp. 297–298.
27. Board of Trustees, National Council on Crime and Delinquency, "Institutional Construction—A Policy Statement," *Crime and Delinquency* 18 (October 1972): 331–332.
28. *1974 California Comprehensive Plan for Criminal Justice* (Sacramento: Office of Criminal Justice Planning, 1974), p. 190.
29. National Advisory Commission on Criminal Justice Standards and Goals, *Report on Criminal Justice System* (Washington, D.C.: Government Printing Office, 1973), p. 165.

chapter fifteen
Delinquency
and the
Justice System

Delinquency refers to the misbehavior of youth. A juvenile becomes eligible for processing by formal agencies in the justice system when his or her behavior coincides with the forms of conduct present in the legal definition of delinquency. Juvenile codes include a wide variety of behavior ranging from true criminal activity to forms of conduct which are not illegal when committed by adults.

CRIMINAL BEHAVIOR

All states are in agreement that a juvenile is a delinquent when guilty of an act that is a crime when committed by an adult. Juveniles account for 22 percent of the arrests for violent crimes such as murder, forcible rape, robbery, and aggravated assault. In the categories of violent crimes, those under eighteen years of age represent 9 percent of all persons arrested for murder, 17 percent of all persons arrested for forcible rape, 34 percent of all persons arrested for robbery, and 17 percent of all persons arrested for aggravated assault.[1] Property offenses are more popular juvenile crimes; 46 percent of those arrested for burglary, larceny-theft, and motor-vehicle theft are under age eighteen. This is divided as follows: 52 percent of all persons arrested for burglary, 43 percent of all persons arrested for larceny-theft, and 53 percent of all persons arrested for motor-vehicle theft.[2] Youngsters between the ages of ten and seventeen make up only 15 percent of the population but they account for fully 42 percent of all persons arrested for these seven crimes.

STATUS OFFENSES

The majority of juveniles appearing before the juvenile court are referred for behavior which would not be a crime if committed by an

THOSE AMERICAN KIDS
WHO KILL AND ROB . . .

WASHINGTON—The trailer park murder of a Phoenix man cut down by rifle fire seemed to be a routine homicide until detectives walked into a third-grade classroom and arrested an eight-year-old boy for the crime.

Similarly, Miami police picked up a twelve-year-old slum youth for the stabbing death of his nine-year-old playmate, who apparently had called him a derogatory name.

In Stockton, in California's San Joaquin Valley, the fifteen-year-old son of a prominent orthodontist was arrested for shooting his father and two sisters to death.

Violence by children. Not a new development to law-enforcement authorities, but more and more a disturbing one. And the list seems endless:

In Philadelphia, a sixteen-year-old student, reprimanded the previous day, serves his photography teacher a cup of coffee laced with hydrochloric acid. A fight between male students on the stairwell of a Chicago high school leaves two wounded by gunfire. A fifteen-year-old girl dies three days later.

In Washington, D.C., and its Maryland suburbs, 112 elderly people were mugged or robbed within the past year by a loosely knit gang of youths who trailed their victims from shopping centers to their homes before assaulting them.

Over the past five years, the number of violent crimes attributed to juveniles has jumped by leaps and bounds.

Source: *San Francisco Chronicle*, 4 May 1977, p. 17. Reprinted by permission.

adult. The term "status offense" is used to identify such conduct. Status offenders are represented by the runaway, the school truant, the person in need of supervision, and the incorrigible youngster. Status-offense categories appear in the juvenile-delinquency laws of all the states; however, their number and range varies and many are worded ambiguously. For example, the delinquency statute in New Jersey provides that the court may have jurisdiction over a child who is: (1) habitually vagrant; (2) incorrigible; (3) immoral; (4) knowingly associating with thieves or vicious or immoral persons; (5) growing up in idleness or delinquency; (6) knowingly visiting gambling places or patronizing other places to which it is illegal to admit minors; (7) idly roaming the streets at night; (8) habitually truant from school; or (9) so deporting himself as to endanger his morals, health, or general welfare.³

One-half of the states place restrictions on juvenile-court handling of status offenders. This handling is limited to detention housing or commitment to the training school or correctional facility. Status offenders are to be housed separately from those charged with more serious offenses who are awaiting a court hearing. Some states prohibit the commitment of status offenders to a state correctional institution, and others require the judge to find the child unamenable to alternative forms of treatment before using this severe disposition.

AGE

There is no standardization of age for juvenile-court jurisdiction in the laws of juvenile delinquency. The statutes may differ in one or more of the following categories: (1) lower age limit; (2) upper age limit; (3) differing upper age limits for males and females; and (4) provisions for concurrent or overlapping jurisdiction of juveniles by the adult and juvenile court.

A lower age limit is seldom found in juvenile codes although six states have minimum ages under which a child cannot be charged with delinquent acts. The minimum age is seven in Massachusetts and New York. It is raised to age ten in the states of Colorado, Mississippi, Texas, and Vermont. The absence of a specific lower age limit in most states can be traced to: (1) a body of common law which holds that a child under the age of seven is granted immunity from prosecution for a crime; and (2) the presence of a juvenile-court philosophy which assists children whose behavior violates adult criminal statutes, children who are in need of supervision as defined in the delinquency statute, and children who are defined as neglected or dependent.

The upper age limit for juvenile-court jurisdiction is always stated in the legal definition of delinquency. The upper age limit is the age under which the juvenile court has original jurisdiction. Most states set *less than* age eighteen as the upper limit. Other states designate the sixteenth or seventeenth birthday as the cut-off point; that is, the court can adjudicate only those who have not yet reached age sixteen or seventeen.

Some states designate different upper age limits for girls and boys. The jurisdiction of the juvenile court is extended an additional year or two for girls when such sex discrimination is noted in the law. Different upper age limits for males and females are found in the juvenile-delinquency statutes of Illinois, Oklahoma, and Texas. These distinctions have been declared unconstitutional in the courts.

The presence of an upper age limit for original jurisdiction is accompanied by provisions for the transfer of serious cases from the juvenile court to the adult court in all states except Vermont. Transfer of such cases is subject to certain conditions. These vary widely but usually include one or more of the following: (1) the youth must be at least sixteen years of age; (2) the charge is a felony involving serious bodily harm to others; (3) there is a prior history of delinquency and an unfavorable response to juvenile-court rehabilitation programs; and (4) the individual is a threat to the community.

In *Kent* v. *United States* (1966) the U.S. Supreme Court ruled that a juvenile is entitled to: (1) a full hearing in the juvenile court on the issue of transfer of his or her case to an adult criminal court; (2) the assistance of counsel at the hearing; (3) the counsel should be granted access to the social records prepared by court personnel in determining whether transfer to the adult court is appropriate; and (4) a statement of the reasons formulated by the judge in reaching the decision for the waiver action. The decision does not question the validity of the laws permitting the transfer of juvenile-court cases to the adult courts for criminal prosecution. The U.S. Supreme Court merely questioned the procedure used in effecting such transfers since the constitutional rights of the juvenile were in question.

Twenty-six states and the District of Columbia require that a juvenile be granted a hearing before he or she is transferred to the adult court.[4] Eighteen states require only an investigation before a waiver decision is made.[5] The waiver decision is not made by the juvenile-court judge in four states, and no waiver is allowed in New York or Vermont.[6]

The juvenile court has sought to consider the welfare of the child and to carry out the goals of rehabilitation. While the criminal courts try to determine whether a defendant is guilty or innocent, the juvenile court asks what can be done to help the juvenile. Unfortunately, the benign efforts of the juvenile court do not always succeed and the youngster must be transferred to the adult criminal court.

JUVENILE COURT PROCESS

The juvenile-court movement emphasizes the protection of children's rights, especially in the areas of physical, moral, and mental development. This basic philosophy has characterized the movement since the establishment of the first juvenile court in Chicago in 1899. The primary function of the court is to protect the community while affording appropriate services to the child.

SENTENCED TO PRISON
Law Writes Off Doomed Boy, 16

DENVER (AP)—When Bobby Magers was born with cystic fibrosis, the doctors told his mother, "Take him home to die."

Bobby, now sixteen, was sentenced this past week to six years in the Colorado State Reformatory for robbery. He faces additional trials, as an adult, for the shooting of a policeman and two other robberies.

Juvenile Court Judge James J. Delaney, who agreed to let Bobby be tried as an adult, said he believes there is little else that can be done by the state.

"It's a tragic thing to say that at fourteen or fifteen or sixteen a kid is almost lost and that you have to write him off," he said. "But that's the case."

One of the things his parents—Judy and Austin Magers—think may have contributed to Bobby's problems is that authorities too often felt sorry for him because of his disease, which affects mainly breathing, and that he learned to manipulate them.

No one really knows why Bobby is alive today. When he was born doctors gave him three months to live, and after three months, they gave him one more month. After two-and-one-half years, he was given eight years to live, and at eight he was given twelve. Most agree he could die anytime.

Some doctors say he is still living because of the tenacious nature of his mother, who contracted a deadly form of cancer six years ago and was given just a short time to live, but is still alive.

Bobby is the oldest of four children. A fifth child, Kathy, died of cystic fibrosis when she was two months old.

Mrs. Magers said her son has manipulated people for so long that he does not know what reality is any more. "Psychiatrists tell me he has an 'unrealistic social concern.' It's like going through your whole life playing games."

Mrs. Magers said she and her husband sometimes suffer guilt feelings, but she also feels society missed a chance to help her boy.

As an example, she said, Bobby stole two cars two years ago and wrecked one. When he was caught, she said, the sheriff read him the riot act, told him he had committed three felonies and would go to jail for up to fifteen years.

Then, she said, "He turns to me and says, 'You can take him home now.'"

Austin Magers, a fireman, said he has tried not to baby his son. "In fact, we probably might have been a little more strict because of it (the disease), to try and make him do more."

Once a judge lectured him harshly but handed down a light sentence. Bobby turned around in court and grinned.

Over the years he grew skilled at running away—from home, mental hospitals, and reformatories—and, his mother said, from himself.

"Bobby is a runner," she said. "That is his way of handling everything. He is searching for something, and it's called himself."

The first time he ran away from home, his mother had scolded him for fighting with a neighbor. He packed a suitcase and walked four miles to a police station, telling the desk sergeant, "My mother doesn't want me. Do you have a place for unwanted children?"

One of the police who took him home told her what Bobby had said. "Bobby was sitting there, holding back a grin," Mrs. Magers recalled. "He had a smirk on his face.

"A psychiatrist I went to said I should have excused the cop, picked up whatever book I was reading, and hit the kid over the head. Tell him what he did wasn't funny and that I didn't like it."

Bobby added stolen cars to his repertoire when he was nine. His parents lost count of how many times he took their cars. The twenty-nine others he stole over the years sometimes led him on out-of-state flights.

At thirteen, Bobby told his mother he wanted to be "put away," and because a psychiatrist recommended it, his parents agreed. He ran away from the hospital repeatedly, and one time he went home and took a pistol his mother kept there.

Returned to the hospital, he immediately escaped again, and held four staff members at bay until his mother took the gun away. She knew it was not loaded.

His I.Q. is in the genius range, but he sometimes flunked subjects he didn't like.

The games ended last fall after he had escaped from a juvenile detention facility. He had stolen a gun from a home and was wandering in Northglenn, a Denver suburb.

When Police Officer Jim Biggins drove up, Bobby stuck the gun through an open car window and forced him to lay down his own gun.

Biggins tried to take Bobby's gun away and Bobby shot him four times. The wound in his stomach nearly killed him.

Biggins said the biggest worry in his life now is an unsettling feeling he had not known before in his six years as a policeman: "I'm scared inside."

"After the Northglenn shooting," Mrs. Magers remembered, "everyone said, 'This boy has used his illness long enough.'

"But the boy didn't use his illness. They did. I wanted to scream in court, 'You guys have used it!'"

Source: *The Sacramento Bee*, 17 April 1977, p. A-1. Reprinted by permission of The Associated Press.

Legislation dealing with jurisdiction determines who is eligible for processing in the juvenile court. The court process consists of four stages: (1) the intake process; (2) the detention hearing; (3) the adjudicatory hearing; and (4) the disposition hearing.

Intake is a procedure to help court personnel decide whether youngsters referred to the court can best be served by it. The most skilled workers in the probation department, which is a part of the juvenile court, are the intake workers. Screening of cases referred to the juvenile court is important because it prevents unnecessary use of the judicial process and it offers the youngster referral services in the community. Unfortunately, many social agencies are reluctant to offer services to youngsters who have been referred to the juvenile court and released for alternate forms of help. There is a prevalent, stereotype of the resistant youth who does not want services imposed upon him. Intake is a voluntary proceeding which determines whether a formal charge will be placed against the juvenile. The charge must be filed in a document known as a petition. Sometimes the worker evaluating the case will decide that a formal petition is not required and the juvenile is "warned and released." Approximately 50 percent of the cases referred to the juvenile court do not move beyond the intake hearing.

The filing of the petition by the court worker, not merely the signing of the document, is the important step in determining whether a youngster is scheduled for an adjudicatory hearing. It should be kept in mind that the decision to file a petition lies with the probation staff. These same people may later be asked to serve as treatment workers for the child. Most parents and youngsters are unable to differentiate the separate roles of the probation staff in filing a petition and in trying later to help the child.

The detention hearing determines whether a youngster will be detained or released while awaiting adjudication. The decision to detain a youngster is the responsibility of an intake worker or the juvenile-court judge. Detention is nothing more than the temporary care of those who require secure custody in order to assure their appearance in court. The holding facility may be an adult jail, juvenile hall, or detention center. The court should provide written guidelines outlining the criteria for detaining children. There are two satisfactory reasons for holding juveniles scheduled for an adjudicatory hearing: (1) need for protection of the youngster or the community; or (2) fear that he or she will run away. The detention hearing is both formal and brief. It is stressful for the juvenile unfamiliar with the justice system. Certainly the youth should be accompanied by his or her parents, all of whom should be told their legal rights by the intake worker. Detention is expensive. It cost $58.97 per day to keep a youngster in the Los Angeles Juvenile Hall in 1977.[7] It is a misuse of detention to lock up children "to teach them a lesson." It should be used only for the most seriously delinquent juveniles. Police in New York City recently arrested a fourteen-year-old boy who was caught moments after beating and robbing a seventy-two-year-old woman of three dollars in the elevator of her building. Table 15–1 shows his arrest record; he is typical of the repetitious offenders who come before the Family Court in New York City. He was first arrested at the age of nine.

The adjudicatory hearing is the next step in the juvenile-court process. The filing of a petition at an intake hearing is followed by the issuance of a summons indicating that a fact-finding or adjudicatory hearing has been scheduled. Each summons to appear should be accompanied by a copy of the petition and a notice of the right to counsel. The summons should reach the juvenile at least one day before the hearing. An adjudicatory hearing is in order when: (1) requested by the complainant or the juvenile; (2) there are substantial discrepancies about, or even denial of, the allegations of a serious offense; (3) protection of the community is a concern; and (4) court attention is required because of the gravity of the offense or the special needs of the youngster.

The adjudicatory hearing was once considered an uneventful interim event between intake and the disposition of the case. It was a time when the court could move from selecting cases to be heard to

TABLE 15-1   A Sample Juvenile Arrest Record

OFFENSE	DISPOSITION
Burglary	Sent home with warning
Robbery (took bicycle at knife point)	Sent home with warning
Robbery (mugging)	Dismissed (no complainant)
Robbery (mugging)	Dismissed (no complainant)
Robbery (mugging)	Dismissed (no complainant)
Robbery (mugging)	Dismissed (no complainant)
Robbery (mugging)	Dismissed (no complainant)
Burglary, possession of stolen property	Pending, youth failed to appear in court; reminder mailed, but no warrant issued
Robbery (mugging)	Pending; youth failed to appear in court; warrant issued
Robbery (mugging), **assault, burglary, possession of stolen property**	Found guilty on all but burglary charge; awaiting sentence

Source: *New York Times,* 11 April 1976, p. 42. © 1976 by The New York Times Company. Reprinted by permission.

determining how it might best serve the child. The introduction of the right to counsel and other changes brought about by the United States Supreme Court have revolutionized the adjudicatory hearing. At this fact-finding hearing, the court decides from legally admissible evidence whether the youngster is guilty of the alleged delinquency, whether he or she is a neglected child, or whether he or she requires supervision.

This hearing is conducted in the informal and sensitive manner characteristic of the juvenile court. The court will presume the innocence of the child at the hearing. It will hear evidence attempting to determine beyond a reasonable doubt whether the juvenile has committed the alleged delinquency. The probation staff will refrain from submitting a social evaluation on the child at the time of the fact-finding hearing. This is necessary so that hearsay and subjective evaluations of the youngster's environment will not influence the actual evidence, which focuses upon the alleged delinquency. The presence of a lawyer at the adjudicatory hearing is helpful. It assures the parents that appropriate procedures for the determination of guilt or innocence are followed in the assessment of available evidence. Some difficulties were encountered when lawyers were initially introduced into the juvenile-court hearing. Traditional training in the adversary procedures of the criminal court had not prepared attorneys for the unique atmosphere of the juvenile court. This problem has been resolved by the passage of time and by the increasing interest in juvenile justice held by those receiving legal training. The informality and privacy of the court hearing often overwhelms parents. They are likely to equate due process of law with the impersonal proceedings characteristic of the criminal court.

When the facts alleged in the petition presented in the adjudicatory hearing have been substantiated the juvenile court will move to the final stage in the proceedings, the disposition hearing. The period between the conclusion of the adjudicatory hearing and the beginning of the disposition hearing is used for gathering and preparing the information necessary for determining the action to be taken by the court. Concern for the child, the basis for the juvenile-court movement, is still expressed in this final stage of the proceedings. The nature of the decision will reveal the sensitivity and skill of the juvenile-court judge. Few individuals have such power in the administration of justice. Communities should pay careful attention when selecting their juvenile-court judges. The juvenile-court movement is fortunate in the quality and probity of the vast majority of its presiding judges.

The most important information prepared by the court for the disposition hearing is the social history. This study focuses upon the child—not on the evidence surrounding the offense. The report familiarizes the judge with the social conditions of the child's environment. Assumptions will be made by the probation officer preparing the report which will influence the decision in the case. A carefully compiled social history will explore a number of areas. The following outline shows the information gathered for the social history.

1. Identifying Information
   a. Name, sex, and age on date of referral to intake.
   b. Birthdate (verified by the agency).

2. Referral
   a. Place referral date, source of referral, or police case number on margin of the social history.
   b. State nature of the complaint (e.g., Joseph was charged with burglary second committed on June 22, 1978) and refer to the police report and petition for specific particulars in the case.

3. Legal Rights
   a. Does the juvenile understand his or her legal rights, particularly right to counsel? Elaborate on the level of understanding or nonunderstanding noted in the interview.

4. Child's Statement
   a. Summarize the following: child's reason for involvement; attitude toward arrest and/or complaint; and identify names and ages of accomplices. Attempt to determine the role of each in the commission of the offense.
   b. Indicate whether the child's statement differs from that reported by the referring agency and, if so, include the child's explanation for these inconsistencies.

5. Detention Report
   a. Summarize detention experience: length of stay; adjustment; attitude; number of previous detention placements; and reports from detention staff.

6. Previous Court or Criminal-Justice Agency Contacts
   a. Briefly summarize any history of family delinquency or criminality.

7. Family History and Environment
   a. Persons residing in the home.
   b. Socioeconomic level of the family.
   c. Cultural background.

    d. Family health problems.

    e. Interpersonal relationships and attitudes to parents or parent substitutes.

    f. Appraisal of parents or parent substitutes.

    g. Appraisal of the family as a unit (e.g., family group activities, sharing responsibilities, and pride in the family as noted in its history and ethnic identification).

8. Child's Personal History

    a. Record any evidence of retardation in mental, physical, motor, or social development. How did the child and his or her parents respond to these problems during the preschool years? Did these attitudes influence the care and training received by the child?

    b. Were there numerous placements outside of the home? If so, why? How did the child adjust?

    c. Medical history: serious illnesses, accidents, operations, and current health status.

9. The Child as a Person

    a. General appearance.

    b. General behavior.

        (1) How does he or she spend the day?

        (2) What are his or her special interests, skills, hobbies, or sports?

        (3) What kind of group activities does he or she enjoy?

        (4) Does he or she participate in religious activities?

    c. Family attitudes and relationships.

        (1) From the child's viewpoint, cite attitudes and manner of relating to: parents and/or the parent substitute; siblings; and close relatives.

        (2) How does he or she react to discipline?

    d. Peer relationships.

    e. Relationships with adults outside the family.

    f. Emotional status.

        (1) How does he or she express and handle happiness, sadness, and anger?

        (2) Identify the situations which readily elicit these emotions.

    g. View of self.

        (1) How does the child describe himself or herself?

        (2) What kind of person would he or she like to be in the future?

      (3) Are most accomplishments viewed as successes or failures?

  h. Antisocial behavior.

      (1) Briefly describe the child's behavior problems. How long have they existed? Did these problems emerge gradually or suddenly?

      (2) How does the child deal with his or her problems (e.g., rationalizes? avoids? minimizes? or sincerely attempts to solve?)?

      (3) Does he or she understand the reason for the antisocial acts? Does he or she have insight, remorse, or guilt?

10. School Report

11. Psychological/Psychiatric Evaluation

  a. Indicate whether the child was referred for formal or informal psychological evaluation and, if so, when, by whom, and why.

  b. Attach written report, if possible.

12. Employment History

  a. Jobs held: how employment was obtained; special training, if any; earnings; and use of income.

  b. Attitude toward work and employer.

  c. Job duration and reasons for leaving.

  d. Significant results of vocational and aptitude tests.

13. Summary

  a. Summarize salient points developed in the preceding sections.

14. Plan of Service

  a. Discuss services—appropriateness and methods for implementation.

15. Probation or Court Officer's Recommendation to the Judge

It is important that the judge have available a carefully prepared social history. Failure to use such information seriously reduces the effectiveness of the juvenile court. For example, a fifteen-year-old youth with three prior arrests was recently taken into custody in one of our largest cities for what the deputy district attorney described as a gangland execution murder. The victim, another youth, had been held to the floor while the subject fired several shots into him with a 22-caliber rifle. Shortly after the shooting, the subject was arrested by police and taken before a probation officer. Requesting that the juvenile court detain the youth pending a court hearing, the probation officer pointed out to the judge that the juvenile was an active gang member and a threat to the community. The judge, however, released the youth to the custody of his mother until the hearing. At the hearing four weeks later, the same judge, without giving any reason, dismissed the case altogether. In response, the deputy district attorney, who described the shooting as clearly premeditated, said it was inconceivable to him that the judge released the youngster. The youth had been charged with the most serious of crimes—premeditated murder. He had an arrest record. He was shown to be a threat to the community. And yet he was released back onto the streets almost immediately after his arrest. Delinquency control requires effort on the part of the judge and court personnel. When the court determines the disposition of a case, it should consider the best interests of the child *and* the community.

The options open to the judge are: (1) dismissal; (2) probation; (3) placement of the child in a foster home or group home; (4) commitment to a county facility when the youngster is considered too sophisticated for a foster-home placement but not in need of the severe sanction represented by placement in a state correctional institution; or (5) sentence to the state juvenile facilities. Whatever disposal the judge makes should be done with the assurance that the service plan recommended for the youngster will be made available. Over one-half of juveniles processed through the juvenile court find their cases dismissed or handled by informal adjustment. Table 15–2 shows the findings of a recent study of delinquency dispositions in the juvenile courts of Denver County (Colorado), Memphis-Shelby County (Tennessee), and Montgomery County (Pennsylvania), illustrating the proportional frequency of occurrence for various dispositions.

The proper disposition in a juvenile case occurs when the court and corrections formulate and implement a program which will develop individual responsibility for lawful behavior and, at the same time, protect society from conduct injurious to persons and property. A fair and equitable juvenile-justice system has an obligation to provide such services.

PROBATION

The major functions of the probation department are supervision and treatment. Supervision is determining the whereabouts of a youngster and accounting for him or her on probation. Caseloads are assigned each officer and he or she may be asked to supervise more than 100 youngsters. A smaller number is recommended, usually fifty cases, but it is seldom possible for a court to reduce the caseload. Unfortunately, the myth of caseload size hampers much that could be done for the child. It is easy to say one cannot provide much time to

TABLE 15-2 Ranking of Disposition Severity in the Three Courts

		DENVER COUNTY	MEMPHIS-SHELBY COUNTY	MONTGOMERY COUNTY
SEVERITY LEVEL 1:	Case adjusted at juvenile court by probation officer or judge—i.e., juvenile counseled and matter closed (also known as "informal adjustment")	66.0%	60.4%	51.5%
SEVERITY LEVEL 2:	Case held open with child to receive special care at private facility or one run by county or state	13.3%	2.8%	5.6%
SEVERITY LEVEL 3:	Formal supervised probation	17.8%	29.0%	36.4%
SEVERITY LEVEL 4:	Case waived to adult court for adjudication or child incarcerated in juvenile institution	2.9%	7.8%	6.5%
		N = 5,684	N = 6,596	N = 1,302

Source: Lawrence E. Cohen, *Delinquency Dispositions,* Utilization of Criminal Justice Statistics Project, Analytic Report SD-AR-9 (Washington, D.C.: U.S. Government Printing Office, 1976), p. 20.

100 youngsters. However, each probation officer will supervise many kinds of children: some require little attention and will be asked to submit periodical reports to the probation officer and to request his or her assistance when needed; others are in need of specific services available at the court and have demonstrated their ability to use such help; and a small number need to be seen by the probation officer weekly.

Supervision requires a great deal of paperwork. Therefore it can get in the way of treatment and service delivery. Too often probation officers must choose between supervising treatment or writing case reports. It is unfortunate when the probation worker is asked to write social evaluations for the judge as a guide in disposing the case and, at the same time, to supervise probationers. There are then too many reasons for not serving the needs of the youngster: the judge wants an immediate social investigation for the court hearing; the caseload is too large; and there are those difficult cases which require an unreasonable amount of time. The probation officer is the worker with the most important role in implementing the philosophy and policies of the judge and the chief probation officer. He or she is the primary contact between the juvenile and the court following the disposition hearing. The court worker represents the formal juvenile-justice system—he or she may act out this role as a sensitive, concerned counselor and advocate or as a punitive figure who views his or her role as one of control.

JUVENILE INSTITUTIONS

The decision to confine a youngster in a state institution requires very serious consideration. Each state should set a minimum age below which a juvenile may not be confined in a state training school. The minimum age should be specified in the statutes. In California no ward of the juvenile court who is under the age of eight may be committed to the state youth authority which administers the institutions. The statute further provides that no youngster who is suffering from an infectious or contagious disease which will endanger other inmates may be confined in such an institution.

Guidelines are needed to determine which youth should be considered for incarceration in a state correctional facility. There are numerous chronic offenders coming before the court who evidence such limited self-control and poor judgment, whose antisocial behavior is so frequent and pervasive, that rehabilitation in a community-based program is a futile and unrealistic effort. Sophisticated delinquents involved in very serious offenses which pose a threat to the lives and property of others are those deemed eligible for this severe sanction. These individuals contribute significantly to the existing crime problem by repetitive and deliberate criminal activity. In addition, they hamper community-rehabilitation programs by instilling fear and reinforcing delinquent values among juveniles amenable to treatment. Confinement protects the community from the delinquent temporarily. However, equating confinement with protection and failing to provide services directed toward changing criminal patterns is shortsighted. The cost of maintaining a youth in a training school ranges from $6,000 to $23,000 per year. Costs are highest in the reception center, less in the long-term institution, and least in the forestry camp.

A recent survey identifies 874 state or locally administered institutions for delinquent children. They range from traditional training schools (189) to forestry camps or ranch facilities (103), detention centers (347), shelters (23), diagnostic or reception clinics (17), and halfway houses or group homes (195). These 874 institutions are augmented by 1,277 privately operated facilities.[8] The daily population of youngsters in all these institutions may reach 74,000. In addition, an estimated 7,800 juveniles are processed through local adult jails daily.[9]

The ideal training school should not house more than 150 juvenile offenders. Forestry camps most often meet this standard. Only 50 percent of the nation's training schools meet this recommendation. Approximately one-third of the juvenile facilities are overcrowded; that figure can increase during some months. The delinquent stays an average one or two months at the reception center, twelve months in the training school, and eight months in a forestry camp. The average term now served by youthful murderers in California is twenty-eight months; for armed robbers it is fourteen months. Adult felons committed to prison for these offenses serve much longer sentences. The average time served for murder in the first degree in California is ten years, and for armed robbery it is forty-two months.

Most juveniles sentenced to institutions are male, members of economically disadvantaged families, products of broken homes, and functioning two years behind their peers in school. Previously they have failed to respond to less severe sanctions such as probation. The California Youth Authority received 3,824 wards from juvenile and criminal courts for incarceration in 1976. A profile of this group by sex, age, race, and offense is shown in Table 15–3.

A state-level agency is responsible for the operation of juvenile institutions in all the states. A majority of the states administer the parole or aftercare services which are required for approximately 60 to 70 percent of released wards. Ideally, the institutions and aftercare programs should be operated by the same agency in order to assure a continuity of services. It is common for the agency responsible for training schools to oversee other state services such as mental health, welfare, and adult corrections. The consolidation of services into superagencies appears to be increasing.

The agency is concerned with responsible programming and supervision of the youth in trouble from the moment of arrival at the reception center until his or her release from parole supervision. This requires a number of special-purpose institutions such as reception and diagnostic clinics, facilities permitting varying degrees of custody control, forestry camps, and other institutions offering special kinds of rehabilitation programs. However, a very large number of states have less than five institutions and it is not uncommon to find only a single facility for juveniles. The state agency administering juvenile facilities can hardly offer a variety of services unless there are special-purpose confinement centers. It would be good to establish

TABLE 15-3 Profile of Juvenile Offenders

SEX	
Male	95.7%
Female	4.3%
AGE	
15 years or less	4.8%
16 years	10.4%
17 years	17.2%
18 years	20.8%
19 years	19.6%
20 years	15.6%
21 years or more	11.6%
RACE	
White	36.1%
Black	36.3%
Spanish surname	25.4%
Other	2.2%
OFFENSE PATTERN	
Homicide	9.1%
Assault	14.5%
Robbery	28.3%
Burglary	20.7%
Theft (except auto)	6.8%
Auto theft	5.1%
Other offenses	15.5%

Source: *Characteristics of California Youth Authority Wards* (Sacramento: State of California, Department of the Youth Authority, 1976), pp. 1 and 18.

some continuity with all the agencies involved in the administration of juvenile justice to offset the isolation which has always characterized juvenile corrections. Recently, the wife of a murder victim filed claims totaling $2 million against four juvenile corrections agencies. The claims allege that the fourteen-year-old murderer had a history of violent crime, as shown by eight previous convictions. He was a ward of the juvenile court and supposedly was confined at a private facility for delinquents on the night of the crime. Thus two county agencies, a state agency, and a private institution have been accused of negligence. The widow's lawyer claims the agencies were mollycoddling the youth because he was neither rehabilitated nor securely confined on the night of the murder. The fourteen-year-old has since been sentenced to the California Youth Authority for second-degree murder.[10] The murder victim was killed as he attempted to enter his automobile after completing his shift at a restaurant in an uptown hotel. The widow and her invalid son, who is one year younger than the murderer, continue to seek justice and accountability from our juvenile corrections system.

The statewide agency responsible for the operation of institutions establishes specific procedures for accepting and processing youth received from the courts. The procedures manual emphasizes custody and service delivery although it is likely that the agency will be more successful in confining the individual than in changing his or her behavior. It is inexcusable to fail on both counts, as in the previous example. Unfortunately, confinement in itself does not protect us from the juvenile after his or her release. Effective services, rather than excessive leisure time, are needed in the institution.

The training schools suffer from a lack of program funds. There are additional handicaps: the institution is often located in a rural area; trained staff will not locate there because of isolation from professional colleagues; line staff are recruited locally and their commitment to juvenile matters is slender while their suspicion of the professional staff is strong; and the juveniles confined are usually from urban areas. There are various signposts which help us identify the well-administered correctional institution. Milton Luger (former Assistant Administrator, Office of Juvenile Justice and Delinquency Prevention, U.S. Department of Justice) provided a group of juvenile-court judges with some guidelines on what to observe when visiting a correctional institution. He asked the following questions.

1. Is the place spotless? If so, it is suspect because all the emphasis is on orderliness.

2. Are we allowed to converse with the juveniles? If we are permitted to speak with only designated wards it is likely that we are communicating with the brainwashed manipulators.

3. What is the demeanor of the youngsters and older youth? They will be spontaneous and exuberant in a well-operated facility.

4. What is the superintendent's response to the juveniles as he or she walks around the grounds of the institution? He or she should know the names of the youngsters and staff and the duties of each worker.

5. Have we observed the bulletin boards throughout the institution? They should include photographs of the juveniles and items of interest outlining various recreational and educational activities. We should find more than copies of the rules and regulations.

6. Have we observed the activities in the cafeteria? Watch the meal being served to you and the wards. Was the food good or bad? If it is bad then you will usually find that youngsters, staff, and visitors have separate dining rooms. Do the wards serve other wards in the cafeteria line? If so, the juveniles serving the food are likely to be the ones who control the institution.

7. Have we asked individual staff members about other personnel in the institution? We should be able to determine whether there is support or rivalry among the staff.

8. Have we asked to review a sample treatment folder for one of the wards? A file which is too meticulous suggests that the facility is preparing the report merely for the purpose of having some paperwork for each juvenile. A file which is cluttered indicates the social-services department deposits everything in it; there is probably no purpose for doing that.

9. Have we attended a group-counseling session? The group counselor should deal with the child's present life and minimize past events.

The success or failure of a juvenile institution is determined by its administrator. Hopefully, the superintendent will emulate the philosophy of the statewide agency. Not that he or she always does. No matter how many facilities are found in a state system, each operates as a separate kingdom under the direction of its superintendent.

PAROLE

Parole is release to the community under supervision. Release from confinement depends on the determination of the agency that the youngster is ready to reenter the free community. Personnel are assigned to help the youth during his or her transition from confinement to freedom. Parole is known as aftercare in some states.

Parole is the most frequent form of release from a training school. The first few months are the most difficult for the new parolee. Release is often based upon good behavior while in the institution. For this reason, the juvenile often needs assistance when he or she is returned to a less structured environment where peer pressures sometimes urge one to return to crime. The parole officer functions as a resource person mediating between the community, the ward, and his or her family. Youngsters experience many difficulties on parole: family problems, school difficulties, problems in the area of work, distrust of social agencies, and pressures associated with the use of alcohol and drugs. Aftercare is more than supervision and control—it is a source of help in the search for community acceptance. Concern for the youngster is the most important consideration. Therefore, the parole agent should devote most of his or her time to actually helping parolees and not to paperwork.

JUSTICE FOR YOUTH

Effective control of juvenile delinquency requires the cooperation of all criminal-justice agencies. They must respond to the priorities of the community they serve. This is best accomplished when each state and local government evaluates its own criminal-justice activities. The passage of the Juvenile Justice and Delinquency Prevention Act of 1974 established the Office of Juvenile Justice and Delinquency Prevention within the Law Enforcement Assistance Administration of the U.S. Department of Justice. The first comprehensive plan for federal juvenile-delinquency programs was completed in early 1976. A number of important goals were formulated: (1) to remove status offenders from detention and correctional facilities no later than 1980; (2) to divert appropriate juveniles from involvement with the juvenile-justice system through maximum use of realistic community-based alternatives; (3) to reduce serious juvenile crime in the schools by establishing a Safe Schools Center within LEAA to provide technical assistance in preventing or reducing delinquency, vandalism, and violence in schools; (4) to reduce serious crime through programs for institutionalized violent offenders; and (5) to prevent delinquency by ensuring the maximum positive development of youth and by altering the environment in ways that lessen the opportunity to commit crimes. Congress has extended the act through 1980 and has appropriated more than $525 million to meet these goals.

The Juvenile Justice and Delinquency Prevention Task Force of the National Advisory Committee on Criminal Justice Standards and Goals has called for a new definition of status offenses—behavior that is legal for adults but unlawful for minors—and recommends that a special court be established to deal with such offenses. The committee limits status offenses to repeated disregard for parental authority, running away from home, use of intoxicating beverages, delinquent acts committed by juveniles under age ten, and truancy. Delinquent acts are those that are violations of criminal law or local ordinance if committed by an adult. A new jurisdiction called "families with service needs" should be established. This could be handled within the family court, which would then have authority over children, parents, guardians, and public institutions such as the school. A school, for example, could be ordered to provide remedial reading for a child.

A representative of the Sacramento County Sheriff's Department visiting a local school in order to familiarize youngsters with the noncoercive role of law enforcement in delinquency prevention. (Photo courtesy of Sheriff Duane Lowe, Sacramento County Sheriff's Department.)

Besides families with service needs, the family-court jurisdiction would include juvenile delinquency, domestic relations, adoptions, civil commitments, neglected or abused children, concurrent jurisdiction over intrafamily crimes, contributing to the delinquency of a juvenile, and criminal nonsupport. Age limits for the court's jurisdiction would be a minimum of ten and a maximum of eighteen. The family court could waive jurisdiction over youths age sixteen or older and transfer them to adult courts in certain circumstances. The implementation of the family-court concept is a leading priority of the Juvenile Justice and Delinquency Prevention Task Force. Family courts should try to develop individual responsibility for lawful behavior, deter bad conduct, maintain the integrity of the law, and contribute to the socialization of the juvenile. Court proceedings should be open to the public when requested by the youngster. Juveniles should be accorded all the rights of a criminal defendant except for bail, grand-jury indictment, and trial by jury. Disposition of cases for those found to be delinquent should be classified as: (1) nominal (reprimand and unconditional release); (2) conditional (conditions imposed by the court but none involving removal of the child from the home); and (3) custodial (removal of the juvenile from his or her home). The task force recommends that state legislatures categorize

400

The lead agency for the International Year of the Child is the United Nations Children's Fund (UNICEF), which has launched programs to help governments improve health, sanitation, and social services in their large cities. For children like these, many governments are planning large-scale programs during the International Year of the Child. (Source: United Nations Children's Fund. Photo by Jean Speiser. Courtesy UNICEF, United Nations.)

delinquent conduct into classes reflecting the substantial differences in the seriousness of offenses. States should develop a state-administered network of community supervision to monitor the behavior of juveniles and to provide other services such as employment counseling. The task force states that juvenile proceedings are no longer nonadversary and the state must therefore receive effective representation. Therefore, family-court prosecutors would comprise a special division in the local office of the prosecutor where special staffing and training would prepare lawyers for the unique problems facing them. Separate counsel should be provided for the child and the parent. This should be provided at government expense if either the youngster or the parent cannot afford a lawyer.

The task force includes recommendations for local governments and police departments. Local governments should develop offices of delinquency prevention to coordinate local prevention efforts. These offices should develop delinquency-prevention programs such as comprehensive public-health services and crisis centers for families with potentially endangered children. These centers would provide family counseling, daycare for working parents, educational services, and recreational activities. Police departments are asked to do more preventive patrolling, and larger departments should set up juvenile investigation units and require at least forty hours of training in juvenile matters for all police recruits.[11]

A number of state legislatures are calling for the passage of a bill of rights for children. The United Nations has designated 1979 as the International Year of the Child in honor of the twentieth anniversary of the publication of its "Declaration of the Rights of the Child." Every year should be the year of the child in the sense that children are our chief investment in the future. Recently, the United States has been made aware of the tragic problems of child abuse, the use of children as transporters of illicit drugs, the exploitation of youngsters in pornography, and unfair child-labor practices. We require greater commitment to juvenile justice from local government and the public. This commitment was found in Janusz Korczak, the greatest champion of the rights of children. He will be honored posthumously during the international year. Janusz Korczak gave up a medical practice to devote himself to the care of children in need. Dr. Korczak was director of an orphanage in Warsaw, Poland, for thirty years before his untimely death. This humble physician became a hero because he chose to die in a Nazi concentration-camp gas chamber with the 200 Jewish children from his orphanage. Two months before he died, Korczak wrote: "I exist not to be loved and admired but to act and love. It is not the duty of those around me to help me, but I am duty bound to look after the world, after man."[12] Such commitment would assure greater justice for youth today.

STUDY QUESTIONS

1. What is delinquency? Who is the juvenile delinquent?

2. Youngsters between the ages of ten and seventeen comprise what percentage of the population in the United States? In your county?

3. Differentiate status offenses from criminal behavior.

4. Does the juvenile law in your state include a lower age limit? Upper age limit? Are there provisions for concurrent or overlapping jurisdiction over juveniles by the criminal court and the juvenile or family court?

5. What is the primary function of the juvenile court?

6. What is the purpose of the detention hearing? Adjudicatory hearing? Disposition hearing?

7. Why is the social history an important resource for the juvenile- or family-court judge?

8. What is a proper disposition in a juvenile case?

9. Identify the typical ward in a juvenile correctional institution.

10. What is parole or aftercare? Probation?

11. What should you observe when touring a correctional institution for juveniles?

12. Has your state achieved one or more of the goals formulated in the first comprehensive plan for federal juvenile-delinquency programs? If so, identify the programs.

13. What is the purpose of the Safe Schools Center?

14. Who was Janusz Korczak? Why will he be honored during the International Year of the Child?

NOTES

1. Federal Bureau of Investigation, U.S. Department of Justice, *Uniform Crime Reports for the United States, 1976* (Washington, D.C.: U.S. Government Printing Office, 1977), p. 183.
2. Ibid.
3. Monrad G. Paulsen and Charles H. Whitebread, *Juvenile Law and Procedure* (Reno: National Council of Juvenile Court Judges, 1974), p. 33.
4. U.S. Department of Justice, Law Enforcement Assistance Administration, *Jurisdiction—Delinquency, A Comparative Analysis of Standards and State Practices,* vol. 4 (Washington, D.C.: Government Printing Office, 1977), p. 21.
5. Ibid.
6. Mark M. Levin and Rosemary Sarri, *Juvenile Delinquency: A Comparative Analysis of Legal Codes in the United States* (Ann Arbor, Mich.: University of Michigan Press, 1974), p. 21.
7. *San Francisco Chronicle,* 13 January 1977, p. 27.
8. U.S. Department of Justice, Law Enforcement Assistance Administration, *Children in Custody: Advance Report on the Juvenile Detention and Correctional Facility Census of 1975* (Washington, D.C.: U.S. Government Printing Office, 1977), pp. 1, 2, and 17.
9. Rosemary C. Sarri, *Under Lock and Key: Juveniles in Jails and Detention* (Ann Arbor, Mich.: University of Michigan Press, 1974), p. 4.
10. *San Francisco Chronicle,* 8 July 1977, p. 17.
11. National Advisory Committee on Criminal Justice Standards and Goals, *Task Force on Juvenile Justice and Delinquency Prevention* (Washington, D.C.: Government Printing Office, 1977).
12. *International Herald Tribune,* 10 June 1977, p. 5.

ILLUSTRATIVE CAREERS IN YOUTH SERVICES

THE YOUTH SERVICES DIVISION

The Youth Services Division is an autonomous unit in the Georgia Department of Human Resources, responsible for the protection, care, and training of youthful offenders. A variety of facilities are operated by the division. Such facilities range from the institutional facilities of the Youth Development Centers to community-based facilities and other community-centered treatment programs. The youth development centers are oriented toward providing care in a stable, controlled environment that is free from external community pressures. Youth development workers provide counseling and therapy. Programs vary, but almost all are involved in remedial education, individual guidance and counseling, indoor and outdoor recreation, and arts and crafts. These therapy programs are designed to modify the behavior patterns of those who are judged to be offenders. Court service workers also provide vital assistance to the juvenile correction system. Court service as a statewide program was established in 1963 to develop and maintain a working relationship with the juvenile courts and the communities in which the children reside. This unit provides intake, probation supervision, detention planning, and aftercare supervision for YDC releases. The court service worker is the key to the preparation of treatment programs. Court service workers prepare intake reports on juveniles which contain social histories of the individual and diagnostic assessments. The court service worker has a vital role in assisting the juvenile judge by deciding upon detailed methods, techniques, and resources to be used in the rehabilitation process, and the court service worker is responsible for carrying out the orders of the court. Court service workers generally supervise around 109 children per year.

Entry Requirements

Youth development workers must possess a high-school diploma or an equivalency certificate. They must be at least seventeen years old. There is no written examination, so individuals possessing a high-school education are automatically qualified for appointment. Court service workers must have a bachelors degree from an accredited university in order to qualify for the entrance examination that is given to all applicants. After the examination, those with qualifying scores are screened in an oral interview.

Career Development

There is a career ladder of increasing job responsibility for both court service workers and youth development workers. At the entry-level position, youth development worker, people ordinarily begin at the level of YDW I which carries an entry-level salary of $6,234. After a year of satisfactory service and with the recommendation of their superiors, youth development workers progress to the level of YDW II, with a salary of $7,782 per year. There is a similar career path for personnel in the position of court service worker. Entry-level personnel begin working as CSW I's at $9,102 annually. Court service workers are eligible for promotion to the designation of CSW II, which carries an annual salary of $11,676. There is a potential for promotion from the position of youth development worker to court service worker, provided that the individual obtains a bachelor's degree.

Glossary*

Abscond (corrections) *v* To depart from a geographical area or jurisdiction prescribed by the conditions of one's probation or parole, without authorization.

Abscond (court) *v* To intentionally absent or conceal oneself unlawfully in order to avoid a legal process.

Acquittal *n* A judgment of a court, based either on the verdict of a jury or a judicial officer, that the defendant is not guilty of the offense(s) for which he has been tried.

Adjudicated *adj* Having been the subject of completed criminal or juvenile proceedings, and convicted, or adjudicated a delinquent, status offender, or dependent.

Adjudication (criminal) *n* The judicial decision terminating a criminal proceeding by a judgment of conviction or acquittal, or a dismissal of the case.

Adjudication (juvenile) *n* The juvenile-court decision terminating an adjudicatory hearing, that the juvenile is either a delinquent, status offender, or dependent, or that the allegations in the petition are not sustained.

Adjudicatory hearing *n* In juvenile proceedings, the fact-finding process wherein the juvenile court determines whether or not there is sufficient evidence to sustain the allegations in a petition.

Adult *n* A person who is within the original jurisdiction of a criminal, rather than a juvenile, court because his age at the time of an alleged criminal act was above a statutorily specified limit.

Alias *n* Any name used for an official purpose that is different from a person's legal name.

*This material has been selected especially for use in this text from SEARCH Group, Inc. *Dictionary of Criminal Justice Data Terminology* (Washington, D.C.: U.S. Government Printing Office, 1976).

Appeal *n* A request by either the defense or the prosecution that a case be removed from a lower court to a higher court in order for a completed trial to be reviewed by the higher court.

Appearance *n* The act of coming into a court and submitting to the authority of that court.

Appearance, first *syn* **initial appearance** *n* The first appearance of a juvenile or adult in the court which has jurisdiction over his case.

Appellant *n* A person who initiates an appeal.

Arraignment *n* The appearance of a person before a court in order that the court may inform him of the accusation(s) against him and enter his plea.

Arrest *n* Taking a person into custody by authority of law, for the purpose of charging him with a criminal offense or for the purpose of initiating juvenile proceedings, terminating with the recording of a specific offense.

Arson *n* The intentional destruction or attempted destruction, by fire or explosive, of the property of another, or of one's own property with the intent to defraud.

Assault *n* Unlawful intentional inflicting, or attempted or threatened inflicting, of injury upon another.

Assault, aggravated *n* Unlawful intentional causing of serious bodily injury with or without a deadly weapon or unlawful intentional attempting or threatening of serious bodily injury or death with a deadly weapon.

Assigned counsel *n* An attorney, not regularly employed by a government agency, assigned by the court to represent a particular person(s) in a particular criminal proceeding.

Attorney *syn* **lawyer** *syn* **counsel** *n* A person trained in the law, admitted to practice before the bar of a given jurisdiction, and authorized to advise, represent, and act for other persons in legal proceedings.

Backlog *n* The number of pending cases which exceed the capacity of the court, in that they cannot be acted upon because the court is occupied in acting upon other cases.

Bombing incident *n* The detonation or attempted detonation of an explosive or incendiary device with willful disregard of risk to the person or property of another, or for a criminal purpose.

Booking *n* A police administrative action officially recording an arrest and identifying the person, the place, the time, the arresting authority, and the reason for the arrest.

407

Burglary *n* Unlawful entry of a structure, with or without force, with intent to commit a felony, or larceny.

Camp/ranch/farm *n* Any of several types of similar confinement facilities, usually in a rural location, which contain adults or juveniles committed after adjudication.

Case *n* At the level of police or prosecutorial investigation, a set of circumstances under investigation involving one or more persons; at subsequent steps in criminal proceedings, a charging document alleging the commission of one or more crimes, or a single defendant; in juvenile or correctional proceedings, a person who is the object of agency action.

Case (court) *n* A single charging document under the jurisdiction of a court; or a single defendant.

Caseload (corrections) *n* The total number of clients registered with a correctional agency or agent during a specified time period, often divided into active and inactive, or supervised and unsupervised, thus distinguishing between clients with whom the agency or agent maintains contact and those with whom it does not.

Caseload (court) *n* The total number of cases filed in a given court or before a given judicial officer during a given period of time.

Caseload, pending *n* The number of cases at any given time which have been filed in a given court, or are before a given judicial officer, but have not reached disposition.

CCH *n* An abbreviation for "computerized criminal history."

Charge *n* A formal allegation that a specific person(s) has committed a specific offense(s).

Charging document *n* A formal written accusation, filed in a court, alleging that a specified person(s) has committed a specific offense(s).

Check fraud *n* The issuance or passing of a check, draft, or money order that is legal as a formal document, signed by the legal account holder but with the foreknowledge that the bank or depository will refuse to honor it because of insufficient funds or closed account.

Chief of police *n* A local law-enforcement officer who is the appointed or elected head of a police department.

Child abuse *n* A willful action or actions by a person causing physical harm to a child.

Child neglect *n* Willful failure by the person(s) responsible for a child's well-being to provide for adequate food, clothing, shelter, education, and supervision.

Citation (appear) *n* A written order issued by a law-enforcement officer directing an alleged offender to appear in a specific court at a specified time in order to answer a criminal charge.

Commitment *n* The action of a judicial officer ordering that an adjudicated and sentenced adult, or adjudicated delinquent or status offender who has been the subject of a juvenile-court disposition hearing, be admitted into a correctional facility.

Community facility *syn* **nonconfinement facility, adult or juvenile** *n* A correctional facility from which residents are regularly permitted to depart, unaccompanied by any official, for the purpose of daily use of community resources such as schools or treatment programs, and seeking or holding employment.

Complaint *n* A formal written accusation made by any person, often a prosecutor, and filed in a court, alleging that a specified person(s) has committed a specific offense(s).

Complaint denied *n* The decision by a prosecutor to decline a request that he seek an indictment or file an information or complaint against a specified person(s) for a specific offense(s).

Complaint granted *n* The decision by a prosecutor to grant a request that he seek an indictment or file an information or complaint against a specified person(s) for a specific offense(s).

Complaint requested (police) *n* A request by a law-enforcement agency that the prosecutor seek an indictment or file a complaint or information against a specified person(s) for a specific offense(s).

Confinement facility *n* A correctional facility from which the inmates are not regularly permitted to depart each day unaccompanied.

Convict *n* An adult who has been found guilty of a felony and who is confined in a federal or state confinement facility.

Conviction *n* A judgment of a court, based either on the verdict of a jury or a judicial officer or on the guilty plea of the defendant, that the defendant is guilty of the offense(s) for which he has been tried.

Correctional agency *n* A federal, state, or local criminal-justice agency, under a single administrative authority, of which the principal functions are the investigation, intake screening, supervision, custody, confinement, or treatment of alleged or adjudicated adult offenders, delinquents, or status offenders.

Correctional day program *n* A publicly financed and operated nonresidential educational or treatment program for persons required, by a judicial officer, to participate.

Correctional facility *n* A building or part thereof, set of buildings, or area enclosing a set of buildings or structures, operated by a government agency for the custody and/or treatment of adjudicated, and committed persons, or persons subject to criminal or juvenile-justice proceedings.

Correctional institution   *n*   A generic name proposed in this terminology for those long-term adult confinement facilities often called "prisons," "federal or state correctional facilities," or "penitentiaries," and juvenile confinement facilities called "training schools," "reformatories," "boy's ranches," and the like.

Correctional institution, adult   *n*   A confinement facility having custodial authority over adults sentenced to confinement for more than a year.

Corrections   *n*   A generic term which includes all government agencies, facilities, programs, procedures, personnel, and techniques, concerned with the investigation, intake, custody, confinement, supervision, or treatment of alleged or adjudicated adult offenders, delinquents, or status offenders.

Count   *n*   Each separate offense, attributed to one or more persons, as listed in a complaint, information, or indictment.

Counterfeiting   *n*   The manufacture or attempted manufacture of a copy or imitation of a negotiable instrument with value set by law or convention, or the possession of such a copy without authorization, with the intent to defraud by claiming the genuineness of the copy.

Court   *n*   An agency of the judicial branch of government, authorized or established by statute or constitution, and consisting of one or more judicial officers, which has the authority to decide upon controversies in law and disputed matters of fact brought before it.

Court of appellate jurisdiction   *n*   A court which does not try criminal cases, but which hears appeals.

Court of general jurisdiction   *n*   Of criminal courts, a court which has jurisdiction to try all criminal offenses, including all felonies, and which may or may not hear appeals.

Court of limited jurisdiction   *n*   Of criminal courts, a court of which the trial jurisdiction either includes no felonies or is limited to less than all felonies, and which may or may not hear appeals.

Credit-card fraud   *n*   The use or attempted use of a credit card in order to obtain goods or services with the intent to avoid payment.

Crime   *syn*   **criminal offense**   *n*   An act committed or omitted in violation of a law forbidding or commanding it for which an adult can be punished, upon conviction, by incarceration and other penalties or a corporation penalized, or for which a juvenile can be brought under the jurisdiction of a juvenile court and adjudicated a delinquent or transferred to adult court.

Crime Index offenses *syn* **index crimes** *n* A UCR classification that includes all Part I offenses with the exception of involuntary (negligent) manslaughter.

Crimes against businesses *syn* **business crimes** *syn* **commercial crimes** *n* A summary term used by the National Crime Panel reports which includes burglary and robbery of businesses, but excludes commercial larceny such as shoplifting and employee theft. One of the National Crime Panel's three major classes of offenses, the others being crimes against persons and crimes against households.

Crimes against households *syn* **household crimes** *n* A summary term used by the National Crime Panel reports including burglary of households, household larceny, and motor-vehicle theft.

Crimes against persons *n* A summary term used by UCR and the National Crime Panel reports, but with different meanings:

UCR

murder
nonnegligent [voluntary] manslaughter
negligent [involuntary] manslaughter
forcible rape
aggravated assault

National Crime Panel

forcible rape
robbery (against persons)
aggravated assault
simple assault
personal larceny

Criminal-history record information *n* Information collected by criminal-justice agencies on individuals, consisting of identifiable descriptions and notations of arrests, detentions, indictments, informations, or other formal criminal charges, and any disposition(s) arising therefrom, sentencing, correctional supervision, and release.

Criminal-justice agency *n* Any court with criminal jurisdiction and any other government agency or subunit, which defends indigents, or of which the principal functions or activities consist of the prevention, detection, and investigation of crime; the apprehension, detention, and prosecution of alleged offenders; the confinement or official correctional supervision of accused or convicted persons, or the administrative or technical support of the above functions.

411

Criminal proceedings *n* Proceedings in a court of law, undertaken to determine the guilt or innocence of an adult accused of a crime.

Culpability *n* A state of mind on the part of one who has committed an act which makes him liable to prosecution for that act.

Defendant *n* A person against whom a criminal proceeding is pending.

Defense attorney *n* An attorney who represents the defendant in a legal proceeding.

Delinquency *n* Juvenile actions or conduct in violation of criminal law, and, in some contexts, status offenses.

Delinquent *n* A juvenile who has been adjudicated by a judicial officer of a juvenile court, as having committed a delinquent act, which is an act for which an adult could be prosecuted in a criminal court.

De novo *adv* Anew, afresh, as if there had been no earlier decision.

Detention hearing *n* In juvenile proceedings, a hearing by a judicial officer of a juvenile court to determine whether a juvenile is to be detained, continue to be detained, or released, while juvenile proceedings are pending in his case.

Diagnosis or classification center *n* A functional unit within a correctional institution, or a separate facility, which holds persons held in custody for the purpose of determining to which correctional facility or program they should be committed.

Dismissal *n* A decision by a judicial officer to terminate a case without a determination of guilt or innocence.

Disposition *n* The action by a criminal or juvenile-justice agency which signifies that a portion of the justice process is complete and jurisdiction is relinquished or transferred to another agency; or which signifies that a decision has been reached on one aspect of a case and a different aspect comes under consideration, requiring a different kind of decision.

Disposition hearing *n* A hearing in juvenile court, conducted after an adjudicatory hearing and subsequent receipt of the report of any predisposition investigation, to determine the most appropriate disposition of a juvenile who has been adjudicated a delinquent, a status offender, or a dependent.

Disposition, juvenile court *n* The decision of a juvenile court, concluding a disposition hearing, that a juvenile be committed to a correctional facility, or placed in a care or treatment program, or required to meet certain standards of conduct, or released.

Diversion *n* The official halting or suspension, at any legally prescribed processing point after a recorded justice-system entry, of formal criminal or juvenile-justice proceedings against an alleged offender, and referral of that person to a treatment or care program administered by a nonjustice agency, or a private agency, or no referral.

Ex-offender *n* An offender who is no longer under the jurisdiction of any criminal-justice agency.

Expunge *v* The sealing or purging of arrest, criminal, or juvenile record information.

Felony *n* A criminal offense punishable by death, or by incarceration in a state or federal confinement facility for a period of which the lower limit is prescribed by statute in a given jurisdiction, typically one year or more.

Filing *n* The commencement of criminal proceedings by entering a charging document into the official record of a court.

Finding *n* The official determination of a judicial officer or administrative body regarding a disputed matter of fact or law.

Fine *n* The penalty imposed upon a convicted person by a court requiring that he pay a specified sum of money.

Fraud *n* An element of certain offenses, consisting of deceit or intentional misrepresentation with the aim of illegally depriving a person of his property or legal rights.

Fugitive *n* A person who has concealed himself or fled a given jurisdiction in order to avoid prosecution or confinement.

Group home *n* A nonconfining residential facility for adjudicated adults or juveniles, or those subject to criminal or juvenile proceedings, intended to reproduce as closely as possible the circumstances of family life, and at minimum providing access to community activities and resources.

Halfway house *n* A nonconfining residential facility for adjudicated adults or juveniles, or those subject to criminal or juvenile proceedings, intended to provide an alternative to confinement for persons not suitable for probation, or needing a period of readjustment to the community after confinement.

Hearing *n* A proceeding in which arguments, witnesses, or evidence are heard by a judicial officer or administrative body.

Hearing, probable cause *n* A proceeding before a judicial officer in which arguments, witnesses, or evidence is presented and in which it is determined whether there is sufficient cause to hold the accused for trial or the case should be dismissed.

Homicide *n* Any killing of one person by another.

Homicide, criminal *n* The causing of the death of another person without justification or excuse.

Indictment *n* A formal written accusation made by a grand jury and filed in a court, alleging that a specified person(s) has committed a specific offense(s).

Information *n* A formal written accusation made by a prosecutor and filed in a court, alleging that a specified person(s) has committed a specific offense(s).

Infraction *n* An offense punishable by fine or other penalty, but not by incarceration.

Inmate *n* A person in custody in a confinement facility.

Institutional capacity *n* The officially stated number of inmates or residents which a correctional facility is designed to house, exclusive of extraordinary arrangements to accommodate overcrowded conditions.

Intake *n* The process during which a juvenile referral is received and a decision is made by an intake unit either to file a petition in juvenile court, to release the juvenile, to place him under supervision, or to refer him elsewhere.

Jail *n* A confinement facility usually administered by a local law-enforcement agency, intended for adults but sometimes also containing juveniles, which holds persons detained pending adjudication and/or persons committed after adjudication for sentences of a year or less.

Jurisdiction *n* The territory, subject matter, or person over which lawful authority may be exercised.

Jury, grand *n* A body of persons who have been selected and sworn to investigate criminal activity and the conduct of public officials and to hear the evidence against an accused person(s) to determine whether there is sufficient evidence to bring that person(s) to trial.

Jury, trial *syn* **jury, petit** *syn* **jury** *n* A statutorily defined number of persons selected according to law and sworn to determine certain matters of fact in a criminal action and to render a verdict of guilty or not guilty.

Law-enforcement agency *n* A federal, state, or local criminal-justice agency of which the principal functions are the prevention, detection, and investigation of crime, and the apprehension of alleged offenders.

Law-enforcement officer *syn* **peace officer** *syn* **policeman** *n* An employee of a law-enforcement agency who is an officer sworn to carry out law-enforcement duties, or a sworn employee of a prosecutorial agency who primarily performs investigative duties.

Model Penal Code *n* A generalized modern codification of that which is considered basic to criminal law, published by the American Law Institute in 1962.

Motion *n* An oral or written request made by a party to an action, before, during, or after a trial, that a court issue a rule or order.

Nolo contendere *n* A defendant's formal answer in court, to the charges in a complaint, information, or indictment, in which he states that he does not contest the charges, and which, while not an admission of guilt, subjects him to the same legal consequences as a plea of guilty.

Offender *syn* **criminal** *n* An adult who has been convicted of a criminal offense.

Parole *n* The status of an offender conditionally released from a confinement facility prior to the expiration of his sentence, and placed under the supervision of a parole agency.

Parole agency *n* A correctional agency, which may or may not include a parole authority, and of which the principal functions are the supervision of adults or juveniles placed on parole.

Parole authority *n* A person or a correctional agency which has the authority to release on parole adults or juveniles committed to confinement facilities, to revoke parole, and to discharge from parole.

Parole violation *n* An act or a failure to act by a parolee which does not conform to the conditions of his parole.

Penalty *n* The punishment annexed by law or judicial decision to the commission of a particular offense, which may be death, imprisonment, fine, or loss of civil privileges.

Plea *n* A defendant's formal answer in court to the charges brought against him in a complaint, information, or indictment.

Plea bargaining *n* The exchange of prosecutorial and/or judicial concessions, commonly a lesser charge, the dismissal of other pending charges, a recommendation by the prosecutor for a reduced sentence, or a combination thereof, in return for a plea of guilty.

Predisposition report *n* The document resulting from an investigation undertaken by a probation agency or other designated authority, which has been requested by a juvenile court, into the past behavior, family background, and personality of a juvenile who has been adjudicated a delinquent, a status offender, or a dependent, in order to assist the court in determining the most appropriate disposition.

Presentence report *n* The document resulting from an investigation undertaken by a probation agency or other designated authority, at the request of a criminal court, into the past behavior, family circumstances, and personality of an adult who has been convicted of a crime, in order to assist the court in determining the most appropriate sentence.

Probable cause *n* A set of facts and circumstances which would induce a reasonably intelligent and prudent person to believe that an accused person had committed a specific crime.

Probation *n* The conditional freedom granted by a judicial officer to an alleged offender, or adjudicated adult or juvenile, as long as the person meets certain conditions of behavior.

Probationer *n* A person required by a court or probation agency to meet certain conditions of behavior, who may or may not be placed under the supervision of a probation agency.

Pro se *syn* ***in propria persona*** *adv* Acting as one's own defense attorney in criminal proceedings; representing oneself.

Prosecutor *n* An attorney employed by a government agency or subunit whose official duty is to initiate and maintain criminal proceedings on behalf of the government against persons accused of committing criminal offenses.

Public defender *n* An attorney employed by a government agency or subdivision, whose official duty is to represent defendants unable to hire private counsel.

Purge (record) *v* The complete removal of arrest, criminal, or juvenile record information from a given records system.

Referral to intake *n* In juvenile proceedings, a request by the police, parents, or other agency or person, that a juvenile intake unit take appropriate action concerning a juvenile alleged to have committed a delinquent act or status offense, or to be dependent.

Release from detention   *n*   The authorized exit from detention of a person subject to criminal or juvenile-justice proceedings.

Release from prison   *n*   A cover term for all lawful exits from federal or state confinement facilities primarily intended for adults serving sentences of more than a year, including all conditional and unconditional releases, deaths, and transfers to other jurisdictions, excluding escapes.

Release on bail   *n*   The release by a judicial officer of an accused person who has been taken into custody, upon his promise to pay a certain sum of money or property if he fails to appear in court as required, which promise may or may not be secured by the deposit of an actual sum of money or property.

Release on own recognizance   *n*   The release by a judicial officer of an accused person who has been taken into custody, upon his promise to appear in court as required for criminal proceedings.

Release, pretrial   *n*   A procedure whereby an accused person who has been taken into custody is allowed to be free before and during his trial.

Release to third party   *n*   The release by a judicial officer of an accused person who has been taken into custody, to a third party who promises to return the accused to court for criminal proceedings.

Residential treatment center   *n*   A government facility which serves juveniles whose behavior does not necessitate the strict confinement of a training school, often allowing them greater contact with the community.

Retained counsel   *n*   An attorney, not employed or compensated by a government agency or subunit, nor assigned by the court, who is privately hired to represent a person(s) in a criminal proceeding.

Revocation   *n*   An administrative act performed by a parole authority removing a person from parole, or a judicial order by a court removing a person from parole or probation, in response to a violation on the part of the parolee or probationer.

Rights of defendant   *n*   Those powers and privileges which are constitutionally guaranteed to every defendant.

Seal (record)   *v*   The removal, for the benefit of the subject, of arrest, criminal, or juvenile record information from routinely available status to a status requiring special procedures for access.

Security   *n*   The degree of restriction of inmate movement within a correctional facility, usually divided into maximum, medium, and minimum levels.

Sentence *n* The penalty imposed by a court upon a convicted person, or the court decision to suspend imposition or execution of the penalty.

Sentence, indeterminate *n* A statutory provision for a type of sentence to imprisonment where, after the court has determined that the convicted person shall be imprisoned, the exact length of imprisonment and parole supervision is afterward fixed within statutory limits by a parole authority.

Sentence, mandatory *n* A statutory requirement that a certain penalty shall be imposed and executed upon certain convicted offenders.

Sentence, suspended *n* The court decision postponing the pronouncing of sentence upon a convicted person, or postponing the execution of a sentence that has been pronounced by the court.

Sentence—suspended execution *n* The court decision setting a penalty but postponing its execution.

Sentence—suspended imposition *n* The court decision postponing the setting of a penalty.

Shelter *n* A confinement or community facility for the care of juveniles, usually those held pending adjudication.

Sheriff *n* The elected or appointed chief officer of a county law-enforcement agency, usually responsible for law enforcement in unincorporated areas, and for the operation of the county jail.

Sheriff, deputy *n* A law-enforcement officer employed by a county sheriff's department.

Sheriff's department *n* A law-enforcement agency organized at the county level, directed by a sheriff, which exercises its law-enforcement functions at the county level, usually within unincorporated areas, and operates the county jail in most jurisdictions.

Speedy trial *n* The right of the defendant to have a prompt trial.

State highway patrol *n* A state law-enforcement agency of which the principal functions consist of prevention, detection, and investigation of motor vehicle offenses, and the apprehension of traffic offenders.

State police *n* A state law-enforcement agency whose principal functions may include maintaining statewide police communications, aiding local police in criminal investigation, police training, guarding state property, and highway patrol.

Status offender *n* A juvenile who has been adjudicated by a judicial officer of a juvenile court, as having committed a status offense, which is an act or conduct which is an offense only when committed or engaged in by a juvenile.

Subpoena *n* A written order issued by a judicial officer requiring a specified person to appear in a designated court at a specified time in order to serve as a witness in a case under the jurisdiction of that court, or to bring material to that court.

Summons *n* A written order issued by a judicial officer requiring a person accused of a criminal offense to appear in a designated court at a specified time to answer the charge(s).

Suspect *n* A person, adult or juvenile, considered by a criminal-justice agency to be one who may have committed a specific criminal offense, but who has not been arrested or charged.

Suspicion *n* Belief that a person has committed a criminal offense, based on facts and circumstances that are not sufficient to constitute probable cause.

Time served *n* The total time spent in confinement by a convicted adult before and after sentencing, or only the time spent in confinement after a sentence of commitment to a confinement facility.

Training school *n* A correctional institution for juveniles adjudicated to be delinquents or status offenders and committed to confinement by a judicial officer.

Transfer hearing *n* A preadjudicatory hearing in juvenile court for the purpose of determining whether juvenile court jurisdiction should be retained or waived over a juvenile alleged to have committed a delinquent act(s), and whether he should be transferred to criminal court for prosecution as an adult.

Trial *n* The examination of issues of fact and law in a case or controversy, beginning when the jury has been selected in a jury trial, or when the first witness is sworn, or the first evidence is introduced in a court trial, and concluding when a verdict is reached or the case is dismissed.

Venue *n* The geographical area from which the jury is drawn and in which trial is held in a criminal action.

Verdict *n* In criminal proceedings, the decision made by a jury in a jury trial, or by a judicial officer in a court trial, that a defendant is either guilty or not guilty of the offense(s) for which he has been tried.

Victim *n* A person who has suffered death, physical or mental suffering, or loss of property, as the result of an actual or attempted criminal offense committed by another person.

Warrant, arrest *n* A document issued by a judicial officer which directs a law-enforcement officer to arrest a person who has been accused of an offense.

Warrant, bench   *n*   A document issued by a judicial officer directing that a person who has failed to obey an order or notice to appear be brought before the court.

Warrant, search   *n*   A document issued by a judicial officer which directs a law-enforcement officer to conduct a search for specified property or persons at a specific location, to seize the property or persons, if found, and to account for the results of the search to the issuing judicial officer.

Witness   *n*   A person who directly perceives an event or thing, or who has expert knowledge relevant to a case.

Youthful offender   *n*   A person, adjudicated in criminal court, who may be above the statutory age limit for juveniles but is below a specified upper age limit, for whom special correctional commitments and special record-sealing procedures are made available by statute.

appendix
Abstracts of
Leading Cases

The cases which follow consist of major Fourth, Fifth, and Sixth Amendment decisions of the United States Supreme Court from the last fifteen years in the area of criminal procedure, applied to the states through the due-process clause of the Fourteenth Amendment. Some cases involve the protection of rights secured by only one amendment to the United States Constitution, while others involve the protections of several. For clarity and ease of organizing this section, each case is placed under the single amendment which is most central to it. It should be noted that this list of cases is illustrative rather than exhaustive.

FOURTH AMENDMENT CASES

Application of the Fourth Amendment to the States
Mapp v. Ohio 367 U.S. 643 (1961)

The Bill of Rights, the first ten amendments to the United States Constitution, limits the power of the federal government from interfering unreasonably in the affairs of its citizens. The Fourth Amendment protects citizens from unreasonable searches and seizures. It requires that, in the usual case, the police obtain a warrant from an impartial magistrate before they (1) search a place or person or (2) seize a person or property.

Prior to *Mapp,* it was thought that these constitutional guarantees applied only to the federal government and not to the states. But by a 6–3 vote, a majority of the Supreme Court decided in *Mapp* that not only does the Fourth Amendment prohibition against unreasonable searches and seizures apply to the federal government, it also applies to the states, through the due-process clause of the Fourteenth

Amendment. The result was that state courts, as well as federal courts, must refuse to admit evidence which was seized illegally.

To illustrate the point, we can review the facts of *Mapp*. Three Cleveland, Ohio, policemen arrived at Mrs. Mapp's house and demanded entrance because they suspected that a bomber was hiding there. Mrs. Mapp called her attorney and on his advice, refused to admit the officers, asking instead that they display a warrant. The policemen then undertook surveillance of the house. Three hours later, after being joined by four or more officers, the police again sought entrance. One door was forcibly opened. Mrs. Mapp again demanded a warrant. A piece of paper was held up and Mrs. Mapp placed it in her bosom. In the ensuing struggle, Mrs. Mapp was handcuffed for being "belligerent" and the paper retrieved from her bosom. Then the Cleveland police thoroughly searched her entire house. No suspect was found, but because the police found certain lewd and lascivious books, pictures, and photographs during their search, Mrs. Mapp was prosecuted under Ohio law, which at the time made it a crime to possess such material. At her trial, no search warrant was produced and no explanation was given by the police of why no warrant was obtained before the search of Mrs. Mapp's house.

Under the Fourth Amendment's "exclusionary rule," all evidence seized during an illegal search and all the fruits of that search are inadmissible against the accused. The Supreme Court reversed Mrs. Mapp's conviction because, although she was technically guilty of possession of obscene material, the police had gathered their evidence illegally, by failing to get a search warrant. The rule of law after *Mapp* thus became: all evidence obtained by searches and seizures, which violates the federal constitution, is inadmissible in a criminal trial in a state court under the mandate of the Fourth Amendment as applied to the states through the Fourteenth Amendment.

Probable Cause
Aguilar v. *Texas* 378 U.S. 108 (1964)

Ideally, when a police officer goes to an impartial judge or magistrate to get a warrant to search or seize a person or property, the officer gives the judge good reasons for believing that a crime is being, or has been, committed. An impartial judge will refuse to sign and issue a warrant if a policeman is too vague or if the evidence is too old. The issue in *Aguilar* was how specific a policeman must be in describing the underlying circumstances to the judge in order for a warrant to be issued.

In *Aguilar,* two Houston, Texas, policemen applied to a local justice of the peace for a warrant to search for narcotics in Mr. Aguilar's home. The justice of the peace issued a warrant solely on the following police affidavit:

> Affiants have reliable information from a credible person and do believe that heroin, marijuana, barbiturates, and narcotics are being kept at the above described premises for the purpose of sale and use, contrary to the provisions of the law.

With the warrant, the police searched Aguilar's home, seized the narcotics, and placed Aguilar under arrest. At trial, Aguilar objected to the introduction of the narcotics as evidence, because he said the drugs were obtained in violation of his Fourth Amendment right to be free of unreasonble searches and seizures, in that the affidavit used by the police to obtain the warrant was too vague, allowed the police too much discretion, and hence was unreasonable.

The Supreme Court agreed in a 6–3 opinion, holding that when the police apply for a warrant on the "tip" of an informer (because they think a crime is being or has been committed) the police must show to the judge facts which reveal why they believe the informer and how the informer got his information. It is not necessary, however, that the informer be identified. By so doing, the police show "probable cause" for a crime having been committed, the judge can reliably issue a warrant, and the suspect can be seized and searched reasonably. One final note: the police may have a warrant issued on the basis of their own personal observations if they are specific in their affidavit for a warrant. But when using informers, the affidavit for a warrant must state how the informer got his information and why the police believe him.

Searches Without Warrants
United States v. *Robinson* 414 U.S. 218
(1973)

Mr. Robinson was convicted in a federal court in Washington, D.C., of possession of heroin. He was arrested on the basis of the following facts: a policeman spotted Robinson driving a car. As a result of a check of Robinson's license four days earlier, the officer believed Robinson was driving without a permit. Robinson was placed under arrest for "operating after revocation and obtaining a permit by misrepresentation." The officer, after the arrest, began to search Robinson, according to police department procedures. During this patdown, the policeman felt an object in Robinson's left breast pocket. It was retrieved and turned out to be heroin, and became the basis of Robinson's subsequent conviction.

At trial, Robinson objected to the introduction of the heroin evidence because he said it was obtained in violation of his Fourth Amendment right to be free of unreasonable searches and seizures. In a 6–3 decision, the Supreme Court disagreed, saying that there is nothing unreasonable about a "patdown" search after a valid arrest. Although under the Fourth Amendment, normally a warrant is required to search a person said the court, nevertheless there is an exception to this rule: when lawfully arrested, the police may search the person of the arrestee without a warrant and may search the area within the control of the arrestee without a warrant. Such searches are reasonable, under the Fourth Amendment, even without a warrant, said the court, to protect police officers from harm by allowing them to search for weapons, and by allowing them to search for fruits of a crime in the arrestee's possession.

South Dakota v. Opperman 428 U.S. 364 (1976)

Opperman's car was parked illegally in a restricted zone. An overtime parking ticket was issued. Hours later, with the car still unmoved, another ticket was issued. Still later, the car was towed to police headquarters. Because the police had had trouble with people getting into the impound lot, breaking into impounded cars, and stealing contents therein, the police regularly made an inventory search of all impounded autos. They would open the car, count and label all items, and then store them inside the police station for safekeeping. During the inventory search of Opperman's car, marijuana was found in the glove box. When Opperman came to retrieve his car, he was arrested for possession of marijuana. At his trial, he said that the search of his car was unreasonable and in violation of his Fourth Amendment right to be free of unreasonable searches and seizures. In a 5–4 decision, the Supreme Court upheld Opperman's conviction, saying that inventory searches of impounded autos are reasonable even without a warrant. The court said that the expectation of privacy in one's auto is much less than the expectation of privacy in the home or the office. As there was no intent by the police to investigate Opperman's car and the police were merely performing a "caretaker" function when they found the drug, then such inventory searches of impounded cars are reasonable under the Fourth Amendment, even without a warrant.

Challenging the Use of Seized Evidence
United States v. Calandra 414 U.S. 338 (1974)

The issue in this case was whether or not a witness summoned to appear and testify before a grand jury could refuse to answer questions because the questions were based on evidence seized illegally under the Fourth Amendment (that is, seized without a search warrant). In a 6–3 opinion, the Supreme Court ruled that a witness summoned to appear and testify before a grand jury may not refuse to answer questions on the ground that they are based on evidence obtained from an unlawful search and seizure.

The facts indicate that the FBI obtained a warrant to search Calandra's business to obtain evidence of illegal gambling. During the search, no illegal gambling paraphernalia was found, but evidence of loansharking was found and seized. When a grand jury called Calandra to testify about loansharking, he refused, saying that the evidence was obtained in violation of his Fourth Amendment right to be free of unreasonable searches and seizure because, although a warrant was obtained, the scope of the warrant was exceeded in that the warrant allowed "gambling" seizures when in fact "loansharking" evidence was seized. Agreeing that the seizure was illegal in that the scope of the warrant was exceeded, nonetheless the Supreme Court, in a 6–3 decision, ruled that the exclusionary rule does not bar the use of illegally seized evidence in *all* proceedings; that allowing petitioner Calandra to refuse to answer questions on the basis of the exclusionary rule would unduly interfere with the grand jury's duties; and that such questions, even though derived from illegally obtained evidence, are only used derivatively against the accused and "work no new Fourth Amendment wrong."

The general rule thus became: although illegally obtained evidence (illegal because the scope of the warrant was exceeded) may be inadmissible for other purposes, a grand jury can consider the illegally obtained evidence, and a grand jury indictment is valid even if based on illegally obtained evidence. A witness cannot decline to respond to questions from the grand jury based on the illegally obtained evidence.

Stone v. *Powell* 428 U.S. 465 (1976)

In a 6–3 decision, the Supreme Court held that where a state fully and fairly allows a defendant to object to evidence admitted against him, which was obtained in violation of the defendant's Fourth Amendment right to be free of unreasonable searches and seizures, then the defendant cannot later raise the same objection in a *habeus corpus* ("give us this body") proceeding in a federal court.

After a person is found guilty at trial and the conviction upheld on all appeals, the government of the United States through the writ of *habeas corpus* allows a prisoner to contest his conviction collaterally (along side of; in addition to) in the federal district courts, on constitutional grounds. In this case, after trial and appeal were exhausted, Powell attacked his California state court conviction in a federal *habeus corpus* action, alleging that his Fourth Amendment rights were violated.

Powell and three companions entered a liquor store in California and got into an argument with the store manager. Powell shot and killed the manager's wife. Ten hours later, in Nevada, Powell was arrested for violation of a local Nevada vagrancy ordinance which made it a crime to loiter or wander aimlessly, to refuse to identify oneself, or to do anything which would indicate to a reasonable man that public safety was endangered. During a "patdown" search subsequent to his arrest, Powell's revolver and six spent cartridges were discovered. It was this gun which had killed the liquor store manager's wife. At trial, Powell contended that the Fourth Amendment guarantee against unreasonable searches and seizures was violated in that the Nevada ordinance used to arrest him was too broad and unconstitutionally vague, making the revolver inadmissible in court. Powell contended that by using such a broad and vague statute, the police were able to exercise too much discretion, in that under the rubric of the ordinance the police could stop, search, and seize almost anyone, anytime, and that to allow such broad discretion was unreasonable under the Fourth and Fourteenth Amendments. So Powell sought to have the evidence of the gun and cartridges suppressed under the exclusionary rule because they were obtained in violation of his Fourth Amendment rights.

The Supreme Court disagreed with Powell. The Court said that a defendant, even though he may be correct on his Fourth Amendment claim, is not entitled to federal *habeus corpus* relief unless he can also show that he was not given a full and fair opportunity to raise the issue in state court. If he had such an opportunity, whether he took it or not, and whether it was accurately resolved if he took it, he is not entitled to relitigate his claim in federal court. So Fourth Amendment claims are deemed waived if, given a full and fair opportunity to raise the issue, the defendant does not raise them at trial or on appeal.

FIFTH AMENDMENT CASES

Self-Incrimination and the Right to Counsel
Gideon v. *Wainwright* 372 U.S. 335 (1963)

Gideon was arrested for breaking and entering a poolroom with the intent to commit a misdemeanor. The offense was a felony under Florida law. At his trial, Gideon asked the court to appoint counsel for him since he had no funds and no attorney. The court denied the request since at that time only prosecutions for crimes carrying a possible sentence of death allowed for appointed counsel. Gideon represented himself, and was subsequently found guilty with a five-year sentence.

The question before the Supreme Court was whether Gideon had a Sixth Amendment right to counsel in a state court proceeding. The Court answered in a 9–0 decision that the right of an indigent to counsel in noncapital criminal trials is a fundamental right which is essential to a fair trial. The Court held that Gideon's trial and conviction without counsel violated the Fourteenth and Sixth Amendments. Left unanswered by *Gideon* was whether counsel must also be provided to indigents arrested and to be tried for misdemeanors.

Escobedo v. Illinois 378 U.S. 478 (1964)

In a close 5–4 decision, the Supreme Court announced in *Escobedo* that where a police investigation is no longer a general inquiry into an unsolved crime, but has begun to focus on a particular suspect in police custody, who has been refused an opportunity to consult with his attorney and who has not been warned of his constitutional right to remain silent, then the accused has been denied the assistance of counsel in violation of the Sixth and Fourteenth Amendments, and no statement obtained by the police during that interrogation may be used against him at trial.

Escobedo was arrested without a warrant at 2:30 A.M. He was a suspect in the killing of his brother-in-law. He made no statement to the police and was released almost sixteen hours later. Eleven days later, Escobedo was again arrested. He made several requests to see his lawyer, who was in the building at that time. Escobedo's request was refused and he was not warned of his right to remain silent. Thereafter, under persistent questioning from the police, Escobedo made statements which were damaging and which were later used as evidence against him at trial. Escobedo was convicted of murder. Because his Sixth Amendment right to counsel was violated, Escobedo's conviction was reversed.

The *Escobedo* decision left many questions unanswered, which subsequent cases filled in.

Miranda v. Arizona 384 U.S. 486 (1966)

To alleviate the confusion created by *Escobedo,* the Supreme Court granted *certiorari* (review) to four cases, all of which come under the heading, *Miranda.* In each case the defendant, while in police custody, was questioned by police officers, detectives, or a prosecuting attorney in a room where he was cut off from the outside world. None of the defendants was given a full and effective warning of his rights at the outset of the interrogation process. In all four cases, the interrogations elicited oral admissions, and in three of them, signed statements as well, which were admitted at trial. All four defendants were convicted.

In a 5–4 decision, the Supreme Court held that when a suspect is "in custody," that is, when not free to leave, warnings must be given to the suspect containing the following elements:

(a) you have a right to remain silent;

(b) anything you say may be used against you at trial;

(c) you have a right to an attorney present during the interrogation;

(d) If you are unable to provide your own attorney, you are entitled to one provided by the state.

If the suspect invokes his right to counsel, interrogation must stop until a lawyer is provided. And if a confession or incriminating statement is made and the *Miranda* warnings not given, the statement is not admissible later at trial. But if the warnings *were* effectively given and a confession made, then the state still must show that the statement or confession was "voluntary" before it will be admitted as evidence at trial. "Voluntary" means the statement was made freely and not induced by coercion, threats, overbearing of the will, or promises of benefit.

United States v. Wade 388 U.S. 218 (1967)

Wade was indicted by a grand jury for robbing a bank. Several weeks later while under arrest, and after indictment, Wade was shown in a lineup to some of the bank employees. His attorney was not informed and was not present. Two bank employees identified Wade at the lineup and this evidence was later used at his trial, where Wade was convicted and sent to jail. His counsel objected to the identification and lineup, saying Wade had the right to the assistance of counsel at the postindictment lineup under his Sixth Amendment right to counsel. The Supreme Court agreed, in a 9–0 opinion.

The Court said a person's Fifth Amendment privilege against self-incrimination is not violated by his being forced to stand in a lineup without counsel. But when made to stand in a lineup, after being formally charged, then the accused's Sixth Amendment right to counsel arises, and counsel must be present. If counsel is not present, then the lineup identification cannot be used later at trial.

The reason counsel is needed at a postindictment lineup, said the court, is because of the great possibility of unfairness (1) because of the suggestive manner in which identification confrontations are usually made and (2) because the accused will often be precluded from reconstructing what occurred at the lineup later at trial and thus not receive a full hearing on the identification issue.

428

Gilbert v. California 388 U.S. 263 (1967)

Gilbert was convicted of armed robbery of a bank and of murdering a policeman. Before trial, Gilbert was placed in a lineup and identified by bank employees as the robber. Gilbert's attorney was not notified of the lineup, so he was not present. The identification was later used to convict Gilbert, who was sentenced to death. Also used to convict Gilbert at his trial were samples of his handwriting, which were compared to the note Gilbert handed the teller at the bank during the robbery. Gilbert claimed these two bits of evidence, the lineup identification and the handwriting sample, violated his Sixth Amendment right to counsel and his Fifth Amendment privilege against self-incrimination.

In a 9–0 opinion, the Supreme Court agreed saying, under *Wade,* that Gilbert had a right to counsel at the postindictment lineup, but that even if counsel was not present at the lineup, if the person who identified Gilbert at the lineup could also identify him at trial without having to rely on the earlier lineup identification for support, then the failure to provide counsel at the lineup was harmless error, making the in-court identification admissible against the accused, but admitted only if independent of the earlier lineup identification.

Second, the court said that taking fingerprints, examples of handwriting, and blood samples are not stages of such critical importance that counsel need be present to represent the accused, nor is one's privilege against self-incrimination impaired by the use of blood, handwriting, or fingerprints at trial since the Fifth Amendment only protects "testimonial" incrimination. It does not protect physical evidence.

In *Gilbert,* then, the handwriting example was properly admitted against the accused, and his right to counsel was not thereby impaired by an independent in-court identification, independent of Gilbert's counsel-less lineup identification.

Stovall v. Denno 388 U.S. 293 (1967)

Stovall was arrested for the murder of Dr. Behrendt. Behrendt's wife was seriously injured in the scuffle at the time of the murder. After his arrest, the police took Stovall to the hospital where Mrs. Behrendt was recovering; she identified Stovall as the murderer. Prior to the hospital identification, Stovall was not given a chance to retain counsel. Therefore, Stovall claimed that this procedure denied him his Sixth Amendment right to counsel and denied him his Fifth Amendment privilege against self-incrimination.

The Supreme Court ruled 8–1 that although showing suspects singly for purposes of identification is a widely condemned practice because it is too suggestive, whether or not such a procedure violates one's right to "due process" depends on the "totality of surrounding circumstances." The Court found the procedure in this case to be warranted, because Mrs. Behrendt was the only person who could exonerate Stovall; because Mrs. Behrendt could not go to the police station for the usual lineup; and because there was no way of knowing how long Mrs. Behrendt would live. The Court, then, found no denial of due process in the hospital confrontation.

Kirby v. *Illinois* 406 U.S. 682 (1972)

The rule contained in *Kirby*'s 5–4 decision was that the right to counsel arises only after the suspect has been formally charged with a crime; that is, when there is in fact an adversary criminal prosecution pending against him. Thus, there is no right to counsel at police lineups conducted prior to the time the accused is indicted, arraigned, or otherwise "formally charged." Of course under *Miranda* and the Fifth Amendment, one is entitled to counsel in any "custodial" interrogation, but this arises from the Fifth Amendment privilege against self-incrimination and not the Sixth Amendment right to counsel.

So, under the facts of *Kirby,* where the defendant is arrested and taken to the police station on suspicion of robbery, and where the robbery victim immediately identifies him as the robber before formal charges are brought, even though Kirby was not advised of his right to counsel, the court said that this was a "regular police investigation" and not a formal prosecutorial proceeding. As such, it was harmless error to use the stationhouse identification as evidence to convict Kirby of robbery, even without counsel present at the identification.

Argersinger v. *Hamlin* 407 U.S. 25 (1972)

Argersinger, an indigent, too poor to pay for counsel, was denied a request for free, court-appointed counsel by a Florida court because "the right to court-appointed counsel extends only to trials for non-petty offenses punishable by more than six months imprisonment." Argersinger was on trial for carrying a concealed weapon, punishable by six months in jail, or a $1000 fine, or both; at trial Argersinger got ninety days. He brought a *habeus corpus* writ, saying his liberty was taken without due process of law in that he was without the assistance of counsel when tried.

The Supreme Court agreed 9–0, saying that anytime a conviction could bring imprisonment, one has an absolute right to counsel and that if counsel is not provided no jail sentence can be imposed, although a fine can be.

Faretta v. *California* 422 U.S. 806 (1975)

Faretta was charged with grand theft. At his arraignment, the judge assigned a public defender to represent Faretta, since he was indigent. Later, but before trial, Faretta asked to be permitted to represent himself. The judge granted the request, but after testing Faretta's knowledge of certain legal rules, the judge ruled Faretta had not made an "intelligent" and "knowing" waiver of his right to the assistance of counsel, and in addition ruled that Faretta had no constitutional right to conduct his own defense.

The Supreme Court reversed this decision. In a 6–3 decision, the Court said that the Sixth and Fourteenth Amendments guarantee that a defendant in a state criminal trial has an independent constitutional right to represent himself. The Court said that once a defendant makes an "intelligent and voluntary" decision to represent himself, the Sixth Amendment demands that he be allowed to do so. The Court ruled that to force court appointed counsel on Faretta was in error.

North v. *Russell* 427 U.S. 328 (1976)

By a vote of 5–3, Justice Stevens taking no part in the decision, the Supreme Court ruled that a defendant in a minor misdemeanor prosecution has no right to have a lawyer for a judge if after his conviction the defendant has a right to *trial de novo* (a new trial) in a court where the judge is a lawyer.

The facts indicate that North was convicted, for a second time, in a Kentucky "police court," of driving while intoxicated. Kentucky law allowed nonlawyers to be judges in police-court cases and also allowed an "appeal of right" if convicted from the decision of a police judge, to a circuit court where all judges were lawyers. In that circuit court, a jury *trial de novo* could be held.

After his conviction, fine, and sentence, North chose to ignore the appeal of right to the circuit court and brought instead a *habeus corpus* petition in state court, challenging the above described scheme as unconstitutional, alleging that his federal due process and equal protection rights had been violated in that he was tried and convicted by a nonlawyer judge. The Supreme Court ruled there was no denial of due process since a *trial de novo* was available but ignored; and there was no denial of equal protection because the court system was justified "so long as all defendants were treated equally."

Brewer v. *Williams* 430 U.S. 387 (1977)

Williams was arrested in Davenport, Iowa, for murdering a ten-year-old girl. Williams, a former mental patient, was deeply religious. On the way to Des Moines for trial, from Davenport after arraignment, and after having been told by his attorneys not to speak to the police without an attorney present, and even after the police agreed not to question Williams on the trip, the police asked Williams where he had hidden the body. Williams made several incriminating remarks and then directed the police to the body. He was convicted of murder partly on the basis of this incriminating evidence obtained on the trip from Davenport to Des Moines.

By a vote of 5–4, the Supreme Court ruled that the evidence had been wrongfully admitted at trial, on the grounds that Williams had been denied his constitutional right to counsel and that by speaking-up under police interrogation Williams had not thereby waived his right to counsel. Under *Kirby, Stovall, Gilbert,* and *Wade,* one has a right to counsel after "formal charges" have been brought. Here Williams was already indicted when he spoke-up without counsel. Also, in order for one to waive the right to counsel, the Supreme Court said that the state must prove "an intentional relinquishment or abandonment of a known right or privilege." No such proof of voluntary relinquishment was shown, so Williams' confession and his "waiver of counsel" could not be used against him at trial. His writ for *habeus corpus* was granted.

Double Jeopardy
Bartkus v. *Illinois* 359 U.S. 121 (1959)

Bartkus and a companion case, *Abbate,* illustrate the same principle: a prosecution in a state court for violation of state law resulting in an acquittal does not bar prosecution in a federal court for violation of a federal law arising out of the same conduct. And vice versa, a federal acquittal does not bar a state prosecution for the same conduct. In other words, the same act may be a crime under both federal and state law. Where this is so, there are, in effect, two distinct crimes committed by the same act, and the acquittal or conviction in one court, federal or state, does not bar "retrial" in the other. The Supreme Court's vote was a close 5–4.

The facts were that Bartkus was tried in a federal court for robbery of a federally insured bank, a federal offense. He was found not guilty. One year later, Bartkus was indicted by the state of Illinois for the same conduct, bank robbery, and received a life sentence. He pled double jeopardy all the way to the Supreme Court. The Court found that the due-process clause of the Fourteenth Amendment had not been violated, and that the Fifth Amendment bar against double jeopardy was not incorporated by the Fourteenth Amendment and so not made applicable to the states. Although subsequent decisions have reversed the latter part of the Court's decision (the Fifth Amendment double jeopardy clause now does apply to the states through the Fourteenth), this holding would not change the result in *Bartkus.*

Abbate v. *United States* 359 U.S. 187 (1959)

Abbate was the reverse of *Bartkus:* here the defendant was found guilty in state court and later found guilty in federal court for the same conduct. In a 6–3 vote, the Court ruled that a federal prosecution was not barred under the double jeopardy clause of the Fifth Amendment, even after an earlier conviction in state court.

During a strike against the Southern Bell Telephone and Telegraph Company, the defendants dynamited telephone company facilities in three states. Thereafter, the defendants were indicted by the State of Illinois for conspiracy to injure or destroy the property of another. They pled guilty and received three months imprisonment. Subsequent to this proceeding, the U.S. Attorney for the Southern District of Mississippi got an indictment against the defendants for conspiring to injure or destroy communications facilities "operated or controlled by the United States," a federal offense. Finding that the efficiency of federal law enforcement must suffer if the double jeopardy clause prevents successive state and federal prosecutions, the Court allowed both the federal and state convictions to stand.

Benton v. Maryland 395 U.S. 784 (1969)

The Fifth Amendment to the U.S. Constitution says "no person shall be . . . subject, for the same offense, to be twice put in jeopardy." In *Benton,* the Supreme Court stated that not only does the Fifth Amendment bar the federal government from twice putting one in jeopardy but, through the Fourteenth Amendment, the Fifth applies to the states as well. The Court found the double jeopardy provision so "fundamental to our constitutional heritage" that it is incorporated into the due-process clause of the Fourteenth Amendment and applies to the states.

The 7–2 decision arose when Benton was tried in Maryland for burglary and larceny. He was found not guilty of larceny but was convicted of burglary. Because part of the Maryland procedure for selecting jurors was shortly thereafter found unconstitutional under the Maryland constitution by a Maryland court, Benton was given a retrial. At the second trial, he was again charged with larceny and burglary, but this time found guilty of both. The judge sentenced him fifteen years for burglary, five years for larceny, the sentences to run concurrently (at the same time).

Because the court earlier in its opinion found that the Fourteenth Amendment incorporates the Fifth Amendment prohibition against double jeopardy, which applies to the states, the question then became: Was Benton twice placed in jeopardy? The Court found that he was, and reversed his larceny conviction. Even though the defendant's sentence was not reduced—he received concurrent sentences of fifteen years for the burglary conviction and five years for the larceny—the Court felt there was an important issue: there may be collateral consequences of an invalid conviction resulting from the double jeopardy, such as loss of civil rights.

Ashe v. *Swenson* 397 U.S. 436 (1970)

Ashe was charged with having robbed one of six poker players, Knight. The trial judge instructed the jury that if it found that Ashe had participated in the robbery with others, the theft of any money from Knight would sustain a conviction against Ashe, and that if Ashe was one of the robbers, he was guilty even though he may not have personally robbed Knight. The jury returned a verdict of not guilty. Thereafter, Ashe was tried and convicted for robbery of another poker player, Roberts. On appeal, Ashe pled double jeopardy, a denial of his Fifth Amendment rights under the Constitution.

In an overwhelming 8–1 vote, the Supreme Court agreed with Ashe. The Court applied the doctrine of *collateral estoppel,* parties who have fully litigated an issue of fact in one proceeding cannot relitigate the same issue in any subsequent proceeding, even though the second proceeding involves a different offense. The Court said that the Fifth Amendment guarantees against double jeopardy, applicable to the states through the Fourteenth Amendment by virtue of *Benton* v. *Maryland,* and embodies *collateral estoppel* as a constitutional requirement. So the issue of fact already litigated in the first trial, that Ashe was not one of the robbers, had been determined in Ashe's favor. As such the state, under the doctrine of *collateral estoppel,* was foreclosed from relitigating the issue in another trial.

Double Jeopardy and Imposition of Harsher Punishment
North Carolina v. *Pearce* 395 U.S. 711 (1969)

Suppose a defendant is convicted and sentenced, but thereafter appeals and obtains a new trial. If he is convicted a second time for the same offense, may he be sentenced to a longer term than he received for the first conviction? In *Pearce,* the Court ruled 9–0 that the trial court can give a more severe sentence the second time if there are "good reasons" for doing so, but that punishment already exacted, jail time served, or fines paid while awaiting a decision on appeal must be fully credited when imposing a new sentence for the same offense.

Pearce involved two cases consolidated for Supreme Court review. In one case, Pearce was convicted of assault with intent to commit rape. He received a twelve-to-fifteen-year sentence. Several years later, he was granted a new trial because his confession was found to be involuntary and thus unconstitutional. Again Pearce was found guilty, and given a new eight-year sentence, which, when added to the time Pearce had already spent in prison, amounted to a longer sentence than that originally imposed.

In another case, Rice pleaded guilty to second-degree burglary, four counts. He received ten years. Two-and-one-half years later, a new trial was granted because Rice had not received his constitutional right to counsel. A new conviction resulted in a twenty-five-year sentence with no credit given for time already spent in jail on the original conviction.

As noted above, the court made a two-pronged decision: (1) the double jeopardy clause of the Fifth Amendment requires that a defendant be given full credit against the new sentence for any time served under the original conviction, and (2) the double jeopardy clause does not bar a more severe sentence upon reconviction provided that there is new objective, factual, and identifiable data on the record, showing a firm basis for a harsher penalty.

Due Process
Mempa v. *Rhay* 389 U.S. 128 (1967)

Probation and parole are prisoner interests protected by the application of the due-process clause of the Fourteenth Amendment. Accordingly, certain procedural safeguards must be afforded in the proceedings to revoke probation or parole. *Mempa,* which consolidated several cases for review, involves one of these safeguards: the right to counsel.

In Case Number 16, the defendant was placed on two years' probation for joyriding. Later the defendant was alleged to have been involved in a burglary and the prosecutor moved to revoke his probation. At the probation revocation hearing, the petitioner-defendant was not represented by an attorney and a sentence of ten years was given. The Supreme Court reversed, under *Gideon* v. *Wainwright,* because the time of sentencing is a "critical stage" in a criminal case, requiring the presence of counsel.

In Case Number 22, the defendant was placed on three years' probation, for burglary. A year later he was arrested for larceny and forgery. At the defendant's revocation of probation hearing, no attorney was present to assist him. He received the maximum sentence of fifteen years. Again the Supreme Court reversed, holding that the Fifth Amendment as applied through the due-process clause of the Fourteenth Amendment requires that counsel be present at sentencing, a critical stage in any proceeding.

The reason counsel is needed at sentencing ruled the court, 9–0, is to ensure that certain rights, such as that of appeal, are reasonably asserted, and to "afford the defendant aid in other situations at that stage."

Morrissey v. *Brewer* 408 U.S. 471 (1972)

Morrissey was convicted of "false drawing of checks" and sentenced to seven years' confinement. He was paroled one year later, but seven months thereafter he was arrested for violation of parole. The question before the Court was whether the due-process clause of the Fourteenth Amendment requires that a state afford an individual some opportunity to be heard before revoking his parole. By a vote of 8–1, the Court said that as a matter of constitutional due process, there must be a two-stage hearing before a defendant's parole can be revoked: (1) a preliminary hearing before an impartial officer to determine whether there is probable cause that defendant violated his parole, the defendant must be given notice of the hearing, he must be entitled to be present and to speak in his own behalf, and the hearing officer must state the reasons for his decision; and (2) a second revocation hearing wherein the defendant must be given written notice of his alleged parole violations, the defendant must be confronted with the evidence against him, the defendant must be given an opportunity to be present and heard, the defendant must be given the chance to confront and cross-examine any adverse witnesses, the decision to revoke parole must be made by a neutral and detached hearing body, and finally, a written record must be kept of the entire proceeding.

Gagnon v. *Scarpelli* 411 U.S. 778 (1973)

Voting 9–0, the Justices decided that, like parole, there must be a two-stage hearing before a defendant's probation can be revoked, as a matter of constitutional process. Scarpelli pleaded guilty to armed robbery and received a fifteen-year suspended sentence, with a seven-year probation. One month later Scarpelli was arrested during a house burglary. His probation was revoked without a hearing. Because of this, Scarpelli claimed his freedom was taken without due process of law, specifically, without the assistance of counsel.

Since a probation order follows sentencing (at which stage counsel is constitutionally required), when probation is revoked and the same sentence reimposed, there is only a limited right to counsel. For a nonindigent, counsel can be present if provided by the defendant. For an indigent defendant, the Court said that the following factors should be borne in mind:

(1) whether due process requires the state to appoint counsel for an indigent defendant is determined on a case-by-case basis;

(2) due process does not require that the indigent be informed of his right to request counsel;

(3) if a request for counsel is made, counsel should be appointed if the indigent either claims he did not commit the alleged violation or alleges mitigating circumstances that would be difficult to show without the assistance of counsel.

Forced Jurisdiction
Ker v. *Illinois* 119 U.S. 436 (1886)

Fredrick M. Ker was indicted by the State of Illinois for larceny and embezzlement. At the time of indictment Ker was in Lima, Peru, so Governor Hamilton of Illinois requested the U.S. Secretary of State to ask the President to extradite Ker from Peru to America under a treaty between the U.S. and Peru. The President issued the warrant and directed Henry G. Julian to receive Ker from Peruvian authorities.

Instead, Julian forcibly and with violence arrested Ker, and placed him on board ship to Hawaii, then transferred to a ship to San Francisco, from which place Ker was transferred by agreement between the Governors of California and Illinois, to Cook County, Illinois, to stand trial. Ker was tried and convicted, but claimed the court had no jurisdiction over him because of the violent way in which he was brought before the court, and because the procedures of the Peru-American extradition treaty had not been followed.

The Supreme Court denied Ker's requests saying "these facts do not establish any right under the Constitution, or laws, or treaties of the United States." Further, the Court said that treaties of extradition should not guarantee a fugitive from justice asylum in another country. Finally, the Court reasoned that the kidnap of a criminal is a dispute between the criminal (Ker) and his kidnapper (Julian) under the law of the place where kidnapped, Peru; and that only Illinois could determine whether it lost jurisdiction over Ker because of the kidnap, which question Illinois had already answered against Ker.

Frisbie v. *Collins* 342 U.S. 519, 865 (1952)

Like *Ker,* the rule of law announced by 9–0 vote in *Frisbie* was that it is immaterial whether defendant, the victim of an illegal arrest or of a kidnapping, was dragged into the state illegally: due process is deemed satisfied by a fair trial. Irregularities in his arrest do not destroy jurisdiction over the defendant.

While he was living in Chicago, and after being indicted for murder, Collins was forcibly seized, handcuffed, blackjacked, and taken into Michigan for trial. He claimed that these "procedures" violated the due-process clause of the Fourteenth Amendment. Finding that there were "special circumstances" in this case which required prompt federal intervention, the Court, under *Ker* v. *Illinois,* found no violation of the due-process clause of the Fourteenth Amendment.

Discovery
Williams v. *Florida* 399 U.S. 78 (1970)

Williams was arrested and indicted for robbery. He claimed an alibi defense, i.e., he was somewhere else at the time of the crime. The Florida Rules of Criminal Procedure required a defendant claiming an alibi to give the prosecution advance notice of his intent to use the alibi defense, and to supply the prosecution with "information as to the place where he claims to have been and with the names and addresses of the alibi witnesses he intends to use." Williams claimed this requirement compelled him to be a witness against himself in violation of his Fifth and Fourteenth Amendment rights.

Second, Williams objected to the six-man jury (provided by Florida law for all but capital cases) used to convict him of life imprisonment, claiming a six-man jury violated the Sixth Amendment.

In a 9–0 opinion, with some Justices dissenting in part, the Court ruled first that the discovery rule on alibi was designed to enhance the search for truth in criminal trials (by giving both the accused and the state opportunity to investigate certain facts crucial to the issue of guilt or innocence) so that it comports with requirements of due process and a fair trial to require a defendant to disclose his alibi witnesses. Further, the court said that the rule of disclosure, at most only accelerated the disclosure of the defendant's alibi defense, as it would come up at trial anyway, and thus did not violate the defendant's Fifth Amendment privilege against compelled self-incrimination. Second, the court said that the six-man jury is constitutional. In other words, there is no constitutional right to a twelve-man jury. The essential feature of a jury is that it be interposed between the defendant on the one hand and the state on the other, to ensure fairness and impartiality. Thus the jury need only be large enough to promote group deliberation. A six-person jury is adequate to promote group deliberation so long as a verdict, found beyond a reasonable doubt, is necessary to convict.

Wardius v. *Oregon* 412 U.S. 470 (1973)

A statute requiring the defendant to disclose the names and addresses of his alibi witnesses prior to trial, without a reciprocal statutory right to obtain the names and addresses of rebuttal witnesses from the prosecution, is fundamentally unfair and violates the due-process clause of the Fourteenth Amendment.

In 1970, Wardius was indicted for unlawful sale of narcotics. At trial, Wardius called one Colleen McFadden who testified that she and Wardius were at a drive-in movie on the night in question. Because Wardius had failed to warn the prosecution of his intent to use an alibi defense, the trial court, as a sanction, prevented Wardius' alibi testimony from being considered by the jury. Wardius got eighteen months in prison and he appealed.

In a 9–0 decision, the Supreme Court said that the due-process clause of the Fourteenth Amendment forbids enforcement of alibi rules and sanctions unless reciprocal discovery rights are given to criminal defendants also. Since the Oregon statute in question did not provide for reciprocal discovery, it was an error for the trial court to impose sanctions on Wardius, and his conviction was reversed.

SIXTH AMENDMENT CASES

Right to Confrontation
Pointer v. Texas 380 U.S. 400 (1965)

Pointer and Dillard were arrested in Texas for having robbed Phillips of $375. At a preliminary hearing, neither defendant had a lawyer. Phillips, the victim, gave his version of the robbery in detail at the preliminary hearing. Because he had no lawyer, Pointer, a defendant, did not cross-examine Phillips. Pointer was indicted and at trial, since the victim, Phillips, had moved to California, the state offered a transcript of Phillips' testimony at the earlier hearing as proof of the crime. Pointer's counsel objected, saying there is no way to cross-examine a transcript, and claiming Pointer's right to confront his accuser under the Sixth Amendment would be denied by admitting the transcript. The court admitted the transcript and the Supreme Court reversed, 9–0.

The Court held that the Sixth Amendment right of a defendant to confront witnesses against him, which includes the right of cross-examination, is a fundamental right essential to a fair trial, and so is made obligatory on the states by the Fourteenth Amendment. The Court found that to allow introduction of the transcript here in question would be a clear denial of the right of confrontation, since the statement by Phillips was made without an adequate opportunity for cross-examination at the earlier hearing.

Bruton v. United States 39 U.S. 123 (1968)

Bruton and Evans were on trial for armed postal robbery. A postal inspector testified that Evans had confessed to the robbery, and implicated Bruton as well. The trial judge told the jury to consider the confession as evidence of guilt against Evans only and not against Bruton. Both were found guilty. On appeal, Bruton argued that even though the judge had instructed the jury to ignore the confession as to Bruton, he (Bruton) was effectively denied his Sixth Amendment right to confrontation because he had no way of cross-examining this out-of-court admission unless his accuser and codefendant (Evans) took the stand, which Evans refused to do. In a 6–2 decision with Justice Marshall taking no part, the Supreme Court agreed with Bruton.

Right to a Speedy Trial
United States v. Marion 404 U.S. 307
(1972)

The Sixth Amendment right to a speedy trial attaches when the defendant has in some way become an "accused." As soon as a defendant has been arrested and held to answer for a criminal charge or has been indicted, then the right to a speedy trial becomes mandatory. The Sixth Amendment demands speed after arrest or indictment, but delay in arresting or delay in indicting are covered by the Fifth and Fourteenth Amendments' due-process requirements.

Marion and a partner were charged with fraudulently conducting a business, misrepresentation, alterations of documents, and deliberate nonperformance of contracts from September 1965, to January 1966. They were indicted more than four years later in April 1970. They claimed this delay denied them their right to a speedy trial.

Voting 9–0, the Supreme Court disagreed, saying that the Sixth Amendment guarantee of a speedy trial is applicable only after a person has been "accused" of a crime, which in this case did not occur until defendants were indicted.

Jury Selection
Swain v. Alabama 380 U.S. 202 (1965)

In every criminal case the defense and the prosecution are allowed a certain number of "preemptory challenges" whereby they can exclude someone from becoming a juror for any reason at all. But if state prosecutors systematically use their preemptory challenges to exclude members of a racial group from all juries in all cases, this violates the equal protection clause of the Fifth and Fourteenth Amendments.

Swain, a Negro, was convicted of rape in Alabama, and sentenced to death. Although available to serve, during the previous fifteen years, no Negro had in fact served on a trial jury in the county where Swain was tried and convicted. Ruling 6–3, the Court said "Total exclusion of Negroes from juries by state officials creates an inference of discrimination." But since Swain could not meet his burden of providing purposeful discrimination, his conviction for rape was left standing.

Unanimous Verdicts
Apodaca v. Oregon 406 U.S. 404 (1972)

In federal courts, the Sixth Amendment right to a jury trial includes the right to a unanimous verdict by the jurors. However, state court convictions have been upheld where the verdict has been less than unanimous, so long as it was based on a "substantial majority" of the jury. This is one of the rare instances in which one of the Bill of Rights rights has been allowed to receive lesser protection in state courts than in federal courts.

In *Apodaca,* Cooper, Madden, and Apodaca were convicted of assault with a deadly weapon, burglary, and grand larceny. Apodaca and Madden were convicted 11–1, Cooper 10–2. Under Oregon law any guilty vote of 10–2 or more was allowed. The three defendants attacked this scheme as unfair, violating their right to a trial by jury under the Sixth and Fourteenth Amendments.

Deciding 6–3 that the Sixth Amendment guarantee of a jury trial does not require a unanimous vote, the Court reasoned that the jury trial's purpose is to interpose between the state and the defendant the commonsense judgment of the layman, which is accomplished despite a lack of unanimity.

Guilty Pleas
Boykin v. *Alabama* 395 U.S. 238 (1969)

In the spring of 1966, within the period of a fortnight, a series of armed robberies occurred in Mobile, Alabama. All the victims were local shopkeepers open at night. A local grand jury returned five indictments against Boykin, a twenty-seven-year-old Negro, for common-law robbery, an offense in Alabama punishable by death. Boykin pled guilty to all five counts. The judge asked no questions of the defendant, and the defendant did not address the court. At his sentencing Boykin did not testify; no character or background testimony was presented for him. There was no prior criminal record. The sentencing jury gave death for each count. The question before the Supreme Court was: Did Boykin do all this voluntarily?

By a 7–2 vote, the Court ruled that we cannot presume from a silent record that Boykin voluntarily waived his privilege against self-incrimination, his right to a trial by jury, and his right to confront his accusers.

Therefore, the Court ruled that acceptance by the trial court of Boykin's guilty plea was in error because the record did not disclose that Boykin voluntarily and understandingly entered his guilty plea. After *Boykin,* the record of every guilty plea had to show clearly that the defendant voluntarily and intelligently waived his constitutional rights to trial by jury, confrontation, and the privilege against self-incrimination.

441

Index

Actus rea, 185
Adjudicatory hearing, in juvenile court, 387–88
Admissible evidence, 211
Age, in juvenile delinquency, 382–83
Agee v. State, 290
Alcatraz, 342
Alfred the Great, 33–34
Allen charge, 220
Altered behavior, due to urban violence, 17
American Bar Association (ABA) standards, 189, 198, 207, 211, 214, 242, 252, 264–268, 306
   on court organization, 233–36
   Defense Function, *199*
   on fair trial and free press, 255–63
   on functions of trial judge, 195–96
   on joint trials, 294
   on lay judges, 245
   on local police departments, 106
   on sentencing, 221–23
   on unions, 164
American Correctional Association, 348
American Federation of Government Employees (AFGE), 159

American Federation of State, County, and Municipal Employees (AFSCME), 157, 159
American Indian Movement (AIM), 24
American Probation and Parole Association, 328
Amnesty, 327
Amos v. State, 280–81
Anti-Castro Groups, 29
Apodaca v. Oregon, 197, 214, 221
Appellate courts, 231
Aquinas, St. Thomas, 176
Arraignment, 212
Arrests, 123–24
   number of, 7
   pattern of, 7
Aryan Brotherhood (AB), 351, 353
Assize of Arms, 39
Assize of Clarendon, 37–38
Atkins v. City of Charlotte, 165
Attorneys
   and client relationship, 266
   colloquy between, 265–66
   recommended conduct of, 257–58
   rights to have, 285
Auburn system, 343
Augustus, John, 306

Auxiliary division, of police services, 106

Bail, 207
  right to, 203
Bard, Morton, 167
Base-expectancy scale, 317–18
Bates v. United States, 272–73
Beccaria, Cesare, 11
Black Guerrilla Family (BGF), 351, 353
Black Liberation Army (BLA), 23
Black Muslims, 21
Black Panther Party (BPP), 22
Boles, Charles E., 52
Border Patrol, 65
Boston police strike, 156–57, 161
Bow Street Runners, 43
Breakthrough, 29
Brewer v. Williams, 200–1
Brockway, Zebulon, 313
Brunson v. State, 279
Bruton v. United States, 291–94
Bureau of Alcohol, Tobacco, and Firearms, 82
Bureau of Customs, 80–81
Burger, Warren E., 250, 356

California Highway Patrol, 90, 94–95
California Youth Authority, 395
Canons of Judicial Ethics (ABA), 252, 253–54
Capital punishment, 203–4
Careers
  in correctional institutions, 359–61, 364–72
  in federal law enforcement, 84–87
  in judicial process, 225–28
  in probation and parole, 330–31
  in state and local enforcement agencies, 115–18
  in youth services, 404–5

Carter, Jimmy, 311
Cassidy, Butch, 50, 51
Certiorari, 246–47
Character evidence, 294–97
Charges, 210–11
  to the jury, 219–21
  right to be informed of, 198–99
Chicano Liberation Front (CLF), 27
Chicago School, 13, 14
Civil Rights Act of 1964, 152
Classical school, 11
Classification in the prison system, 344–48
Clemmer, Donald, 350
Close custody prisons, 342
Closed courtroom, 195–96
Cloward, Richard and Lloyd Ohlin, 13
Codefendants, 219, 290–94
Code of Judicial Conduct, 253
Coercion, 283–84
Collateral estoppel, 193
Collective bargaining, for police, 157–59, 161–63
Colloquy between attorneys, 265–66
Colquhoun, Patrick, 43–44, 176
Commission on Revision of the Federal Court Appellate System of the United States, 245
Committee on Uniform Crime Records of the International Association of Chiefs of Police, 3
Community-based corrections, 372–76
Community Relations Service, 67–68
Commutation of sentence, 327
Confessions, 278–94
  requirements of, to be admissible, 288–90
Confrontation of witness, 215–17, 302
Consolidation of police services, 107–9
Constable, 39, 40–41, 103, 105
Constitutional safeguards, 190–204

Contempt power, 266–67
  recommended use of, 263
Contract forces, 110
Convict, 350–51
Coroner, 39, 41, 101–3
  vs. medical-examiner system,
  102
Coroner's inquest, 101–2
Correctional institutions, 2, 142
  careers in, 359–61
Correctional Rehabilitation Study
  Act, 364
Counsel
  arguments to the jury by,
  217–18
  right to, 199–202, 213–14
Counterfeit, 74–76
Court administrator, 236–38
  career as, 226
Court information systems, 238–41
Court system, 2, 142, 206–23, 229–50
  careers in, 225–28
  public attitudes toward, 229–30
  recommended conduct within,
  260–63
  reorganization proposals,
  232–50
Cressey, Donald, 13
Crime
  amount of, 3–10
  cost of, 1–3
  definition of, 185–86
Crime Control Act of 1973, The, 10
Crime Index, 4, 5, 7
Crime in the United States, 3, 64
Crime prevention, 175–80
  English revival of, 177–79
Criminal behavior, 183–85
  of juveniles, 380
Criminal-history record, 8–10
Criminal justice, 10–16
  administration, 2
  for juveniles, 399–402
Criminal-justice system, 2–3, 140–44
Criminal Man (Lombroso), 11
Criminology, 11

Crisis intervention, 165–71
  in New York City, 166–68
Crofton, Sir Walter, 313
Cross-examination, 215–17
Cruel and unusual punishment,
  203–4
Cuban Action Commandos, 29
Custody, 278–79
Custody Classification Preprocessing
  Center, 337–38

Dade County Department of Public
  Safety (Florida), 98–99, 108
Davis v. Alaska, 215–17
Delinquency, 380–402
  definition of, 380
Delli Pooli v. United States, 291–92
Department of the Treasury, 74–82
  Bureau of Alcohol, Tobacco, and
  Firearms, 82
  Bureau of Customs, 80–81
  Internal Revenue Service, 79–80
  Interpol, 77–79
  Secret Service, 74–77
Detention hearing, in juvenile court,
  386–87
Determinate sentencing, 313
Deviance, 120–21
Disaster Squad, 64
Discharge from prison, 325
Disposition hearing, in juvenile
  court, 388–92
Domestic-disturbances, 123–24,
  165–66
Double jeopardy, 191–94, 219
Dozie v. State, 274
Drug Enforcement Administration,
  71–74
Due-process provision, 194–95
Due-process revolution, 128–31

Edward the Confessor, 35–36
Eight amendment, 202–4
Emiliano Zapata Unit (EZP), 27–28

England
   development of policing in,
   33–40, 42–46
   revival of crime prevention in,
   177–79
Evidence, 271–302
Eyewitness identifications, 217–78
   Wall's danger signals in, 277

Face-to-face confrontations, 272–74
Fair trial, 195
   and free press, 255–57
Family Crisis Intervention Unit
   (FCIU), 166, 170
Federal Bureau of Investigation
   (FBI), 3, 4, 5, 61–65
Federal Bureau of Prisons, 342, 359,
   373
Federal court system, 232, 245–50
Federal law enforcement, 59–82
   careers in, 84–87
Felony, 122
Fielding, Henry and John, 43, 176
Fifth amendment, 191–95
First appearance, 206–7, 210, 211
Fitzpatrick, Mary, 311–12
Florida Highway Patrol, 115–16
Foster v. State, 300
Fourth amendment, 190–91
Frankpledge system, 35
Fraternal Order of Police (FOP), 160
Freedom of the press, 195
   and fair trial, 255–57
Fuerzas Armadas de Liberación
   Nacional, 23
   Puertorriquena (FALN), 23
Function of the Trial Judge, The, 252

Generalist model, in crisis
   intervention, 168, 170
Generalist-specialist model, in crisis
   intervention, 168, 170
Georgia Game and Fish Division, 117

Grand jury, 191, 211
Gun Control Act of 1968, 82

Habeas corpus, 244
Hassell v. State, 294
Hastings v. Cardwell, 273
Hayner, Norman, 318–20
Hearst, Patricia, 26, 102–3
Hindelang, Michael J., 5
Hoffman-Bustamante, Dale, 341
Hoover, J. Edgar, 61–62
Hung jury, 220
Hypothetical questions, 300–1

Identification Division, 64
Immigration and Naturalization
   Service, 65–66
Impartial jury, 196–98
Incriminating statements, 194
Individual jurisdiction, 187
Individual styles of policing, 138–40
Inherent power, 233–45
In-house forces, 110
Inmate, 350
Intake process, in juvenile court, 386
Internal Revenue Service, 79–80
International Brotherhood of Police
   Officers (IBPO), 160
International Brotherhood of
   Teamsters, Chauffeurs,
   Warehousemen, and Helpers of
   America (IBT), 160
International Conference of Police
   Associations (ICPA), 160–61
Interpol, 77–79
Interpretational safeguards, 189–90
Intent, 185

Jails, 333–39
   inspection of, 255
   reform of, 338
   surveys of, 334, 337
   types of prisoners in, 334

Jewish Defense League (JDL), 23–24
Joint Commission on Correctional
   Manpower and Training, 363, 364
Joint Economic Committee of the
   United States Congress, 1
Joint trials, 290–94
Judge, 219, 248–49, 252–68
   and admissible confessions, 288
   contempt power of, 266–67
   in juvenile court, 388, 391–92
   pretrial duties of, 255–64
   qualities of, 253–54
   and sentencing, 267–68
   trial duties of, 264–68
Judicial behavior, 252–68
Judicial-conduct commission, 268
Jurisdiction, 186–87
Jurors, 196–97, 214–15
Jury trial, right to, 214–15
Justice of the peace, 38, 41
Juvenile court, 383, 386–92
Juvenile delinquents, 380–402
   and police, 126–27
   profile of, 396
Juvenile institutions, 394–98
Juvenile Justice and Delinquency
   Prevention Task Force, 399–401

Kansas City Study, 173–75
Kent v. United States, 383
Kirby v. Illinois, 272
Korczak, Janusz, 402
Ku Klux Klan (KKK), 28

Law Enforcement Assistance
   Administration (LEAA), 68–71,
   152, 156, 334, 362
Law Enforcement Education
   Program (LEEP), 364
Law-enforcement officers, 258–59.
   See also Police Officer
Law enforcement(s), 2
   effect of due-process revolution
   * on, 129, 131*
   public opinion of, 363–64

Lay justice, 244–45
Legal context, for policing, 122–31
Legalistic style of policing, 136–37
Legion of Justice, 28
Line units, of police services, 106
Lineups, 277–78
Local policing. *See* Municipal
   policing
Lombroso, Cesare, 11
London, "new police" of, 42–46
Lopez-Rey, Manuel, 12–13
Luger, Milton, 397–98

McCormick, 296
McGee v. state, 295
McMillan v. U.S., 280
Maconochie, Captain Alexander, 313
Magistrate, 242
Mala in se, 185
Mala prohibita, 185
Mandatory release, 310, 325
Manpower, 362–77
   correctional requirements, 366
   development, 376–77
   educational level of, 365
   outlook for, 367–69
Manslaughter, 184
Manuel, Wiley, 15–16
Maximum-security prisons, 342
Medical-examiner system, 102
Medium-custody prisons, 342–43
Melton v. City of Atlanta, 165
Melville, Sam, 25
Mexican Mafia (EME), 351–53
Michigan v. Tucker, 287–88
Minimum-security prisons, 343
Minutemen, 28
Miranda warnings, 194, 278–88
   form of, 284–85
Misdemeanor, 122
Mississippi Supreme Court, 291, 295
M'Naghten rule, 184
Model Sentencing Act, 316
Morrissey v. Brewer, 324
Motive, 183

Muir, William Ker, 138–39
Municipal policing, 105–9
   alternative methods of, 107–9
   careers in, 118
   divisions of, 106
   responsibilities of, 106–7
Murder, 184–85
   cost of, 2

Narcotics Traffickers Project, 80
National Academy (of the FBI), 62,
   64
National Advisory Committee on
   Criminal Justice Standards and
   Goals, 21, 110, 179, 221, 233, 242,
   252, 315, 320, 362
   on correctional priorities,
      375–76
   on court information systems,
      238–41
   on parole supervision, 323–24
   on state court administrator,
      236–38
National Center for State Courts,
   229, 242
National Clearinghouse for
   Correctional Programming and
   Architecture, 343
National College of the State
   Judiciary, 253
National Conference of State Judges,
   267
National Court of Appeals, 245–47
National Crime Information Center
   (NCIC), 64
National Crime Panel for the Law
   Enforcement Assistance
   Administration, 18
National Crime Prevention Institute,
   179, 180
National Criminal Justice Directory,
   366, 369
National Criminal Justice
   Information and Statistics Service,
   70–71

National Criminal Justice Reference
   Service (NCJRS), 70, 371
National Fraudulent Check File, 64
National Institute of Corrections, 371
National Institute of Law
   Enforcement and Criminal
   Justice, 69
National Prisoner Statistics, 373
National Socialist Liberation Front
   (NSLF), 29–30
National Strategy to Reduce Crime,
   A, 362
National Union of Police Officers
   (NUPO), 159
Nevels v. State, 280
New criminology, 12
New Jersey State Police, 116–17
New Police
   in America, 46–49
   in London, 42–46
New York City Police
   careers in, 118
   crisis-intervention program,
      166–68
New World Liberation Front
   (NWLF), 26–27
NIC Jail Center, 339, 340–41
Noguchi, Dr. Thomas, 103, 104
Nolo contendere, 263, 264
Normans, The, 36–37
Norris, Clarence, 326–27
Nuestra Familia (NF), 351, 353

Offender-Based Transaction
   Statistics System (OBTS), 8, 9
Office of Juvenile Justice and
   Delinquency Prevention, 399
Ohlin, Lloyd and Richard Cloward,
   13
Omnibus Crime Control and Safe
   Streets Act of 1968, 68, 69, 97, 362
Omnibus hearing, 212
On Crimes and Punishments
   (Beccaria), 11
One-man showup, 273

On-the-scene exception (to Miranda warnings), 279–81
Opinion evidence, 297–301
   expert, 299–301
   nonexpert, 297–99
Organizational context, for policing, 131–40

PACE (Programmed Activities for Correctional Education), 336–37
Parajudges, 241–44
Pardons, 326–27
Parmelee, Maurice, 13
Parole, 310–25
   conditions of, 320–22
   decision to, 315–20
   hearings, 316–20
   history of, 313–14
   for juveniles, 398–99
   revocation, 324–25
   supervision, 322–24
Parole board, 314–15
   consolidation model, 314
   hearings, 316–20
   independent, 314
Parole officer, 322–24
   career as, 330
Part I offenses, 4, 64
Part II offenses, 5, 64–65
Peace and Freedom Fighters, 30
Peel, Robert, 43–46, 176
Penal Institutions, Probation and Parole, 372
Pennsylvania State Police, 53–55, 92–93
Pennsylvania system, 343
Photographic identification, 274–77
Pitt, William, 43, 176
Platt, Tony and Paul Takagi, 12
Plea negotiation, 263
Police
   arrest authority of, 123
   attitudes toward policewomen, 154–55

   in criminal-justice system, 142, 143
   discretionary power of, 124–28
   and juveniles, 126–27
   and unions, 156–65
Police officer
   determinants of behavior of, 133–36
   requirements to become, 91, 131
   separation from conventional world of, 131–33
Police Officer Standards and Training Commission (POST), 91, 96
Policewomen-on-patrol experiment, 152–55
Policing
   growth of, in America, 40–42, 46–55
   historical development of, in England, 33–40, 42–46
   in legal context, 122–31
   in organizational context, 131–40
   in societal context, 120–22
   styles of, 136–40
   vs. team policing, 171–73
   United States Supreme Court and, 128–31
   Women in, 148–56
Positive school, 11
Posse Comitatus, 30
   sheriff's power of, 36
Praepositus, 36
Prearrest screening, 337
Precedent, 231–32
Preliminary hearing. *See* First appearance
Presentence investigation, 307–8
Presentence report, 222, 307
President's Commission on Law Enforcement and Administration of Justice, 233, 244, 252, 362, 365, 372
Pretrial conference, 213

Pretrial discovery, 212–13
Pretrial proceedings, 211–13
Pretrial publicity, 196
Price v. Georgia, 192
Prisoners, 339–44
    rights of, 353, 355–56
    social system of, 350–51
    women, 341–42
Prison gangs, 351–53
Prisons, 339–44
    life in, 350–51
    new, 344
    types of, 342–43
    violence in, 351–53
Private police, 109–14
    factors spurring growth of, 111
    future of, 113–114
    personnel of, 112–13
    role perspectives of, 111–12
Probation, 305–10
    conditions of, 308
    for juveniles, 392–94
    supervison of, 308–10
Probation officer, 309
    career as, 330–31
Programmed inmate activities,
    335–37, 348–49
Property crimes, 4
Public opinion
    of justice system, 363–64
    of policewomen, 154
Punishment, 11
    crime prevention and, 175–76

Rape, cost of, 1–2
Reasonable grounds, 123–24
Recidivism, 312–13
Red Guerrilla Family (RGF), 27
Regionalization of police services,
    107–9
Rehabilitation programs, 336, 348,
    375
Reid v. State, 284

*Report of the Task Force on Disorders
    and Terrorism, 21*
Republic of New Africa (RNA), 22
Res gestae, 301–2
Revolutionary Action Movement
    (RAM), 22
Rights, 190–204, 285
    of inmates, 353, 355–56
    to remain silent, 286–88
    waiver of, 282–83, 285

Safe Schools Center, 399
Schneble v. Florida, 292–93
Schober, Dr. Johann, 77, 78
Seasonal safeguards, 188–89
Secret Army Organization (SAO), 29
Secret Service, 74–77
    Executive Protective Service, 77
    Treasury Security Force, 77
Sentencing, 221–23, 267–68
Service Employees International
    Union (SEIU), 159–60
Service style of policing, 137
Sheriff, 35–38, 41, 49, 97–101
    functions of, 100
    grounds for removal of, 101
    optional responsibilities of, 101
Showups. *See* Face-to-face
    confrontations
Simmons v. United States, 275
Sixth amendment, 195–202
Social deviance, 121
Social history, of juvenile, 388–91
Social institutions, 120
Societal context, for policing, 120–22
Specialist model, in crisis
    intervention, 168, 170–71
Speedy trial, 189
Spurlin v. State, 286
Staff division, of police services, 106
*Standards Relating to the Function of
    the Trial Judge, 253*
Stare decisis, 231, 232
State, power of, 186

State patrol, 90. *See also* State police forces
State police forces, 53–55, 90–105
   careers in, *115–17*
State Trial Judge's Book, The, 252
Statistical deviance, 121
Status offenses, 380–82
Statute of limitations, 188–89
Stone v. Powell, 244
Stovall v. Denno, 272
Student Nonviolent Coordinating Committee (SNCC), 21–22
Students for a Democratic Society (SDS), 24
Subject-matter jurisdiction, 186–87
Survey of Inmates of Local Jails, 335
Sutherland, Edwin, 13
Symbionese Liberation Army (SLA), 26, 102–3
Systems Development Divison, 71

Tacitus, 176
Takagi, Paul and Tony Platt, 12
Task Force Report: The Courts, 252
Team policing, 171–75
Territorial jurisdiction, 187
Terrorism, 21–31
Texas Syndicate, 351, 353
Theory of delinquency and opportunity (Cloward and Ohlin), 13–15
Theory of differential association (Sutherland), 13–14
Three-judge courts, 249–50
Treatment programs, 348–50
Trial, 213–21
   proof difference between civil and criminal, *271*
Trial de novo, 193, 194
Trial judge, 253–54, 264–68

Unconditional release. *See* Discharge from prison

Unified court system, 233–36
Uniform Crime Reporting Program, 3
Uniform Crime Reports for the United States, 3, 4, 64
Unions, 156–65
United States Marshals Service, 67
United States Supreme Court, 190, 200, 201–2, 232, 287
   police and, *128–31*
United States v. Ash, 275
United States v. Roth, 273–74
Unreported crime, 5, 18
Urban violence, 16–20
U.S. Bureau of the Census, 2
U.S. Cultural Organization (US), 22–23
U.S. Department of Justice, 2, 59, 60, 61
U.S. v. Calandra, 211
U.S. v. Marion, 189
U.S. v. Robertson, 280

Venue, 187
Verdict, 220–21
Victim
   compensation, *19–21*
   treatment of, *18–19*
Victimless crime, cost of, 1
Victim of Crimes Act of 1977, 20
Violent crimes, 4
Voir dire, 197, 215
Vollmer, August, 48, 49, 177
Voluntary and spontaneous statement, 281–84

Waiver of right to remain silent, 282–83
Wall, Patrick M., 277
Warrant, 206
Warren Court, 128–29
Warren, Earl, 130
Watchman style of policing, 137–38
Watergate, 263, 265

Weather Underground Organization
  (WU), 24–25
Weekend sentences, 337
Wells, Alice, 149
White-collar crime, cost of, 1
Wickersham Report, 372, 376
Wilson, James Q., 136
Witness, 264
  confrontation of, 215–17

  expert, 299–301
  nonexpert, 297–99
Women
  in policing, 148–56
  in prison, 341–42
Work-release programs, 337

Yankelovich study, 230
Year-and-a-day rule, 193